THE ART OF WALTER ANDERSON

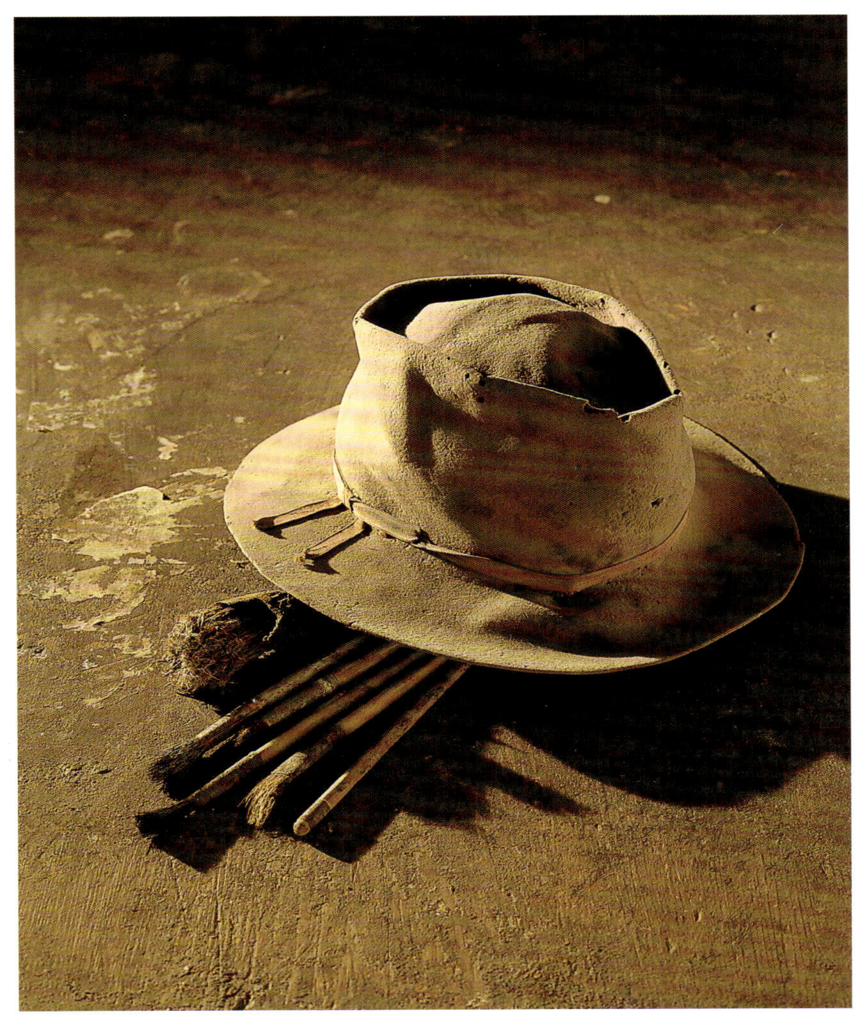

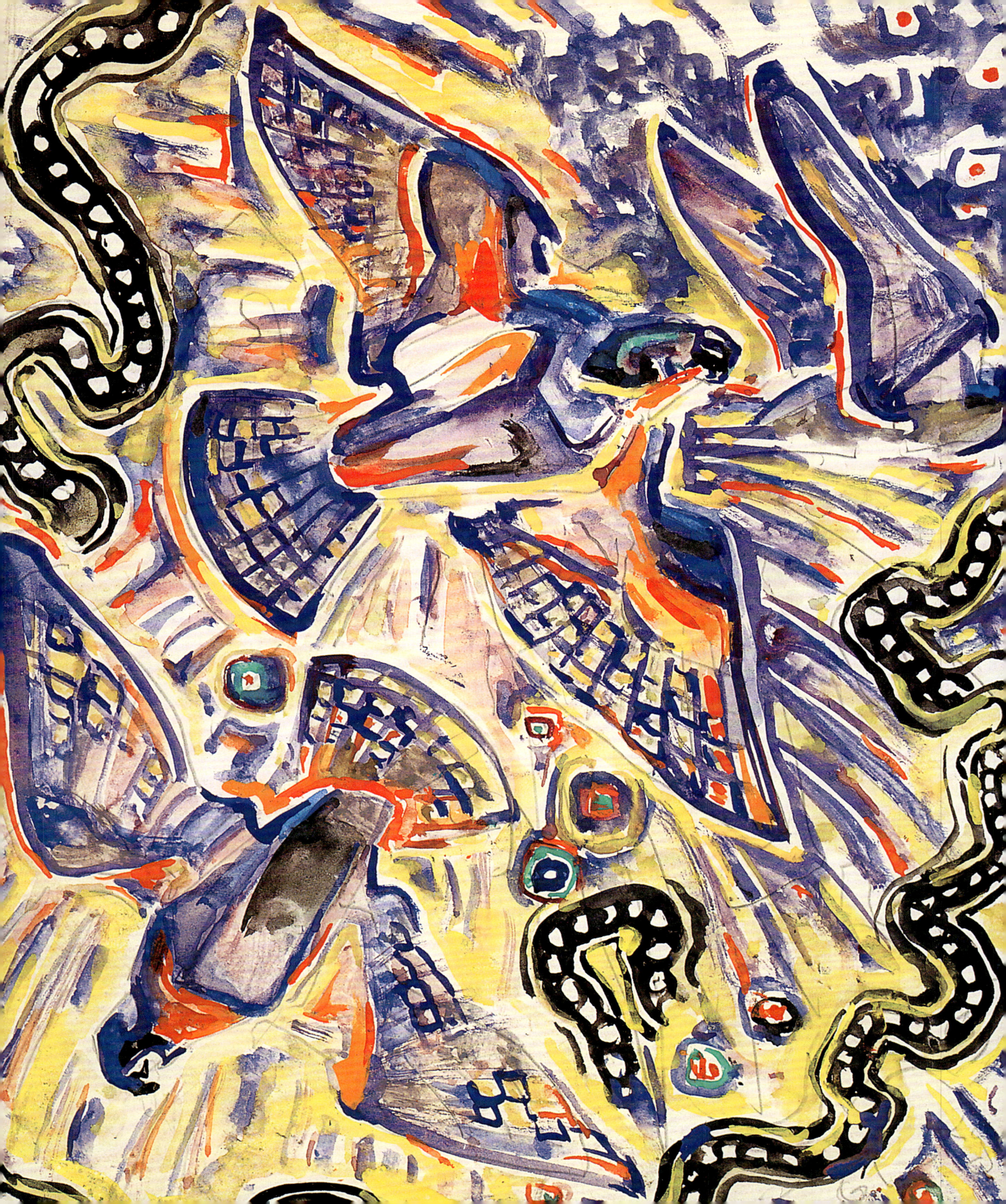

THE ART OF WALTER ANDERSON

EDITED BY PATRICIA PINSON

Contributions by

COLIN EISLER

SUSAN C. LARSEN

CHRISTOPHER MAURER

FRANCIS V. O'CONNOR

MARY ANDERSON PICKARD

ERNEST PINSON

LINDA CROCKER SIMMONS

UNIVERSITY PRESS OF MISSISSIPPI
AND THE WALTER ANDERSON MUSEUM OF ART

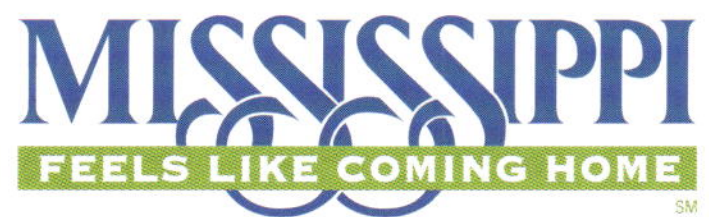

PUBLICATION OF THIS BOOK IS MADE POSSIBLE IN PART BY FUNDING FROM
MISSISSIPPI DEVELOPMENT AUTHORITY, DIVISION OF TOURISM

WWW.UPRESS.STATE.MS.US
WWW.WALTERANDERSONMUSEUM.ORG

The University Press of Mississippi is a member
of the Association of American University Presses.

Manufactured in China
Designed by John A. Langston

06 05 04 03   4 3 2 1

Library of Congress Cataloging-in-Publication Data

Anderson, Walter Inglis, 1903–1965.
The art of Walter Anderson / edited by Patricia Pinson ; contributions by Colin Eisler . . . [et al.].
p. cm.
Includes bibliographical references and index.
ISBN 1-57806-600-X (cloth : alk. paper) — ISBN 1-57806-601-8 (pbk.)
1. Anderson, Walter Inglis, 1903–1965. I. Pinson, Patricia. II. Title.
N6537.A48A4 2003
709'.2—dc21   2003004270

British Library Cataloging-in-Publication Data available

Frontis: *Hawks at Sunrise,* Watercolor on paper, 11 x 8½ in.,
Mary Anderson Pickard, 98.1.1

Photographs on pages 88, 92, 99, 106, 111, 112, 140, 143, 147, 149, 152, 153, 155, 183, 184, 192, 193, and 213 were made by Owen Murphy.
Photographs on pages 102, 103, 104, 162, 165, 166, and 167 were made by John Lawrence.
Photograph on page 177 was made by an unknown photographer.
Photograph on page 162 was made by Harold Head.
All other photographs of Walter Anderson works were made by Kevin Berne.

Decorative line art on essay opening pages: Walter Anderson Museum of Art
and the Family of Walter Anderson
Decorative art on catalogue section pages: Ceramic tiles, 1950s, Walter Anderson Museum of Art

CONTENTS

PREFACE AND ACKNOWLEDGMENTS

True art consists of spreading wide the intervals so that imagination may fill the space between the trees.
—Walter Inglis Anderson

Few artists from any period of art history have ever communicated the essence of the natural world, literature, and mythology so vividly and with such passion as Walter Inglis Anderson (1903–1965). His art easily captivates the imagination of audiences of all ages, from the art connoisseur to the casual observer.

Anderson described himself as an "artist who preferred nature to art." After completing his studies at the Pennsylvania Academy of the Fine Arts and in Europe, he chose a life path that took him far from the lights, galleries, and streets of New York, Paris, and other centers of the art world. He found inspiration all around him as he explored the rich world of the flora, fauna, sea, earth, and sky of the Gulf Coast.

An unquenchable thirst for solitude and discovery eventually led Anderson to Horn Island, a narrow and fragile place along Mississippi's coast. This barrier island became for him a metaphor of the natural world—a balanced system that was simultaneously harsh yet delicate. It was here that the man was transformed by his discoveries, his realizations, from an observer to a participant on nature's stage.

In all of his work, Anderson is recognized for evoking a "sense of place" that is at once naturalistically accurate yet universal in its poetic and artistic appeal. This sense of place constitutes the heart of the centennial celebration of the artist and his work.

The centennial catalogue, *The Art of Walter Anderson*, and the traveling exhibition, *Walter Inglis Anderson: Everything I See Is New and Strange*, were developed by the Walter Anderson Museum of Art (WAMA), in collaboration with the Family of Walter Anderson, to commemorate the centennial of Anderson's birth, September 29, 2003. Projects of such monumental proportions are never accomplished without assistance.

The Smithsonian Institution made possible an extraordinary opportunity to reveal the many facets and influences of Anderson's creative spirit through the exhibition *Everything I See Is New and Strange*. WAMA is indebted to Seetha Srinivasan at University Press of Mississippi for her strong commitment to this project and to Anne Stascavage and John Langston for kind direction and unstinting patience.

Gratitude is due Dr. Patricia Pinson, WAMA Curator of Collections, for her ability to undertake such endeavors with verve and pragmatism; Dennis Walker, Registrar, for his infectious enthusiasm for getting things done; and museum colleagues for extraordinary gifts of time and mind. We are indebted to Mary Anderson Pickard for a sea of information, Joan Gilley for tireless searches for images and documents, Dr. Christopher Maurer for his critical eye, Dr. Ernest Pinson for his comprehensive pen, and Kevin Berne for his cross-country trips with cameras and lights to achieve his inimitable photography.

It is because of the vision and diligence of Courtney Blossman and the early Friends of Walter Anderson, Inc., that we are able to celebrate this artist and his works on a national level. They are commended for their perseverance and dedication.

The following sponsors are acknowledged for their generous support:

BellSouth, Inc.
Chisholm Foundation
Milton R. Kaack and Ethel Reilley Kaack Philanthropic Trust
Community Foundation of Greater Jackson
Mississippi Arts Commission
Mississippi Development Authority, Division of Tourism
Mississippi Power Foundation
Northrop Grumman
City of Ocean Springs, Mississippi
The Elizabeth Irby Foundation
Members of the Centennial Circle
Board of Supervisors, Jackson County, Mississippi

The realizations that Anderson experienced during his journeys into nature and into his own inner *terra incognita* continue to inspire people. If we are fortunate, we may discover, like the artist, that we are not just observers but truly a part of that grand journey.

Clayton Bass
Walter Anderson Museum of Art
Executive Director, 1996–2002

Marilyn Lyons
Walter Anderson Museum of Art
Executive Director, 2003

THE ART OF WALTER ANDERSON

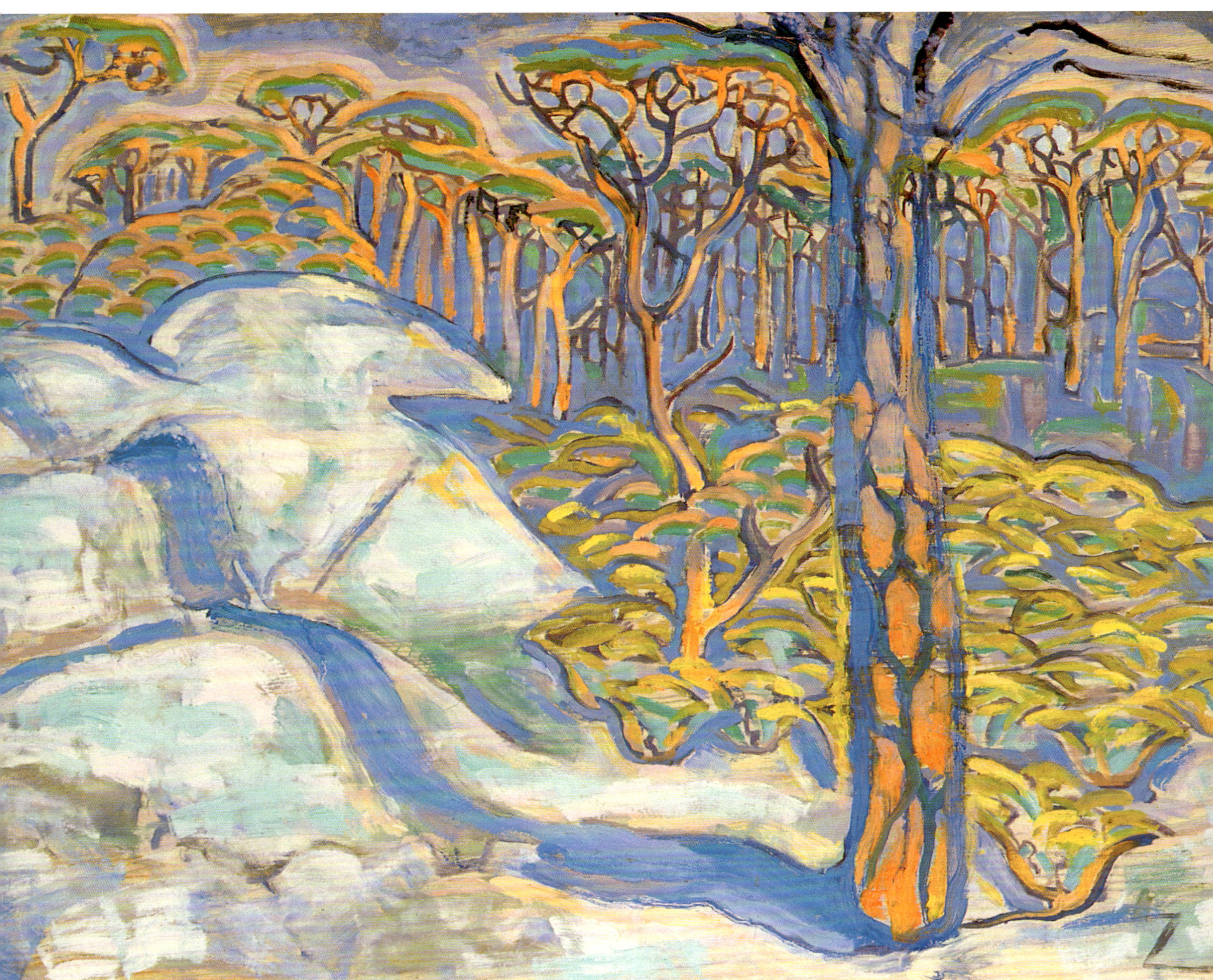

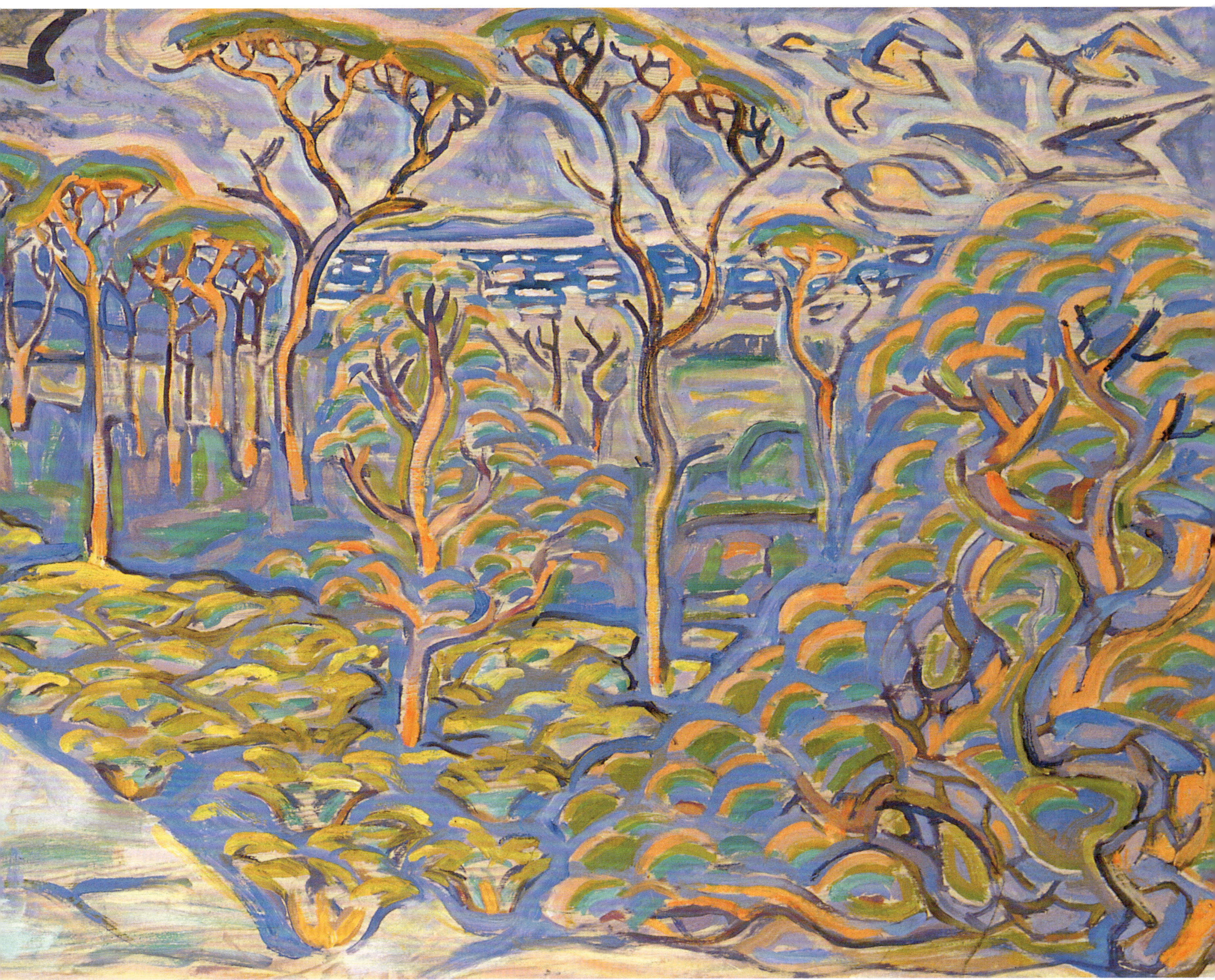

Horn Island, 1960

Oil on wood, 25 x 60 in.

John Anderson

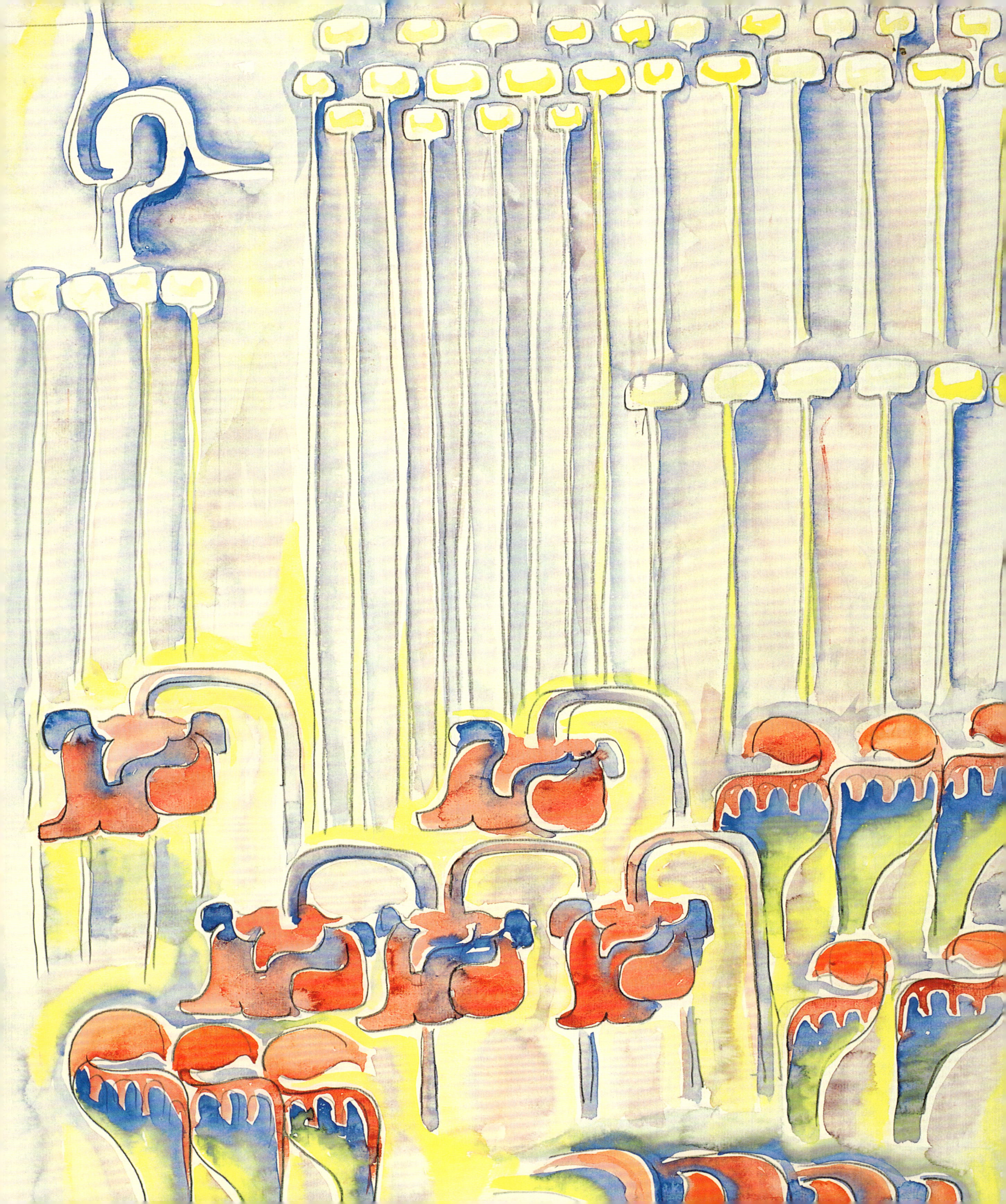

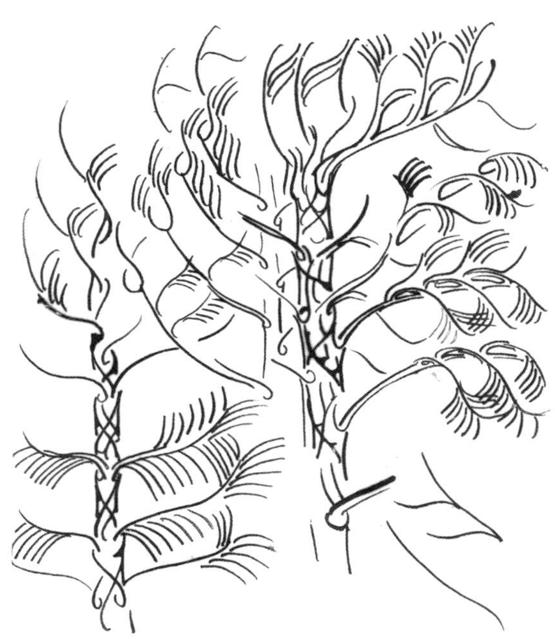

THE WORLD OF WALTER ANDERSON

MARY ANDERSON PICKARD

Worlds away from the bustle of Washington, D.C., a narrow barrier island lies between the coast of Mississippi and the open Gulf of Mexico. Low dunes formed by shifting sands are stabilized by golden grasses and sea oats. Pines, palmettos, and rosemary bushes anchor the higher dunes which protect marshy brackish lagoons. Beyond the lagoons, old relic dunes offer secret interior spaces carpeted in lichen and pine needles and encircled by thickets of yaupon, sumac, and greenbrier.

When hurricanes come, the raccoons, rabbits, wild hogs, and small rodents must survive by finding shelter here. The permanent reptile population, snakes, turtles, frogs, and alligators, huddle on the marshes or submerge in the deepest lagoons.

Surrounding the island are waters rich with marine creatures. In seasonal cycles, crabs, shrimp, and fish school and spawn and crowd the open ponds. Oysters thrive. Porpoises play. Great sea turtles drag themselves ashore to lay their eggs where the first dunes rise. Shells, starfish, sand dollars, swollen moon jellies, iridescent Portuguese man-of-wars, octopi, and sea horses all wash up along the south shore.

Myriad busy shorebirds scavenge there alongside the larger stronger gulls. Fishing pelicans plunge, terns pattern the clouds. Boat-tailed grackles strut along the tide line. At the back of the lagoons, red-winged blackbirds punctuate the rustling canebrakes, their persistent songs swept up by the gulf wind. From the wax myrtles along the marsh's edge, heedless blue-green tree swallows hurl themselves at the sky where osprey and eagle soar.

Herons, bitterns, and egrets nest on the island, as do the waterfowl—coots,

Pitcher Plants, ca. 1943
Watercolor on paper, 24 x 19 in.
Walter Anderson Museum of Art, 93.3.1 (B)

gallinules, and rails; terns and skimmers lay their eggs on the open sand. In winter come grebes and loons and great flocks of geese and ducks. In spring and fall, the many-colored migrants—hummingbirds, warblers, all the passerines—rest there from their arduous flight.

From the 1940s until his death in 1965, the artist Walter Anderson found sanctuary on Horn Island in all seasons of the year. He rowed or sailed a small skiff ten miles from Ocean Springs on the mainland to camp near a free-flowing artesian spring. In his skiff he carried minimal supplies in a metal garbage can—paint, paper, pencils, brushes—and foodstuff such as rice and coffee, apples, raisins, peanut butter and bread, canned fruit and vegetables, as well as extra clothes and bedding and insect repellant with which he defended himself against Horn Island's most numerous population. He slept under his boat and reveled in his world. "A magic carpet," he called it, or "the back of Moby Dick surrounded by strange inhabited space." Today Horn Island is preserved as a valuable wilderness area, protected by the Gulf Islands National Seashore.

Walter Anderson was well prepared for his island. His natural gifts were honed by training and discipline and enriched by his assimilation of art history and his studies of literature, folklore, myth and legend, symbol, and music.

On Horn Island, he lived to paint—or painted to live. He kept logs of his days there. "This morning I drew bulrushes while the flies stung. Later I made a watercolor under my boat while the rain poured. Such is the life of an artist who prefers nature to art. He really should cultivate art more but feels his love of art will take care of itself as long as it has things to feed upon."

His love of art fed on the infinite images of sea, earth, and sky. The island became a microcosm of indivisibility, a comprehensible unity of interconnected parts, a wholeness that he conveyed in thousands of drawings and watercolors. His expansive and concentrated vision embraced and reconciled the dualities of life and death, of good and evil, of sand and water, of matter and spirit.

Born in New Orleans and educated in the East, trained at the Parsons School of Design and at the Pennsylvania Academy of the Fine Arts, Anderson was familiar with the same ideas and influences that shaped his well-known peers. He sought and attained the sensual acuity with which Georgia O'Keeffe explored the depths of flowers or used her brush to caress the nuances of form in bone or desert landform. He understood and used the magic of rhythm, of cycle, of pattern and synesthesia which occupied Burchfield. He shared a mastery of technique with Demuth, abstraction with Marin, the secret symbols of Dove, and the exuberant creativity of Picasso. Recognizing the validity of primitive art which sprang alive from a way of life, he evoked the same ancient rhythms that danced the paint onto Pollack's canvas.

Walter Anderson is recognized and acclaimed in his native South. In Ocean Springs a museum built and supported by the public stands witness to his community's appreciation, attracting visitors from all the states and many different countries.

A New Orleans businessman brings friends and confides, "Before I saw his watercolors, I had never looked at a pine tree." Gazing at a colorful watercolor of an obscure sea creature, a marine biologist laughs with appreciative recognition. "He's not only gotten a good likeness of the sea hare. He's captured its personality." A sophisticated tourist from Paris stands in shocked delight in the middle of the murals of the Ocean Springs Community Center. Before the Venus panel, a shy eight-year-old girl spontaneously dances. An art professor, moved by the Anderson oeuvre, organizes an interdisciplinary course incorporating science, art, and journal keeping. Schoolchildren are introduced to Walter Anderson's art in the primary grades and regularly tour the museum. Literary drawings from the classics, which Anderson made as he read, are used by teachers to stimulate reading and visualization. Art students sketch in the galleries. Musicians, poets, and artists find impetus for their own work and come to share it there.

Now, one hundred years after Anderson's birth, the Walter Anderson Museum of Art has organized an exhibition and created a catalogue to offer him to the larger world. His name is still missing in most annals of twentieth-century American art. Perhaps the centennial events will change that.

Today our country stands balanced between a newly perceived vulnerability and the weight of power. Perhaps the vision of an unlikely hero could offer guidance. Joseph Campbell once wrote that it is the duty of the artist "to provide the myth for modern man." Anderson's world offers a lesson in interconnected wholeness and strength, a recognition of our community with all who share the precarious balance of life on this planet.

This hero arrives in the city in ragged sun-bleached trousers, a salt-stained sweatshirt, a shapeless felt hat, and who knows what shoes. In the words of the Stephen Sondheim song, "There won't be trumpets. . . ." But perhaps, transcending time and place, the watercolors will sing of wind in the pines, the plash of waves, a gull's cry.

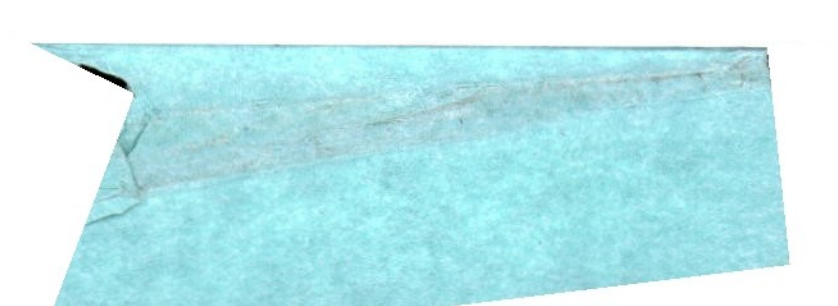

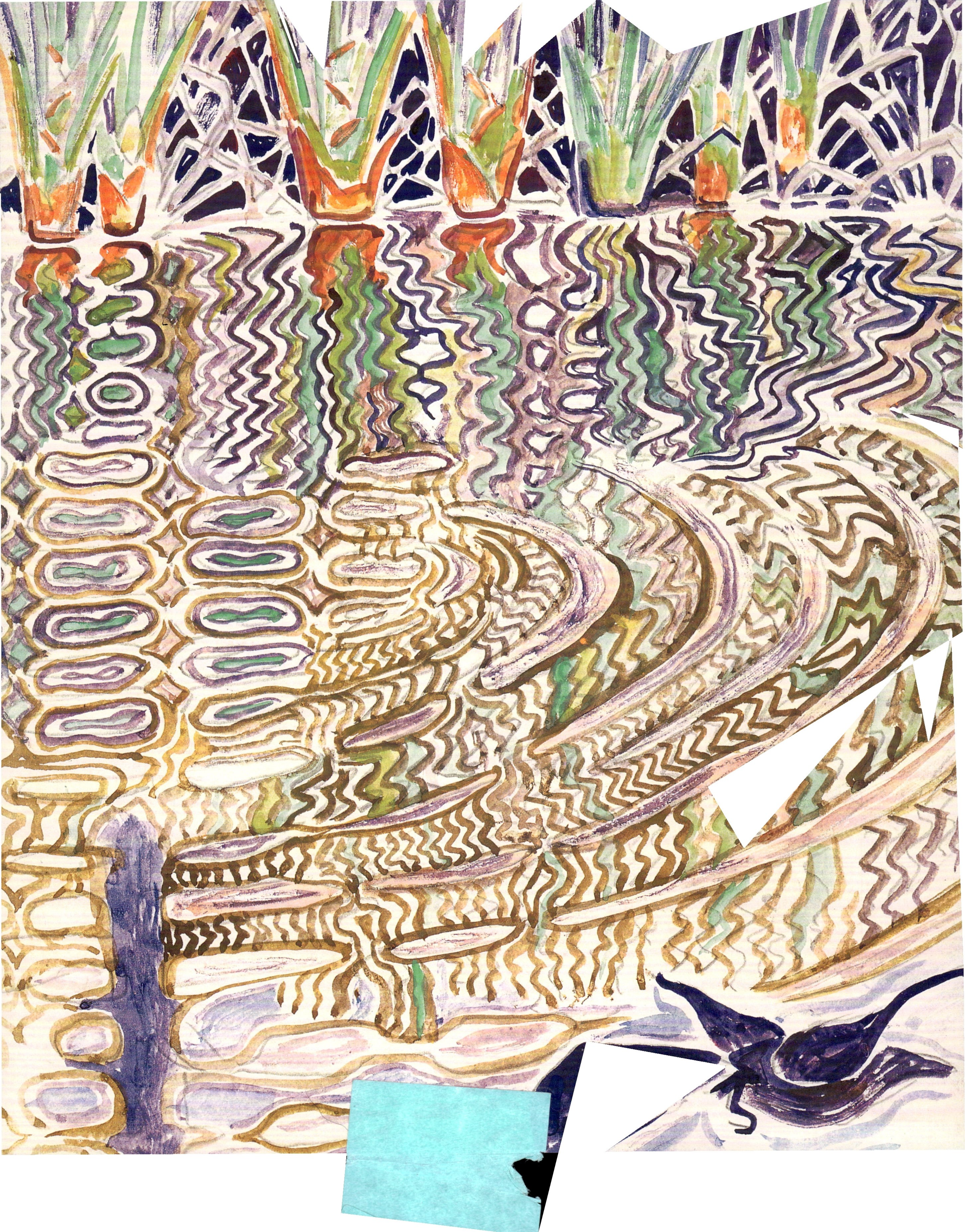

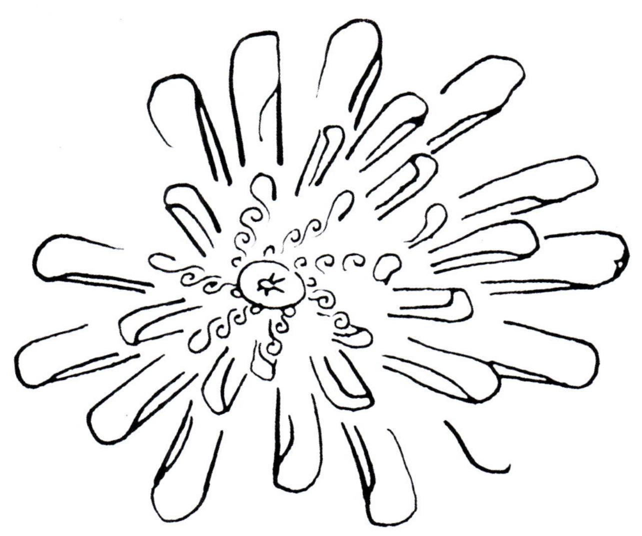

THE HARMONIOUS ART OF WALTER ANDERSON

PATRICIA PINSON

"A genius is amongst us," exclaimed Guy Northrop, art critic for the Memphis *Commercial Appeal*, when he reviewed the 1950 exhibition at the Brooks Memorial Art Gallery. "Never before has a city seen such a show as this. . . . Anderson stands as tall as Marin but on different terrain."[1] In 1999, the writer of "Capturing the Magic of the Gulf Coast" in *The Chronicle of Higher Education* still noted that he was in the "presence of genius" when he looked at the Ocean Springs Community Center murals. He compared Anderson's mural to the journals of Meriwether Lewis for their boldness and sense of wonder, concluding that Anderson's paintings "pass the test of greatness."[2] Patti Carr Black, author of *Art in Mississippi, 1720–1980*, refers to him as the most outstanding artist the South has produced. He has been called a "regionalist" and then a "southern" artist; clearly an appreciation of the scope and universality of this man's oeuvre has been late in coming. But, as in the case of J. S. Bach, whom he revered, awareness of his contribution to art has steadily grown since his death. His significance in the broader context of American art is now being established, and comparisons are being drawn with van Gogh and Kandinsky in Europe.

His output was astounding. He painted watercolors and oils and drew in pen and ink, pencil, and crayon. He sculpted in wood, carved furniture, cut large linoleum blocks for printing, painted murals, carved and decorated earthenware. He also kept copious journals (ninety of them) that contained his observations, his ideas, and his poetry, compelling the viewer to stop and to see the natural. His reputation today, however, rests on his murals in Ocean Springs, Mississippi, and the thousands

Reflections in a Bull Rush Pool, ca. 1960
Watercolor on paper, 11 x 8½ in.
The Family of Walter Anderson

of watercolors that he produced during the last sixteen years of his life. The watercolors are on 8½-x-11-inch paper, but they are not small in scope. Like haiku or illuminated manuscripts, they vibrate with broader connotations; they are microcosms of universal meaning. Because most of these works were on typing paper, much of his output was lost during his life due to his own neglect and self-critical attitude (it was the process that was important, not the completed work), and many other works have been purchased and disappeared onto the walls of homes throughout the South. So it is difficult to get a very clear idea of the total scope of his work and, consequently, many of the brilliant moments of his "realizations" are surely lost to us.

Yet, in the thousands of works left, it is possible to trace the dark brilliance of a mind which worked itself relentlessly to see, to understand, and to merge with the miracle of creation that surrounded him. Perhaps his bouts with the terra incognita of the mind both sharpened the inner vision and intensified the compulsion to capture the fleeting image.

What is it that makes this artist exceptional? All great art has its own uniqueness and its own "strangeness"; otherwise it would not stand apart. Writers as disparate as E. A. Poe and Francis Bacon believed that there is no exquisite beauty without some "strangeness."[3] Anderson often recorded haunting instances when "everything I see is new and strange." Such freshness of vision gives a new appreciation of the exceptional nature of the ordinary. This ability to back away from the commonplace and see it with new perception was one of the characteristics of Anderson's work. Indeed, when he returned from the journey into mental illness in 1940, he did many drawings from a bird's-eye view, looking down at himself and his world from a place apart. In a larger sense, he seemed to feel some identity with a particular bird—the pelican. (Leonardo da Vinci had a similar response to the vulture.) The identification of the pelican with the coastal areas, its strange awkward beauty, and its absolute mastery of the air made it especially appealing to Anderson. He wrote one of his most poetic logs and a beautiful essay on life among the pelicans. The fact that the bird almost became extinct and yet returned during his lifetime is also no small similarity. Anderson, too, seemed awkward in the company of the citizens of Ocean Springs, and his mental illness threatened a kind of extinction, but he was able to return with an uncanny mastery of his own ability to explore new and strange vistas.

The compulsion to seek the unity of all existence became Anderson's raison d'etre. He broke the boundaries between himself and nature and sought to merge with it. He ignored many of the traditions set up by civilization which called for a man to socialize and to lead as comfortable an existence as possible. Instead, he weathered the elements for weeks at a time on an island alone and without shelter or when traveling by bicycle sometimes for hundreds of miles. Whereas Thoreau sought to experience Walden Pond by observing nature from a small house, Anderson sought to experience nature by living in it. This acceptance of nature in all its forms and all its cycles is what produced the works that would have been otherwise unattainable. Composer Toru Takemitsu approaches music the same way: "Rather than on the ideology of self-expression, music should be based on a profound relationship to nature" and "[H]ow wonderful it would be if the incomplete composer could be made whole by this act of performing his own music."[4] Takemitsu would merge with sound and the silence surrounding it as Anderson wished to blend into the natural world surrounding him through his act of painting it. "I drew it in ecstasy. It was a concentrated image that nothing could take from me."[5]

When he found out that Einstein was dead, he commented that he felt a real kinship with Einstein's search for the unifying factor, and respected him for seeking out the answers to deep, fundamental questions. Anderson felt that the answers he and Einstein had found were the same—that everything was part of a larger unity.[6] Not only did Anderson see the unity in the senses and the sciences, but in the matter, air, and water of the earth, as well. In the block prints and in the murals, he often used the same design for the movement of air, the wings of birds, and the waves. They became extensions of the same compulsion of fluid motion.

Anderson saw the history of art as having a certain cohesion as well. His travels and his study of art history opened up the imagery of the past. In the murals of 1934[7] he captured the simplification and elongation of form from Egyptian and Minoan wall painting. But he intuitively drew on the mystical power of size and shape rather than using the ancient styles to create an effect. One finds references to cave painting, to Gothic art, to Mesopotamia, and to Greece as well. They were absorbed into his own style. "I've had very good training, you know. I've studied and profited from all of art history. I think few people are better qualified to paint the appearance of things than I. Yet, that is not really what I want. The heart is the thing that counts, the mingling of my heart with the heart of the wild bird; to become one with the thing I see. . . ."[8]

Anderson also continually made alliances with music—he often seemed to see the structure of music visually. "There are constant qualities in art and music which go thru all paintings or music regardless of the name underneath."[9] Many composers, writers, and artists have experienced a synesthesia particularly of color and sound, but Anderson often saw the environment as a musical score with the spaces (measures) defined by pine trees, and birds on power lines as melody. He wrote that "harmony is not just a word, it is literally true."[10] He saw the movement of flocks of birds as if they were a polyphonic segment of music with the constancy of a figured bass beneath. "I was greatly impressed by their beautiful form, and the tremendously musical harmonies of rising from the ground at my approach, some returning in one direction and dropping to their nest and hundreds of others soaring in the opposite direction. . . .There was a definite order in the rising, soaring, and returning. . . . Minor motifs of gulls on the water. . . ."[11]

This description could easily refer to the contour and dynamics of a musical phrase, or describe the polyphony of a Baroque chorus. He said that the order (in nature) is there if we just see it. On the other hand, most classical music is built on natural movement in its composition and in performance. Anderson's line and its subtlety is as refined as a melody by Bach or Brahms. The harmony is the space into which it is placed to provide its context.

The structure of an idea can be similar whether in two dimensions of height and width or in the dimensions of time and its organization. Anderson composed the early murals[12] like a Haydn symphony, with clear melodic phrases across the regularity of marked-off spaces. Other compositions from the 1940s are rather polyphonic in their organization. Of course, he had studied music and was a devoted listener to the New York Philharmonic on the radio and to his own records; he also attended performances, including traveling to Pennsylvania for the Bach Festival, after which he "levitated for days."[13] His wife wrote of an instance when he was able to complete a movement of Beethoven's *Emperor Concerto* in his mind after the radio performance was interrupted by a power failure.[14] He returned to her feeling that he had captured the sound with paint. So, like Paul Klee and Arnold Schönberg, he felt at home in both fields of art.[15]

His sensitivity to sound extended into the verbal as well. "I am continually arriving from some strange planet and everything I see is new and strange."[16] This freshness of approach and breadth of resource worked equally well in grasping an image or an idea. He painted verbal pictures of a cat who left flowers for footprints, spoke of the turtle as having the flowers above its head as we do the stars, and said that thoughts are like yellow butterflies (whoever would catch them "must have a net with a long handle").[17] We seek harmony with the environment so that "we are part of the music instead of an unwelcome interruption" to the divine symphony.[18] Such handling of words is closely akin to the handling of line and color. As a poet refines his idea by keeping only the necessary words, the artist rejects the unnecessary to identify the most essential aspect of the image. If he can add information by alluding to an unexpected image, he gets the attention of the viewer or reader, who is surprised. Anderson wrote with metaphors as fresh as his water-mixed paint. He handled the language in some instances as deftly as he drew one line and captured a bird or a cow. Sometimes he drew on the literature of the past just as he did in art. His poems on Columbus and Leif Eriksson recall the drama of a firelit night with a bard weaving a story with repetition and sonority, just as he referred to the cave paintings or Minoan wall paintings to restate the age-old truths which change only in the language used.

Regardless of the breadth of his ability in parallel fields and his encompassing vision, his significance as an artist lies in the visual way he conveys his ideas. He is one of the greatest masters of line in the twentieth century. The exploration of line as the basic element of communication runs through the history of humankind. Paul Klee describes line as a point going on a journey, and Adolfo Best-Maugard summarizes visual history into seven basic lines or linear motifs. One of the key elements of Anderson's style is his exploration of these lines and the building of his own vocabulary of meaning through the passage of the point. Anderson's use of line is similar to improvisational jazz, which allows each soloist to interpret freely, but within the structure of an armature. The pressure of the thumb is translated into the brush or pencil that makes the lines so sensitive that you feel the form with the eye. He often pushes the reduction of the figure to its essence or to the most economic presence that identifies its idiosyncratic movement in a line—a cow or bird. The line drawings are lyrical, matching movement with rhythm, and often use repetition and variation. They often capture the momentary, the fleeting image that few even register. It was mainly on line and lyrical design that Anderson made his living decorating the pots at Shearwater. The style of the watercolors in the 1930s and 1940s also emphasizes repetition of line and shape and limits the palette to delicate primary colors.

Beyond his virtuoso use of sheer line, he developed the three-dimensional quality of the line as edge with equal genius, employing an open marking system similar to that of Willem de Kooning. When line defines the outside of the edge, or the inside of it, or even the center or top of the edge, a kinetic energy develops. Edges are as descriptive of the space that they inhabit as is the throwing of the voice so it emerges at another point in space. The edges of a figure sink in and out of an image, and the crispness of that edge can denote whether it is going to move inside or outside. There is a gestural quality that allows the space to evolve as if it is coming out or pushing back in. It is this quality of line and edge that gives an animal its life, rather than being just a static image.[19]

Anderson also uses negative space as a positive element. As with a musical instrument, the sound travels beyond the (positive) strings into the (negative) space of the hall. That negative space gives the positive space its context and, therefore, its life. Anderson uses lines of color or auras to define the areas, or he overlaps the positive and the negative by opening the boundary lines between. He makes a figure of a cat or cow fit into and fill the shape of a page by working the negative spaces with color, making negative space become positive forms or outlines, or opening the edges between the two where the space becomes ambiguous.

During the 1950s and until his death in 1965, he was intrigued with color. When he sometimes had to draw with a pencil because he did not have his color available, he wrote the colors on the drawing. The Little Room, for example, vibrates with intense pinks and yellows as if he were awakening from a monochromatic dream, and the watercolors take on a chromatic intensity they had not had before. Even the most ephemeral color of a wet oyster shell and the iridescence of a grackle's black feathers suddenly take on a life of their own.

Line, shape, edge, color—these are the tools that Walter Anderson used to explore his relationship to his world. For an artist to be significant in history, he or she must have something of consequence to say to the rest of the world, and then the labor-intensive experience of skill takes over. The discipline of sound training and of rational thought must form the envelope in which the message is sent. Here is where Anderson's excellent training in art and his quick mind gave him the tools that would serve him wherever he explored—whether as a "decorator" of objects for the public to purchase at a low price or as a voyager into uncharted regions.

But there must be a bit of "strangeness," too, to give the image or message a bit of ambiguity or delight. When one looks at an artwork, one can see the mind of the artist there, playing, directing, cajoling, leading us to see through his eyes or to discover something new through the merging of our visions. Walter Anderson's rare gift of curiosity about the other side of the world or about the crab by his foot whetted his hunger to explore, to discover. "All that I see is new and strange." He lets us see the wonders and ambiguities of his (our) world by holding the door ajar. He lived voraciously, moving where his mind led him, drinking life in great gulps, leaving thousands of artworks and words. Perhaps he burned himself out, dying at a youthful sixty-two when his heart stopped after a bout with cancer surgery. But his own death was just as he saw it with the creatures on the island—death is a part of life and it in turn nourishes the living. Nothing is lost. His death came after a life spent in the most honorable of human explorations—life with some understanding of its meaning—and we, the living, replenish our spirits on the fruits of his mind.

NOTES

1. Guy Northrop, Jr., "Sheer Genius Flavors Show by Anderson," Memphis *Commercial Appeal*, 17 September 1950.

2. "Capturing the Magic of the Gulf Coast," *The Chronicle of Higher Education*, 3 September 1999.

3. Quoted by Robert K. Wallace in *Jane Austen and Mozart: Classical Equilibrium in Fiction and Music* (Athens, GA: University of Georgia Press), 1983, p. 23.

4. Toru Takemitsu, "Nature and Music," in *Confronting Silence: Selected Writings (*Berkeley, CA: Fallen Leaf Press, 1995), p. 8.

5. Redding S. Sugg, Jr., ed., *The Horn Island Logs of Walter Inglis Anderson*, rev. ed. (Jackson: University Press of Mississippi, 1985), p. 139.

6. Agnes Grinstead Anderson, *Approaching the Magic Hour: Memories of Walter Anderson*, ed. Patti Carr Black (Jackson: University Press of Mississippi, 1989), p. 140.

7. There were six parts to a mural created for the Ocean Springs High School that were funded under the Federal Art Project of the Works Progress Administration. See Francis V. O'Connor, "The Murals of Walter Anderson: An Encompassing Vision," in this volume.

8. Anderson, *Approaching the Magic Hour*, p. 140.

9. From Walter Anderson's handwritten manuscripts at the Mississippi Department of Archives and History, Jackson, Mississippi, collected by Patricia Pinson, 23 May 1996.

10. Archives.

11. Sugg, *Horn Island Logs*, p. 44.

12. The murals *Ocean Springs: Past and Present* were done as a commission from the Public Works of Art Project, part of the New Deal art programs during the Depression. The agency later became the Works Progress Administration (WPA).

13. Archives.

14. This is a particularly charming story in *Approaching the Magic Hour* (p. 54). Sissy Anderson concludes by saying, "Bob was equating music with color and form. The *Emperor* became extravagant sunsets with dark, violet clouds."

15. Swiss artist Paul Klee (1879–1940) had intensive training in music as a child and incorporates the linear designs of musical symbols and string instrument shapes in his artwork. Austrian composer Arnold Schönberg (1874–1951) was one of the innovators of serial music and a skilled painter. For an in-depth study of the relationship of art and music in the twentieth century, see Karin v. Maur, *The Sound of Painting: Music in Modern Art* (New York: Prestel, 1999).

16. Mary Anderson Pickard, "Yellow Butterflies: A Reading of Excerpts from the Writings of Walter Inglis Anderson" (Ocean Springs, MS: The Walter Anderson Estate, n.d.), n.p.

17. "Yellow Butterflies," n.p.

18. Walter Anderson, *A Symphony of Animals* (Jackson: University Press of Mississippi, 1996), p. 1.

19. I am indebted to Ted Rose, author of *Discovering Drawing* (Worcester: Davis, 2000), for his insights on Walter Anderson's style.

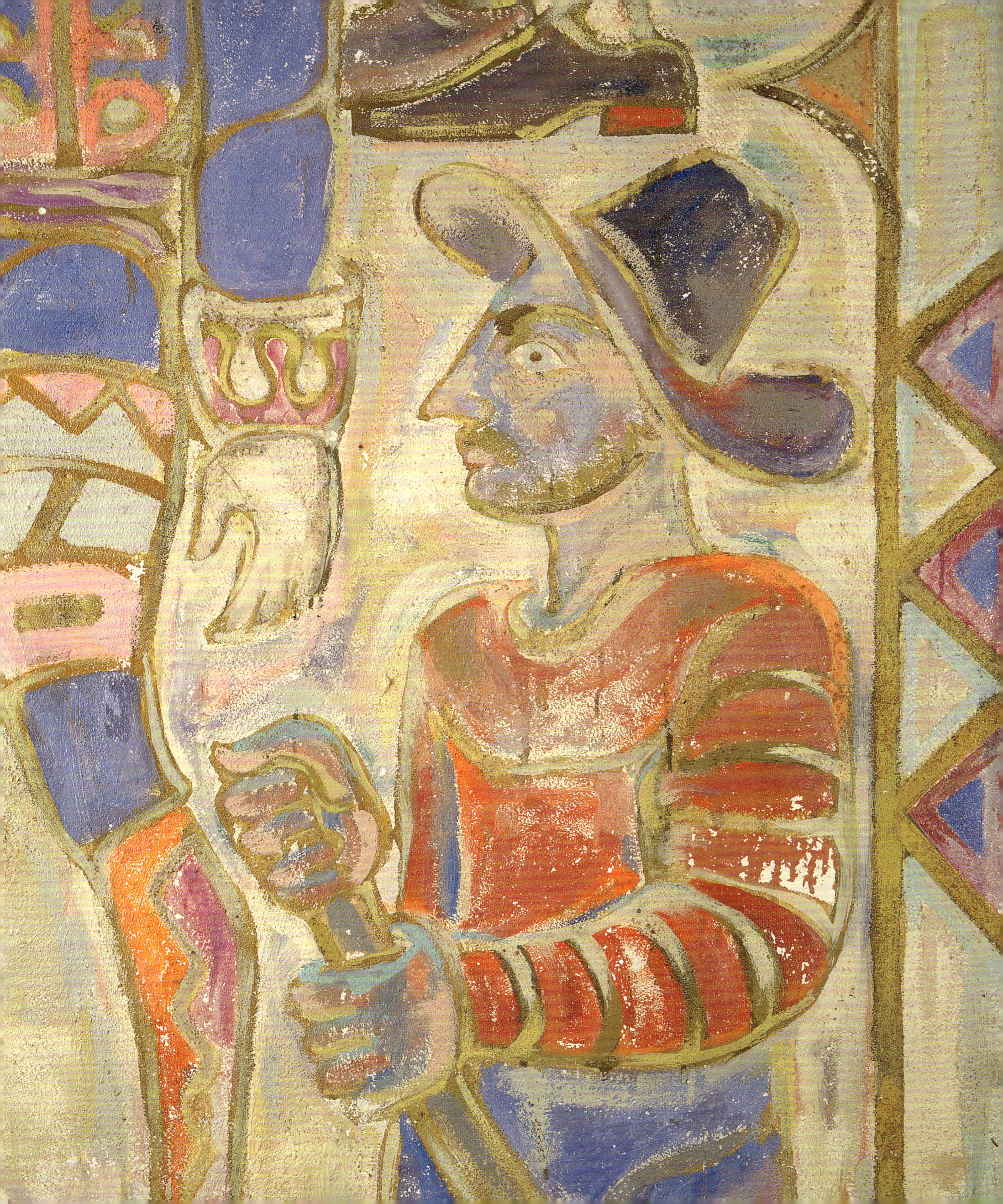

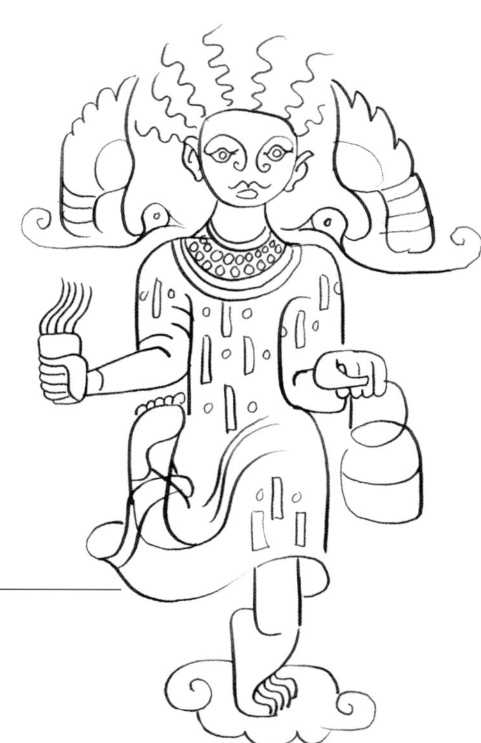

THE SEEKER BECOMES A SEER: "MY EYE IS STRANGE TO THEE"

SUSAN C. LARSEN

He who would catch my thoughts must have a net with a long handle.
—Walter Anderson[1]

Walter Inglis Anderson had no great need for the world's acclaim or for the approval of art critics. If he could see the present exhibition, he might be surprised and delighted to witness our great admiration for his artistic legacy. One hundred years after the artist's birth, his watercolors, murals, ceramics, prints, and drawings refuse to settle into a comfortable familiarity. Their restless and impolite intensity is so seductive that they rebuke standard historical analysis. What can we say of an artist who sought no career advantage beyond the esteem of a few friends and the opportunity to earn a simple wage in his family's pottery studio? How can we compare Walter Anderson to others of his generation when he found his own artistic world so entirely self-sufficient? The commonplace ambitions of our art world seem predictable and pale beside the cosmic sweep of Anderson's daily communion with birds, turtles, the sky, and the earth of his beloved Mississippi coastal waters. We are challenged to rethink the purposes of art as we witness the reach and the struggle of his never-settled and luminous mind.

Self-portrait from the Community Center mural, 1951–1952
Oil and tempera on stucco
The City of Ocean Springs, Mississippi

Walter Anderson's self-documentation in the form of his handwritten diaries and logbooks have drawn thousands of seekers into his now dark, then light-filled world. A vivid and vulnerable soul, he sought personal redemption through direct experience of the worst and the best that human consciousness can sustain. Akin to the wanderings of a spiritual pilgrim or a penitent, Anderson's travels over the earth to places near and far yielded fleeting moments of enlightenment. To this earth, he left a body of work illuminated by glimpses of his transcendent moments as he struggled to express his ecstasy and pain in paint, in clay, and in words.

It is clear that Walter Anderson was a difficult person for his family and his community to understand and to sustain. It is also very clear that they loved him and struggled to enable him while he was alive. They continue to revere his capacity to create beauty. They remember his unique ability to inspire daring and fantasy in the midst of ordinary life. Walter Anderson is still beloved among his family and the townspeople of Ocean Springs. His spirited unconventionality, his spontaneity, and his odd naturalness have become the very soul of that engaging and uniquely appealing town.

Walter Inglis Anderson is an almost exact contemporary of the seminal figures of the New York school of painting and sculpture. Born in 1903, Anderson would have been part of a generation of American artists including Adolph Gottlieb (b. 1903), Mark Rothko (b. 1903), Willem de Kooning (b. 1904), Isamu Noguchi (b. 1904), Arshile Gorky (b. 1904), David Smith (b. 1906), and others. It is almost impossible to consider Walter Anderson in this company because the assumptions and outcomes of his art are so very different and his life experiences so separate from the mainstream issues of his day. While Anderson's contemporaries worked to build cultural bridges between American art and European modern movements, especially Surrealism, Walter Anderson worked in geographical, social, and mental isolation in Ocean Springs, Mississippi.

Anderson's artistic program has more in common with that of a previous turn-of-the-century generation schooled in a scientific appreciation of nature, tutored in world literature and ancient mythology, and brought up to admire American transcendentalist poetry and prose. To his contemporaries working in New York City during the 1930s and 1940s, Surrealism offered a persuasive and timely set of ideas. Aspects of the Surrealist program enabled the individual to explore the unconscious, to discover secular pathways to spirituality and to flirt with the inner world of mental illness, among other things. Walter Anderson, perhaps ignorant of Surrealist doctrine, was destined from birth to live through the most trying and tragic dimensions of human consciousness on a daily basis without giving it a literary or artistic name.

Anderson's art is modest in scale and touchingly earnest; it whispers and laughs and shouts and gently persuades. The art of his contemporaries is boldly declarative, worldly and ironic, confident and monumental. Walter Anderson speaks of the fragility of each living creature, including himself. The artist struggled to describe each bird, turtle, fish, or flower and to place it within a boundless eternal cycle of nature. Anderson's work is sometimes abstract, but it is never completely an abstraction. It has a sophistication born of a useful set of ideas and circumstances afforded to the artist by his unique upbringing and education. Anderson also had the ability to retain and remain loyal to a few cherished artistic principles. In one respect, he did resemble others of his generation of American artists. He let loose the undeniable force of his explorative personality and pushed life's experiences to the very limit.

> To be inspired. That is the thing.
> To be possessed; to be bewitched.
> To be obsessed. That is the thing.
> To be inspired.[2]
> —William Baziotes

The life and work of Walter Anderson would not have its strange richness were it not for the cultural vitality of his parents' home in New Orleans. A patient and successful father, George Walter Anderson, a grain dealer, provided a secure economic life while the artist's mother, Annette McConnell Anderson, filled the household with world literature, music, art, and lively conversation. Their home at 553 Broadway in the Garden District afforded Walter and his two brothers easy access to local parks and libraries. Annette Anderson often took them to Newcomb College where a thriving art department promoted an aesthetic outlook in every facet of modern life. The ideas of John Ruskin, William Morris, and other luminaries of the Arts and Crafts movement would provide the backbone of artistic philosophy in the Anderson household. Classical world literature fueled the imaginations of the Anderson children as they read and quoted from *Don Quixote*, *Paradise Lost*, "The Rime of the Ancient Mariner," *Alice in Wonderland*, and countless other works in an ample and often consulted family library. Emerson, Melville, Thoreau, and Whitman were among the American writers read by children and adults alike. Handsome three-dimensional vessels adorned with subtle glazes and carved decorations from the Newcomb Pottery were a feature of daily life in the Anderson home.

There was little distinction between art and decoration in this culturally privileged environment. It was just as important to create a beautiful ceramic pot as to decorate it with color and lively narrative forms. Annette Anderson was herself a gifted painter who respected the application of painting techniques and principles to other endeavors such as textile design, the carving and decorating of furniture, mural painting, book illustration, and other forms of art. It is little wonder that the art of Walter Anderson takes so many forms so naturally without apparent self-consciousness or hesitation. He had the ability to acquire technical skills as he needed them and enough self-confidence and practicality to focus upon the eventual outcome of the work without letting technique get in the way.

George Walter Anderson emphasized the practical necessities of life and supported efforts to acquaint his three sons with the industrial arts, business, and physical culture. One such effort involved the sending of Peter and Walter Anderson to St. John's School in Manlius, New York. Walter would spend four perhaps painful years (1915–1919) acquiring an academic and military education away from the supportive environment of his mother's artistic circle. The deepening of World War I created concern about having the boys so far away from home. Peter and Walter came back to New Orleans and enrolled at the Isidore Newman School, which offered a curriculum of practical arts such as furniture making, pottery, metalwork, mathematics, and English. These studies reinforced connections between art, high-level craft, and business, concepts which would prove important to the success of the Anderson family's Shearwater Pottery in a few years to come.

As Walter Anderson grew into young manhood, his gifts as a draftsman were evident to all who knew him. With his parents' support, he traveled to New York City and enrolled in the autumn of 1922 at what would later be known as the Parsons School of Design. He struggled to accommodate to urban life and found the school narrowly focused upon the practical and application of artistic principles to commercial advertising. Christopher Maurer's excellent new historical study of the Shearwater Pottery places Walter Anderson as a spectator at the 1923 Independents Exhibition in New York City.[3] As a young art student, Anderson also frequented exhibitions of the Hispanic Society of America. Like many of his peers, he haunted the galleries of the Metropolitan Museum of Art. On several occasions, Walter Anderson remarked upon the work of a little-known Mexican modernist, Adolfo Best-Maugard. The Mexican painter and filmmaker's pedagogical essays published in English by Knopf in 1925 would have an effect upon Walter Anderson's style and artistic outlook in the 1930s and would soon shape his formal vocabulary for a lifetime.[4]

Walter Anderson's sojourn in New York City was brief, and it occurred at a time when the impact of the historic 1913 Armory Show was perceived to have passed. In the opinion of many, modernism was over and sanity had returned to American art. Collectors of advanced European modernist art were few, even in New York City. American modernists like Patrick Henry Bruce, Arthur Dove, Marsden Hartley, and many others struggled to earn even a subsistence living.

It is not surprising that Walter Anderson's understanding of modern art should rest upon his own rich personal background of late-nineteenth-century sources. The diagrams and essays in Adolpho Best-Maugard's *A Method for Creative Design* would have easily fulfilled Anderson's desire to be modern. An elegant and seemingly simple system of abstract notation, it featured seven motives: the spiral, circle, half-circle, S-curve, wavy line, zigzag, and straight line. Moreover, many of the ideas would be familiar from Anderson's studies of decorative arts. Their possible application to his own life and art would have been quite clear and inviting.

Walter Anderson and his generation took part in a revolution in the visual training of artists. As the spoils of empire poured into the great museums of England, France, Germany, and the United States, a breathtaking array of world art was spread before the public. The nineteenth-century passion for encyclopedic learning and cross-cultural synthesis led to a long sequence of revival styles: the Classic Revival, the Gothic Revival, the Egyptian and Etruscan revivals, and other original syntheses of historical periods. Scholars and publishers produced handsome engraved volumes that were quickly circulated among artists and architects. Creative minds embellished the basic vocabulary of historical styles and suggested sometimes fanciful ethical and psychological programs for individual periods and civilizations.

Artists and designers were often charmed and intrigued by the novelty of antique styles and made wide use of such volumes as Owen Jones's *Grammar of Ornament* published in England in 1856.[5] It offered splendid color plates of formal decorative designs from China, India, Egypt, Byzantium, Persia, Tibet, Oceania, and many other places and cultures. In effect, these became the intellectual property of the Victorian world to use as it pleased without subscribing to the social and philosophical systems out of which each style and civilization had arisen. Selected as source material for decoration and architecture, many of the beautiful pages of Jones's *Grammar of Ornament* feature flat patterned, allover surfaces suitable for adaptation to fabrics, furniture, architectural ornament, and wallpapers. These would, in turn, influence the artists and designers of the Arts and Crafts movement in England, Europe, and America. By the 1880s and 1890s, nativist American architects and designers such as Louis Sullivan and Frank Lloyd Wright emerged as innovators who were able to construct a new American ornament based upon local flora and fauna. Even the stricter realist style of John Audubon inspired artists eager to take local beauty from the particular to the universal.[6]

Best-Maugard reflected this revolution of taste and thought when he wrote, "It is the intention of this method of teaching graphic art to return to the sources, to begin with basic symbols, and little by little to establish in the mind of the student his own sense of, and his kinship with, these laws: he is the natural heir of all the stored wisdom accumulated in Time, and he can better use his heritage if he knows its boundaries . . . The past is an apparently formless body, carrying in it all that we are, our knowledge and experience, and all that we may draw upon to strengthen our own contribution to the present."[7]

Among the paradoxes of this overwhelming richness of source material was a growing cultural relativism as historical styles lost their power to stand for a body of ideas, specific places, times, and meanings. Artists could freely borrow from the Egyptian, the Greek, or the Chinese visual lexicon without considering formal elements as specific cultural signifiers. The reductivism of modern art arose, in part, from the elementalist philosophies of the late nineteenth century. Finding the root causes of human creativity and vocabulary of universal visual symbols offered a pathway to an evolved modern personality. Best-Maugard's seven elements provide an inventory for such a quest. The cross-cultural visual comparisons of Carl Jung also helped to open artists to other civilizations and styles while giving them a grander contemporary meaning.

Walter Anderson made the surprising choice to enroll in the degree program for artists at the Pennsylvania Academy of the Fine Arts in late 1923. For a young man of his imaginative powers and strong temperament, the strict curriculum based upon the principles of classical antiquity and a commitment to a carefully studied form of realism would have seemed a poor fit. However, at the age of twenty, Walter Anderson had enough maturity to profit from the academy's teachings while remaining independent of its somewhat restrictive curriculum.

Fellow student Frank Baisden described Anderson's drawing style as a "romantic and broad drawing technique."[8] He said that Anderson "employed color in flat decorative areas."[9] Hours of drawing the required plaster casts of antique sculpture gave Anderson's style an added sureness and precision. Timeworn academic approaches were enlivened by the influence of Professor Henry McCarter. His lectures on Impressionist color and the creation of light in a painting would have a profound influence upon the young Walter Anderson. The existence of Cubism, Dada, and the entire modern revolution in art seems curiously absent from Anderson's classroom experience at the Pennsylvania Academy of the Fine Arts.

The strong pull of the natural world would assert itself before Anderson finished his formal studies. Seeking living creatures to draw, he spent many hours watching and describing the animals in the Philadelphia Zoo. Abstracted into curves, straight lines, circles, and spirals, his spirited animal drawings contain the sinewy force of an antelope, the impossible mass of an elephant, and the elegant physical prowess of a tiger. Adept at describing, characterizing, and transforming from nature, Anderson continued a tradition of naturalism exemplified by artists as diverse as John James Audubon and Martin Johnson Heade. His animal studies earned Walter Anderson the Packard award for animal drawing in 1924. He won the coveted Cresson prize in 1927, which offered him the opportunity to take a longed-for trip to France.

Anderson's eagerness to travel to Paris arose from several motives, not all of them related to his artistic studies. We know from the testiment of Baisden and also from Anderson's later narratives to his family that he wished to present himself to the Institute for the Harmonious Development of Man at the Chateau du Prieuré near Fontainebleau as an aspirant for instruction and enlightenment.[10] During the 1920s, many American intellectuals and artists in particular fell under the spell of esoteric doctrines arising from the Russian expatriate community in world capitals including Paris and New York. Helena Blavatsky presented her synthetic fusion of the world's religious texts with strongly occult dimensions under the name theosophy.[11] She claimed to have received instruction from lamas in Tibet, and her mission on earth was to disseminate their teachings for the betterment of humanity. Blavatsky's ideas circulated widely in numerous books and periodicals. She toured the world giving lectures and had many active disciples. She stimulated many spiritual seekers to travel to India and Tibet for instruction. When Walter Anderson suddenly left on a trip to China in 1949, he revealed that the ultimate goal of the journey was to visit and study in the lamaseries of Tibet.

The writings and ideas of Peter Demianovich Ouspensky, based in part upon theosophical principles, were also very appealing to Walter Anderson. Ouspensky proposed the existence of a Fourth Dimension, an unseen level of reality uniting all creation which might be sensed by persons evolved, open-minded, and openhearted enough to perceive it. Ouspensky proposed that three-dimensional reality was indeed an illusion and that plants and animals perceived the world quite differently from how humans did, something closer to two-dimensionality. Ouspensky also speaks of life forms evolving in space according to an unfolding spiral, for example, in the growth of trees, the motion of a bird in flight, the contours of a seashell. According to theosophical teachings and those of Ouspensky, the goal of life was not fame nor profit nor love of family and country, but enlightenment and fusion with the universal Oversoul. Artists had a special role in the development of human consciousness, according to Ouspensky: "The artist must be clairvoyant; he must see that which others do not see; he must be a magician: must possess the power to make others see that which they do not themselves see, but which he does see."[12]

These ideas are complex, many say unsystematic, and they lost currency in intellectual circles after World War I. While a student at the Pennsylvania Academy of the Fine Arts, Walter Anderson attended off-campus lectures by A. R. Orage, a prominent figure in the movement who explained Ouspensky's ideas of the Fourth Dimension. He also introduced his audience to the spiritual practices of George Ivanovitch Gurdjieff.[13] It is likely that Walter Anderson was receptive, in part, because he had loved the writings of Emerson, Whitman, and much of the American transcendentalist literature throughout his childhood.

Arriving in Paris, Anderson traveled to Prieuré and presented himself as an applicant to the Institute for the Harmonious Development of Man. But Anderson soon realized that the institute had become an elegant salon of Russian expatriates, French aristocrats, and other wealthy students. It was not the kind of place that would welcome an earnest young American artist of modest means. One aspect of the teachings of Gurdjieff may have stayed with Walter Anderson and become a part of his own mode of addressing nature. Gurdjieff advocated a trance-like ecstatic dance as a method of spiritual awakening. The "Gurdjieffian Dances" were taught worldwide as a unique and very physically demanding form of spiritual observance. The logbooks of Walter Anderson frequently describe his own ecstatic dances as an outlet for his joy and wonder and perhaps also as a way of communicating with the spirits of natural creatures.

The charms of Paris, its great museums and proud architecture, held little allure for Walter Anderson once he realized that his other purposes for the trip could not be achieved. Surely he saw many of the world's masterworks in Paris, but his own taste for the raw and elemental drew him away from the city. Anderson saw truth, beauty, and forthrightness in the Gothic cathedrals of France. He loved the cave paintings of Les Eyzies in the Dordogne. His was an interesting choice because cave paintings were yet to be widely admired by artists and intellectuals as complete and legitimate works of art. They were more often studied as fragmentary archaeological curiosities.

We have dwelt upon the intellectual and spiritual resources that Walter Anderson was able to bring to his art by 1930, because these would provide the direction, the precious stability, and the emotional balance he needed so very much in his later life. He would not have a usual career as an artist. He did not seek a gallery, a dealer, an urban studio, or even the secure life of a teacher of art. Walter Anderson returned to his family possessing a formal education but one shaped by the artist's strong preferences and inclinations. The creation of works of art became, for Anderson, not a job but a spiritual calling.

When Walter Anderson returned home in 1929, he came into a new and stimulating environment. His parents had moved to a twenty-five-acre residence in the Mississippi town of Ocean Springs. His brother Peter had already established Shearwater, his pottery studio on the lovely peninsula near the Mississippi shoreline. Romantic yearning for the hand of Agnes Grinstead encouraged Walter to go to work with Peter on a commercially successful line of small sculptures. Their "widgets" took the form of animals, sports figures, scenes of southern Negro life, and other highly charged, odd, and whimsical subjects.

Shearwater vessels decorated by Walter Anderson reflect the scope of his education and the eclecticism of his interest in world civilization. Sinuous repeated forms weave around plates, vessels, and the borders of Peter's other ceramic creations. Some works recall the energy of Minoan vases and others the layered hierarchy of Greek amphoras; still other vessels have a Persian or a Chinese vocabulary of form. Some of the Shearwater ceramic vessels and sculptures of the 1930s, especially the leopards, lions, and other stylized beasts, conform loosely to the vocabulary of international Art Deco which by now was a popular consumer taste. A few designs are quite similar to the sample drawings from Best-Maugard. More often, though, Anderson's sources are utterly transformed by his inventiveness and the imprint of his Dionysian touch.

The Great Depression found its way to Ocean Springs as it had to every other part of America by the early 1930s. Walter Anderson looked for opportunities from the Works Progress Administration and submitted designs for several murals. His panoramic history of Mississippi for the Ocean Springs High School gave the young artist his first taste of a public audience and his first serious standing in the local community. These murals exemplify the careful draftsmanship and sophisticated formal training Anderson had acquired in his long years of study. Their abstraction does not come from the usual Cubist and Expressionist sources common to most twentieth-century American modernists. Strong outline, flat forms, and frequent but subtle quotations from antiquity all contribute to an otherworldly tale of primitive and modern man settling the Ocean Springs area in harmony with nature's undeniable bounty. Anderson is very successful in these panels where his sense of timelessness and multiculturalism is quite appealing and appropriate.

Walter Anderson had yet to work out his important relationships with nature by the mid-1930s. Early oil paintings such as *Androcles and the Lion* (ca. 1935) and *Horse and Rider* (ca. 1935) place man in a paradoxical position, one of vulnerability even as he struggles for dominion over the earth's living creatures. The strong curves, vivid color, and healthy impasto of *Horse and Rider* suggest that Anderson may have been familiar with the Blue Rider period paintings of Franz Mark and Wassily Kandinsky. Anderson's style moved back and forth. For example, he used a different and perhaps more comfortable vocabulary, flat broad planes of color and curvilinear geometry, in *Jockeys Riding Horses* (ca. 1935).

A fateful trip to Baltimore introduced Walter Anderson to Dr. Ned Park, whose ornithological work stimulated Anderson to begin a series of detailed anatomical studies of birds native to the Southeast. Dr. Park showed Walter and his wife, Agnes, a copy of Chapman's *Color Key to North American Birds* and explained that illustrations for a volume devoted to the Southeast would be most welcome and useful.[14] According to Mary Anderson Pickard, her father and his brother gathered specimens but often had to kill the birds in order to study them. Walter Anderson's lovely and careful watercolors such as *Chimney Swift* (ca. 1935), *Nighthawk* (ca. 1935), and many others demonstrate the artist's powers of observation and something of his tenderness toward these creatures. They project a pathos and an elegiac chill that Anderson found deeply disturbing. The entire project was a dark turning point in Anderson's life. The memory of living birds killed in the service of knowledge and art would haunt him for the rest of his life.[15]

The birth of children is generally an event welcomed with joy in the life of a young father. It was not to be the case in the marriage of Walter Anderson and Agnes Grinstead Anderson. Walter was already institutionalized with terrifying mental illness when his daughter Mary was born in 1937. Perhaps still convinced that an artist needed to be utterly free to be "a magician," Anderson may have dreaded the growing bonds of family and the duties of a householder. In a larger sense, Anderson may have feared losing his vocation as clairvoyant and creator of otherworldly beauty. According to Mary Anderson Pickard, her father sometimes identified with the wild birds he began to paint in his highly charged wonderfully original style. Birds need to soar above man's creations, and Anderson envied and admired their freedom from artificial boundaries, their sensitivity to the seasons, and their life in the sunlight and the open air.

The period from 1937 to 1940 was terrible and artistically unproductive as Anderson struggled for mental and spiritual equilibrium. His wife, Agnes, bravely kept the family together and bore a second child, William Walter Anderson, in 1939. Her ability to nurture and provide for her children while caring for her troubled spouse was most heroic and extraordinary.[16] She brought her entire family, two young children, her ailing father, and her troubled husband, together in 1940. Through a wise insight, she guessed that they might perhaps flourish at her family's farm called Oldfields. And so they did for a time.

Several familiar sources reappeared in the art of Walter Anderson as he put his life back together at Oldfields. The clear and reassuring theories of Jay Hambidge and his ideals of dynamic symmetry gave Anderson's work an immediate sense of order and an underlying beauty of proportion.[17] The ideas of Best-Maugard reasserted themselves as Anderson achieved a new level of confident abstraction in his painting. There is a great deal of pattern and repetition in the work Anderson created in Oldfields. Surely aspects of his work at Shearwater informed his paintings, but the new drawings and paintings had larger narrative ambitions and more emotional range, and, as time went by, they were grander in scale. Like stacked figures in an Egyptian tomb frieze, Anderson's parade of geese, cattle, sheep, pigs, and farm cats make their way across the pages of his watercolors. Sometimes they run and gambol; in other works they stand as elegant symbols of biological continuity, the one and the many, throughout countless time.

Despite all of his formal training, Walter Anderson now eschewed conventional perspective in favor of a primitive, vertically stacked space, akin to the spaces of Chinese and Egyptian painting, of Mayan reliefs, of Assyrian sculpture, and of children's art. He now had the power and the means to address the larger issues of life through his art. Anderson's trees are alive with spiral movements, decorated with geometries like the stylized feathers of a painted Chinese peacock or the flame-like halo in a Buddhist sculpture. His repetition of motives, so characteristic of his art, stands for the eternal cycle of life in the biological world. In Anderson's artistic realm, everything is alive, part of a grander whole, aglow in a universe where dynamic order rules.

Anderson hoped to share his beautiful vision of the orderly, living universe with the American public. Finding a source for inexpensive long rolls of wallpaper, he made elegant and multilayered block prints using the motives he developed at Oldfields. He hoped these would serve as decorative embellishments in numerous young households established after World War II. Anderson was willing to sell these at very low cost and offered them like cloth by the yard, so eager was he to share his art with the average citizens of Mississippi.

Anderson's celebrated Calendar Drawings were made during his time at Oldfields. One for each day of the year, they are emblematic of the seasons, the flora and fauna, anniversaries and birthdays and special moments. Anderson liked to describe his "halcyon" moments as days made special by some new and surprising delight. The Calendar Drawings are among his most endearing works cherished by a public able to appreciate the artist's calmer, more ebullient moods, his sense of fun, and his literary turn of phrase. So, too, his volume of drawings *An Alphabet* is a children's classic from a man who truly appreciated the child's innocence and openness to the world.

The larger artistic contribution of Walter Anderson came at great cost to the artist's emotional stability. By 1946, no longer able to sustain an everyday communion with his family, he moved into a cottage on the property and lengthened his periods of wandering and his voyages out to the offshore islands. His work intensified and its space seemed to fragment and shatter into a kaleidoscopic sun shower of color. The pages of his watercolors shine with a brave transparency. No longer dependent upon theories of form or space, Anderson invented each page anew. He shows us a universe full of detail and dizzying incident. It is not the world most of us see through our own human eyes.

Ordinary life requires the suppression and ordering of the constant stream of sensory input, from the beating of our hearts to the intake of our breath to our constant awareness of small shifts of sunlight in a room. Were we to stay fully aware of every sensate impression, the crush of information might entirely overwhelm us.

Some of Anderson's greatest and most original works seem to offer up the full array of nature's sensate realm. Works such as *Oak With Squirrel* (c.1955), where every last fiber of the page is filled with bark, leaves, reflections, and shadows, assault our senses with impossible detail and radiant color. When we find him at last, the tiny squirrel in the lower central portion of the work is a welcome refuge for the eye. Was Anderson's visual abundance a form of camouflage or was it his true picture of the universe?

Walter Anderson's mature works seldom bother with ordinary optical perspectives. He felt free to place his birds, turtles, and elegant shorelines of stylized trees on a blank, open piece of paper. He had no need to fill up every inch of the page; he knew that the universe was already full. His notations point to one man's experience, one soul's agony and delight. His art of the 1950s and early 1960s satisfied the artist's need to be clairvoyant and original. He especially loved "the magic hour before sunset," when the world was bathed in a glow of unifying color. At such times, outward appearance perhaps came close to the lovely and terrifying images of Anderson's inner eye.

Walter Anderson bore mental and physical torment in order to spend days and weeks on the outer coastal islands, especially Horn Island, in raw communication with the birds, fish, turtles, and other living creatures. In perpetual transit, subject to tides, weather, and time, they fly and swim and crawl through his watercolors, leaving traces as vivid and unrepeatable as they did on the sandy beaches. Starting around 1950, Anderson abandoned his studied geometries, his formulas and learned ideas; he was at one with nature's flow.

Where, then, does the art of Walter Anderson fit into the larger history of American art? He has much in common with our greatly admired artistic visionaries such as Charles Burchfield, Morris Graves, and Joseph Stella. He shares the raw nativist voice of his own generation of American painters even though his spiritual program is from another earlier time in our cultural history. Most American children of the twentieth century grew up reading the transcendentalist literature of Emerson, Thoreau, and Whitman. While we admire such illuminating and otherworldly ideas, most of us never aspire to live them in time and space. Like Burchfield, whom biographer John I. H. Baur called "the last pantheist,"[18] Walter Anderson lived outside of the big city world of art and found his sources in nature's lexicon.

It is time to place the art of Walter Anderson with that of his artistic and spiritual peers. He belongs with that wonderful and uniquely valuable group of artistic and literary visionaries who time and time again sustain one of our deepest connections to the American natural landscape.

These artists and writers have enriched our lives for more than two hundred years, building upon our national attachment to the land, to our wild creatures, and to our unique sense of space. As in the life and work of Walter Anderson, each artist and writer had to find the thread again, to discover it in another time and place and in so doing discover a new artistic purpose. Writing of Burchfield, John I. H. Bauer drew upon a statement from the naturalist John Burroughs which might also apply to the life and the triumph of Walter Anderson. "The great artist is identified with his subject; it is *his* subject; he does not merely write about it; he *is* it; it fuses and blends with his personality. The lesser poets search for a subject, to the great poet the subject comes; he stands in his place and it finds him."[19]

Today it is virtually impossible to stand along the shores of Mississippi and look across the bay to the outer islands without thinking of Walter Anderson, his art and his great spiritual adventure. He has deepened our regard for the mysteries of his homeland, lightened our outlook on work and play, opened our eyes to a light that truly exists. Indeed, he was and still is "a magician."

NOTES

1. Mary Anderson Pickard, *The Walter Anderson Birthday Book* (Jackson: Mississippi State Historical Museum, 1986), unpaged.

2. William Baziotes, "To be inspired. . . ," *Tiger's Eye*, no. 5 (October 1948): p. 55.

3. Christopher Maurer with María Estrella Iglesias, *Dreaming in Clay on the Coast of Mississippi: Love and Art at Shearwater* (New York and London: Doubleday, 2000), p. 65.

4. Adolfo Best-Maugard, *A Method for Creative Design* (New York: Alfred A. Knopf, 1926).

5. Owen Jones, *Grammar of Ornament* (London: Day and Son, 1856).

6. John James Audubon, *Birds of America*, 7 vols. (Philadelphia: Bowen, 1840–44).

7. Adolfo Best-Maugard, *A Method for Creative Design* (New York: Dover Publications, 1990), pp.112–113.

8. Redding Sugg, Jr., ed., *The Horn Island Logs of Walter Inglis Anderson*, rev. ed. (Jackson: University Press of Mississippi, 1985), p. 12.

9. Sugg, *Horn Island Logs*, p. 12.

10. Conversation with Mary Anderson Pickard, Ocean Springs, Mississippi, November 2002.

11. Helena Petrovna Blavatsky, *The Secret Doctrine* (London: The Theosophical Publishing Company, 1888).

12. Piotr Demianovich Ouspensky, *Tertium Organum: A Key to the Enigmas of the World* (St. Petersburg: TRUD, 1911), p. 162. Quoted in Linda Dalrymple Henderson, *The Fourth Dimension and Non-Euclidian Geometry in Modern Art* (Princeton: Princeton University Press, 1983), p. 251.

13. Sugg, *Horn Island Logs*, p. 13.

14. Chapman, *Color Key to North American Birds* (New York: D. Appleton, 1912).

15. Mary Anderson Pickard, introduction to *Birds*, by Walter Anderson (Jackson: University Press of Mississippi, 1990), p. xi.

16. Agnes Grinstead Anderson, *Approaching the Magic Hour: Memories of Walter Anderson*, ed. Patti Carr Black (Jackson: University Press of Mississippi, 1989).

17. Jay Hambidge, *The Elements of Dynamic Symmetry* (New York: Dover Publications, 1967).

18. John I. H. Baur, *The Inlander: Life and Work of Charles Burchfield* (Newark: University of Delaware Press, 1982), p. 257.

19. Baur quoting from Clara Barrow, ed., *The Heart of Burroughs's Journals* (Boston and New York: Houghton, 1928), p. 175.

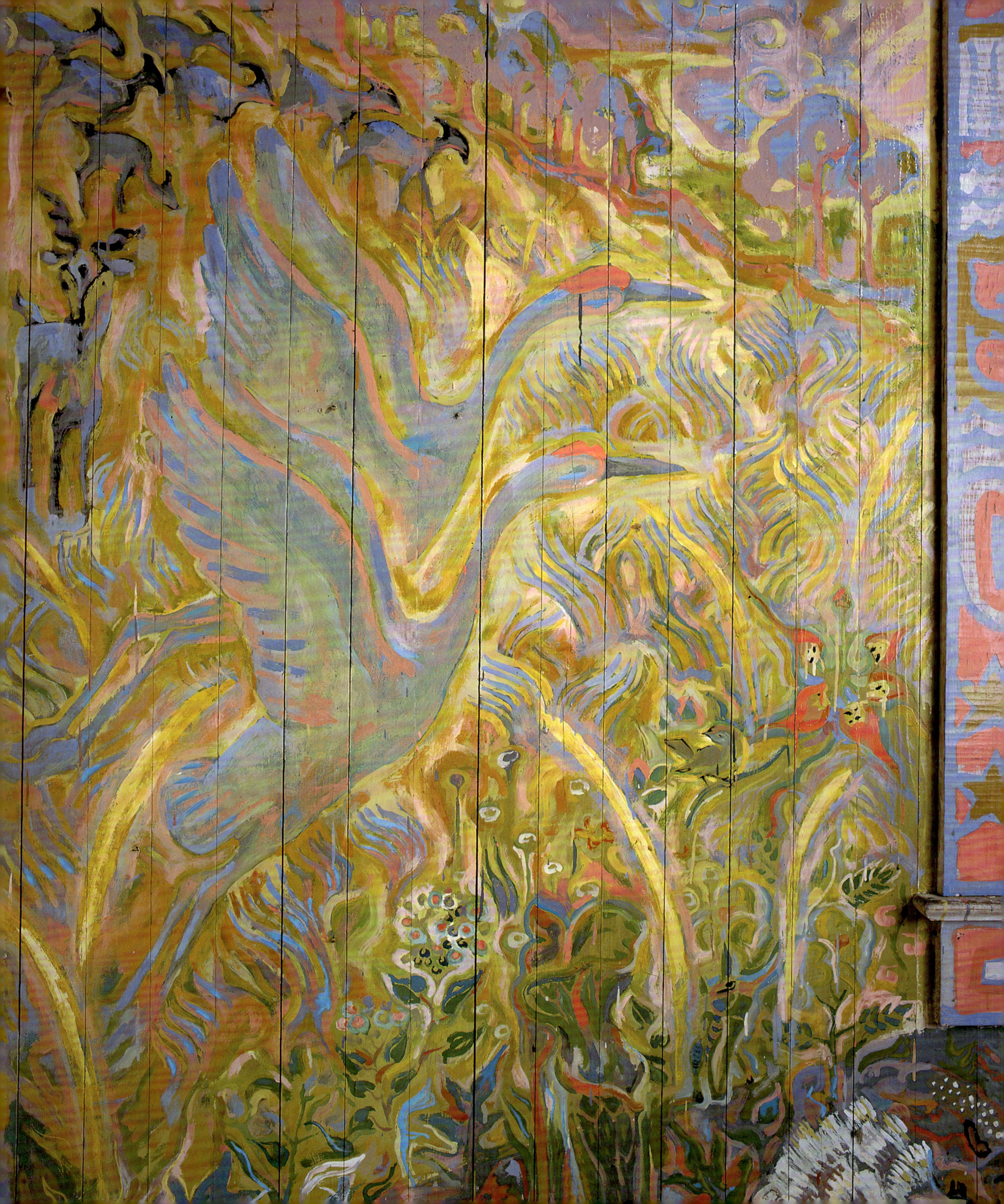

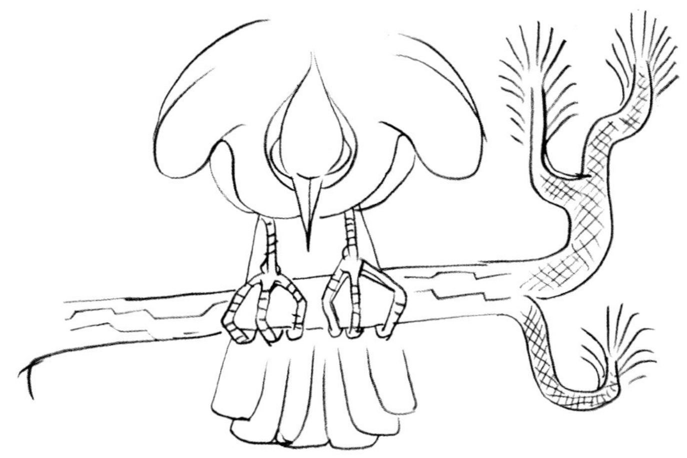

WALTER ANDERSON AND THE AMERICAN TRADITION OF NATURE PAINTING

LINDA CROCKER SIMMONS

Walter Anderson has been labeled an outsider, an eccentric, an artist whose life and artistic career seem unrelated to those of his contemporaries. The existing literature discusses him in terms of the isolation in which he lived mentally and socially, with the assumption that such isolation excludes him from the rest of American art. The time is now propitious to reconsider this view. Walter Inglis Anderson can continue to be admired by artists, scholars, and critics for the originality of his vision and the singleness of purpose with which he pursued it, but he must also be accorded recognition for the content of that vision, which links him to the rest of American art as well as prophetically looking ahead to its future. Although his physical distance from the art centers of Philadelphia and New York City he once knew is acknowledged, this essay is intended to show that since much of his career focused on nature combined with an awareness of the fragility of the natural world, in his art can be found a continuation of themes and elements central to American art not only of the twentieth century but of the centuries which preceded it.

In the more than three decades since his death Walter Inglis Anderson (1903–1965)—"Bob" to his family—has been written about as "mythmaker, local legend, mystic poet and painter, man of light, inveterate voyager."[1] His extensive creative abilities have been chronicled, and the variety of media in which he expressed himself is usually noted. His drive to create was prodigious, resulting in the production of thousands of watercolors, hundreds of different print images, at least three complete mural cycles, hundreds, perhaps thousands, of decorated pots, innumerable molded

Sandhill cranes from the East Wall of the Little Room, ca. 1951–1953
Oil on wood
Walter Anderson Museum of Art

pottery figures, and various other decorative objects such as furniture, rugs, textiles, and clothing, as well as over one hundred known oil paintings and three-dimensional sculptures.[2]

Anderson's fascinating but sadly tempestuous life story is told with sensitivity from the close perspective of his wife, Agnes Grinstead Anderson (1909–1991) known as "Sissy," in her memoir *Approaching the Magic Hour: Memories of Walter Anderson*,[3] and is told in a broader narrative about the Anderson family at Shearwater Pottery by Christopher Maurer with María Estrella Iglesias in their enthralling book, *Dreaming in Clay on the Coast of Mississippi: Love and Art at Shearwater.*[4] The artist's fascination with the visualization of the images of great literature, mythology, and fairy tales is focused upon, in part, by Ellen Douglas in her book *The Magic Carpet and Other Tales.* It is a selection of fairy tales retold by Douglas and published with the related linoleum prints cut by Anderson incorporated as illustrations into the design of the volume.[5] More recently the murals he planned and executed are the subject of the book *Walls of Light: The Murals of Walter Anderson* by Anne R. King.[6]

Since the opening of the Walter Anderson Museum of Art in 1991, Anderson's admirers have had the opportunity to view his artwork as a part of the permanent collection and changing art exhibitions in the context of the community where he lived and worked for nearly all his life.[7] Located in Ocean Springs, Mississippi, the museum building was designed and so located that it is bracketed by structures containing two of Anderson's mural cycles: the Ocean Springs Community Center, painted in 1951, and the mystically beautiful "Little Room," moved intact from the artist's cottage near the pottery.[8] The museum is itself located not far from the Shearwater Pottery and the remaining group of residences where many of the extended new generations of the Anderson family still reside.

With the publication of *The Horn Island Logs of Walter Anderson*, edited by Redding S. Sugg, Jr.,[9] Anderson's reputation as an outstanding painter of nature subjects was established. This beautifully designed and illustrated volume chronicles his depictions of the flora and fauna of the Mississippi Gulf Coast—more specifically the land, water, air, sky, and animals of the Mississippi Sound and the barrier islands that stretch along the coast from Pascagoula west towards New Orleans.

Walter was the middle of three sons, born between Peter (1901–1984) and James McConnell (1907–1998). The brothers remained close, often residing in proximity to each other and the Shearwater Pottery as each pursued his own career in the arts. The young Andersons grew up in an atmosphere of art, music, literature, and culture, with financial security provided by the successful New Orleans business of their father, George Walter Anderson (1865–1937). Their mother, Annette McConnell Anderson (1867–1964), trained as an artist at Newcomb College, from which she graduated at age thirty-three; she pursued additional studies with Julian Alden Weir in Branchville, Connecticut, and William Merritt Chase at Shinnecock Hills on Long Island.[10] Her art was shown at the New Orleans Art Association as well as the Isaac Delgado Museum of Art.[11]

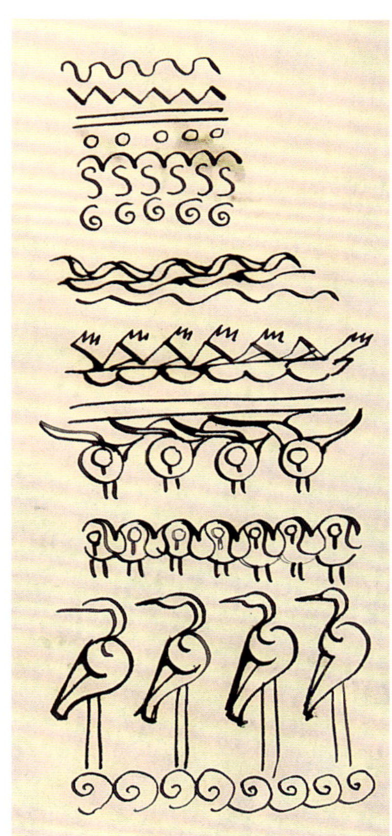

Fig.1. Walter Anderson, *Seabirds and Motifs*, ca. 1942, ink on paper, 11 x 8½ in., The Family of Walter Anderson.

The strengths and characters of both parents provided a childhood focused on intellectual and creative pursuits for all three boys. One constant running through the family's early life was a respect for the creative impulse and a commitment to steady efforts to discipline oneself in the arts. Like his brother Peter, who followed a clearly defined path of training to become a potter, Walter pursued a course of study through some of the finest art institutions of the day. In September 1922 he began the study of design at the New York School of Fine and Applied Arts, later known as the Parsons School of Design, in New York City.[12]

Either as part of a class assignment during these years, or by chance, he began to read and absorb some current theories of design. He delved into Jay Hambidge's 1919 publication *Elements of Dynamic Symmetry*, attempting to apply to his own art the principles addressed about the use of orderly arrangements of units of form. Hambidge's theories articulate that in nature there is "a clear understanding of law and order and a passion for its enforcement," and he advocates its application in art as a visual system suited to expressing life and movement with line.[13] Hambidge states, "Symmetry provides the means of ordering and correlating our design ideas."[14] His observations about art and natural form were to provide a written description of what Anderson would later come to appreciate in Karl Blossfeldt's photographs published in *Art Forms in the Plant World*.[15]

Further reading in *A Method for Creative Design* by Adolfo Best-Maugard introduced Anderson to a method of drawing which utilized the repetition of what the author identifies as the seven basic motifs needed to create all forms: the spiral, the circle, the half-circle, the two half-circles, the wavy line, the zigzag and the straight line.[16] Over the next few years, from these two theories the young Anderson drew the elements to create his own unique style as a draughtsman—one that rhythmically repeated lines and forms in a distinctive palette of restricted colors chosen as much for decorative purposes as for direct representation—which he would continue to utilize throughout his career.

Eager to pursue his art training, Anderson entered the Pennsylvania Academy of the Fine Arts, one of the most venerable of American art schools, in 1924. Art instruction provided by the faculty of the academy in the early twentieth century included a strong respect for the mastery of draughtsmanship as the foundation upon which all other artistic skills would be based. Anderson's fellow student and friend Frank S. Baisden was to later observe that Anderson "came to the Academy with a romantic and broad drawing technique . . . essentially illustrative in feeling."[17] Anderson worked hard, and in his second year of studies, in 1924, he received the Packard Award for drawings of animals. Anderson's abilities were further recognized with the conferral of a Cresson Traveling Scholarship of one thousand dollars.[18]

The art of Europe was thus made available to him. He went to Paris, but, not finding the art in the museums as exciting as he had expected, he made a number of other trips, including visits to Chartres, Mont-Saint-Michel, and, most significantly, to see the cave paintings at Les Eyzies in the Dordogne, which appealed strongly to him. Back in the United States he completed his studies at the Pennsylvania Academy in 1928 before moving back to Ocean Springs. His family now resided there permanently following his father's retirement and the opening in 1928 of the Shearwater Pottery by his brother Peter. He came home planning to be an artist, but he soon found it necessary to be involved in the production of ceramic figurines in the pottery to establish himself financially in anticipation of marriage. Although rarely enthusiastic for anything that took attention, time, and energy away from his true calling as an artist, Anderson did continue to work for the pottery on a regular basis, decorating—besides the figurines—ten dollars' worth of pots per week. Such labor provided a tiny income, and it satisfied his desire to produce objects of high artistic quality for the public. This was the same motivation which lay behind much of his printmaking and mural painting.

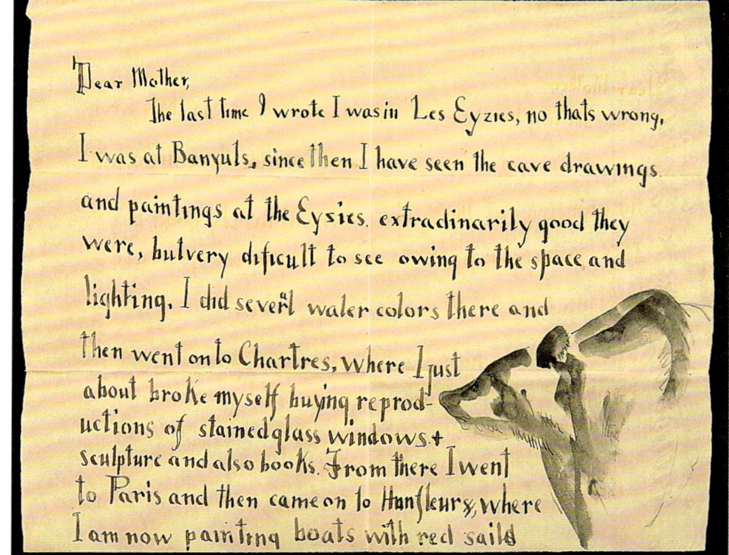
Dear Mother,
The last time I wrote I was in Les Eyzies, no thats wrong,
I was at Banyuls, since then I have seen the cave drawings
and paintings at the Eysies. extradinarily good they
were, but very dificult to see owing to the space and
lighting. I did severl water colors there and
then went on to Chartres, where I just
about broke myself buying reproductions of stained glass windows +
sculpture and also books. From there I went
to Paris and then came on to Hanfleurs, where
I am now painting boats with red sails

Fig. 2. Walter Anderson, *Letter from France*, 1927, ink on paper, 8½ x 10½ in., The Family of Walter Anderson.

Following his marriage to Agnes Grinstead, in 1933, the couple set up housekeeping in a small cottage on the property given to them by his parents. Married life initially appeared to be fine, but within a few years the disruptiveness and severity of the young artist's mental illness necessitated a series of hospitalizations in Maryland and Mississippi.[19] Treatments of various types were tried, with limited success. The recommendation finally was made to keep him home and to have as part of his ongoing care the avoidance of "divisive pressures."[20] In growing social isolation he joined his wife and their two young children at her family's summer home, Oldfields, at Gautier, located about twelve miles from Ocean Springs. There the family lived between 1940 and 1947, sometimes together with the artist, and sometimes physically and socially separated from him. Finally in 1947 he moved by himself back to the cottage at Ocean Springs.[21] He spent the remainder of his life living there alone. He occasionally made trips of varying length to places as far away as China, but he went most frequently to the barrier islands out in the shimmering water visible through the trees from his cottage windows.

During the final seventeen years of his life, Anderson withdrew almost completely from his family. His energies and artistic activities were almost entirely focused on nature; he visited and observed life in its many forms and rhythms in the world around him, most specifically on Horn Island. He fancied himself an explorer and naturalist, "an artist of the known as well as the unknown," as Jessie Poesch aptly describes him.[22] He kept journals, or "logs," as he called them, for many of his journeys. The word "log," which he used for these accounts, is derived from one of his favorite types of literature, journeys of exploration such as *The Voyage of the Beagle.*[23] Although the logs seem to have been at the core of his artistic, physical, and even spiritual existence, he rarely shared them with his family, their content and extent becoming known only later. Estimates vary as to how many may once have existed. Redding Sugg, Jr., theorizes that there must have been more than ninety, while Jessie Poesch notes eighty-two found after Anderson's death in an old cabinet in his cottage along with thousands of watercolors.

Anderson's drawings, paintings, and watercolors combine with his logs to present the story of his life as an artist of nature and to chronicle his adventures with his fellow inhabitants on Horn Island.[24] In them is found an almost daily recitation of his activities, often filled with passion, excitement, joy, and pleasure. The numerous characters of the drama he describes in both words and images are of nature—the animals, the plants, the weather, the island, the sea, and the sky. He calls himself "the islander," and his relationship with the other participants in this natural world changes over time as he goes from the role of artist as spectator or observer to become the essential participant, performing the function of what the artist calls "realizing" nature through his act of painting.[25] Sugg suggests that Anderson came to view himself in the role of "Adam" witnessing the "Eden" of Horn Island. Nature and specifically the places he knew and loved along the Gulf Coast assume almost a spiritual quality in his art. On one trip Anderson wrote that the island was accessible only to "celestial beings" and beyond the reach of mortals. Wryly the artist observes, "Providence made an exception in my case."[26]

In this is found the unifying thread which links Anderson to American art history, his love of, fascination with, depiction of, even participation in nature, the natural world of the New World, which he sees again much as it must have been presented, fresh and wonderful, to newly arrived European eyes. Walter Anderson needs to be seen as the intellectual heir not only to those earlier visions of nature but also to those artists whose artistic abilities are amplified much as his were by their powers of observation, curiosity, respect, courage, and imagination.

Nature has long been an engaging subject for American artists, and Anderson's predecessors are many. One might consider such early individuals as John White in the sixteenth century, Mark Catesby and then William Bartram in the eighteenth and early nineteenth centuries, joined by the wonderful and remarkable John James

Audubon. The nineteenth century is remarkably full of various groups and schools of painters visually consuming images of nature and the American land, often presenting not only the wonders of what they discovered, but also reporting or predicting the changes and losses that were occurring. By the end of the nineteenth century and throughout the twentieth century awe and wonder continued to be expressed in the work of painters like Arthur Dove, Georgia O'Keeffe, and Marsden Hartley. Over and again, the sense of loss and the urge to record, to preserve, and to protect is seen in the work of artists as diverse as photographer Edwin Hale Lincoln and painter and printmaker Edgar Dorsey Taylor. A discussion of some of these artists relating their art and lives to Anderson will demonstrate their commonality.

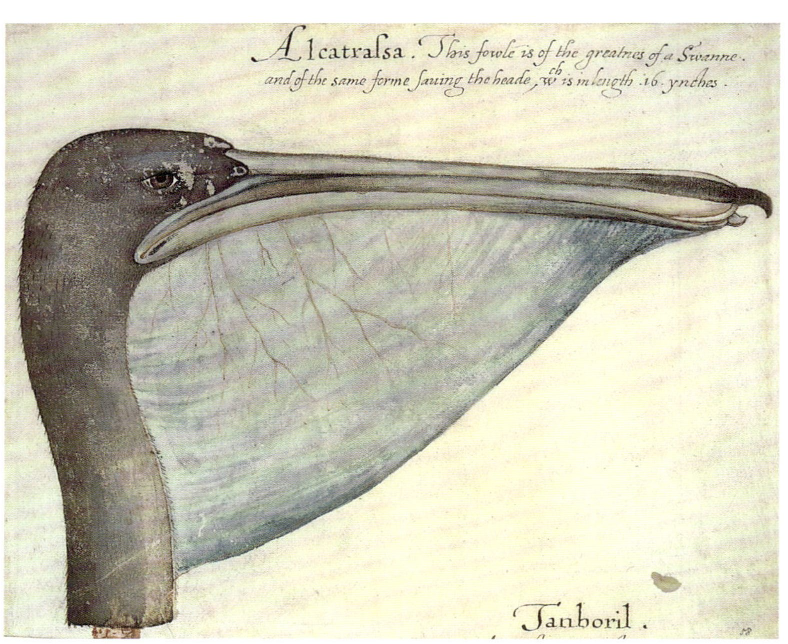

Fig. 3. John White, *Pelican*, watercolor on paper. The British Museum.

One of the earliest artists active in the South, John White (1540/50–1606?), painted watercolors in the 1580s that depict scenes of Florida, some of which include various aquatic creatures still seen today.[27] Although naïve in manner of representation, his works were clear, uncluttered, and realistic in coloration. They were painted in a medium that was to continue to be the one preferred not only by Anderson but by many other artists working out-of-doors. Although no record of White's working methods survives, he must have faced conditions similar to those Anderson described when he faced the elements on Horn Island. There he lived in the open without shelter, except for his overturned boat, while pursuing and depicting his subjects, and he sometimes suffered from the bites not only of mosquitoes and other insects but of poisonous snakes and various predators.

Almost a century later, Mark Catesby (1682–1749) traveled through some of the same regions White had, painting the flora and fauna found in the tidal regions of Virginia and going further inland through the piedmont and south into the Carolinas, Florida, and on to the Bahamas.[28] Catesby painted each bird or animal in a separate composition providing an appropriate natural setting, the first artist in the New World to do so.[29] His images, more vigorous than White's and characterized by a "dynamic freedom," were unlike any seen before, according to naturalist and author Robert Elman.[30]

William Bartram, the first native-born American artist among these early painters of nature, demonstrated his artistic talent at a young age. Even Benjamin

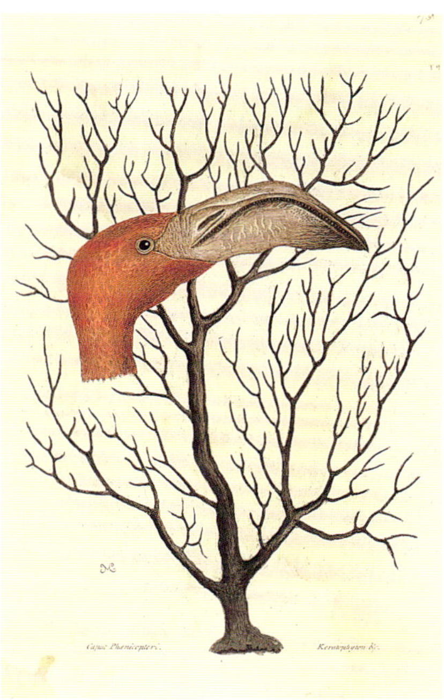

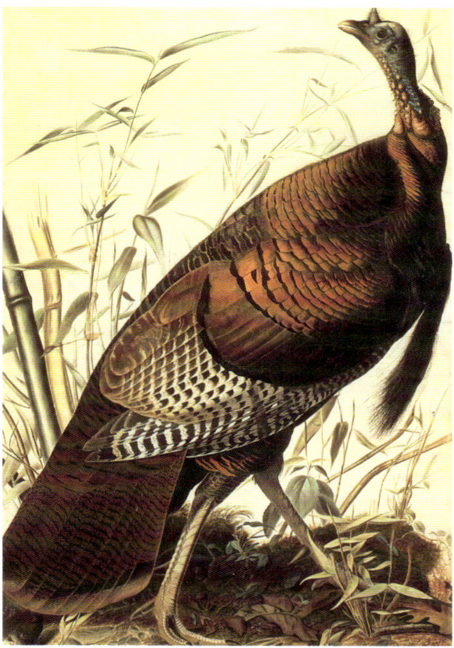

Fig. 4. Mark Catesby, *The Bill of the Flamingo in its full Dimensions and Keratophyton fruiticis,* from *Natural History of Carolina, Florida and the Bahama Islands,* Vol. I, 1754, engraving with watercolor on paper, 13¾ x 10⅛ in., collection of Robert Hilton and Linda Crocker Simmons.

Fig. 5. John James Audubon, *Wild Turkey*, ca. 1825, watercolor and graphite on paper, 52 x 38 in., Collection of The New-York Historical Society (1863.17.1).

Franklin encouraged him to learn to paint and produce prints.[31] Like Anderson, William Bartram grew to love his chosen subject of the natural world so much that he feared more greatly for the preservation of his gardens during the British occupation of Philadelphia than he did for his own life. Bartram's observation—"in essence that plants animals and man all operated on the same God-given principles and were thus intertwined of the intimate interrelationship"—prefigures late-nineteenth-century theories of ecology that Anderson would come to understand and note in the twentieth century.[32]

John James Audubon (1785–1851) is a name virtually synonymous with the genre of nature painters in American art. He is included in this discussion because his achievements in the art field are regarded by some as greater than his work in the scientific field. Relevant to this discussion are a variety of ways in which Audubon and Anderson can be related through their working methods, career details, and art.

After attempting and failing in business, Audubon decided to commit himself to what was to become his life's work: depicting America's avifauna. Leaving his wife and family, he traveled down the Mississippi River to New Orleans, and he sought the professional art instruction he had never had and the opportunity to work as an artist without interruption. From 1820 to 1827 he lived apart from his wife, by agreement each fending for him- or herself. Audubon writes, "My wife determined that my genius should prevail. . . ."[33]

Audubon frequently worked alone, occasionally with apprentices, in rugged conditions not unlike those endured by Anderson. As L. Clark Keating says,

"Audubon was, in a word, a born outdoorsman. . . . From the outset the woods were his element. . . . For Audubon the rain, the wettings, the sleet, the cold, the snow—in short, all the discomforts of the trail—were to be taken in stride, enjoyed, and frequently, laughed at."[34] Nature for Audubon offered much he did not find in human society: "Nay during my deepest troubles I frequently would wrench myself from the persons around me, and retire to some secluded spot of our noble forests."[35] Although both men faced nature and their subjects in similar situations, Anderson's process of working was different. He too speaks of living out in the open, working under his boat on the beach. He used a mangled umbrella to mute the glare of brilliant sunlight, kept his brushes in the band of his battered hat, and rapidly brushed images on sheet after sheet of typewriter paper. Audubon's work was stylistically very different. Linear and replete with details, Audubon's birds were reproduced with the artist paying careful attention to their natural colors and physical features. Anderson, on the other hand, was not restricted by the nineteenth-century need for photographic reproduction of nature. His images were broadly painted. They glowed with color and were compositionally strengthened by the repetition of both color and forms.

Early in his campaign to see and paint every American bird, Audubon decided on a few basic design elements. Every bird would be painted life-size and shown in a setting suited to it. His working method involved using dead birds whose bodies were wired into position in realistic poses in front of graph paper. Their profile forms were the basis for the images he then painted. Both artists were aware of the need to paint swiftly to capture the impermanent color of bird feathers or of other living things. Once the animal was dead, that freshness of color would be lost. Audubon maintained that "feathers lose their brilliance almost as rapidly as flesh or skin itself . . . a bird alive is 75% more rich in colors than 24 hours after its death."[36]

The two men shared certain compositional elements in their work. Often Audubon would include multiple views of a species, such as the Carolina parakeet, using the forms to tell the viewer various things about the animal. The multiple birds not only represented the great numbers in which these small creatures were known to exist but also demonstrated visually their lively vibrant nature. Enough birds are provided to show subtle variations according to gender and age. Anderson's paintings frequently included more than one animal or bird. These repetitions may be the same creature shown more than once, as he noted he had done in images of a scaup named "Simy," his pet. In his 1959 log Anderson notes, "Yesterday afternoon I did him in a composition twice. He composes well together."[37]

Both artists are noted for their powers of observation, Audubon especially for the veracity of his depictions. Such accuracy came at a time when American ornithological knowledge was limited, and some images were challenged, with the artist

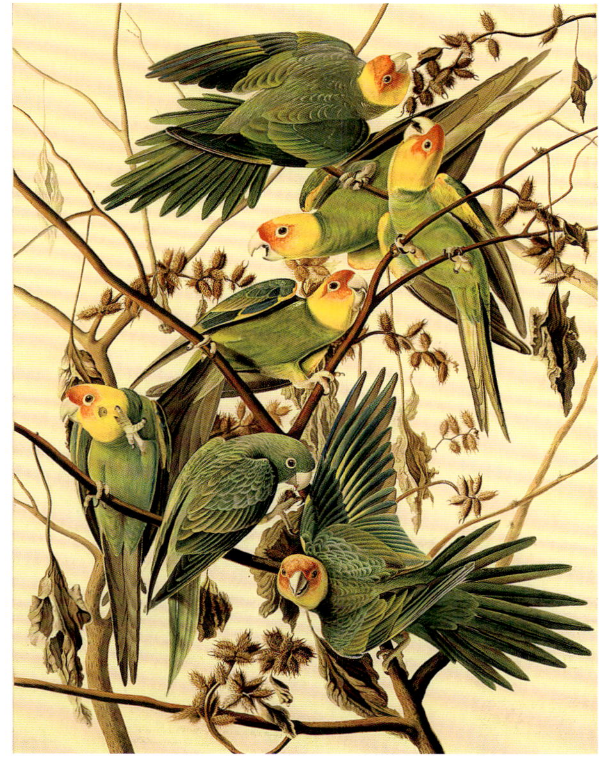

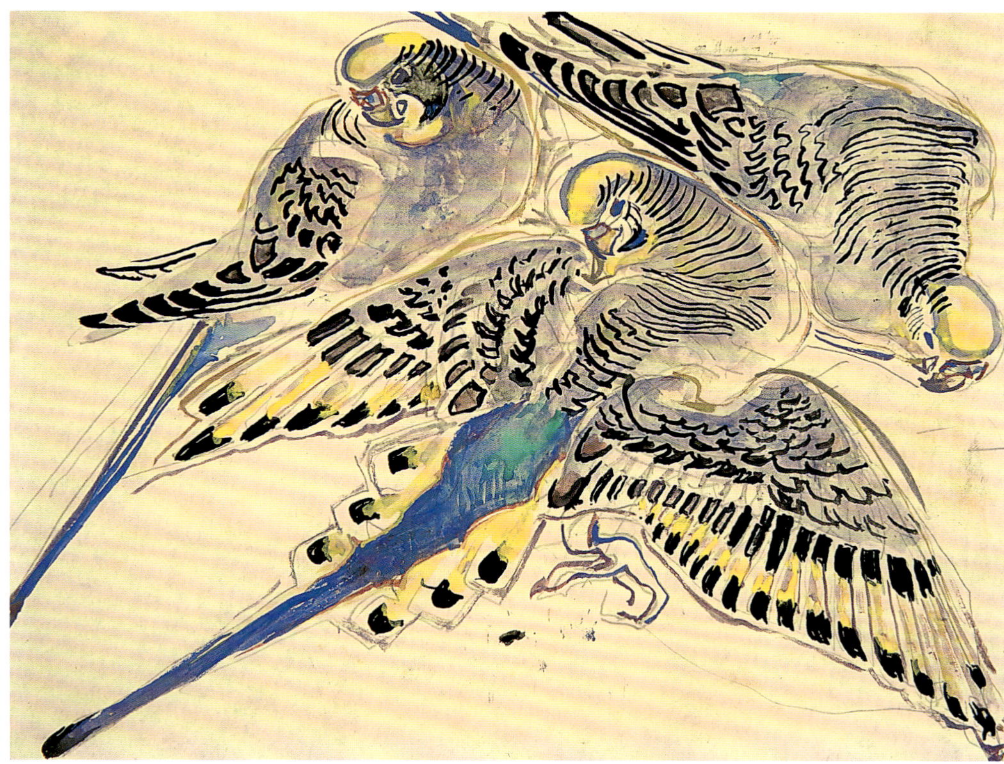

Fig. 6. John James Audubon, *Carolina Parakeets*, 1825, watercolor, gouache, pastel, and crayon on paper, 29 11/16 x 21 3/16 in., Collection of The New-York Historical Society (1863.17.26).

Fig. 7. Walter Anderson, *Toby*, ca. 1952, watercolor on paper, 8½ x 11 in., Walter Anderson Museum of Art (98.11.2).

being accused of inaccuracies. In one instance, his image of mockingbirds, painted in 1821, was criticized as a gross exaggeration. When it was published as a print, claims were made that rattlesnakes do not climb trees, nor do they have outward-curving fangs as Audubon had painted them. Subsequent investigation proved Audubon to be correct in his observation and depiction.

Both men were generally unsentimental about their subjects. Anderson was unflinching as he observed life and change in nature, although sadness sometimes clouded his view when the death of some animal or bird was the result of his actions. In the earlier years of his logs, he might mourn a death: "the little seahorse died several days ago—never to be forgotten."[38] He seems more chagrined than overwhelmed with sorrow when some creature which he had captured and held as a model died, as in this entry of July 1959 when a frog did not survive: "he's like an albatross and I shall draw carefully and well but without pleasure."[39]

Audubon empathized with his subjects, but that did little to deter him from killing birds to paint. His fondness for hunting is well documented.[40] Even so, he could be surprised when some small creature allowed his attentions without protest. In May of 1812 he noted how he had caught a live broad-winged hawk and taken it to his room: "I measured the length of its bill with the compass, began my outlines, continued measuring part after part as I went on, and finished the drawing without the bird ever moving once. My wife sat at my side, reading to me at intervals but our conversation had frequent reference to the singularity of the incident."[41]

Unlike Anderson, Audubon very much valued his own works of art. When a trunk full of more than two hundred watercolors was destroyed by the residency of a family of Norway rats, he was at first angry, then resigned, and finally determined to begin again and produce even better paintings.[42] He had begun initially to produce his portraits of birds for his own pleasure in the face of public criticism of what was thought to be a lazy way of life that allowed the neglect of business in favor of art. In *The Story of My Life*, Audubon states, "Birds were birds, then as now, and my thoughts were anon turning towards them as objects of my greatest delight. I shot, I drew, I looked at nature only, my days were happy beyond human conception, and beyond that I really cared not. . . ."[43] These sentiments were recorded a century later in the logs of Walter Anderson.

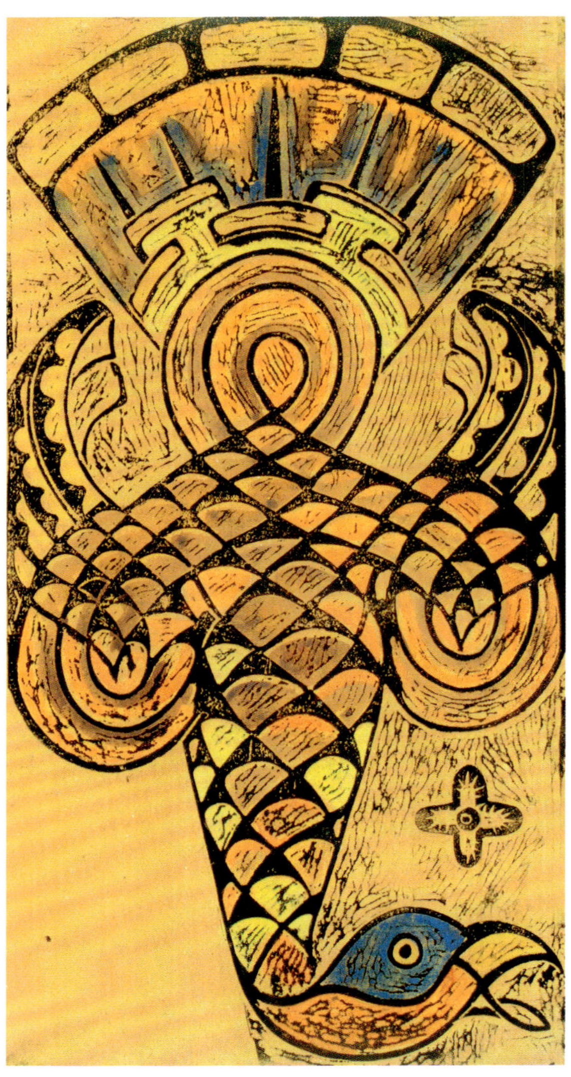

Fig. 8. Walter Anderson, *Turkey*, linocut with watercolor on paper, 36 x 19 in., Walter Anderson Museum of Art (76.2.1).

At one time Anderson had contemplated producing an illustrated guide for the birds of the Southeast.[44] He made a few tightly painted drawings, not in his characteristic repetitive style of draughtsmanship. However, he soon dispensed with the idea because he abhorred the need to work from dead specimens obtained by hunting. Although his brothers and father had hunted with him as a child, the artist could not tolerate the idea.[45] Even so, painting birds continued to be a significant part of his art; thus it is probably not surprising that one of the single-artist exhibitions during his lifetime was *Fledgling Birds by Walter Anderson* at the Brooks Memorial Art Gallery in Memphis in 1964. His daughter Mary observed, "My father believed that man's salvation lay in his awareness of the natural world and his recognition of his own role in it. He wrote: 'The bird flies and in that . . . fraction of a second man and bird are real. . . . He is the only man and that is the only bird and every feather, every mark, every part of the pattern of its feathers is real and he, man, exists and he is almost as wonderful as the thing he sees.'"[46]

Both painters, Anderson and Audubon, although separated by a century of time, captured something else in their depictions of nature, the dynamic of change. Both were alarmed about the destruction they saw in the habitat each knew best.

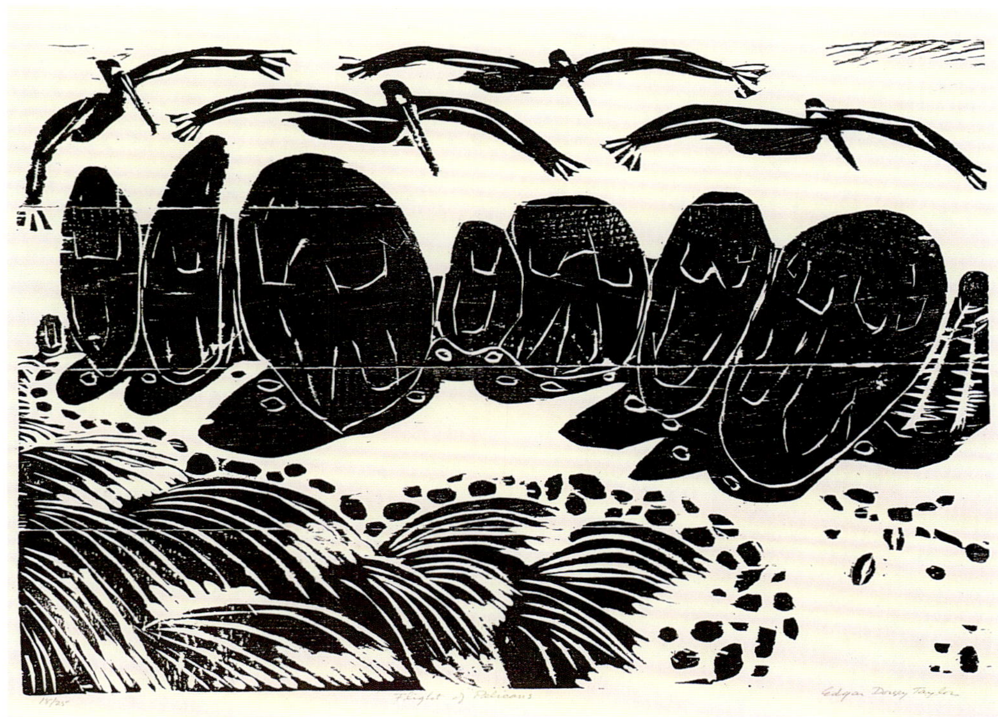

Fig. 9. Edgar Dorsey Taylor, *Flight of Pelicans*, 1959, woodcut on paper, 14 x 20¼ in. plate size, Collection of Robert Hilton and Linda Crocker Simmons.

Audubon saw the beginning of the end for the carrier pigeon as well as the Carolina parakeet, and Anderson witnessed the decline of the pelicans on the Chandeleur Islands. Before the 1950s they were plentiful; by the 1960s they had become a rare sight. He was jubilant in 1965 when he saw more than one: "17 in one flock!"[47] He was to die in November of that same year, just three short years after Rachel Carson's *Silent Spring* sounded the warning against the destructiveness of DDT, which Anderson had correctly identified as what was killing the pelicans.

Far away from Anderson, on the west coast in California, his contemporary, Edgar Dorsey Taylor (1904–1978), painter, printmaker, sculptor, and artist in a variety of decorative arts, shared some of the same concerns for the damage man was doing to our environment. Both artists depicted pelicans in their very different environments. In a descriptive note for a print of flying pelicans Taylor writes, "Always the wind modifies the environment. When blowing cool and fresh from the north up over the steep bluff of alluvium, it is a buoyant path for soaring pelicans, ospreys, gulls and buzzards in their search of sustenance, with shiny ravens coasting slowly past to cast appraising eye on camp culinary activities."[48]

Taylor was born in Grass Valley, California, and attended the University of California at Berkeley, receiving a B.A. in 1928 and an M.A. in 1932. After many years of teaching college art courses, he was drawn to the black-and-white woodblock print for its drama and visual strength, and he produced a large body of work, including hundreds of images of Baja California and the Gulf of California.

Taylor, a longtime resident of Los Angeles, made his first journey to Baja California in December 1934. He returned often, traveling the peninsula either in a four-wheel-drive vehicle or along the coast in an eighteen-foot, two-seated German kayak.[49] His traveling companions varied, sometimes including his wife, Mildred, Maurice Conrad, or Robert Hilton Simmons, Sr., all fellow artists and enthusiasts of the beauty of that place. Taylor, like many artists observing and recording nature, kept a written record: "Each of my journeys, either by water or by land has made some contributions of ideas, thoughts and sketches recorded in a notebook and log, and some of these have been expressed in woodcut."[50] His artistic engagement with Baja continued throughout his life, and he noted that with repeated trips the place "seems to grow in size and become ever more intriguing and elusive."[51] A small volume featuring fifty reproductions of Taylor's woodcuts was published by Plantain Press in 1969 with an introduction by Simmons.[52]

Like the barrier islands along the Gulf Coast, the peninsula of Baja California is a wonderful magical place in its combination of geography, isolation, and wildlife. The Pacific Ocean lies to the west, the Gulf of California to the east, and the land between those two bodies of water is stark, desert-like, and rich in wildlife and birds. Nearly half a century ago it was sparsely populated. Simmons thinks Taylor found a subject in Baja analogous to the woods and ponds Thoreau wrote of in his journal: "old meandering, dry, uninhabited roads which lead us . . . to forget what country you are traveling, . . .[noting] how much virtue there is in simply seeing."[53]

Although not stylistically similar to those of Anderson, neither are Taylor's woodcut images a detailed photographic record of nature. Both artists' work might be described as Simmons writes of Taylor: "descriptive in an imaginary rather than a literal sense."[54] Both artists produced works that exist on the edge of the abstract, retaining basic identifiable elements of form, shape, line, and texture appropriate to the subject. Those ingredients have been reconfigured by each artist's personal experience and stylistic development, as each utilized his chosen medium in the manner most distinctive for it. Taylor uses the edges of the block almost like line or contours to define form, to articulate bulk, and to suggest motion. Anderson uses the dynamics of his linear style as well as the repetitive patterns and the medium of watercolor to create jewel-like swaths of color suggestive of what he saw before him, but his work is not restricted to the mere replication of nature.

Like Anderson, Taylor was "saddened by evidence of waste and pollution . . . appalled by the litter left everywhere in unthinking gesture of contempt for the environment and for other humans. . . ."[55] Taylor was upon occasion touched by his chosen subject. "We were lunching on butter clams and repeating the gestures of ancient aborigines, throwing shells on the midden formed long ago. All of a sudden one of the active lizards whose antics we were enjoying made a prodigious leap to my hand relaxed for a moment on my knee, caught a recently alighted fly, did three lizard push-ups, then jumped off again, tail twitching to and fro in apparent satisfaction. He has loomed large ever since in my catalogue of pleasures and memory."[56]

The canon of American art history has tended to dismiss the idea that artists continued to focus on landscape and nature after the end of the nineteenth century. Nature as a subject has been overlooked, and it was replaced by an emphasis on the ideas and developments of styles and modernism. Across the country, in regions often removed from the centers of art, landscape and nature persisted as subjects in distinctively different ways and styles in parts of the Southwest, California, the South, and New England. In these separate places, artists worked, thought, and immersed themselves in nature, maintaining strong ties to their own regions.

Further comparisons could be made to other artists of the twentieth century such as Georgia O'Keeffe, noted for her career-long focus on nature as seen in her floral subjects and the many paintings of her beloved Southwest. Anderson was not alone in his interest in and commitment to nature, nor should he continue to be viewed as standing outside American art. Works that must rank among his masterpieces are the murals he painted in secret on the interior walls of his cottage. They are now referred to as the "Little Room" and are on permanent display at the museum. Those images are rightly interpreted as the artist's ultimate psalm to nature, to the dawn of creation on the first day on the Gulf Coast. Ranged about the walls are the creatures with which he shared his existence and from which he derived the realization of himself as an artist. Of Walter Inglis Anderson it has been singingly said, "For Anderson, art was not a product but a process, a means of experiencing the world. His significance in the history of art may lie in his perception of fundamental reality: the interconnectedness of the world, the dynamism of matter, the knowledge that man is a participant in nature rather than an observer."[57]

NOTES

1. Anne R. King, *Walls of Light: The Murals of Walter Anderson* (Jackson: University Press of Mississippi and the Walter Anderson Museum of Art, 1999), p. 13.

2. No catalogue raisonné exists for Anderson's art, the bulk of which remains in the possession of the Anderson family under the curatorial direction of daughter Mary Anderson Pickard, with the assistance of friend and advisor Joan Gilley. Although the collection they care for numbers in the thousands, what survives is thought to be only a portion of what the artist produced during more than four decades of artistic activity. In the medium of watercolor alone family members recollect or have recorded numerous works casually discarded, destroyed by acts of nature or by the artist himself, and in occasional instances given away or sold.

3. Agnes Grinstead Anderson, *Approaching the Magic Hour: Memories of Walter Anderson*, ed. Patti Carr Black (Jackson: University Press of Mississippi, 1989).

4. Christopher Maurer with María Estrella Iglesias, *Dreaming in Clay on the Coast of Mississippi: Love and Art at Shearwater* (New York: Doubleday, 2000).

5. Ellen Douglas, with the illustrations of Walter Anderson, *The Magic Carpet and Other Tales* (Jackson: University Press of Mississippi, 1987). See also Redding S. Sugg, Jr., ed., *Walter Anderson's Illustrations of Epic and Voyage* (Carbondale: Southern Illinois Press; London: Feffer & Simmons, 1980).

6. King, *Walls of Light.*

7. One and a half million dollars were raised by the Anderson family and others to create the museum. The building was designed by nationally known architect Edward Pickard, at that time married to Mary Anderson, daughter of the artist. Bil Gilbert, "Stalking the Blue Bear: The Fine Art of Walter Anderson," *Smithsonian*, October 1994, p. 118.

8. The "Little Room" was moved to the museum as a gift of the artist's family in 1991, the year his widow, Sissy, died. Maurer, *Dreaming in Clay*, p. 298; Gilbert, "Stalking the Blue Bear," p. 118.

9. Redding S. Sugg, Jr., ed., *The Horn Island Logs of Walter Anderson* (Memphis: Memphis State University Press, 1973; rev. ed., Jackson: University Press of Mississippi, 1985).

10. Maurer, *Dreaming in Clay,* p. 44.

11. Maurer, *Dreaming in Clay*, p. 45.

12. Maurer, *Dreaming in Clay,* p. 64.

13. Jay Hambidge, *The Elements of Dynamic Symmetry* (1926; reprint, New York: Dover Publications, Inc., 1967), p. xvii; Sugg, *Horn Island Logs*, p. 15.

14. Hambidge, *Elements of Dynamic Symmetry*, p. xvii.

15. Karl Blossfeldt, *Art Forms in the Plant World* (1928; reprint, New York: Dover Publications, Inc., 1985).

16. Adolfo Best-Maugard, *A Method for Creative Design* (1926; reprint, New York: Dover Publications, 1990), pp. 1–2.

17. Quoted in Sugg, *Horn Island Logs*, p. 12.

18. Maurer, *Dreaming in Clay*, p. 66; Sugg, *Horn Island Logs*, p. 13.

19. For a discussion of his illness and treatment see Maurer, *Dreaming in Clay*, pp. 166–214, and Anderson, *Approaching the Magic Hour*, pp. 50–82.

20. Anderson, *Approaching the Magic Hour*, p. 75.

21. Sugg, *Horn Island Logs*, p. 19.

22. Jessie Poesch, "Growth and Development of the Old South, 1830–1900," in *Painting in the South: 1564–1980* (Richmond: Virginia Museum of Fine Arts, 1983), p. 132

23. Anderson, *Approaching the Magic Hour*, pp. 70–71. Agnes Anderson describes how he shared one he wrote on paper bags while returning home from Baltimore in 1939.

24. Maurer, *Dreaming in Clay*, p. 261.

25. Sugg, *Horn Island Logs*, p. 26.

26. Sugg, *Horn Island Logs*, p. 175.

27. John White produced sixty-three watercolors which were later engraved and published upon his return to England. Carolyn T. Weekley, "The Early Years 1564–1790," in Poesch, *Painting in the South*, pp. 5, 7. White's watercolors were widely known after being published in *A Brief and True Report of the New Found Land in Virginia, 1590* (English language edition) engraved illustrations by Theodor de Bry after John White, text by Thomas Harlot. Cited in Weekley, "The Early Years," p. 170.

28. Weekley, "The Early Years," pp. 13–14.

29. Weekley, "The Early Years," p. 14.

30. Robert Elman, *America's Pioneer Naturalists, Their Lives, and Their Times, Exploits and Adventures* (Tulsa: Winchester Press, 1982), p. 20

31. Elman, *America's Pioneer Naturalists*, p. 32.

32. Quoted in Elman, *America's Pioneer Naturalists*, p. 35.

33. Quoted in Phillip Drennon Thomas, "Painter of the Feathered Tribe," *Natural History* 94, no. 4 (April 1985): 99.

34. L. Clark Keating, *Audubon: The Kentucky Years* (Lexington: University Press of Kentucky, 1976), pp. 11, 86, 87, 90–92.

35. Quoted in Keating, *Audubon*, p. 85.

36. Thomas, "Painter of the Feathered Tribe," p. 95.

37. That animal did not survive Anderson's artistic efforts. He left the bird tethered in a marsh, and "When I went to take him in afterwards he was dead, with his head under water. I suppose he drowned trying to get away. I got very fond of him during the six days I had him. He made no pretense of liking me." Sugg, *Horn Island Logs*, p. 92.

38. Sugg, *Horn Island Logs*, p. 92.

39. Sugg, *Horn Island Logs*, p. 24.

40. The irony of the carnage done by this father of American conservation is legendary. It must be remembered that he lived at a time when the consumption of all manner of birds was a regular part of the diet, before the existence of game laws, nature parks, or refuges and well before the conscious articulation of an environmental ethic. It would only be in later years that he would recognize the damage being done and see the impending loss in the extermination of such birds as the carrier pigeon and the Carolina parakeet. In his writings he sounded mournful at the change, as when he wrote in 1843 that "the woods are disappearing fast under the axe by day and by fire at night. . . ." Quoted in Keating, *Audubon*, p. 92.

41. *The Original Watercolor Paintings by John James Audubon for the Birds of America Reproduced in Color for the First Time from the Collection of the New York Historical Society*, vol. 2 (New York: Heritage Publishing Co., 1966), facing pl. 259.

42. Keating, *Audubon*, p. 57.

43. Keating, *Audubon*, p. 26.

44. Dr. Ned Park gave him his first guidebook, *Chapman's Color Key to North American Birds*, in 1935, and Anderson discussed doing one for the Southeast. Walter Anderson, *Birds* (Jackson: University Press of Mississippi, 1990), p. xi.

45. Anderson, *Birds*, pp. x, xi.

46. Anderson, *Birds*, p. xxvi.

47. Anderson, *Birds*, p. xix.

48. Robert Hilton Simmons, Sr., introduction to *Baja California Woodcuts, with Notes by the Artist*, by Edgar Dorsey Taylor (Los Angeles: Plantain Press, 1969), facing pl. 34.

49. Simmons, introduction, *Baja California Woodcuts*, p. viii.

50. Simmons, introduction, *Baja California Woodcuts*, p. x.

51. Simmons, introduction, *Baja California Woodcuts*, p. x.

52. Robert Hilton Simmons (1922–1998), artist, writer, art collector, and ship's officer in the merchant marine, was a close friend of Taylor and his wife from the 1940s until Taylor's death in 1978. Simmons was the publisher of three print portfolios of Taylor's woodcuts: *The Gulf of California* (1959), *The Boulevard* (1965), and *Baja California* (1969). Simmons is also the late husband of the author of this essay.

53. Quoted in Simmons, introduction, *Baja California Woodcuts*, p. xiii.

54. Simmons, introduction, *Baja California Woodcuts*, p. xiv.

55. Simmons, introduction, *Baja California Woodcuts*, p. xvi.

56. Simmons, introduction, *Baja California Woodcuts*, facing pl. 11.

57. Patti Carr Black, introduction to Anderson, *Approaching the Magic Hour*, p. viii.

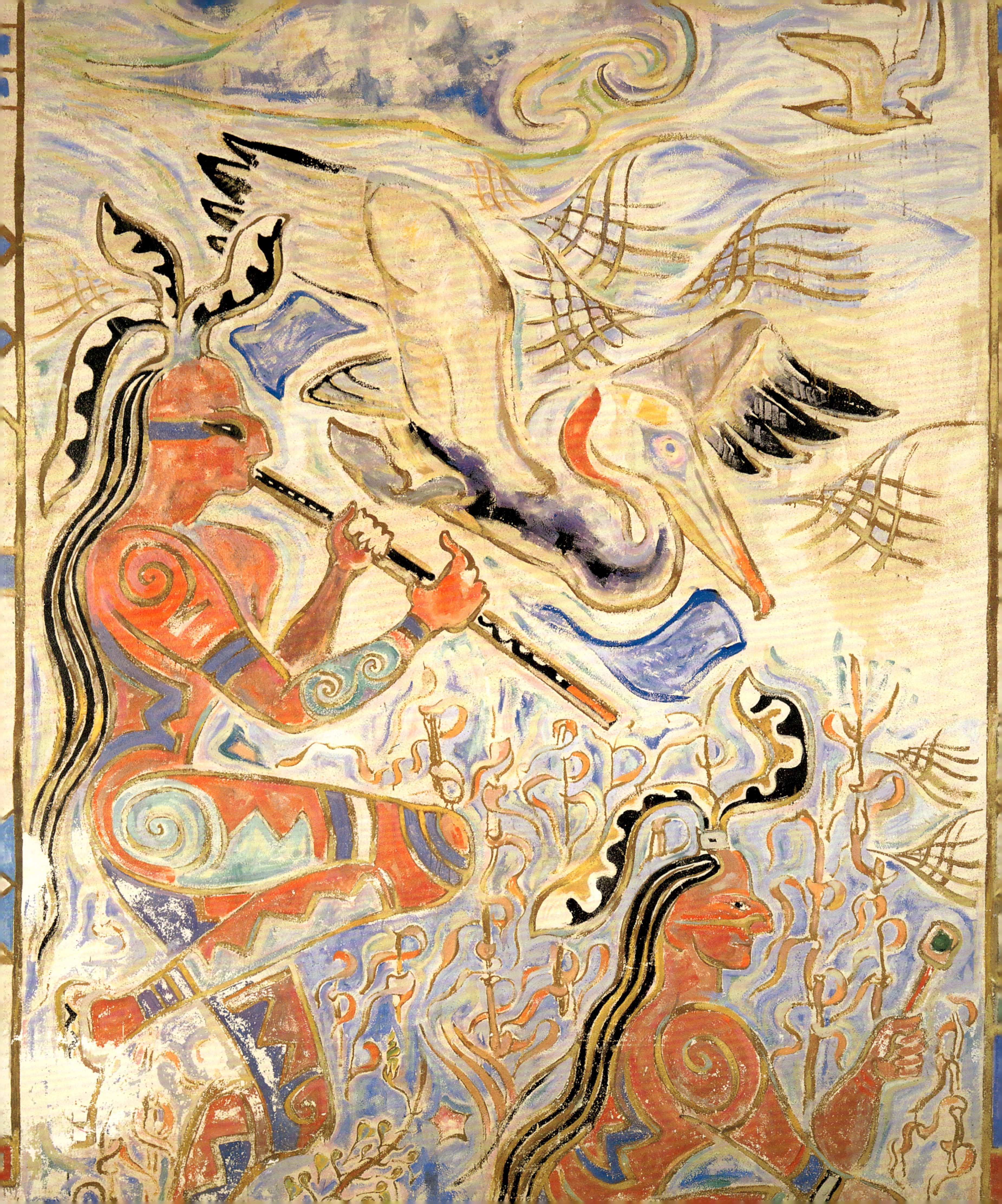

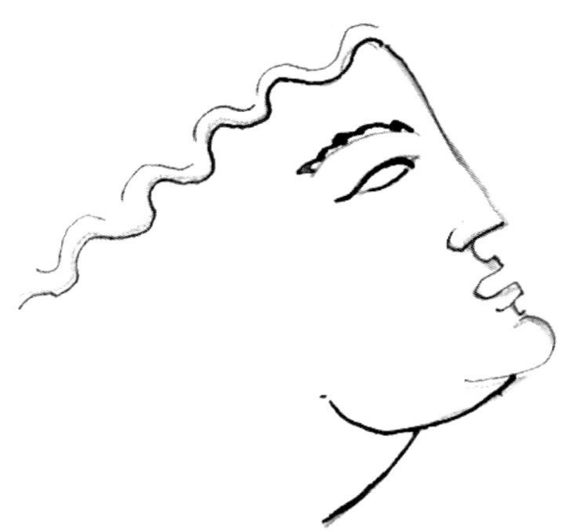

THE MURALS OF WALTER ANDERSON: AN ENCOMPASSING VISION

FRANCIS V. O'CONNOR

Only those who are dissatisfied may be content. I am beginning to learn the truth of paradox.[1]

INTRODUCTION

Walter Inglis Anderson created three exceptional mural environments and a number of studies for unexecuted wall paintings. The first mural and several studies were created between 1934 and 1936 under New Deal art programs. Later in life, after recovering from a mental breakdown and establishing a new life for himself close to nature, he created two fully developed mural cycles, one in the Ocean Springs Community Center in 1951–52 and another in his cottage at Shearwater in the years up to his death in 1965.[2] A trained artist, he seems to have learned more from nature. His is a vision at one with its encompassing phenomena, which it is rare to find in art and rarer still to find so lyrically expressed in wall painting.

Given the many murals painted in the Americas during the thirty-odd years involved, his walls reveal no particular influence of any one artist or school. On the other hand, he studied at the Parsons School of Design and the Pennsylvania Academy of the Fine Arts between 1922 and 1928, and knew the history of art. There is also evidence that the ideas of Adolfo Best-Maugard and Jay Hambidge, the botanical photography of Karl Blossfeldt, and the art of like-minded artists helped to inform his methods and sensibility.

Biloxi Indians from the Community Center mural, 1951–1952
Oil and tempera on stucco
The City of Ocean Springs, Mississippi

Adolfo Best-Maugard (1891–1960s?) headed Mexico's Department of Art Education in the early 1920s when the Mexican mural movement was born. In 1926 he published *A Method for Creative Design*, which became a popular textbook.[3] Its first part offered a theory of seven primordial motifs: spiral, circle, curve, s-curve, wavy line, zigzag, and straight line, as elaborated and applied to everything from decorative borders to landscape and the human figure. Its second part contained chapters on the creative imagination, archetypes, the whirling spiral, and the psychology of creation. These in effect summed up the aesthetics of the era, including a collectivist approach to art inspired by the author's experience in Mexico, Henri Bergson's concept of creative intuition, John Dewey's social view of art, C. G. Jung's archetypal psychology, and Jay Hambidge's theory of dynamic symmetry.

The theory put forth by Hambidge (1867–1924) is mentioned by Best-Maugard and by Anderson while he was at Parsons.[4] Hambidge developed a popular method of composition based on the proportions implicit in the mathematical ratio of 1:1.618, first manifest in Pythagorean theory and the spiral of the Greek Ionic column and later in modern art by the French Section d'Or movement and in murals by Maxfield Parrish, José Clemente Orozco, and Diego Rivera. Anderson seems to have experimented with dynamic symmetry in school and in some of his designs for murals during the 1940s, but so rigorous a method was not in keeping with his character as an artist.[5]

Karl Blossfeldt (1865–1932) was a leader in the New Objectivity photography movement in the 1920s and became famous with his *Art Forms in Nature*.[6] His 240 close-up images of plants offer a range of powerful shapes that any artist would find fascinating and look for in nature, which Anderson may well have done.[7]

These influences, along with affinities to artists of his time, provide a background for understanding aspects of Anderson's murals.

NEW DEAL MURALS: 1934–1936

All popular expressions of art are the fruit of a collective ideal; national collectivity is necessary before there can be unity in the national art.[8]

Anderson began as a muralist in 1934. He had married in 1933 and no doubt saw the New Deal's art programs as one way to survive the Depression. Like his brothers, Peter and James McConnell, he joined the very first of these, the Public Works of Art Project (PWAP), which had begun in December 1933 and continued through the spring of 1934. His brothers were potters and created tile murals for the Ocean Springs Public School. Walter, a painter, was assigned a mural in its auditorium.[9] There, in keeping with the PWAP's policy that murals represent local themes, he created what

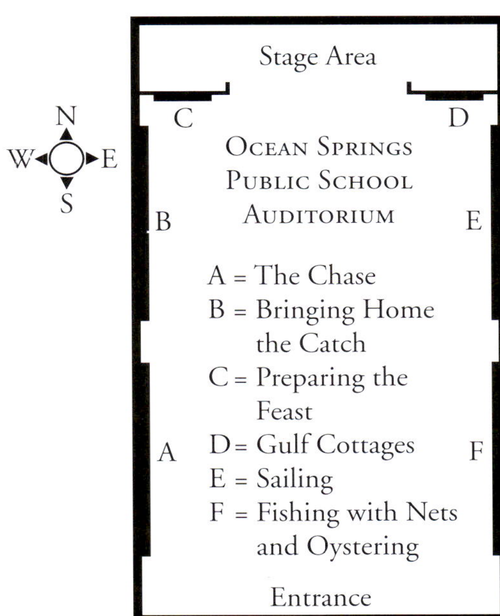

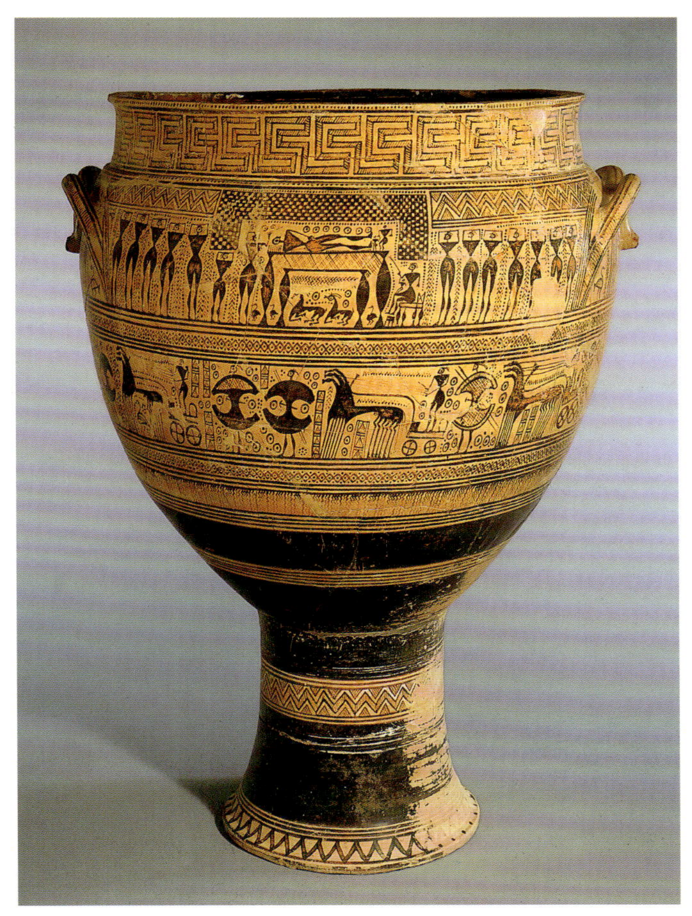

Diagram 1. Ocean Springs Public School mural, 1933–1934

Fig. 1. Geometric Dipylon krater, 8th century B.C., terra cotta 42⅝ x 28½ in., The Metropolitan Museum of Art, Rogers Fund, 1914 (14.130.14).

was to become a typical government-sponsored dichotomy: Gulf Coast life then and now.[10]

The mural consisted of six panels around the side and proscenium walls of the school's auditorium (Diagram 1 and pages 102–4).[11] They started with two panels arranged on the west wall in a frieze located between the lower and upper windows. Here Biloxi Indians fish, hunt prey, and bear home their catch (A&B). This side concluded at the bottom of a tall, vertical panel to the left of the stage which depicted preparations for a feast amid the Indians' domed dwellings (C). On the right, in the same arrangement around from the stage, one saw typical Gulf Coast cottages next to it (D), and then a frieze of settlers oystering, spearfishing, and sailing (E&F). Both walls indicated the presence of the gulf's shoreline.

Two things are striking. First, there are the gracefully stylized human and natural forms. The pine trees are not only reduced to a lively row of identical patterns but also show their roots under the transparent ground. And the human figures are

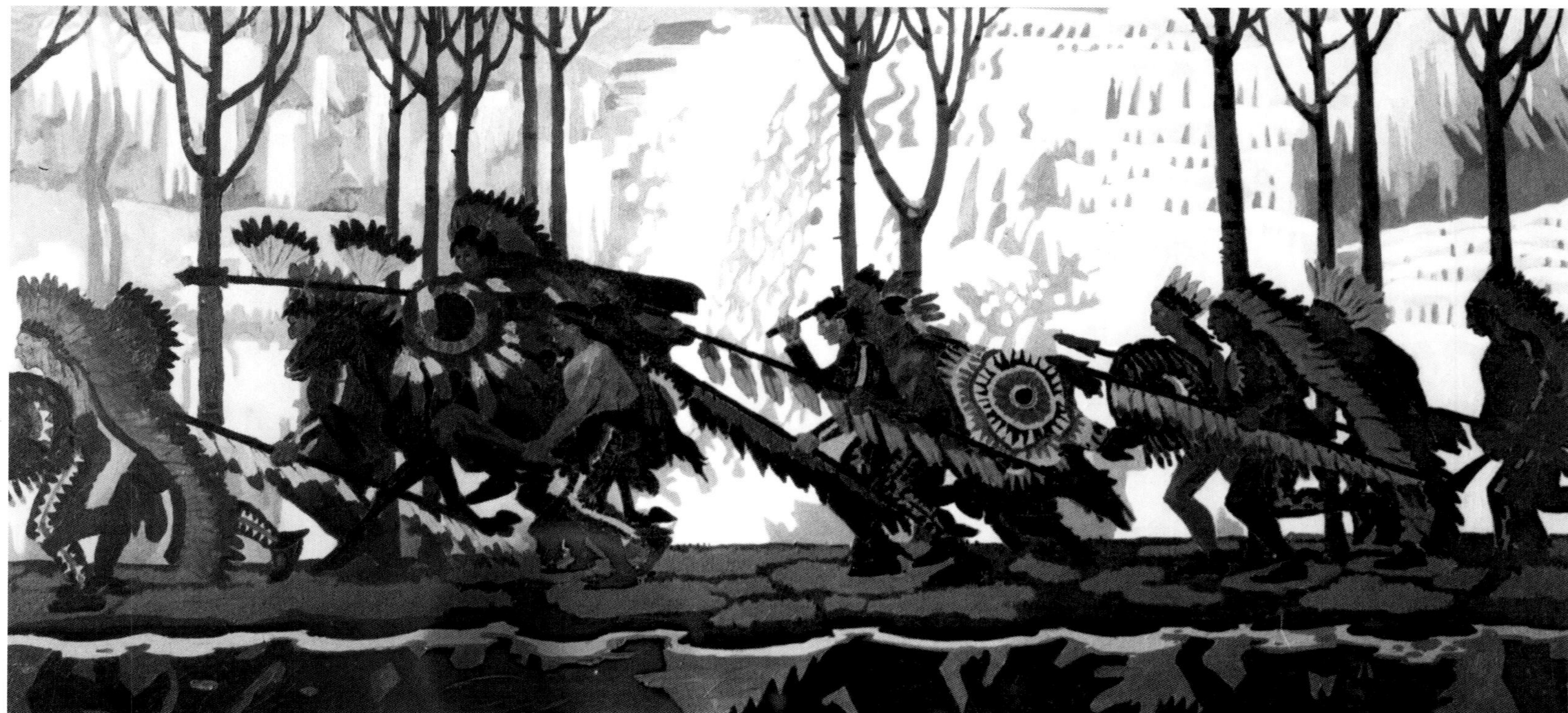

Fig. 2. Charles Burchfield, *Hiawatha's War Party*, 1916, 27 x 40 in., collection unknown, photograph courtesy of the Burchfield-Penney Art Center, Buffalo State University, New York.

abstracted to forms readily found on early Greek pottery—motifs he might well have brought to his brothers' attention (Fig. 1).[12]

It is notable that Anderson emphasized the Indians' relation to nature by depicting them walking in the same earth plane as the trees' roots. He showed them integrated with the land, whereas his settlers do not get their feet too wet in the sea's depths.[13]

There is a precedent for his design of the Indian panels. In 1916, Charles Burchfield, an artist whose work Anderson knew, created a mural on the theme of the Native American legend of Hiawatha (Fig. 2). It shows a row of Indians, reflected in a still stream in the foreground, passing right to left across a stand of vertical trees. The composition is uncannily similar to Anderson's arrangement of under, on, and above the earth. While there is no evidence Anderson saw Burchfield's mural or the sketches of it,[14] the similarity raises an issue to be encountered throughout his oeuvre. When considering a nature-oriented sensibility like Anderson's and Burchfield's, do we presume direct influences between artists or similar awarenesses of natural phenomena? It is best to suggest possible influences while at the same time not underestimating the possibility of independent perceptions of the same realities under the earth, upon it, and above it.

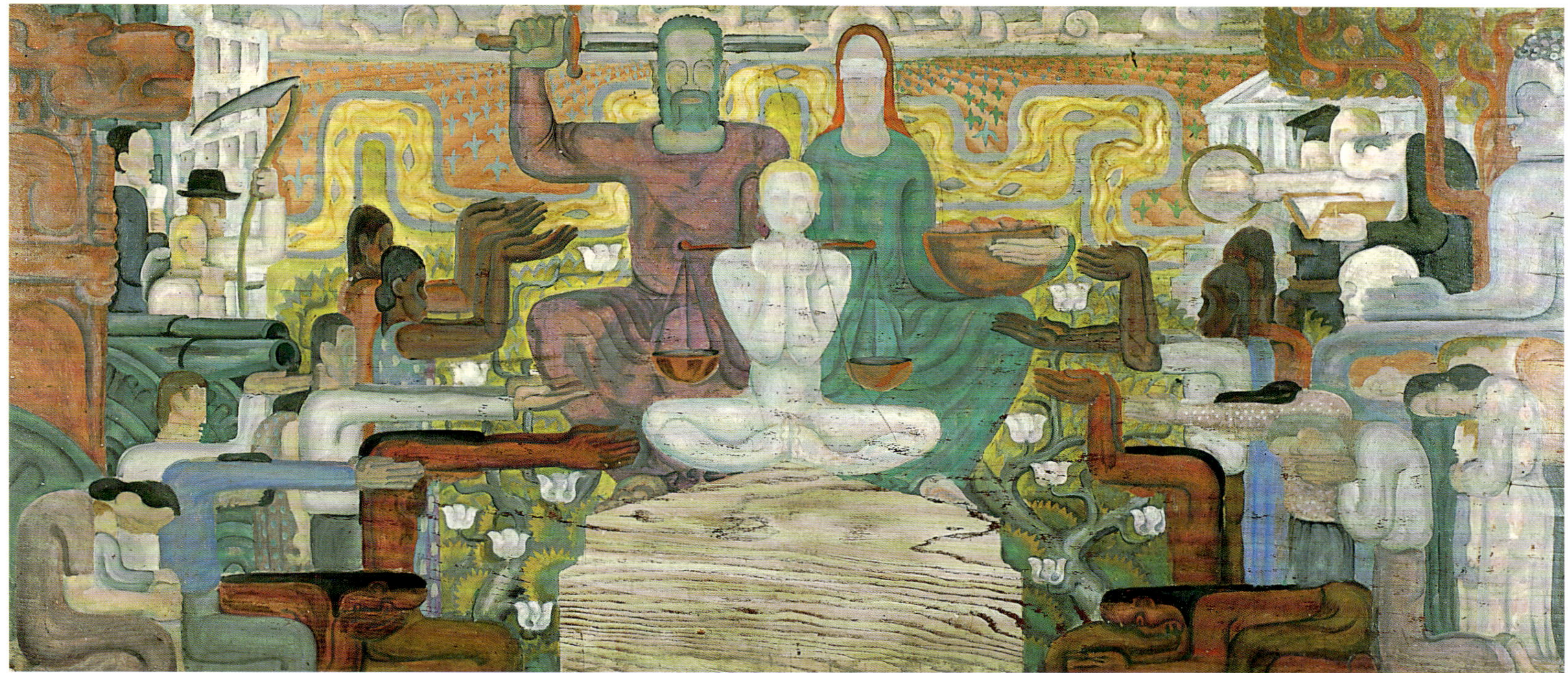

Fig. 3. Walter Anderson, color design for Jackson courthouse mural, 1935, oil on plywood, 27½ x 61⅛ in. Walter Anderson Museum of Art (87.2.1).

How long Anderson worked on these murals is indicated in a letter from his mother to him and his wife, who were vacationing in Maryland. It was dated May 9, 1934. "The school board came last night to inspect the murals. . . . Judge Davidson said the tiles were better than he expected. He was very definite about which were the best, and he pointed out the off color ones [i.e., tiles]. He said they should be put where they would be safe."[15] Since the PWAP was terminated about April 1934, it would seem that Anderson finished his panels in about five months.[16]

Starting about the fall of 1935, Anderson sought mural commissions under the Treasury Department's Section of Painting and Sculpture (1934–1943).[17] While the PWAP assigned murals on the basis of sketches and an available community wall, the Section held formal competitions for its commissions. Anderson first submitted a design for a commission in the federal courthouse in Jackson, Mississippi. In December 1935 he was asked to redesign his submission so it would be "suitable for a court room," to change its colors, and to put in "more dignified" subject matter. It noted that people in Jackson had objected "to the use of a negroid type as the dominant figure in the panel." This apparently referred to the boy holding the scales and possibly to the African American god holding a skull to the right. Anderson seems to have repainted both white while leaving the negroid features (Fig. 3).[18] It is not surprising

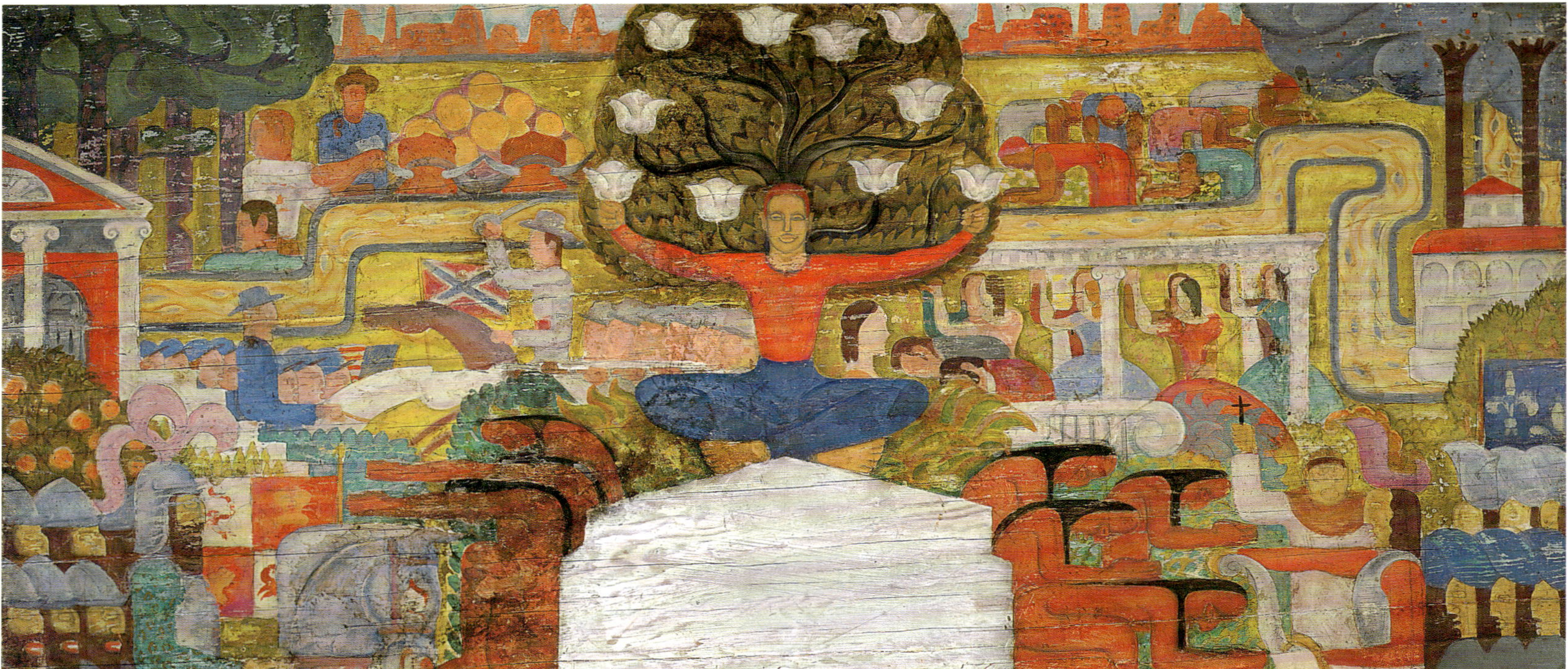

Fig. 4. Walter Anderson, color design for Jackson courthouse mural (with boy and tree), oil on plywood, 27½ x 61 in., The Family of Walter Anderson.

he did not win, since his studies show a surprisingly idiosyncratic conception of his task.

Traditional courthouse iconography had been determined by academic murals centered on a female personification of Justice in classical robes and identified by one or more of three attributes: the blindfold of impartiality, the sword of retribution, and the scales that weighed evidence. Anderson replaced this image with a family. The father held the sword, the mother wore the blindfold, and the naked, negroid son took a Buddha-like pose holding the scales. This astonishing motif is flanked by eleven magnolia blossoms, Meso-American and African American idols (the latter holding a skull), cannons, ancient and modern buildings, men with a scythe and a book, and a multicultural crowd including African Americans and others in the form of Meso-American glyphs, bent in prayer or gesturing in fealty toward the central figures. The background shows farmland and an undulating river.[19]

One finds here an autobiographical depiction of what any good Freudian would call Anderson's "family romance." The father figure brandishes the sword so it passes behind (through?) his head. Anderson would later be hospitalized for suicidal tendencies.[20] Freud defines suicide as taking revenge on the father, especially in a family where the mother might be blind to a son's emotional needs. Establishing that displaced desire for retribution, and viewing himself as inferior, the boy/artist prays for justice as a nature-oriented, negroid Buddhist. Indeed, his entire mythic world of

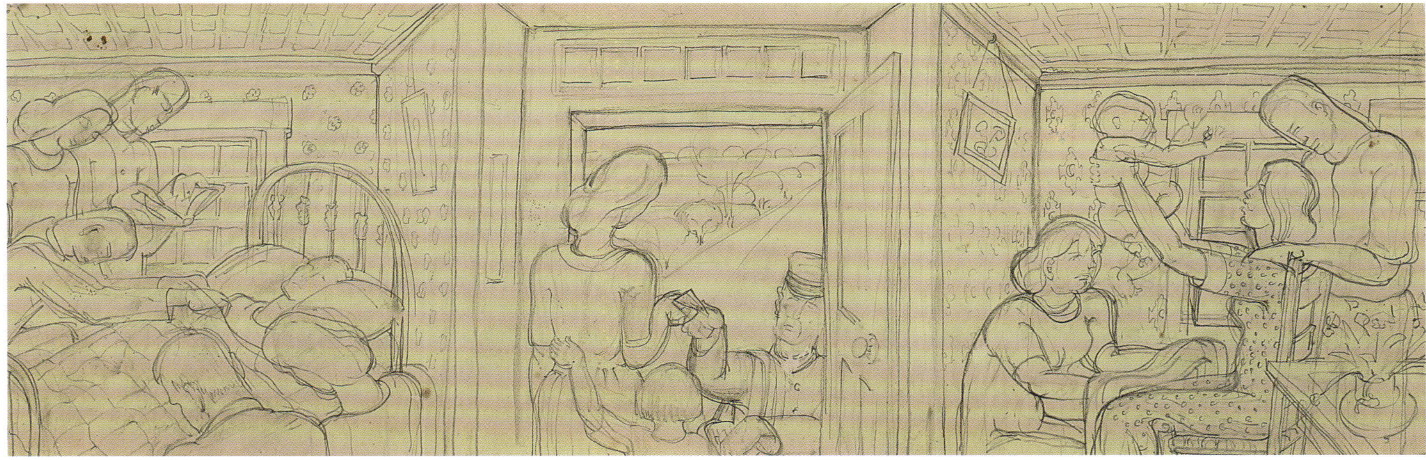

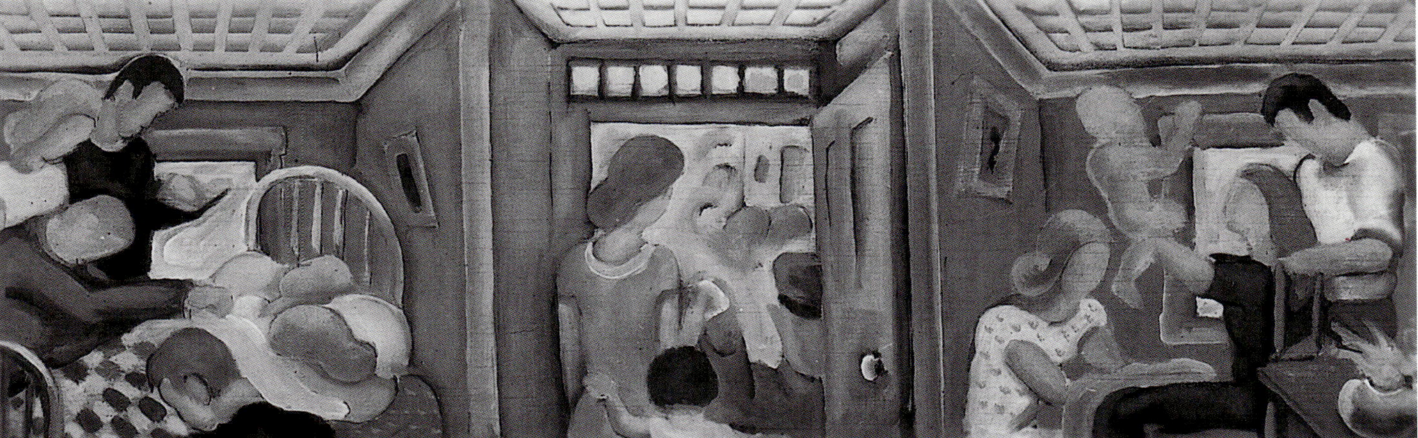

Fig. 5. Walter Anderson, pencil sketch for Indianola mural, 1936, pencil on paper, 3 x 23¾ in., The Family of Walter Anderson.

Fig. 6. Walter Anderson color design for Indianola mural, medium and dimensions unknown, photograph from National Archives, College Park, Maryland.

natural, artistic, and cultural interests—including the racism of his era—joins with him as he seeks a justice only therapy, art and his sense of unity with nature would ultimately provide.

Another undated study for the same courthouse exists and appears to be an equally misguided attempt to make a more acceptable design (Fig. 4). Here a young man—clothed and clearly Anderson's self-portrait—assumes the lotus position as the trunk of a tree bearing ten flowers, two of which he touches. The background is somewhat simplified, with more modern and industrial buildings, and praying glyph-figures are turned away from the central motif. But it is still too autobiographical for a public mural, and it is unclear if it was ever submitted to the Section. It does suggest that Anderson's hold on practical reality was by now seriously diminished.[21]

In August 1936, the Section invited Anderson to compete for a mural in the Indianola, Mississippi, post office on the basis of "a competent design" for the Jackson courthouse and to submit designs in the form of pencil sketches for the Indianola post office.[22] He submitted two sketches which were rejected. The Section admired one for the idea "of the mailman delivering mail on either side of a long street," but rejected it because "the abstractions and decorative qualities of the human figures are too extreme." This suggests he had reverted to the figure style of the PWAP panels. He tried again with five sketches, one of which (Fig. 5) was tentatively accepted, and, after he submitted several color designs, one was approved in January 1937 (Fig. 6). But the Section noted that the scale of the figures was too large for the intended wall, that some colors were too bright, and that he ought to revise the left section of the mural to show a sickbed scene rather than a deathbed.

The mural's subject suggested that the mails brought both good and bad news. Anderson, of course, was thinking of his father, George Walter Anderson, who was dying of cancer at this time and would die on February 21, 1937. He began work on it early in 1937, but this mural was never executed because of Anderson's mental breakdown. On April 22, 1937, his wife informed the Section that her husband was ill and asked that the contract be delayed; the commission was withdrawn in February 1938.

Anderson remained institutionalized at various times from April 1937 to 1940, and would not execute another mural until 1951.[23]

THE OCEAN SPRINGS COMMUNITY CENTER MURALS: 1951–52

History . . . is like a life in the midst of all lives. It is the natural world that counts, primarily the universal world, the world of planets and climates.[24]

In 1951 Anderson agreed to paint murals in the new Ocean Springs Community Center, and again chose the "then and now" theme: the founding of the town in 1699 by the French explorer Pierre Le Moyne, Sieur d'Iberville, opposite the eternal cycle of the seasons. Despite the choice of historical and symbolical subjects, the resulting overall theme was the exuberance of natural forms in which human and animal figures merge, countered by the geometric patternings around the window and door frames (Diagram 2 and pages 162, 165–67).[25]

The historical theme begins in the southeast corner of the Community Center's meeting room with an elaborate wall of geometric designs flanking the stage (A). It is crowned by a spiralic "rose" that suggests both the flower (its thorny stem can be seen below it) and the rose window of a French Gothic cathedral. The historical theme consists of two panels separated by windows showing Biloxi Indians welcoming the French explorers with pipe, drum, and a turtle (B). The scene is continued over the kitchen area with an appropriate frieze of birds feeding on fish (C), and continues in the last two panels with Iberville raising the French flag, followed by a cross-bearing monk, five soldiers, and Anderson himself guiding their boat to harbor (D).

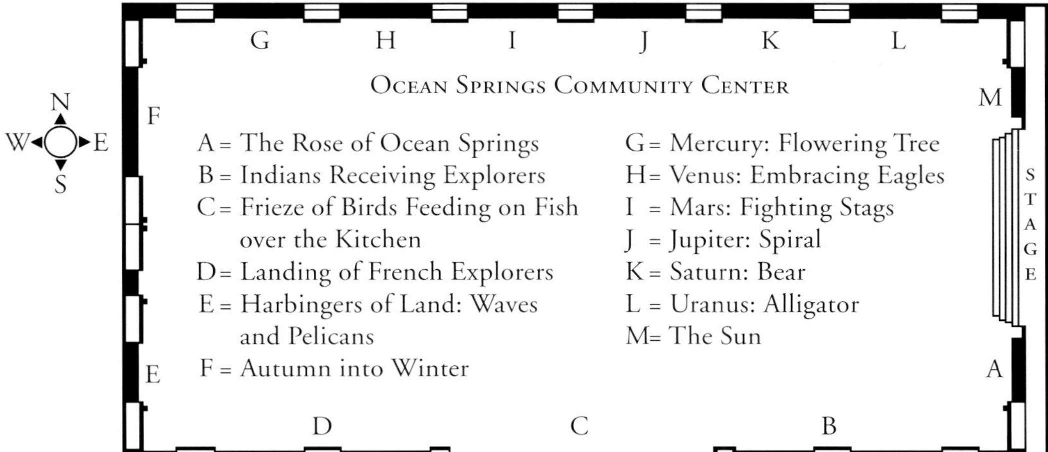

Diagram 2. Ocean Springs Community Center mural, 1950–1951.

Around the corner the west wall's left panel (E) depicts a lively scene of those harbingers of land, waves and pelicans, which guide explorers to shore. The west wall to the right of the central doors is devoted to the start of the seasonal cycle: an autumnal tree and one set in a winter landscape crowned by an iridescent crescent moon (F). The cycle continues on the north wall with panels, separated by windows, devoted to the natural and planetary iconography of spring and summer couched in the artist's personal symbology.

Thus Mercury and a flowering magnolia tree represent the beginnings of spring (G) and Venus with rising fish, gulls and terns, and embracing eagles its fruitfulness (H). Stags fight for a mate under Mars (I), while the shape-shifting Jupiter presides as a whirling spiral over the start of summer (J). As the season progresses, Saturn is seen as a black bear hunting honey in a tree (K) and Uranus with a lightning bolt, blue jays, and an alligator (L). At the corner the wall turns east to an image of the summer sun (M) blazing forth exactly opposite the winter moon back on the west wall, which completes the seasons' cycle.

There are four things to consider about this mural cycle: its compass orientation, its pictorial style, the symbolism of the planets, and the use of geometric patterns.

For a nature lover like Anderson, the four directions were the coordinates within which heavenly bodies moved, seasonal cycles proceeded, and life was lived. Their relationship to the daily cycle of dawn, day, dusk, and dark defined the continuity of existence. The east was of greatest importance as the source of the sun's light and took on a positive symbolism: like the spring, it illuminated and regenerated. The west reduced light to dark. It is thus a place of opposites: light and darkness and by exten-

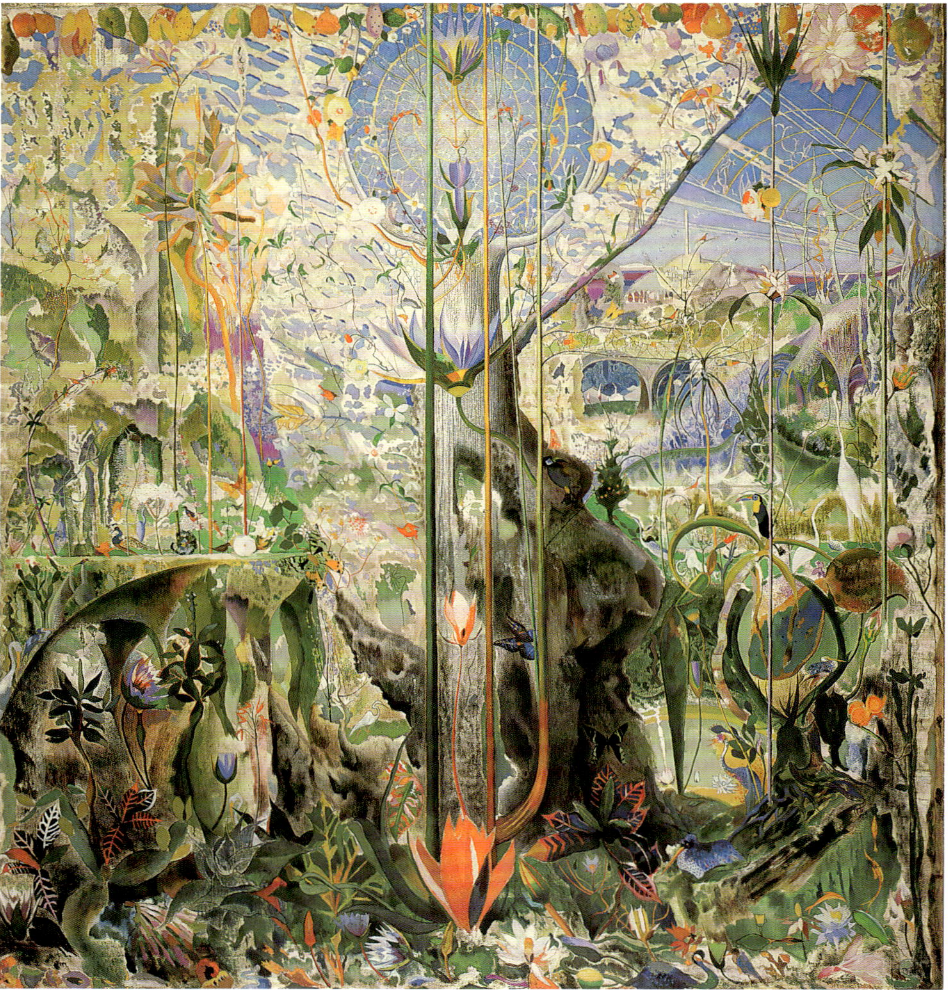

Fig. 7. Joseph Stella, *Tree of My Life*, oil on canvas, 83½ x 76½, 1919–1920, Mr. and Mrs. Barney A. Ebsworth Foundation and Windsor Inc., St. Louis, Missouri.

sion life and death—as at autumn. While the east and west were clearly defined in terms of the solar passage, the north and south found universal import in contrast to each other. The sun shone from the south and was associated with fertility and a wide range of positive and everyday values. It was the direction of daylight, noon, bright skies, human enterprise—and summer. In contrast was the cold, lightless, mysterious north that was associated most frequently with nocturnal powers, their impenetrable mysteries—and winter. It was within these encompassing coordinates that Anderson found a coherent model of the cosmos to image on walls.[26]

At the Community Center, the cosmos had to be adjusted to the architecture, with the result that the east wall, appropriately, is the place of the sun and rose motifs and the west the opposition of autumn into winter. But the seasons of spring and summer, most appropriate to the east and south, had to go to the north because of the kitchen's intrusion into the south wall. One advantage of this, however, was that an everyday historical event was put to the south, while Anderson's most impressive paintings about the seasonal birth, nurturing, and maturing of life, while placed to the north, faced south and received its light directly.

Anderson's pictorial approach here was extraordinary in its vigor, inventiveness, and simplicity. As with Burchfield's *Hiawatha* mural, however, there is an affinity here with Joseph Stella's 1919 *Tree of My Life* (Fig. 7), with its many vertical elements, exuberant foliation, and rich colors. Stylistically, of course, its carefully rendered details are very different from Anderson's forceful painterliness on the Community Center's concrete walls.

Lending to the power of these murals is Anderson's typical refusal to idealize nature: autumn elides into the deadly cold of winter, and out of winter comes spring, whose fertility is symbolized by embracing eagles and fighting stags. Summer's growth finds the god Jupiter in a whirlwind, and its decline is indicated by marauding animals. Nature's drama is not without its violence and dangers, and Anderson does not let the viewer forget that most fundamental of its lessons.[27]

One of the great strengths of these murals was the way in which Anderson countered his natural forms with the geometric patterns around the doors and windows. In both cases, the dimensions of the aperture is extended onto the mural surface, so there is a tripartite frame, with the elements on the mural plane decorated with every conceivable variation of Best-Maugard's seven universal motifs, the middle elements left white, and the inner plane more often than not set with the spare patterns of line and squares first employed by the Scottish Art Nouveau architect and designer Charles Rennie Mackintosh (1868–1928). These decorations were not all completed, but where they were, they balance the forms in the murals and harmonize with their colors.

After a somewhat frustrating year at the Community Center, when he had to endure his neighbors' suspicions about his sanity and the quality of his murals, which some would have destroyed, he retired to his cottage at Shearwater for the rest of his life.

THE SHEARWATER COTTAGE MURALS: 1951ff.

I go for a walk in the woods nearly every day and I have special places where I go and read and draw.[28]

In 1939, Anderson had built an extension on the south side of his home to be used as a nursery. Now he determined to paint a mural in it for himself that would embody, on his own terms, his place in nature.[29]

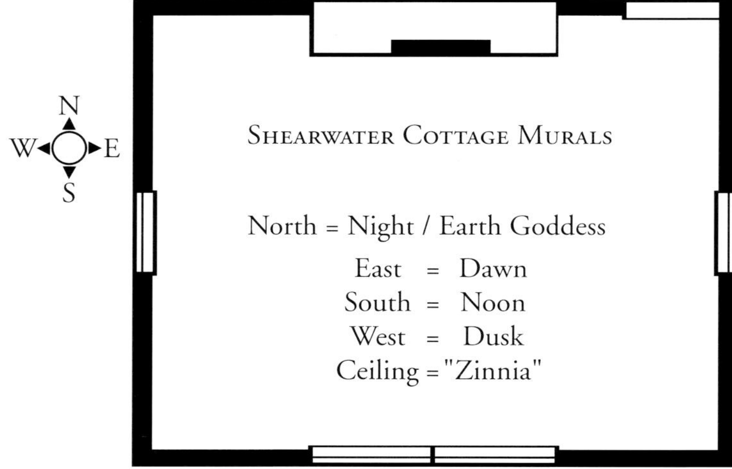

Diagram 3. Shearwater Cottage mural, 1951ff.

The room had a double window facing south and others on the east and west walls. The north wall was dominated by the back of the fireplace and chimney that heated the rest of the cottage and had a door in the northeast corner that led into it (Diagram 3 and pages 168–73).[30]

Here Anderson had a perfectly oriented architectural setting in which to integrate the directions (as discussed above) with the times of day. The window in the east wall glows with the sun at dawn, the south wall with the glory of the day, the west with the dying of the dusk, and the north with the brilliance of moths brightening the dark. Each wall has its own perspectival ground plane that extends the floor of the room. On the white background of the chimney to the north is an ethereal evocation of the primordial earth mother—a horned young woman rising up from a glowing font of flowers.

Crowning this private temple was a strange, mandala-like circle of forms centered on the room's light fixture. This image has been identified as a zinnia, but seems, from its style, more an evocation of some Meso-American glyph or calendar stone. It also resembles Karl Blossfeldt's photograph of saxifrage.[31] This brings Anderson full circle back to his mural studies for the Jackson courthouse, where similar glyph figures surrounded his autobiographical fantasies.

AN ENCOMPASSING VISION

Mysticism is not only an experience but is also a creative process in which this experience is given shape in language, pictures, worldview, and behavior. . . . The mystic has the most disturbing awareness that something is not quite right. The social order . . . [makes it] hard to see or accept any alternative. The [mystic] must have a talent of some sort. . . . Only when a thing has been given form, will its value be demonstrated.[32]

"Oh darling, don't be surprised at what the years may bring. Know that I live under a different compulsion. I must be in harmony with this . . ." He waved his arm, encompassing the earth. "Not only must I be in harmony, I must make it manifest."[33]

Toward the end of his recovery in the early 1940s, Anderson made a drawing of himself seen from the back struggling against enclosing walls of hospitals (see page 113). It is clear from his later murals that he came to see the art form as a way of breaking through walls to reveal the unity within the all-encompassing natural world beyond them. He wanted the interior and the exterior to be one environment.

The fact of his mental illness and its consequence in an isolated life and intense art should not make us view his art any differently from how we would if he had been perfectly "normal." We too often see mental anomalies as craziness, weakness, or some sort of failure, when the history of art is replete with those who took their mental afflictions and made them assets, integrating themselves through creativity—as did Vincent van Gogh and Jackson Pollock. This is why it would be unfair to categorize Anderson as an "outsider," just as it is unfair to include under that unnecessary rubric "folk artists," "primitive artists," or "occult artists."

At a time when many curators, critics, and collectors are coming to see serious modernist art petering out in contemporary mannerism, pastiche, and fin de siècle angst, and scholars are recognizing the validity of third world and minority group artistic expression, interest in the art of the mentally ill is part of this healthy quest for justice for the most literally alienated among us. Indeed, such art, so long segregated and ignored in favor of "high" art, can be seen more justly as one of many "styles of sanity."[34] This requires a certain sense that there are different ways of being sane—just as Anderson came to understand himself as both alienated and normal.

What then was Anderson's style of sanity? For him it was a hard-earned vision of being at one with nature. He was a nature mystic, emerging from his illness as from a shamanistic initiation, to feel he could make his own, unified world in nature and make it manifest to others. He could not ignore the natural world around him for the family world into which he was born. It is hard to trace this inner evolution. But it is quite possible that he early on saw more in natural phenomena than most[35] and was, by midlife—his illness began at about the age of thirty-five[36]—so torn by the contradictions between "normal" life and his needs as an artist to express what he could see, that he could no longer function.

Later he came to see the world as divided between the "concentric"—those controlled by narrow subjective realities—and the "excentric" [*sic*], who lived in the objective world of nature.[37] He sought totalities, whereas most are content with elementalities; he sought transcendent unity while others are satisfied with putting things in order. Like Jackson Pollock, he could say "I am nature," while everyone else was saying "I must be a civilized citizen." But nature is an amorphous, indifferent, and dangerous environment, and to create a world within nature, Anderson found the surrounding mural to be his ideal art form, since its traditional conventions, going back to the cave paintings he had seen as a student, had already established a style of sanity capable of containing and manifesting his relentlessly encompassing awareness.

ACKNOWLEDGMENTS

I am indebted to Mary Anderson Pickard, Walter Anderson's daughter, as well as to Dr. Patricia Pinson and Dennis Walker, the curator and registrar respectively of the Walter Anderson Museum of Art, for their help while writing this essay. Thanks are also due to William Creech and Gene Morris of the National Archives for help with New Deal records, and to Professor Christopher Maurer for sharing his ideas for the biography of Walter Anderson he is writing. I am also grateful for the assistance of Avis Berman, Professor John Charlot, Mildred Constantine, and Helen Harrison.

NOTES

1. Walter Anderson Papers, Archives of American Art, Smithsonian Institution, letter to his mother while he was an art student at the Parsons School of Design in New York, March 6, 1923, Reel 4867, frame 143–44. Hereafter: AAA.

2. I am indebted to Anne R. King's pioneer study of Anderson's murals, *Walls of Light: The Murals of Walter Anderson* (Jackson: University Press of Mississippi and the Walter Anderson Museum of Art, 1999). Hereafter: *Walls of Light*.

3. Adolfo Best-Maugard, *A Method For Creative Design* (New York: Alfred A. Knopf, 1926). This book went through five English editions between 1926 and 1930. Hereafter: *A Method*. See also Jay Hambidge's two most widely published books: *Dynamic Symmetry in Composition As Used by the Artist* and *The Elements of Dynamic Symmetry* (New York: Brentano's, 1923 and 1926 respectively). Anderson owned these books in various editions.

4. Best-Maugard, *A Method*, p. 162, and Anderson's letters to his mother while at he was at Parsons in New York, January 30 and February 2, 1923, AAA Reel 4867, Frames 132–34.

5. Conversation with Professor Christopher Maurer, December 1, 2002. Further, the idea that the 8½-x-11-inch stationery Anderson used for many of his watercolors is related to dynamic symmetry seems incorrect; only "legal" paper, which is 8½ x 13 inches, would conform to the required proportions. The many spirals in Anderson's work may well have been inspired by Best-Maugard's book (see *A Method*, Part V, "The Whirling Spiral," pp. 154–63), but are not worked out in strict accordance with Hambidge's methods.

6. First published in English by E. Weyhe, New York, 1929. Anderson owned several editions of these books. References here are to *Karl Blossfeldt: Art Forms in Nature, The Complete Edi-*

tion (Munich: Schirmer Art Books, 1999), which contains a useful introductory essay by Gert Mattenklott.

7. His daughter, Mary Anderson Pickard, believes the Blossfeldt books were of primary importance because they validated what her father had already discovered—the deep unities in nature. Communication from Dr. Patricia Pinson, November 22, 2002.

8. Best-Maugard, *A Method*, p. 103.

9. All three brothers are listed among Mississippi's twelve PWAP artists in the Final Report of the Public Works of Art Project (Washington, DC, 1934), p. 54, and they all did murals for the same school in Ocean Springs after submitting proposals to the project's regional director, Ellsworth Woodward, who was a friend of their mother. See Anne King, *Walls of Light*, p. 20.

10. It ought to be stressed that these murals were not done on the famous WPA Federal Art Project, as Anne King states (*Walls of Light*, p. 19). In 1935 a Works Progress Administration cultural program was established in Mississippi that supported projects for artists, writers, actors, and musicians. There were, however, so few artists in the state—the three Anderson brothers constituted a quarter of the State's PWAP cohort!—that the art project did not start until 1939 when the WPA was put under state control.

11. The side panels each measured 4 feet 7½ inches x 14 feet 4 inches; the two front panels were 11 feet x 6 feet 1 inch; each was painted in oil on heavy canvas.

12. In a letter of August 20, 1930, Anderson mentions to his fiancé "doing ducks on a pot for Peter in a more or less Cretan manner." AAA Reel 4867, Frame 265. It is surprising that Anderson was allowed such a daring feat of abstraction. The PWAP was the first New Deal art program and there was probably little supervision, especially since its local director was a friend of the Anderson family. Unfortunately, the records of the PWAP in the National Archives contain no mention of this mural.

13. This is in contrast to his brothers' tile murals in the same school that are richly decorative but symbolically neutral: birds fly in the air; fish swim in the sea. See Anne King, *Walls of Light*, p. 21, Figs. 8 and 9.

14. There is a sketch for a wood carving in a letter of January 1924 that shows a frieze of Indians similar to the Burchfield work in that they are all heading right to left. See AAA Roll 4867, Frame 171.

15. His mother also reported on May 10 that the PWAP would not pay for the installation of his brothers' murals. See AAA Roll 4867, Frames 959 and 960. All three artists eventually paid for the installation themselves.

16. Given the limited range of flat colors—red, yellow, blue, and brown—and many repeated figure and plant motifs in these murals, it seems that Anderson used a stencil system to facilitate their completion.

17. What follows is based, unless otherwise noted, on documents from the National Archives, Record Group 121, Records of the Public Building Service, Entry 133, Records Concerning Federal Art Activities, Case Files Concerning Embellishments of Federal Buildings, Box 55, Folder for Jackson, Mississippi Post Office & Court House [1935–1936] and Box 54, Folder for Indianola, Mississippi Post Office [1936–1938].

18. There are several color studies for this submission extant in which he blocks out his colors. One omits the right side of the design entirely. It is impossible to determine their chronology. The one in the collection of the Walter Anderson Museum of Art (Fig. 3) was probably the first submitted and later repainted, although it is unclear if that version was resubmitted.

19. The landscape there is strongly influenced by Best-Maugard. See *A Method,* p. 39, for a similar treatment of hills and trees.

20. Agnes Grinstead Anderson, *Approaching the Magic Hour: Memories of Walter Anderson*, ed. Patti Carr Black (Jackson: University Press of Mississippi, 1989), pp. 53–58. Hereafter: Agnes Anderson, *Approaching.*

21. One might speculate that this design, given the central role Anderson takes in it, was cre-

ated after his father's death in February 1937. Note that the magnolia blossoms in his first courthouse sketch (Fig. 3) numbered eleven, but in the second (Fig. 4) they numbered ten. Conspicuous, countable items in a painting often signify emotion-laden personal reality. There were, in 1935–36, eleven immediate members in Anderson's family cohort: his parents, his wife and her father, his two siblings and their wives, two nieces and a nephew. After February 1937 there were ten. Further, young men who discover themselves no longer sons often identify with trees—with new roots.

22. This was standard operating procedure, especially in states without many artists. The New Deal's cultural programs were as interested in publicly promoting art as they were in procuring it for the government. See Ralph Purcell, *Government and Art: A Study of the American Experience* (Washington, DC: Public Affairs Press, 1956), passim.

23. About 1945, Anderson made a number of mural studies for the house in which he was living with his wife and father-in-law at Oldfields in Gautier, Mississippi. They were never executed, and since how the murals were to be arranged is unclear, they will not be discussed here. See Anne King, *Walls of Light*, pp. 41–49, for reproductions at Figs. 21–30, and her commentary on them. See also Agnes Anderson, *Approaching*, pp. 83–120.

24. Agnes Anderson, *Approaching*, pp. 135–36.

25. The room is 84 feet long by 42 feet wide by 11½ feet high. The mural panels are continuous around the doors and windows, the latter being 4½ feet wide, although they appear larger because of the decorative bands around each.

26. He would realize this fully in his Shearwater Cottage mural. See below. For a fully developed discussion of directional symbolism in murals, see Francis V. O'Connor, "An Iconographic Interpretation of Diego Rivera's *Detroit Industry* Murals in Terms of Their Orientation to the Cardinal Points of the Compass" in *Diego Rivera: A Retrospective*, Detroit Institute of Arts / W. W. Norton, 1986, pp. 215–17.

27. One thinks of the old aesthetic contrast between the superficially *elegant* and the emotionally charged *sublime* when viewing any work by Anderson. Further, he was very much involved in music. Regarding this, see Dr. Patricia Pinson, "Symphonies in Paint," unpublished lecture for a symposium titled "Elements of the Whole: Walls of Light," Nov. 11, 1999, at the Walter Anderson Museum of Art (hereafter Pinson, "Symphonies"). But given that we are dealing with an artist who loved to dance to Beethoven, his use of planet symbolism suggests he knew a work by English composer Gustav Holst (1874–1934), the famous musical suite *The Planets* (1914–16). This consisted of seven movements, one for each of the planets known in Holst's day (which omits Pluto), based on their astrological rather than mythological connotations which determined keys and rhythms. For instance, he leaves out Neptune, which in Holst's suite might well describe musically the panel on the west wall showing the eliding of dying autumn into the stillness of winter. But such an elaborate interpretation of the mural is best left to a musicologist. For an interpretation of the mythological aspects of the murals, see David J. Johnson's unpublished essay "Symbolic and Mythic Potential in Nature's Images: A Perspective on Walter Anderson's 'Community Center Murals.'"

28. Walter Anderson, age twelve, when starting his first year at St. John's School, Manlius, New York, to his mother in New Orleans, August 5, 1915, AAA Reel 4867, Frame 6.

29. Regarding the Shearwater murals, I have relied on Anne King, *Walls of Light*, pp. 91–103, and Redding S. Sugg, Jr., *A Painter's Psalm: The Mural from Walter Anderson's Cottage* (Jackson: University Press of Mississippi, 1992), passim. Hereafter: Sugg, *A Painter's Psalm.*

30. The room was 13 feet long by 11 feet wide and 10 feet high.

31. See *Art Forms in Nature,* First Series, plate 30.

32. Bruno Borchert, *Mysticism: Its History and Challenge* (York Beach, Maine: Samuel Weiser, Inc., 1994), pp. 16–17.

33. Agnes Anderson, *Approaching*, p. 116.

34. I first used the phrase "styles of sanity" in a review of two books on the art of the insane:

"The Styles of Sanity," *Medical Humanities Review* 5:2 (July 1991): 51–57.

35. Note, for instance, the iridescent rendering of the auras of the sun and moon in the Community Center murals. Anderson is known to have experimented with such phenomena around flowers. See Agnes Anderson, *Approaching*, p. 88. It is also possible that he was synesthetic. His wife recalls that "He was always connecting tone with color and rhythm with pattern, until I think he saw a Beethoven symphony almost as he would see a painting, or a series of paintings matched to the movements of the symphony [and] that he often equated music with color and form." Quoted in Pinson, "Symphonies."

36. For an essay about the developmental psychology of artists that deals with such situations, see Francis V. O'Connor, "The Psychodynamics of the Frontal Self-portrait," *Psychoanalytic Perspectives on Art 1*, 1985, pp. 169–221.

37. See Sugg, *A Painter's Psalm,* pp. 78–80.

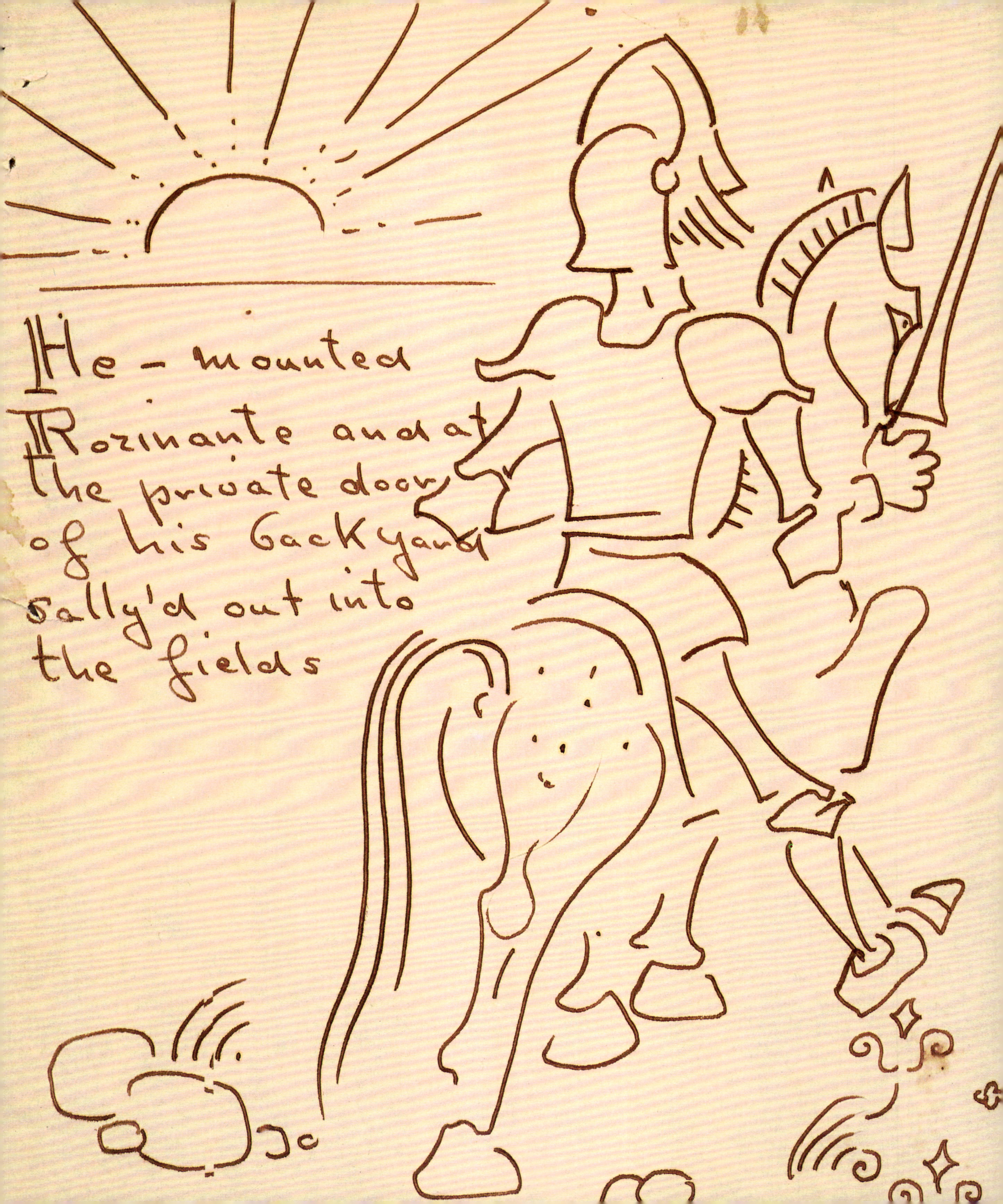

He-mounted Rozinante and at the private door of his backyard sally'd out into the fields

JC

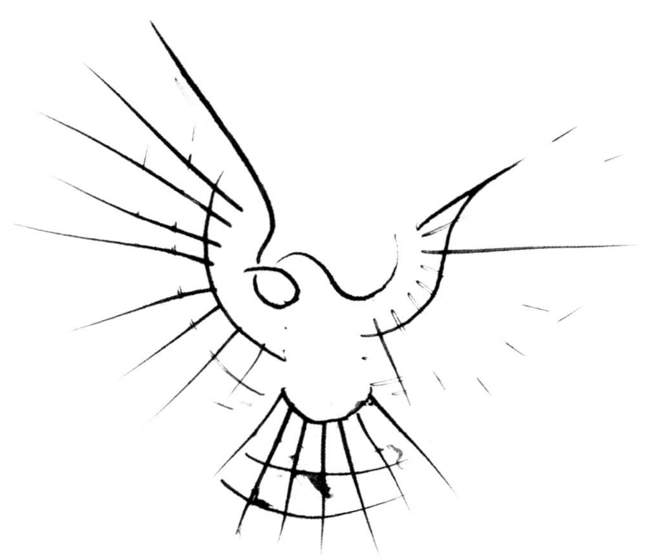

WALTER ANDERSON AS EXPLORER AND DISCOVERER

COLIN EISLER

. . . every movement, each discovery,
Is a part of the heavenly music,
If my ears were functioning properly
I would hear not just the wind in the grass.
The two or three different rhythms of insects,
The piping of a frog, the call of a nightjar,
But an orderly and recognizable harmony
Which might or might not have been written.
—Walter Anderson

Of the artist's poems,[1] among his longest are two concerned with the challenge of exploration: *Columbus* is an epic in prose; the other, *On Leif Eriksson*, in verse, is devoted to the Norse voyager, inspired by the earliest Greek verses of maritime adventure—Homer's *Iliad* and *Odyssey*. He illustrated Pope's translation of *The Iliad*,[2] and was so at home with the Homeric heroes that he made a large model of Ulysses' ship with working oars, possibly for his children's pleasure. Anderson's liveliest biblical cycle, by way of *Paradise Lost*, was devoted to another maritime adventure, his series being based upon Milton's vision of the flood.[3]

Anderson must have thought of Ulysses when, according to legend, he lashed himself to the mast of his sailboat to avoid drowning in Hurricane Betsy.[4] So close was the artist to the westward-oriented voyages of Eriksson that he named his third

He Mounted Rozinante, ca. 1941
Ink on paper, 11 x 8½ in.
The Family of Walter Anderson

child—not the hoped-for son but a daughter—Leif when she was born in 1944. "The Rime of the Ancient Mariner" by Samuel Taylor Coleridge (1772–1834) provided another of Anderson's favorite readings, which he also furnished with hundreds of illustrations.[5]

Of all explorers, William Beebe (1877–1962) may have been particularly close to the artist since that American combined the rare gift of narration with his other fields of interest, including going down to the depths of the sea in his bathysphere and acting as chief curator of ornithology at the New York Zoological Society.

Water's infinite mysteries, so involved with Anderson's seagoing and the subject of many notes in his logs, are closely related to the miracle of flight, the subject of some of the artist's most beautiful studies. These tangential areas, of adjacent motion above the earth and below the waters, were of equal interest to the world's greatest artist-explorer-discoverer, Leonardo da Vinci. Essentially loners, both men often applied their arts to mediate between the twinned investigations and magical manifestations of the air- and the seaborne. Two pages drawn for *Paradise Lost*, showing how "the floating Vessel swum uplifted," "and secured with beaked prow Rode tilting o'er the Waves,"[6] show the wonder and terror of water's domain.

With a mythic, archaic sense of self, a bardic exploration and identification with the natural world around him, Anderson recited some lines from G. K. Chesterton (surprising in their passion from that somewhat tame poet in their return to the genesis of life's discoveries), using them to convey to his wife his sense of primeval autogenesis:

> When fishes flew and forests walked
> And figs grew upon thorn,
> Some moment when the mood was blood
> Then surely I was born.[7]

Both of Anderson's longest poems deal with the discovery of the New World, being devoted to the Viking's finding of Labrador and Nova Scotia and to the Italian's journey to Central America. *The Voyage of the Beagle* by Charles Darwin and the travel records of New World traveler Alexander von Humboldt were among the artist's favorite readings. Many drawings were made of the English evolutionist's scientific voyage, almost as if Anderson were a witty fellow member of the *Beagle*'s crew, some of these pages depicting British naval officers, gauchos lassoing a wild cow in Patagonia, Fuegians greeting the *Beagle*, or tattooed Tahitians.[8]

It was within a scene of discovery and conquest in his painting *The Landing of the French Explorer Pierre Le Moyne, Sieur d'Iberville* (the explorer is shown being greeted by the Biloxi Indians in 1699) for the walls of the Ocean Springs Community Center that Anderson chose to include one of his few highly finished self-portraits. Did he, yearning for the role of painter rather than that of commercially successful artisan, wish himself into this subject as a form of vicarious conquest? Though he cherished the notion of an idealistic role as producer of low-cost art for a large audience, this necessitated the mass manufacture of Art Deco novelties, many of these rightly disparaged by him as "widgets," which kept him from working on a higher level. They took up the time and energy he would have preferred investing in experimentation toward the production of a more challenging, individualistic oeuvre.

For Walter Inglis Anderson, exploration may always have been uppermost in his life and work. The most successful discoverer must also be prepared to get lost, leaving a known sense of self and place in favor of finding others. A drive, a compulsion, a passion, exploration is often driven by need or greed. But it can also be extravagantly quixotic or nonobjective, an irrational concern limited to a looking for the "there." Elements of risk, vulnerability, and exposure are built into adventure's strange seductions, these often outstripping any possible financial or other reward.

Linked to search as well as research, exploration always deals with discovery, with uncovering, revealing, bringing to the eye, to the surface, what has not been known or seen before, represented on an extravagant or an intimate scale. Finding such life forms was another of Anderson's key concerns. Whether uncovering a pattern, carving or painting a pot, cutting a linoleum block, or watching and painting the life of nature, he acted as its first secret witness, then its sharer and perpetuator through his art.

Having won a travel prize from the Pennsylvania Academy of the Fine Arts, the artist went to France and Spain in 1927. Later he went to China (1949) and Costa Rica (1951). According to him, logs were just notes, preparatory to the "third poetry." The first was always written by sailors and farmers who sang with the wind in their teeth, the second by scholars, students, and inspired drinkers. The third was sometimes unwritten "but when it is, it is written by those who have brought nature and art into one thing."[9]

Inner journeys, as important as those covering "surface space," were also among the artist's definitive experiences. A visit with the influential Armenian mystic (and probable conman) George Ivanovitch Gurdjieff (1877?–1949) near Fontainebleau exposed Anderson to that charismatic figure, known as a brilliant "awakener" of his followers. He too was a traveler, claiming journeys to northeast Africa, the Middle East, India, and central Asia in search of spiritual enlightenment.[10] Among the first of the twentieth-century "Questers," Gurdjieff taught intially in Russia, beginning his Institute for the Harmonious Development of Man there in 1919. After the Russian

Revolution, the Russian moved to the comfortably monastic housing at Prieuré d'Avon, where his disciples' lives were punctuated by ritual exercise and dance to the music written by the master's associate.

Close to later concepts of transcendental meditation, the cathartic, contemplative adventures engendered by Gurdjieff must have constituted a form of emotional/spiritual release, yet these journeys into uncharted waters may have had potentially mixed consequences for so volatile a character as Anderson. With the American dancer Isadora Duncan, the Russian guru shared an almost messianic attachment to the importance of movement. Some of his theories also approached those of the innovative Russian drama teacher and theorist Konstantin Stanislavsky.

Abandoning the restrictions and supports of convention, an artist such as Anderson needed the freedom to discover, to find a nature often invisible to others, to follow a privileged path. Increasingly important for his life and work was the way in which exploration usually meant a going away, letting him leave his domestic as well as his professional cares. Exchanging the known for the hazards and encounters of the unknown, Anderson took off for the Far East or Central America, in the certain knowledge that his parental resources would bail him out when need be.

Whether by boat, bicycle, car, or on foot, the artist became a constant explorer of his own land as well, with travels to Texas, Florida, Tennessee, and New York. As much as possible, he became one with the elements, sleeping outdoors, washing in rivers. Poetic journals show a romantic, transcendental merging with the world around him. In his Texas journal—significantly described by him as a log, not a diary—he wrote, "It was one of those rose and blue sunrises with white herons and large pink mallows just opened and with a landscape swept clean by the river, and all the willows apparently planted according to plan. I took a swim and had breakfast of rice and oranges. I had a little trouble with the fire because the wood was wet. Then afterwards wrote up the log."[11]

Even his visiting New York City brought out a discoverer-like dimension. He turned the clock back to the ancient Near East in his Manhattan log, the first page of which records the city's residents: "Then I explored and saw more Sumerians everywhere . . . I kept being reminded of Queen Shubad."[12]

With his brothers Peter (1901–1984) and James (1907–1998), Walter Anderson realized one of the last, dynastic representatives of the vibrant Arts and Crafts movement, so strong throughout the United States near 1900, stimulated by the great popularity in America of John Ruskin and William Morris. The marvelously eccentric potter George Ohr and Joseph Fortune Meyer both worked in Biloxi, near the three brothers' future home at Ocean Springs. There too America's major nineteenth-century architect and theorist Louis Sullivan had built a summer cottage on the beach.

With increasing economic difficulties, the artist felt less entitled to travel, since his brothers were working so hard to maintain the family's major source of revenue, Shearwater Pottery. It had been founded in 1928 by Peter, who broke down temporarily under the enormous financial and creative burden of the pottery's direction during the Depression.

Among the key aspects in the life of the artist is his seeing himself as a voyager, and the keeping of logs or journals of his travels to Horn Island and to China.[13] Ceaseless activity—an enormous physical participation that characterized Anderson's role in art and life—was the wellspring of his painting, potting, woodcarving, walking, cycling, and sailing. This dynamic may have been both stabilized and stimulated by Gurdjieff's guidance. Always "fascinated by ideas dealing with expanding consciousness," the artist's mother, Annette McConnell Anderson, a vibrant, wealthy, autocratic, and artistic New Orleans aristocrat, must have laid the groundwork for her son's exploration of mystical frontiers in art and life.[14]

Young Anderson and his two equally handsome and talented brothers, along with their wives, were all arresting for their striking good looks and physical grace. His beautifully coordinated presence allowed Anderson to throw himself into Gurdjieff's world of spiritual and physical discovery and self-realization in 1927 both in France and at the spiritual retreats run in New Jersey by the mystic's follower, the pseudonymous A. R. Orage (1873–1934). That Englishman had begun with Shavian concerns, editing *The New Age*, and then moved in more mystical directions, going from London to Gurdjieff's French colony, then coming to preach his gospel in America.

Though Anderson's adventures may be compared with those of many artist-travelers, the man closest in many ways to the American's empathic, mystical drives is the great Muscovite master Wassily Kandinsky (1866–1944). His membership in Russian anthropological societies and study of Siberian art are close to Anderson's love for the caves at Les Eyzies and his passion for nature.

Concerned, like so many artists of his day, with the mysticism of Madame Blavatsky, the founder of theosophy, Kandinsky long consulted her publications, moved by her theories of correspondences among color, sound, spirit, and shape.[15] Theosophy was well established in the United States by Blavatsky's successor, Krishna Murti, who settled in this country for many years. Anderson's mother, the matriarch known to her family as Mère, was a devotee of similar theories, following some theosophical interests in equivalences between color and sound. She also pursued the revelations of a card game where the player was to predict which geometric shape lay on the other side of a card, to be sensed by touch alone.

Mary Anderson Pickard recalled how her paternal grandmother "liked to talk to us . . . about the geometry of form and of composition, of proportion and of the Golden Mean.[16] These and other esoterica like numerology, vertical/horizontal oppositions, sequences of color and auras, of geometries underpinning form were lively topics of conversation whenever Mère and my father were together." [17]

Newcomb College in New Orleans, which the talented Annette McConnell Anderson had attended, was long distinguished for the teaching of arts and crafts. Her strong personality ("I and the Lord are one") influenced all three of her sons in becoming artists and artisans. She treasured the internationally popular German photographic publication by Karl Blossfeldt, with its provocative title, *Urformen der Kunst* (*Primeval Art Forms*) (1928). Using microscopic photography Blossfeldt produced compelling studies in which plant elements were so seen and printed as to suddenly resemble structural, functional, symmetrically "designed" forms. These memorable photographs removed the accident and the incident from plant life, allowing plants to assume a magical, spooky quality with strangely strong, intimate effects that are all their own, so turning their viewers into Lewis Carroll–like discoverers traveling on some mysteriously shrinking and expanding spaceship.[18] That English writer's *Alice in Wonderland*, an eccentric explorer of the imagination, would be the subject of hundreds of Anderson's drawings.

In anticipating the geometrical drive to regularize life forms in terms of pattern and clarity of definition of Art Deco, Blossfeldt's seductive photographic reducing of nature's seemingly infinite variety provided an enormous stimulus to a new graphic language. It proved of compelling concern to the young Walter Anderson, and to the writer of this study—seen as a form of initiation, a private voyage into nature's secret ways.

For the artist, the linear repertoire of all cultures, including the caves of Les Eyzies (reflected in one of his earliest and finest pots), the arts of Crete, Greece, and Egypt, the pre-Columbian arts of Mexico, and folk themes from Central and South America, were an empire of his domination, if not discovery, and were found throughout his oeuvre. Anderson even saw the courting of his future, brilliant wife in terms of cosmic dominion rather than of an individual love conquering all!

Tormented during much of his adult life by mental illness, the artist was able to work despite the restrictions usually entailed by such affliction. This was made possible by the powerful intelligence and compassion of both his mother and his wife—each a tower of strength, of independent character and of equally independent determination. Anderson's parents had known mental illness on both sides of the family, and his wife's father proved be arteriosclerotic with psychotic episodes. Agnes "Sissy" Grinstead Anderson's account of life with her artist husband, *Approaching the Magic Hour: Memories of Walter Anderson,*[19] is among the most unflinching, clear-minded, and stirring of all memoirs, itself a stoical, loving odyssey of the experience of marrying into both genius and madness.

Exile can be a form of exploration all its own. Unlike those wrenching departures imposed by others, Anderson's sudden, self-engendered voyages out, to escape his own violent dictates, were brought on by psychotic pressures. Usually, when the artist felt a lack of control coming on, he would simply slip away. He would take his sailboat to Horn Island, twelve miles by sea from Ocean Springs. There the artist made many of his finest watercolors, escaping the wild within by communing with the beauties of the surrounding wilderness, finding therapy in its recording. The results of these flights were often as memorable and beautiful as their motivation was tragic. Birds in flight, fish parting the waves, vegetation enlivening the shore, pelicans diving in search of fodder—all preserved on the watercolored page, all evoked as if by sympathetic magic.

The family's major concern was to let Anderson work, love, and live as freely as possible. He had moved back to the cottage at Shearwater for his last nineteen years, for freedom from commercial and domestic pressures. Anderson's great gift for language—analogous to his graphic eloquence with line—made the artist's need to leave for Horn Island clear in the most original fashion;[20] he wrote in one of the Horn Island logbooks, "So much depends on the dominant mode on shore, that it was necessary for me to go to sea to find the conditional."[21] Here, he explains quite literally, in terms of the grammar of life, just what going to sea signified in the most personal sense—an escape from the dominant by taking refuge in the conditional. On Horn Island the artist could lead a hermetic life, not one resembling Robinson Crusoe's, since he so seldom wanted or needed rescue or companionship, but rather the residing on a doubled island, including the troubled one within.[22]

During Anderson's years of enforced hospitalization (1937–40) he read Homer, Beebe, and Darwin. The Englishman's revolutionary literature of voyage may have encouraged the artist's escapes from institutionalization. From the best of his hospitals, the Phipps Clinic at Johns Hopkins University, he seems not to have desired respite. But from the Sheppard Pratt Hospital, in the same state, Anderson fled on a homeward journey taking no less than six months, making an odyssey from Maryland to his studio at Ocean Springs, Mississippi, by following the railway tracks. Two other escapes, made from the Mississippi State Hospital at Whitfield, required his walking the two hundred and ten miles home.

Art history abounds in complex, often rewarding episodes of escape and discovery—among them Delacroix's and Delaroche's Romantic absorption in and transcription of North African life. Gauguin's South Seas adventures were inspired by his dealer; his search for freshly profitable exotica offered convenient flight from family and creditors alike. The rediscovery of Brittany was key for the fresh color and exotic approaches characteristic of the Pont Aven school, whose Arts and Crafts aesthetic was close to Anderson's. The Expressionists' "primitivistic" wanderings in Far Eastern waters led them to new kinds of ornament and to nature.[23] Yet the American's work is also reminiscent of some of the early works of the Norwegian Edvard Munch, himself so seminal a figure for the German avant-garde.

Leading American nineteenth-century artists often chose getting away from it all as their way of life, preferring distant to domestic destinies. They found security in distant adventure preferable to the hazards of home, the chancy comforts of the unknown better than familiar and familial demands. Often misogynistic loners, these artists chose a self-imposed, sometimes even remunerative exploration, close to exile, often sharing the lives and works of cowboys and Indians. Some of these painters discovered the bird and plant life of the Amazonian jungles or the glacial rigors of Alaskan ice floes. One thinks of George Catlin, George Caleb Bingham, Martin Heade, Albert Bierstadt, Frederic Remington, Thomas Moran, and Winslow Homer. A Canadian whose work comes close to Anderson's in the depiction of the passionate, evocative freedom of some of her native British Columbia wildernesses is Emily Carr. Her work too is steeped in a sense of fierce communion with nature, she seemingly hearing as well as seeing the eerie, daringly discovered depths of the forest primeval. Canoeing alone down the Ohio and Mississippi rivers during his brilliant art-student days, Anderson was the very model of the American artist-explorer. Under more romantic circumstances, this journey was to be repeated on his belated honeymoon, after he married Agnes Grinstead in 1933.

Sometimes, especially in his later works, there is a sense of graphic code cracking, one of discovery and sudden admission to an impossibly regularized superworld—that of an Art Deco dream carried beyond the wildest devices of the elegantly formularized. Such pages border upon an irrational insistently patterned quality, presenting a dividing line between insight and insanity. Their repetitive conventions are recognized among psychologists as coming close to the messages that some schizophrenics claim to receive from secret voices or visions. These drawings by Anderson are startlingly like those of his companion in illness, Vaslav Nijinsky. That great Russian dancer, long sequestered in a Swiss asylum, showed a similarly passionate devotion to the repeated lines of graphic movement.

Ancient writers on art noted how creativity stemmed from the inspiration dictated by poetic fury. Special spirits—benevolent "daemons"—provided the requisitely frenzied sources for the generation of all the arts. Madness, ecstasy, and fantasy were three elements, as closely linked as the Three Fates, collectively crucial for expression in all forms of literature and art. Transcending the limitations of the mundane, madness also lifts the veil to the sublime.

Though a fiercely powerful mental illness can wreak havoc upon artist and family alike, it too can be seen as a form of dreadful exploration. In a state of sudden release, of extreme, uncontainable violence, a dreadful triad climbs aboard—the irrational, the cruel, and the terrifying. Those three devastating shipmates sometimes mislead the artist on an anarchic voyage of discovery, occasionally one of relentless search and destroy. With its aspects of abandon and of letting go, such qualities of sudden vulnerability and exposure to cruel elements, working from within, may still be seen as part of the special explorer's fate.

The artist's brilliant transcription of illumination in his too few large wall paintings suggests both "divine" and possibly daemonic inspiration. With his fellow sufferer, Vincent van Gogh, the American was unusually open to the mystique of light and color, to the vibrancy of life and motion, to the wilder shores of expression. A sort of redoubled seeing and hearing, a self-induced, dangerously heightened consciousness, may accompany the etiology of schizophrenic episodes, which, in creative terms, can yield extraordinarily vibrant, unforgettable artistic consequences.

Another fellow sufferer with severe mental affliction, Virginia Woolf, noted, "[H]ow astonishing, when the lights of health go down, the undiscovered countries that are then disclosed, what waters and deserts of the soul, what precipices and lawns . . . what ancient and obdurate oaks are uprooted in us by the act of sickness. . . ."[24] So, to see the artist's "troubled" mind as being limited by illness is often erroneous. Sickness may open, or reopen, the creative eye. Anderson could have shared Woolf's view that disturbance can result in having "the whole landscape of life lie remote and fair, like the shore seen from a ship far out at sea, and he [the patient] is now exalted on a peak and needs no help from man or God."[25] Painter and writer alike should be seen as explorers, sailing into the distance to witness the world in its entirety or rising to the mountaintop, they now endowed with an incomparable, scintillating independence.

Anderson, possibly in view of his partially unstable heritage, never "wanted" children, though fathering four. He stayed with Agnes at her family's beautiful plantation, Oldfields, at Gautier, close to Ocean Springs, near the mouth of the Pascagoula River. He remained there from 1940 to 1946–47, years his daughter Mary Pickard recalls with great happiness, describing how "he gave generously of himself to his children, producing an abundance of work, so much of which survives to delight all children today."[26] Yet on hearing that their fourth child (John) was on the way, he moved back to the cottage at Shearwater in 1946, often sailing to Horn Island, later commuting between the pottery and the island until his death in 1965.

In her memoir, Agnes Grinstead Anderson recalled, "I could never reconcile Bob's reverence for life with some of the things he did . . . So many small creatures . . . sacrificed to what? Curiosity? Art? Does the act of creation become so transcendent that it can be carried on without regard for anything else? Yet I knew he suffered deep conflicts about it."[27]

Reverence for nature's life, though close to so many of Anderson's magnificent artistic discoveries, seems especially so in his beautiful bird studies. He, like his best-known forerunner in American animal studies, John James Audubon (1785–1851) specialized in depicting birds and smaller mammals. Yet both *animaliers*, in an effort to understand, explore, and record the complex characters of those beautiful creatures, went in for mass slaughter of bird and beast before perpetuating the animals in art. This form of fatal exploration comes close to so many journeys of discovery, even, as in early brain surgery, almost always involving exploitation and often accompanied by destruction. Paradoxically—if necessarily—most of the greatest master explorers of life in art worked surrounded by death. That greatest of all *animaliers*, Leonardo da Vinci, whether exploring animal-like man or man-like beast, waited and watched impatiently, almost stalking an ailing old man, so eagerly did he anticipate his human quarry's death so that the artist could finally dissect and draw him. Three centuries later, his peer, George Stubbs, drew his equestrian studies after exploring the anatomy of horses by surrounding himself with their dead bodies, conveniently flayed and sent to the artist from the local tanneries.

Often obsessed by their own creativity, artists, under the most ideal of circumstances, seldom make the best husband material. But among all of that vocation, *animaliers* may be some of the worst family men. The unique power of most of Leonardo's magnificent nudes and anatomical studies is reinforced by their curious absence of personhood. Conversely, the equally great strength of his magnificent animal studies is enhanced by a warm sense of humanity.

A similar situation holds true for Dürer's most moving renderings—those of animals, such as his well-known *Hare* (Vienna, Albertina). Though these were treated with singular sensitivity, the German master's sympathy for the animal kingdom seldom extended to his peers.[28]

Oscar Wilde, as usual, knew just the answer to Agnes's anguished question concerning the *animalier's* divided state, in which he was caught between annihilation of and veneration for those he perpetuated in art.

Yet each man kills the thing he loves,
By each let this be heard,

Some do it with a bitter look,
Some with a flattering word.
The coward does it with a kiss,
The brave man with a sword!
—*The Ballad of Reading Gaol*

Anderson's strikingly empathic approach to animal "portraiture" could be seen as the verso of an otherwise often blank coin. As Mary Anderson Pickard recalled, her father "seems to have identified so strongly with his subjects that he actually saw himself [in them]. The possum's face is his face. He feels the fear that paralyzes, and his hair stands out like white fire."[29] As was true in the lives of the earlier great *animaliers*, that degree of intense observation and ability to translate was seldom given to his fellow humans, who were often reduced to decoratively witty, incisive outline.

Anderson had a personal piety, a prayer to God's creativity (Psalm 104), transcribed in his exquisitely Deco script, these lines possibly the inspiration for the magnificent wall paintings of his cottage/studio.[30] America's most majestic river, the Mississippi, was another of Anderson's deities. He carved an awesome eight-foot-tall male human/animal idol from an oak downed in the hurricane of 1947 and gave it the river's name. Now largely lost, this haunting totem, *Father Mississippi*, with carved animals, birds, and fish, was installed in his studio/cottage garden at Shearwater.[31] Anderson's painting of the same river, inside the cottage, is on its north wall, now seen as an image of night. Given his wife's youthful features, the painted Mississippi, now shown as a river-woman, recalls their honeymoon on that river.[32]

If, in terms of discovery, the depiction of humanity was most definitely Anderson's road *not* taken, his birds[33] and beasts will always remain among the major zoological explorations of New World art. Just as the artist had a pantheistic dimension, his work too has a Pan-like quality, in which the kingdoms of man and beast are brought together in a uniquely sympathetic, vibrant fashion. He believed that "unless man be bird, beast, fish as well as man he may not escape."[34] Anderson added an evolutionary dimension to his belief in the divinity of nature, found in a poem tracing a Darwinian progression to man, but a rise in which all the animal predecessors were, and remain, part of a "divine symphony."[35] The artist's investigation of animal life concluded: "An animal always does the intelligent thing because he can't help it. A man very seldom does because he must assert his will and do foolish things. If a man could literally be guided by animals without losing his manhood or will, he would act intelligently."[36]

Blakean mysticism pervades the Andersonian perspective—so many of his visions are close to the English poet's. It might just as well have been in Mississippi that the lines "Tyger! Tyger! burning bright" were written.

It would be far too simple and sentimental to see this artist as a Noah-like figure, gathering and preserving the animal world together with his own, although Anderson did draw the Noah sequence from *Paradise Lost* with predictable vivacity. Yet his theology was far from biblical.[37] As Mary Anderson Pickard stated, her father's views meant that "Man's salvation depended upon his discovery of the natural world and his recognition of his own role within it." It was the artist's belief that "The bird flies and in that . . . fraction of a second man and bird are real. . . . He is the only man and that is the only bird and every feather, every mark, every part of the pattern of its feathers is real and he, man, exists and he is almost as wonderful as the thing he sees.[38]

Anderson's exploration of animal nature yields a pictorial paradise regained, one all of us can share. It is not surprising that Milton's celestial text meant so much to him. As the artist wrote in one of his most unforgettable lines: "Dogs, cats, birds are holes in heaven through which man may pass."[39]

ACKNOWLEDGMENTS

I am very grateful to Mary Anderson Pickard, herself an artist, for writing to me about the interests of her grandmother, Annette McConnell Anderson, which are so relevant to the perspective on Walter Anderson given here.

Sharon Chickanzeff, librarian at the Institute of Fine Arts at New York University, has helped me track down sources, as has Linda Seckelson, readers' services librarian at the Watson Library of the Metropolitan Museum of Art. Pat Pinson and Joan Gilley, curators at the Walter Anderson Museum of Art and of the Family of Walter Anderson collections, have also been generous with their assistance.

The many publications on Walter Inglis Anderson by Redding S. Sugg, Jr., introduced me to Anderson's art, and I am most grateful to this writer for his infectious enthusiasm, sensitivity, and insight.

NOTES

1. Transcribed from his logs by Pat Pinson and kindly shared with me.

2. Redding S. Sugg, Jr., ed., *Walter Anderson's Illustrations of Epic and Voyage* (Carbondale, IL: Southern Illinois University Press, 1980), pp. 3–7, 33–38, 63–86. Sugg, p. xii, notes that, including illustrations of epics and classics, the artist left ninety-five hundred such drawings.

3. Sugg, *Walter Anderson's Illustrations of Epic and Voyage*, pp.105–114.

4. Christopher Maurer with María Estrella Iglesias, *Dreaming in Clay on the Coast of Mississippi: Love and Art at Shearwater* (New York: Doubleday, 2000), p. 266.

5. See Sugg, *Walter Anderson's Illustrations of Epic and Voyage*, plate 51, for Anderson's drawing of Pt.V, II, lines 335–340. Such scenes of sailing were particularly close to the artist in his later life, so much of which was spent at sea.

6. Sugg, *Walter Anderson's Illustrations of Epic and Voyage*, plates 111–112.

7. Agnes Grinstead Anderson, *Approaching the Magic Hour: Memories of Walter Anderson*, ed. Patti Carr Black (Jackson: University Press of Mississippi, 1989), p. 8.

8. Sugg, *Walter Anderson's Illustrations of Epic and Voyage*, p. xvii. For the gauchos, see plate 54 and for the Fuegians plate 55.

9. Maurer, *Dreaming in Clay*, p. 261.

10. See the fine entry by Michel de Salzman in the *Encyclopedia of Religion*, 6, pp. 139–140.

11. The Texas log of Walter Inglis Anderson, typescript, pp. 2–3. Kindly provided by Joan Gilley, curator for the Family of Walter Anderson.

12. New York log, pp. 1ff.

13. See Redding S. Sugg, Jr., ed., *The Horn Island Logs of Walter Inglis Anderson* (1973; rev. ed., Jackson: University Press of Mississippi, 1985). He estimates that more than ninety journals about the islands were kept, but only about forty survive. See also Maurer, *Dreaming in Clay*, p. 260. I am indebted to Pat Pinson for letting me see the diary/logs concerning the artist's travels to Costa Rica and China. Joan Gilley kindly sent me those for Texas, Tennessee, New York, and Florida.

14. Anderson's mother's interest in this area was described to me by his daughter Mary Anderson Pickard.

15. See Roger Lipsey, *An Art of Our Own: The Spiritual in Twentieth-Century Art* (Boston: Shambhala, 1988).

16. Presumably these pertain to the popular text by Jay Hambidge, *The Elements of Dynamic Symmetry*.

17. Mary Anderson Pickard, letter to the author.

18. Information communicated by Mary Anderson Pickard.

19. Anderson, *Approaching the Magic Hour*. For important biographical information, see also Mary Anderson Pickard's equally remarkable text, the introduction to *Birds*, by Walter Anderson (Jackson: University Press of Missisippi, 1990).

20. See Sugg, *Horn Island Logs*.

21. Sugg, *Walter Anderson's Illustrations of Epic and Voyage*, p. xiv.

22. His daughter Leif saw the island within her father. Maurer, *Dreaming in Clay*, p. 261.

23. See William Rubin with Kirk Varnedoe, *Primitivism in Twentieth Century Art: Affinity of the Tribal and the Modern* (New York: The Museum of Modern Art, 1984).

24. Virginia Woolf, *On Being Ill* (Ashfield, MA: Paris Press, 2002), p. 1.

25. Woolf, *On Being Ill*, p. 8.

26. Mary Anderson Pickard, afterword to *Robinson: The Pleasant History of an Unusual Cat*, by Walter Anderson (Jackson: University Press of Mississippi, 1982).

27. Anderson, *Approaching the Magic Hour*, p. 29. See p. 31 for a similar episode.

28. See Colin Eisler, *Dürer's Animals* (New York: Smithsonian Press, 1987).

29. Walter Anderson, *A Symphony of Animals* (Jackson: University Press of Mississippi, 1996), p. xix.

30. See Redding S. Sugg, Jr., *A Painter's Psalm: The Mural from Walter Anderson's Cottage* (1978; rev. ed., Jackson: University Press of Mississippi, 1992).

31. Sugg, *Walter Anderson's Illustrations of Epic and Voyage*, p. xvii. Reproduced in its entirety in *A Symphony of Animals*, p. xviii.

32. Anne R. King, *Walls of Light: The Murals of Walter Anderson* (Jackson: University Press of Mississippi and the Walter Anderson Museum of Art, 1999), fig. 69, p. 95.

33. Maurer, *Dreaming in Clay*, p. 218

34. Anderson, *A Symphony of Animals*, p. xx.

35. Anderson, *A Symphony of Animals*, p. 101.

36. Anderson, *A Symphony of Animals*, p. 67.

37. Sugg, *Walter Anderson's Illustrations of Epic and Voyage*, plates 105–114.

38. Anderson, *Birds*, p. xxvi.

39. Remembering my Pearl, beyond price, beyond compare, beyond forgetting.
For another version of Anderson's line, see *Birds*, p. xx.

FOLLOWING PAGE:

Pitcher Plants, ca. 1943

Watercolor on paper, 24 x 19 in.

Walter Anderson Museum of Art, 93.3.1 (A)

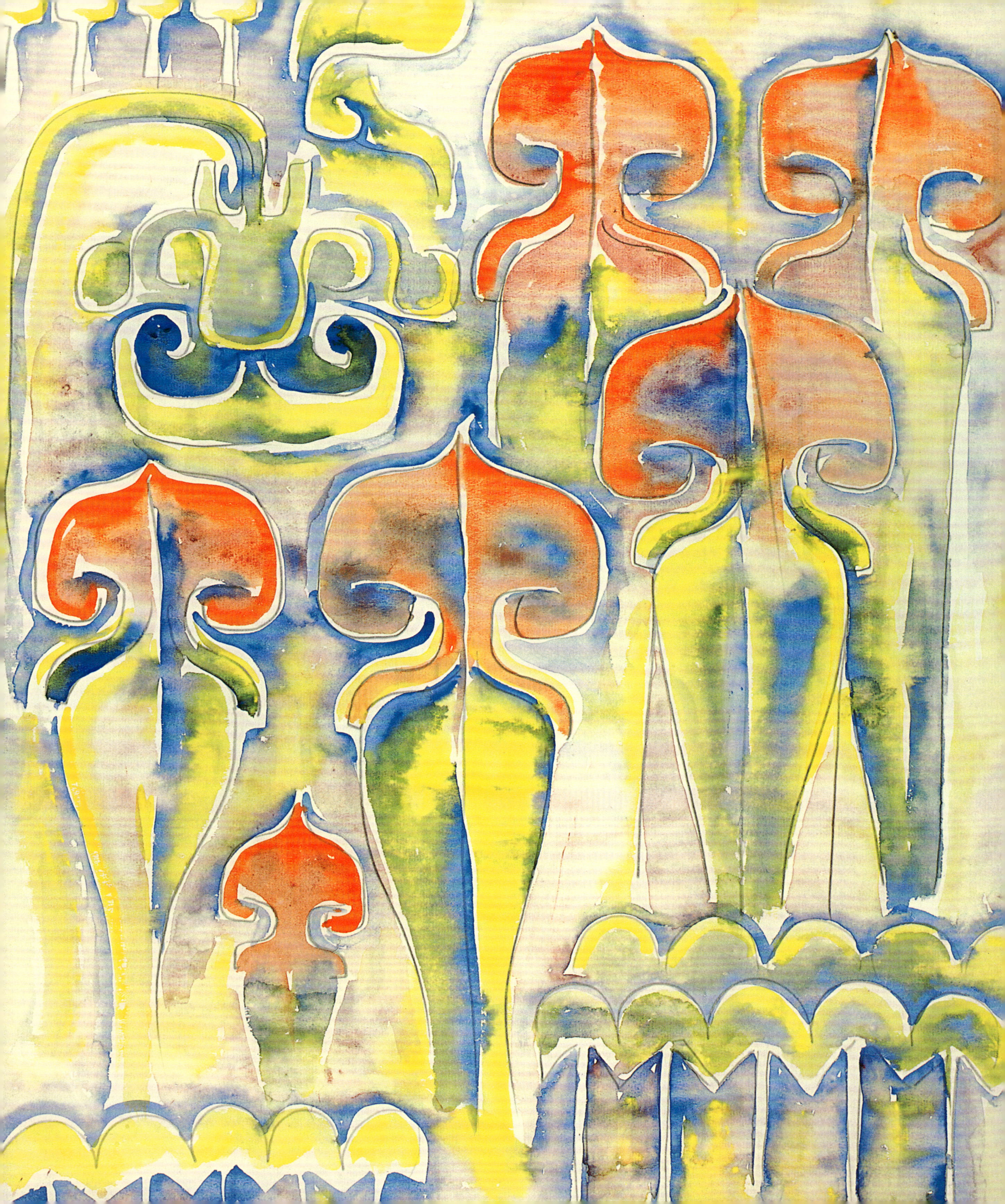

THE ART OF WALTER ANDERSON

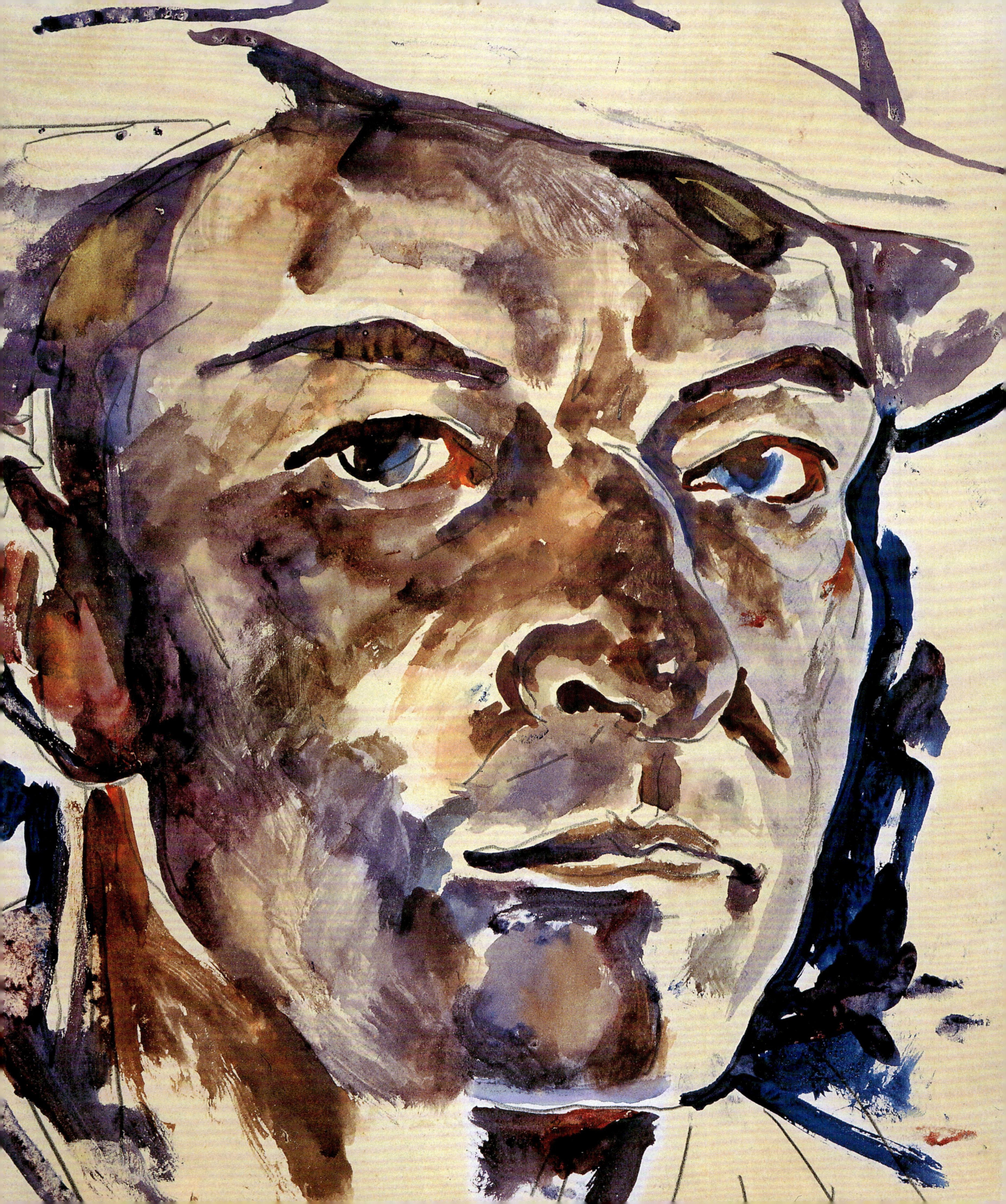

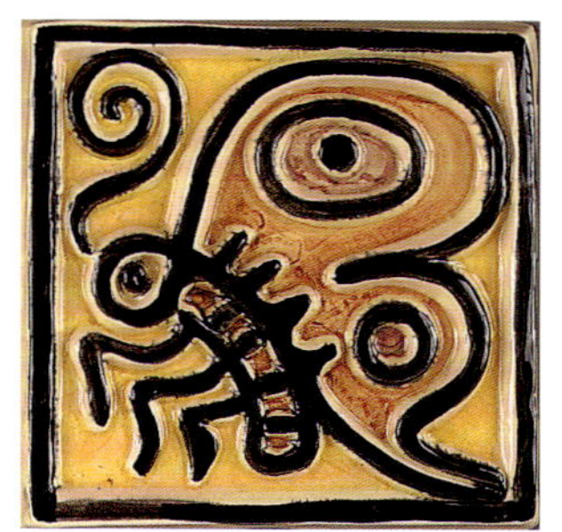

STUDENT AND EARLY PROFESSIONAL YEARS: 1920S AND 1930S

Self Portrait, 1960

Watercolor on paper, 11 x 8½ in.

The Family of Walter Anderson

Walter Inglis Anderson was born in 1903 in the Garden District of New Orleans, the second son of George Walter Anderson, a well-educated, prosperous grain merchant, and Annette McConnell, who came from a prominent, civic-minded New Orleans family. As children of eleven and thirteen, he and his older brother, Peter, were sent to St. John's School, a military academy in Manlius, New York, where they were to receive a classical education. Back in New Orleans, Walter Anderson attended the Isidore Newman Manual Training School, where he studied woodworking and carpentry. His enthusiasm for art was such that he persuaded his reluctant father—who had hoped that his sons would follow him into the world of business—to allow him to attend the New York School of Fine and Applied Art (now known as the Parson's School of Design). His letters to his parents from New York speak less of his studies than of his extensive reading, the concerts he was attending, and the marvels of local museums, including the Metropolitan Museum of Art and the American Museum of Natural History. In 1924, he entered the Pennsylvania Academy of the Fine Arts, and studied drawing and painting under Arthur B. Carles, Henry McCarter, Hugh Breckenridge, and Daniel Garber. His ability in drawing won him the Packard Award for animal studies and a Cresson scholarship for travel in Europe, and in the summer of 1927 he went to France and Spain.

When Walter Anderson returned to Ocean Springs in 1928, he began to work at Shearwater Pottery, and over the next eight years, he and his younger brother, James McConnell Anderson, decorated bowls, vases, cups, and plates that were thrown by Peter. In 1931, the two younger brothers opened the Annex, where they created several series of figurines: pirates, baseball players, and a picturesque series of blacks. All of these series were produced in quantity; they were molded, painted, fired, and sold in the Shearwater showroom, in New Orleans, and in department stores in the North, helping the pottery—and the family—weather the depression. Walter Anderson also produced other, larger molded figures: *Chesty Horse*, *The Bust of Allison Rochon,* pelican bookends, and a series of lamp bases, e.g., *Totem*. Plates were decorated with natural motifs characteristic of the area, showing the many possibilities of circular design. The vases and large bowls were sometimes incised with sgraffito or carved into elaborate patterns.

In 1933, Walter Anderson married Agnes (Sissy) Grinstead, the daughter of a Harvard-trained Pittsburgh investment banker who had a second home in Gautier, twelve miles east of Ocean Springs. Agnes Grinstead had graduated cum laude from Radcliffe, where she had majored in art history; as a young woman she had also studied for two years in France. In the cottage at Shearwater, which they had been given as a wedding present, Walter worked on furniture and rugs, providing evidence of a lifelong interest in design and of his belief, shared with William Morris, that "the best joy was the joy of making things and knowing that you made them well. In this spirit . . . a man should be able to make all that he needs: not only his house and his furniture, his tools and utensils, his tapestries and pictures, but even his music and song."

During his first years as a professional artist, Anderson painted in oils, sketched the wildlife around him, and created small block prints to sell in the Shearwater showroom. In the little time available to him for painting, he did several oil portraits using a rather dark palette, influenced, perhaps, by Cézanne and the German Expressionists. In 1934—a year when he canoed down the Ohio and Mississippi from Louisville to Arkansas on a belated honeymoon with Sissy—he was commissioned by the Public Works of Art Project to paint a series of murals for the Ocean Springs High School. After competing unsuccessfully for a public-works mural in Jackson he designed a mural for the Indianola, Mississippi, post office, but he was unable to complete it because of mental illness and intermittent hospitalization from 1937 to 1940.

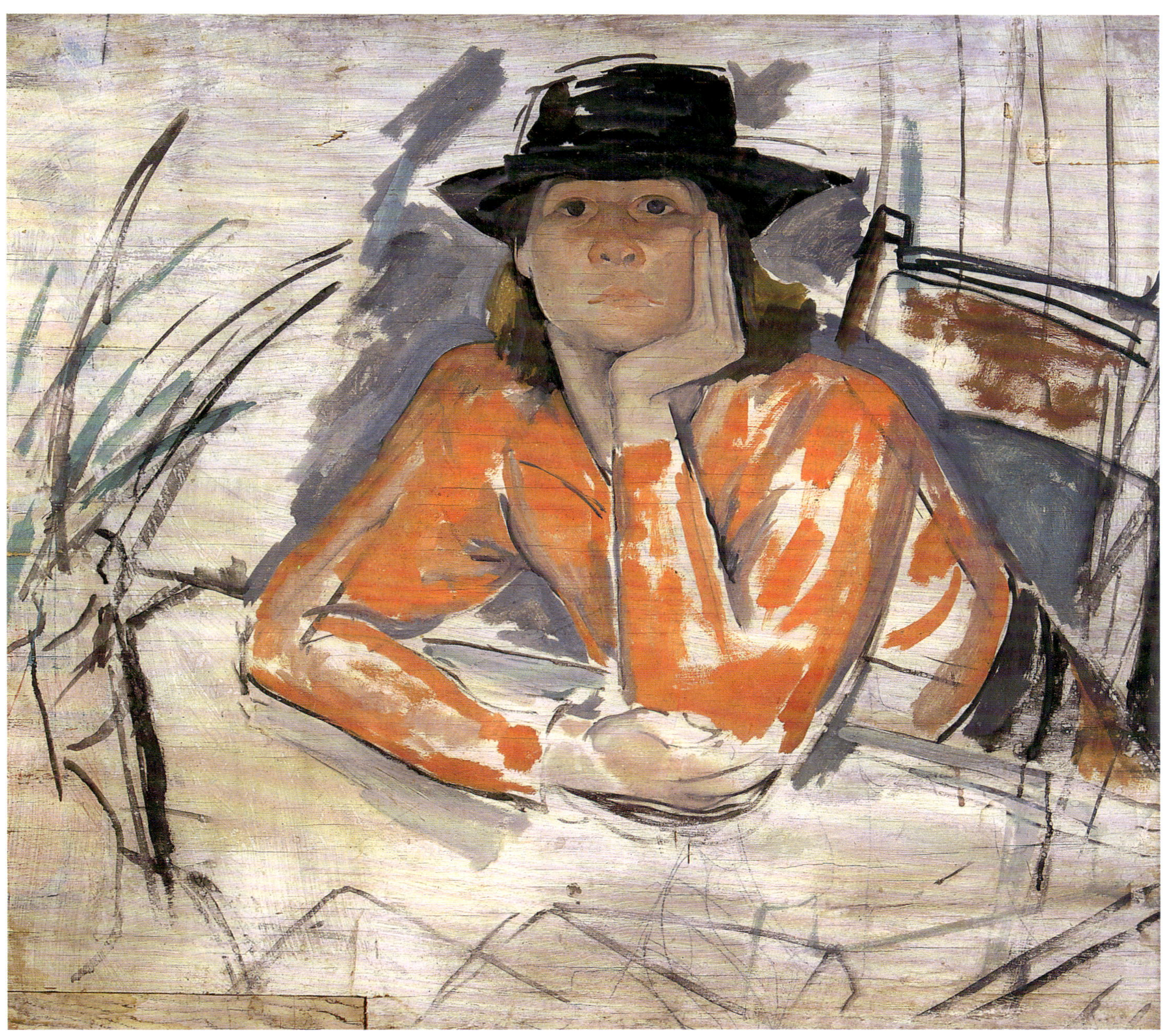

Sissy at Table, ca. 1933

Oil on wood, 37 x 41½ in.
The Family of Walter Anderson
Agnes Grinstead at the time of her marriage to Walter Anderson

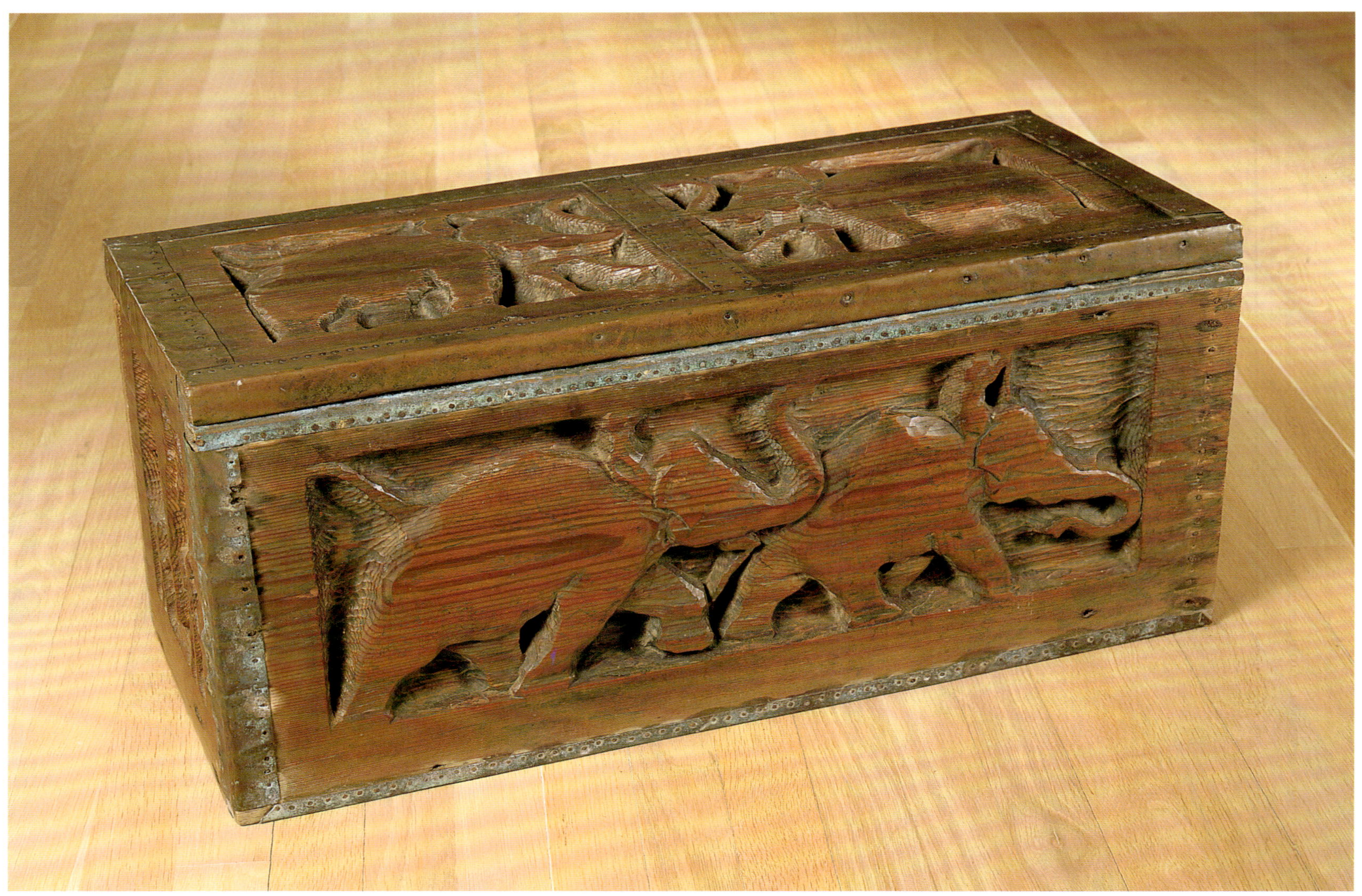

Elephant Chest, ca. 1922

Carved wood chest, 12½ x 28 x 12 in.
The Family of Walter Anderson
From the age sixteen until he was nineteen, Anderson was a student at the Isidore Newman Manual Training School in New Orleans. To persuade his father to send him to art school, he carved this chest, making a reference to *The Jungle Book* by Rudyard Kipling, his father's favorite writer.

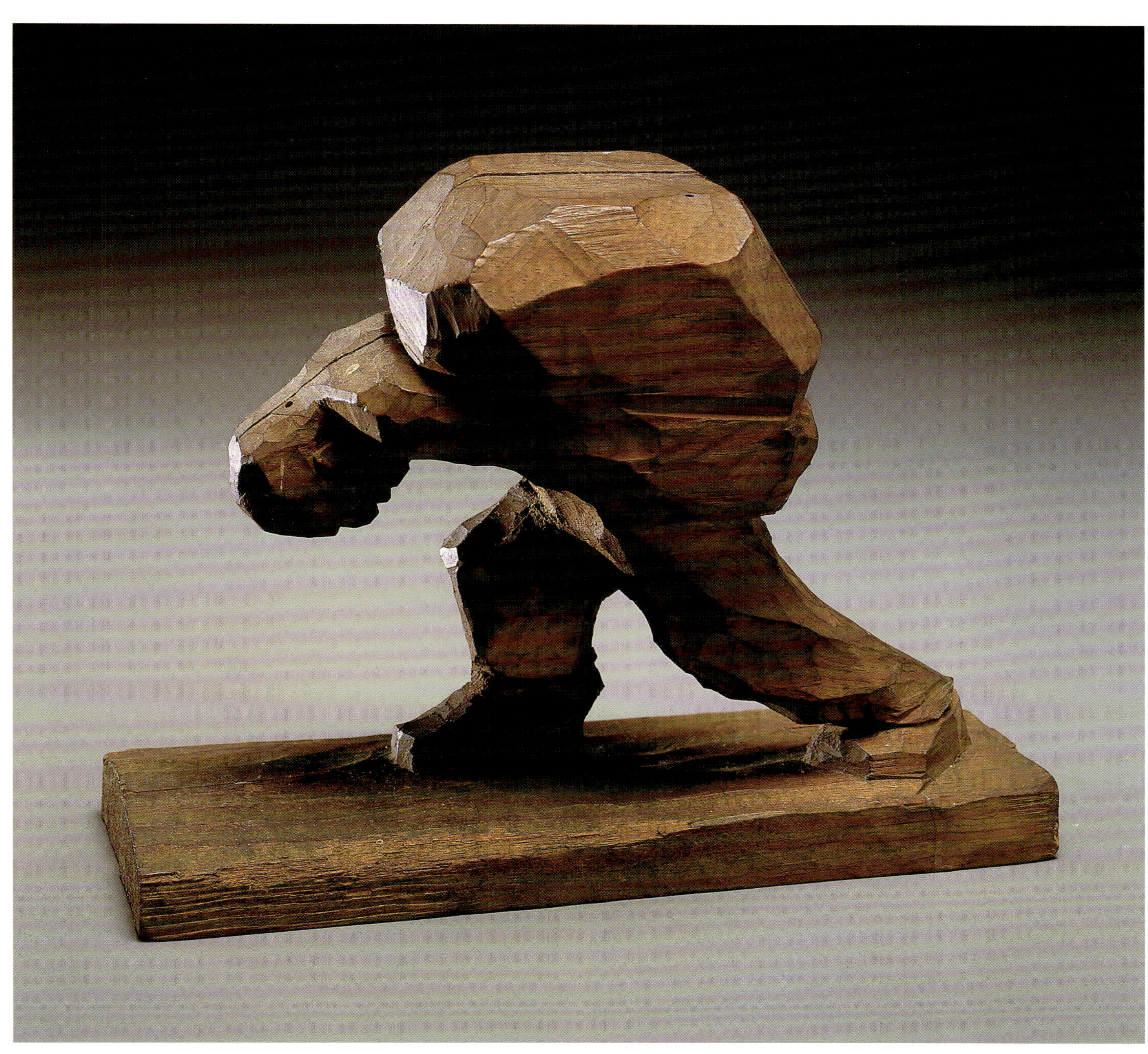

Man Carrying Burden, ca. 1923

Wood sculpture 7½ x 3½ x 10 in.
Walter Anderson Museum of Art, 92.3.17
While an art student, Anderson carved wooden figures in order to make pocket money and sold them in Philadelphia, Ocean Springs, and New Orleans.

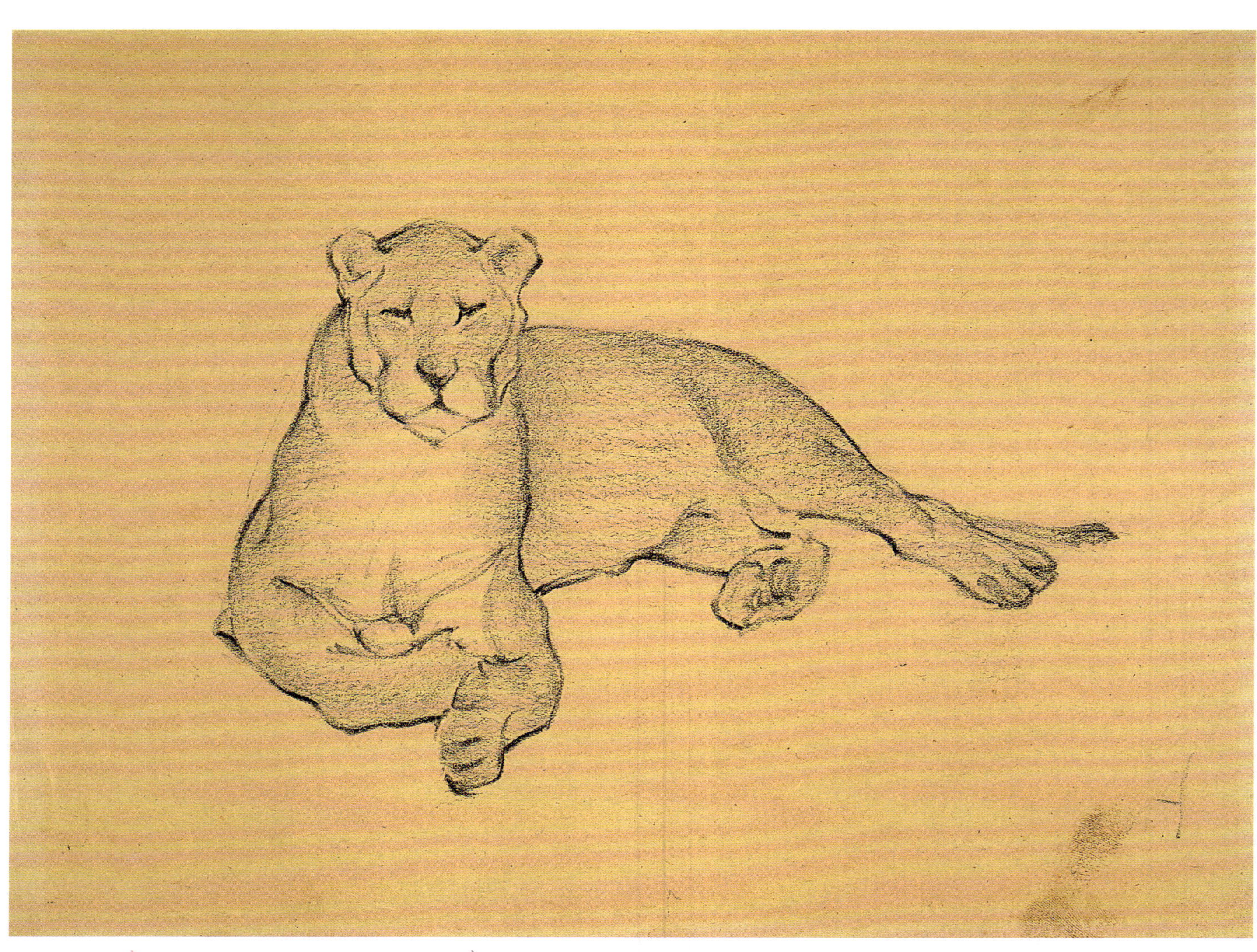

Lion, 1924

Charcoal on paper, 9 x 11¾ in.
The Family of Walter Anderson
When Anderson was a student at the Pennsylvania Academy of the Fine Arts, he often went to the Philadelphia Zoo to draw the animals. These were part of the series of drawings for which he won the Packard Prize for animal drawing.

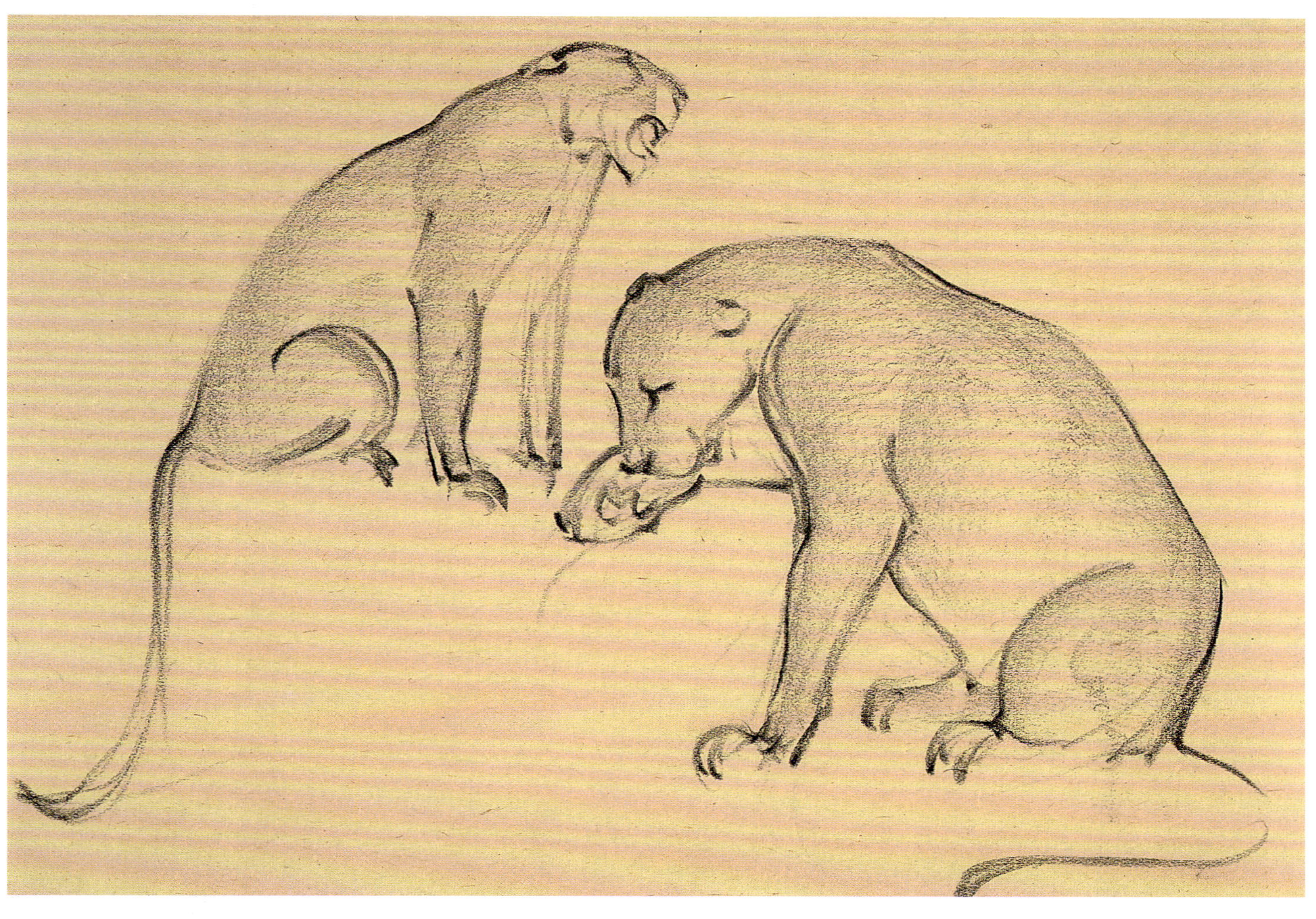

Lions, 1924

Charcoal on paper, 9 x 11¾ in.
The Family of Walter Anderson

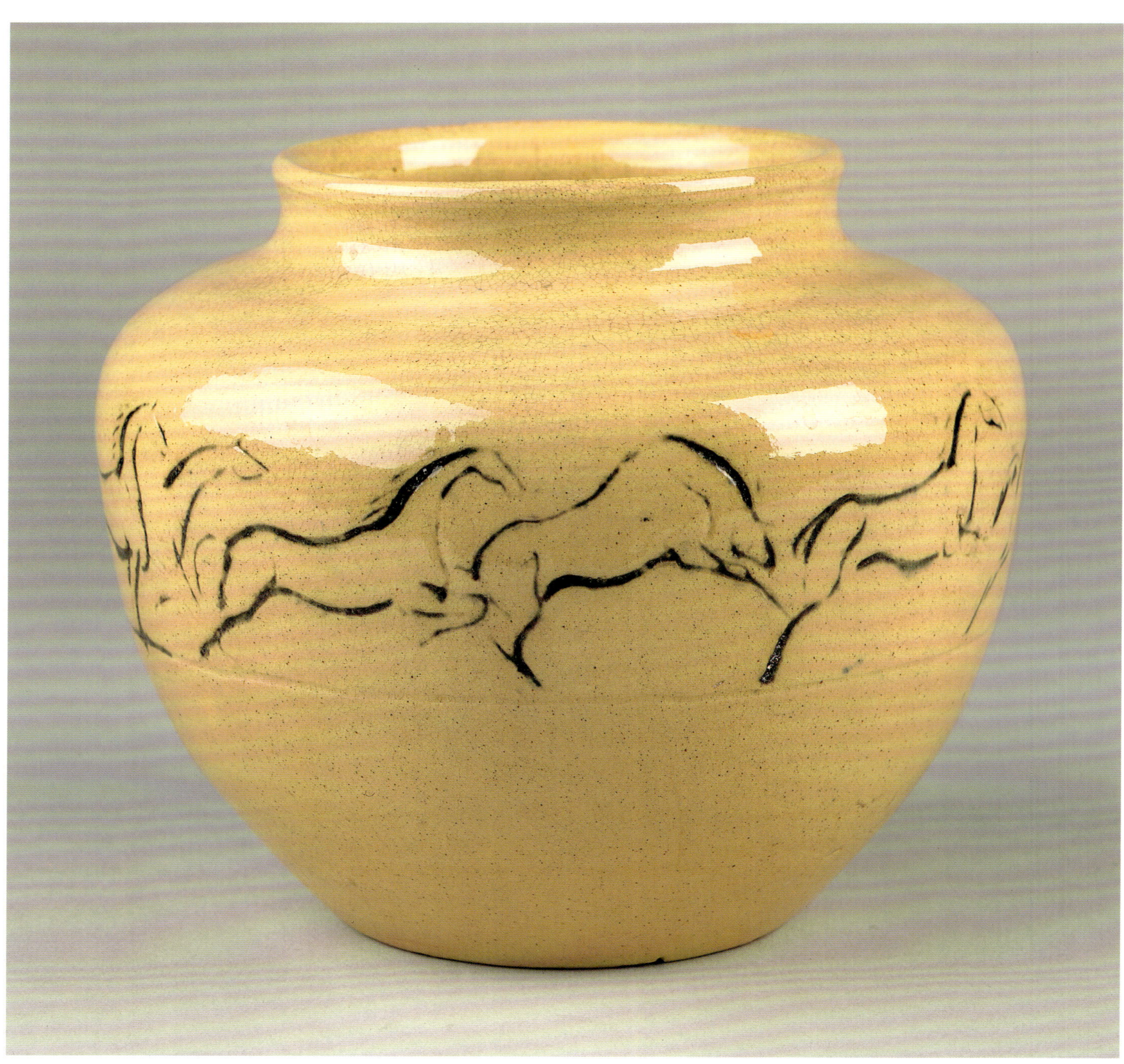

Running Horse Vase, 1929

Ceramic, 6½ x 7 x 7 in.
Mary Anderson Pickard
Thrown by Peter Anderson, decorated by Walter Anderson
In 1927, while in France on a Cresson Traveling Fellowship from the Pennsylvania Academy of the Fine Arts, Anderson went to the Dordogne region to see the paintings in the numerous caves and shelters near Les Eyzies. The impressive images he saw drawn on stone later influenced him in his painting of the frieze of horses.

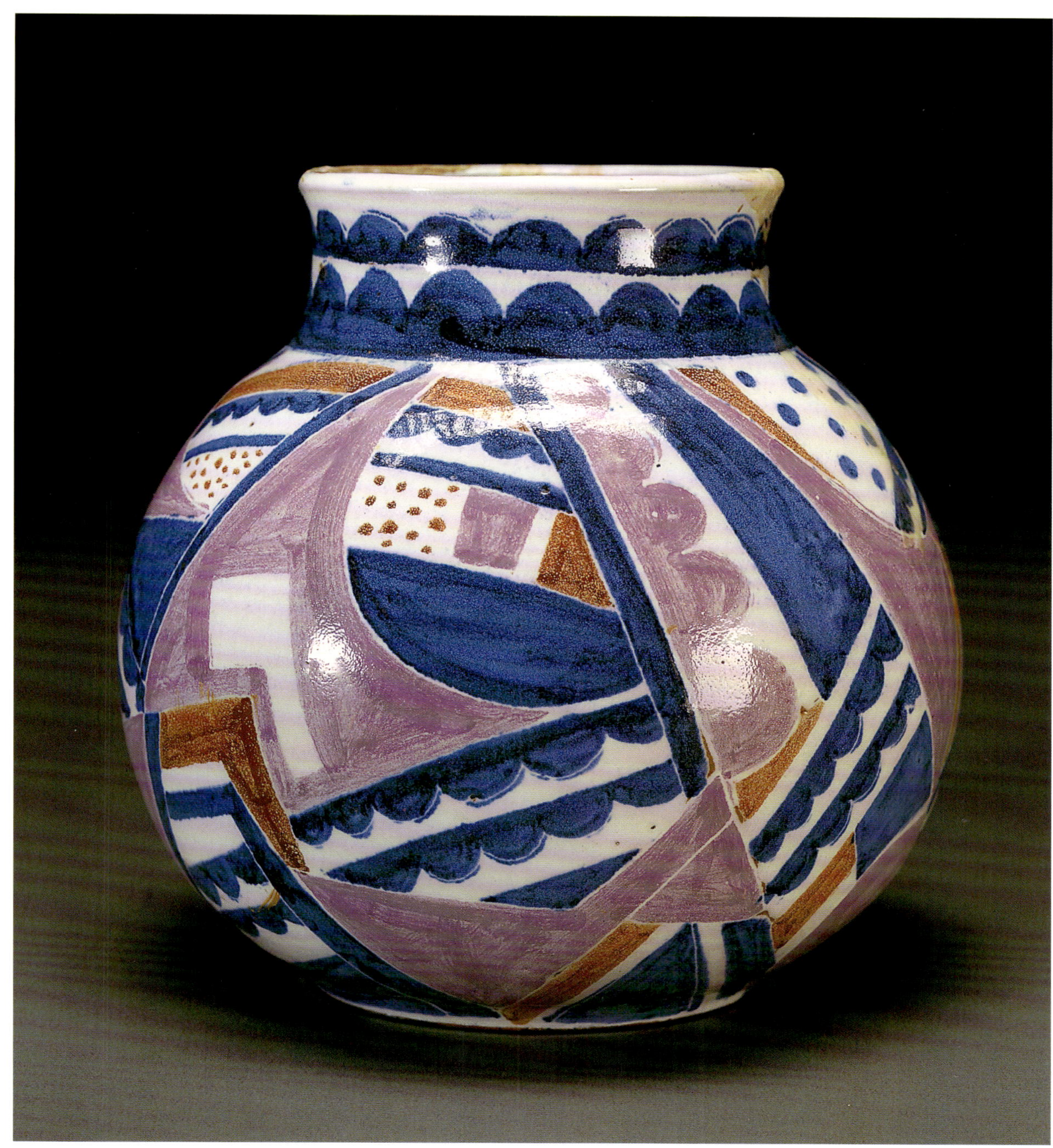

Cubist Design Vase, ca. 1930

Ceramic, 8 x 7½ x 7½ in.
Louise Lehman Collection
Thrown by Peter Anderson, decorated by Walter Anderson
This color palette and abstract "modernist" style of decoration was used only around 1930 at Shearwater Pottery.

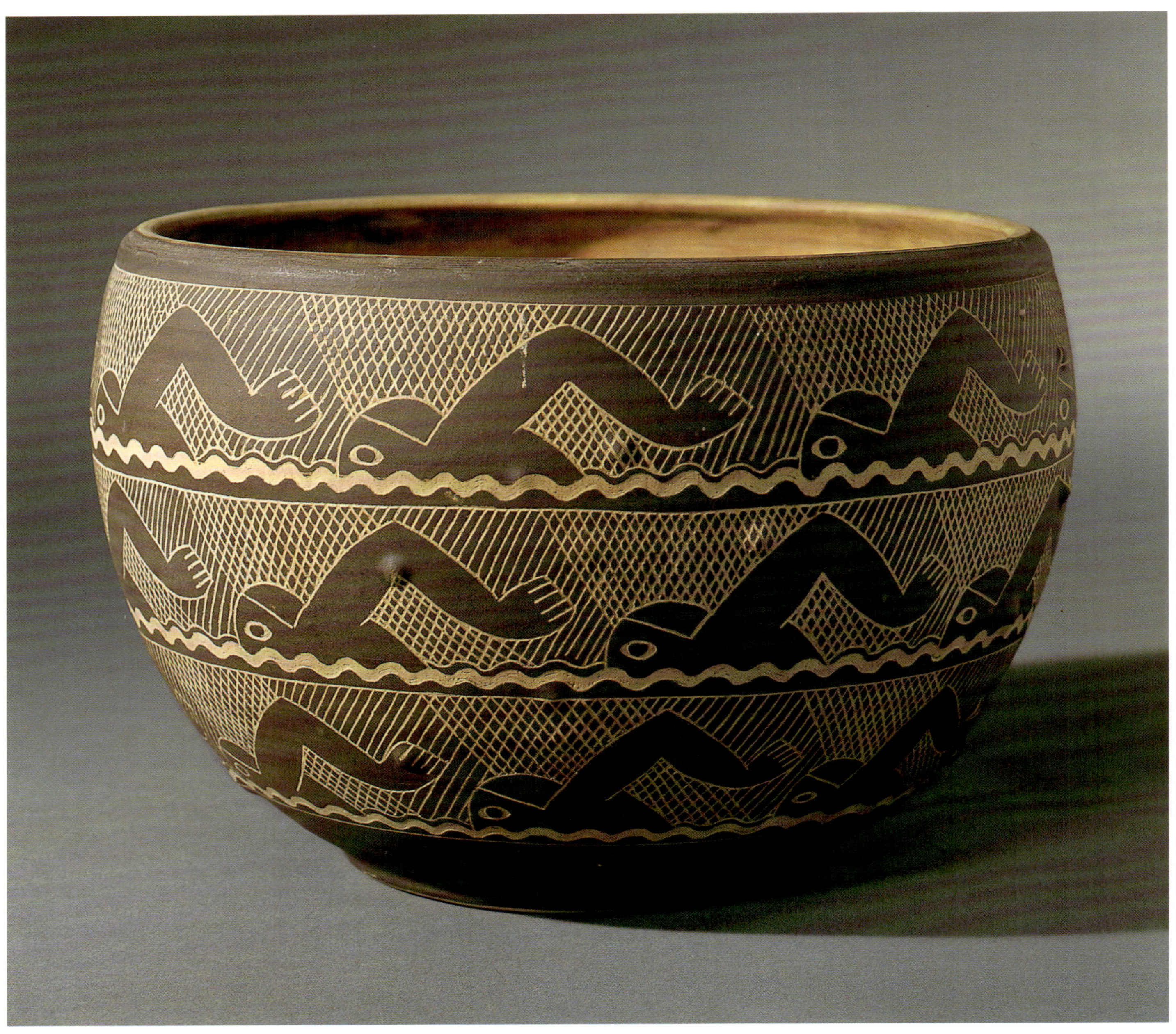

Swimmer Bowl, ca. 1935

Ceramic, 7½ x 11 x 10½ in.
The Family of Walter Anderson
Thrown by Peter Anderson, decorated by Walter Anderson
Sgraffito is the method of carving through the layer of slip (clay in suspension) to expose the color of the clay body beneath.

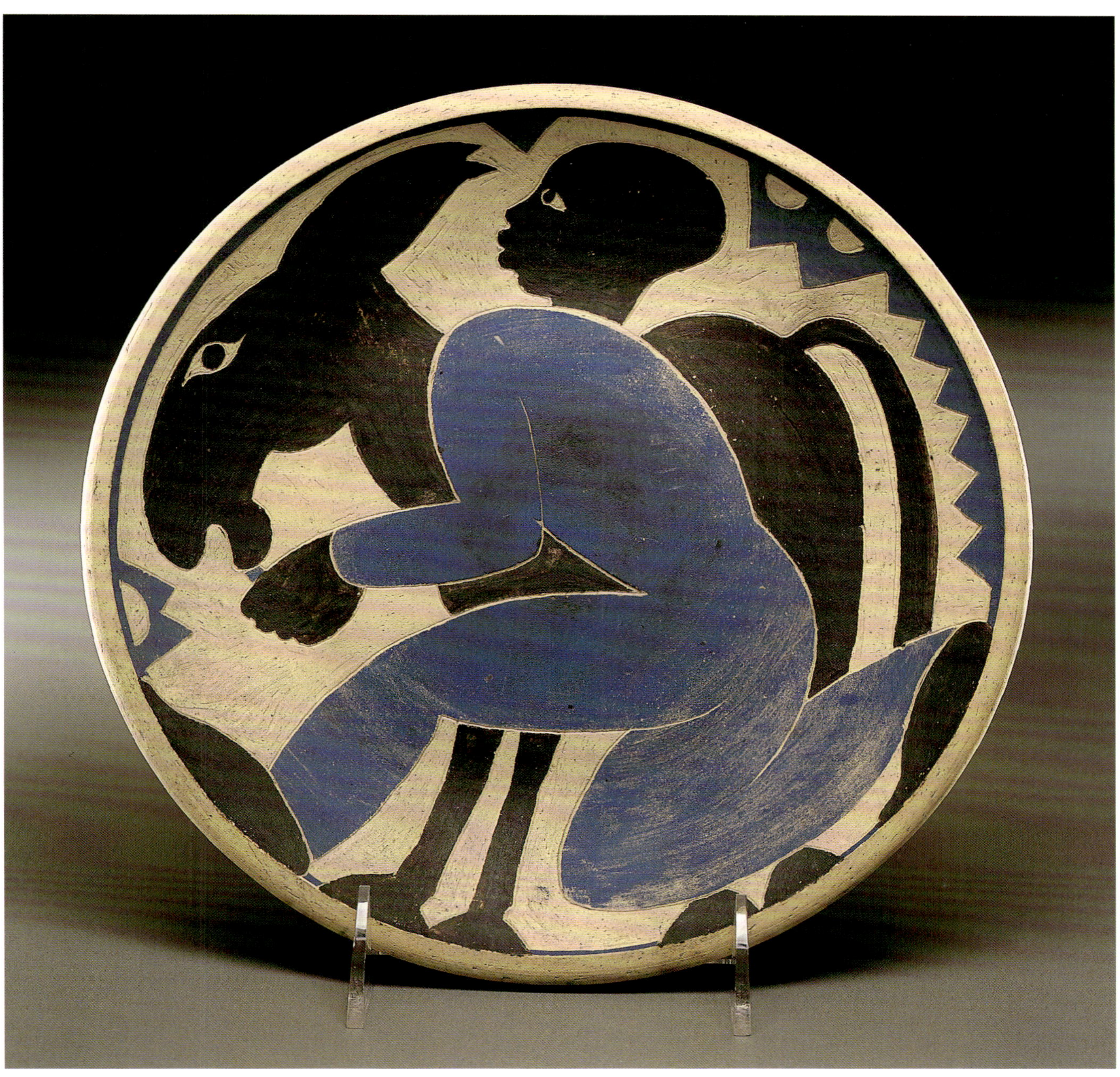

Man and Donkey Plate, ca. 1935

Ceramic, 9½ x 9½ x 1¾ in.
The Family of Walter Anderson
Thrown by Peter Anderson, decorated by Walter Anderson.

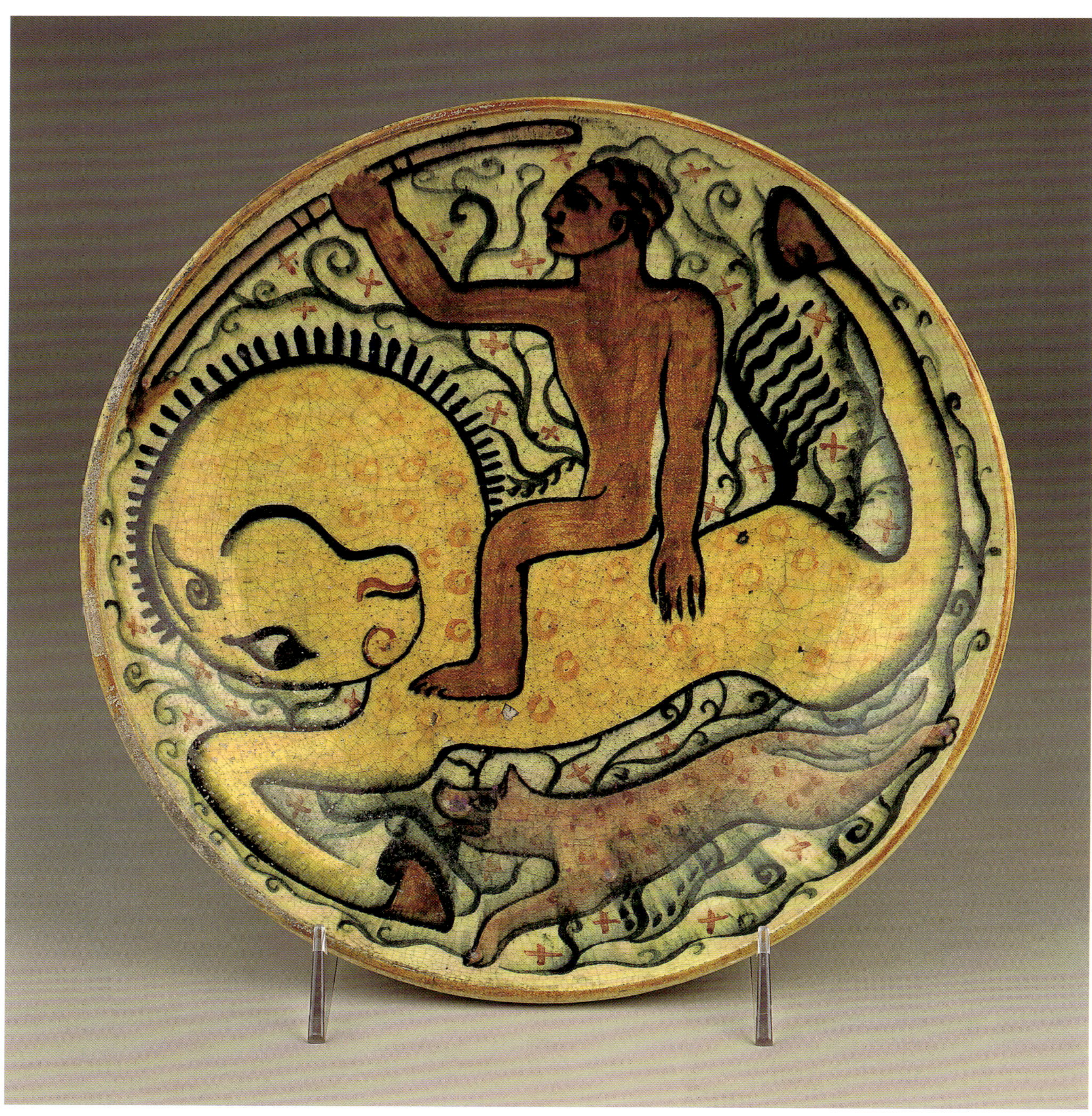

Hunter Plate, ca. 1935

Ceramic, 10 x 10 x 1½ in.
The Family of Walter Anderson
Thrown by Peter Anderson, decorated by Walter Anderson

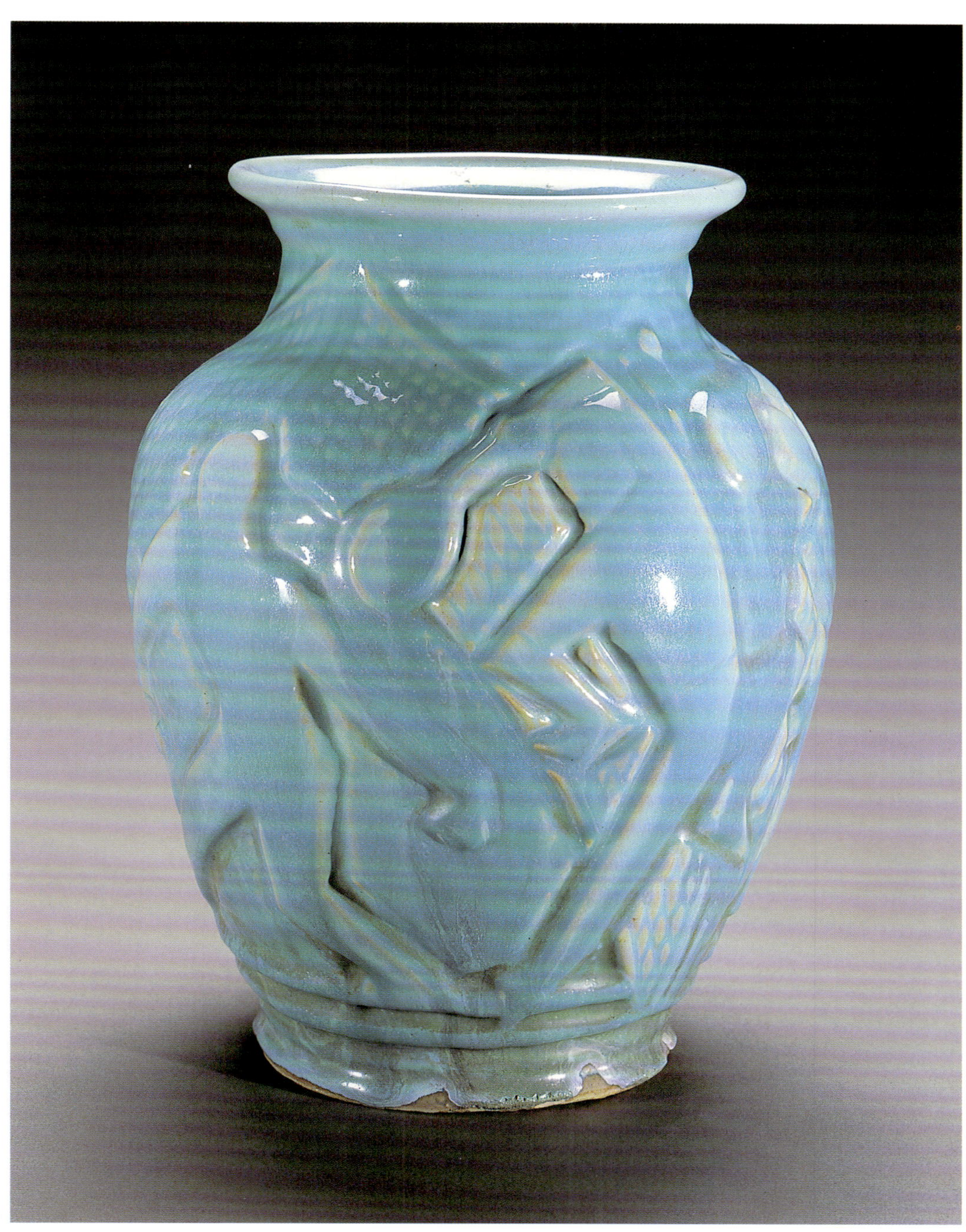

Tennis Players Vase, ca. 1935

Ceramic, 9½ x 7½ x 7½ in.
Walter Anderson Museum of Art, 01.1.1
Thrown by Peter Anderson, decorated by Walter Anderson

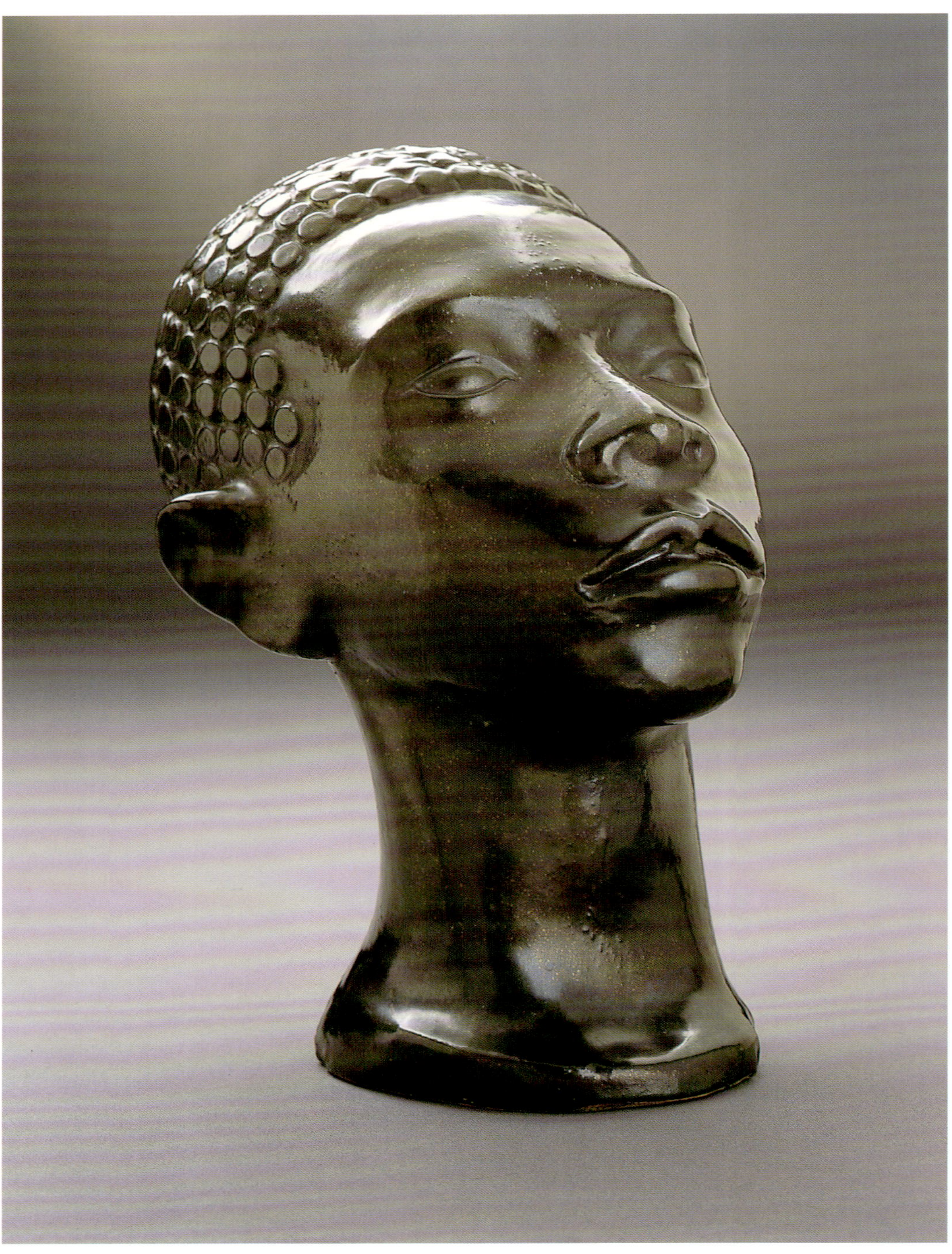

Bust of Allison, ca. 1930

Ceramic, 8½ x 5½ x 7 in.
Walter Anderson Museum of Art, 94.12.1
Allison Rochon worked at the pottery in the 1930s, when this bust was first made. This one was probably cast and glazed in bronze in the 1950s.

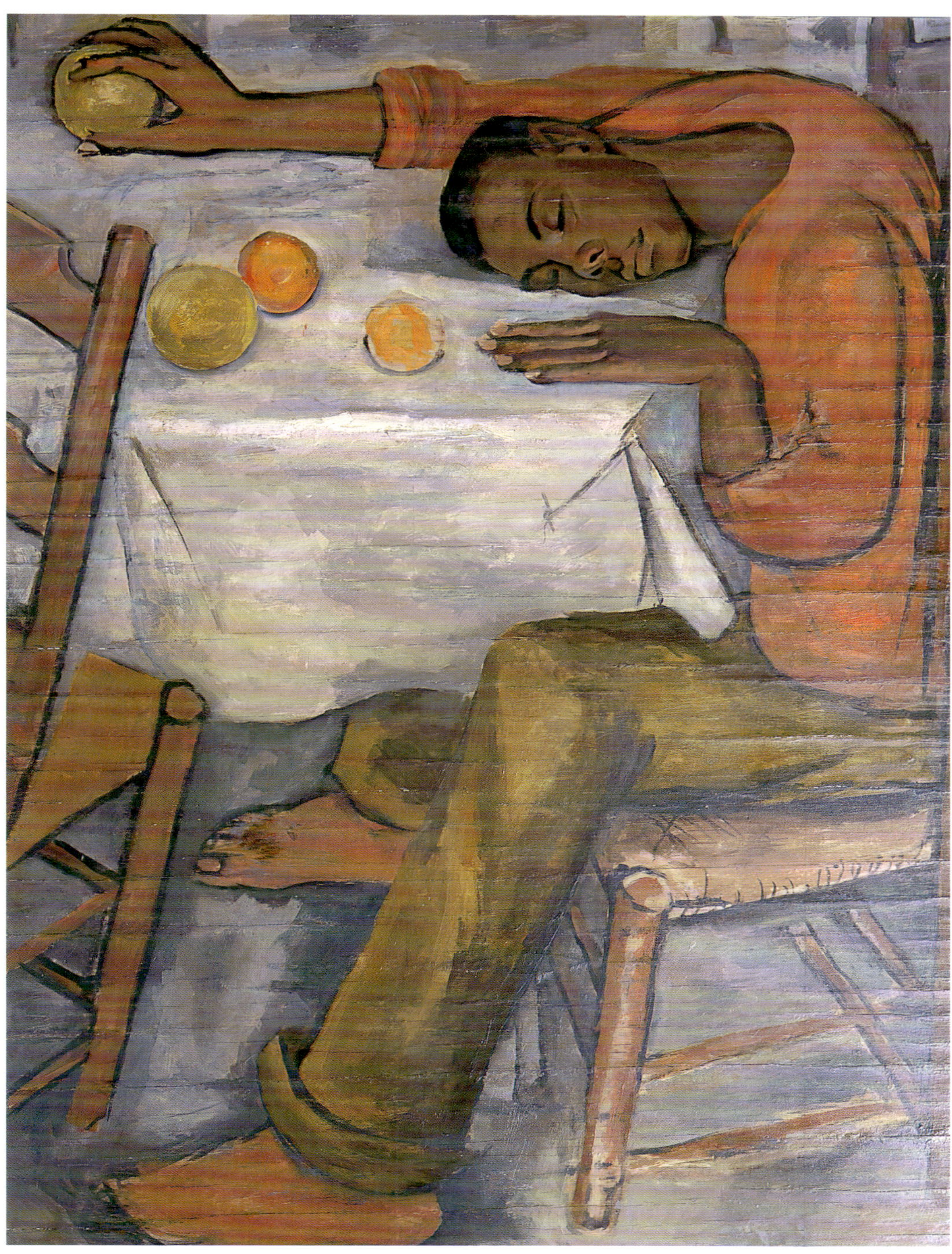

Allison Sleeping, ca. 1930

Oil on wood, 48 x 35 in.
The Family of Walter Anderson

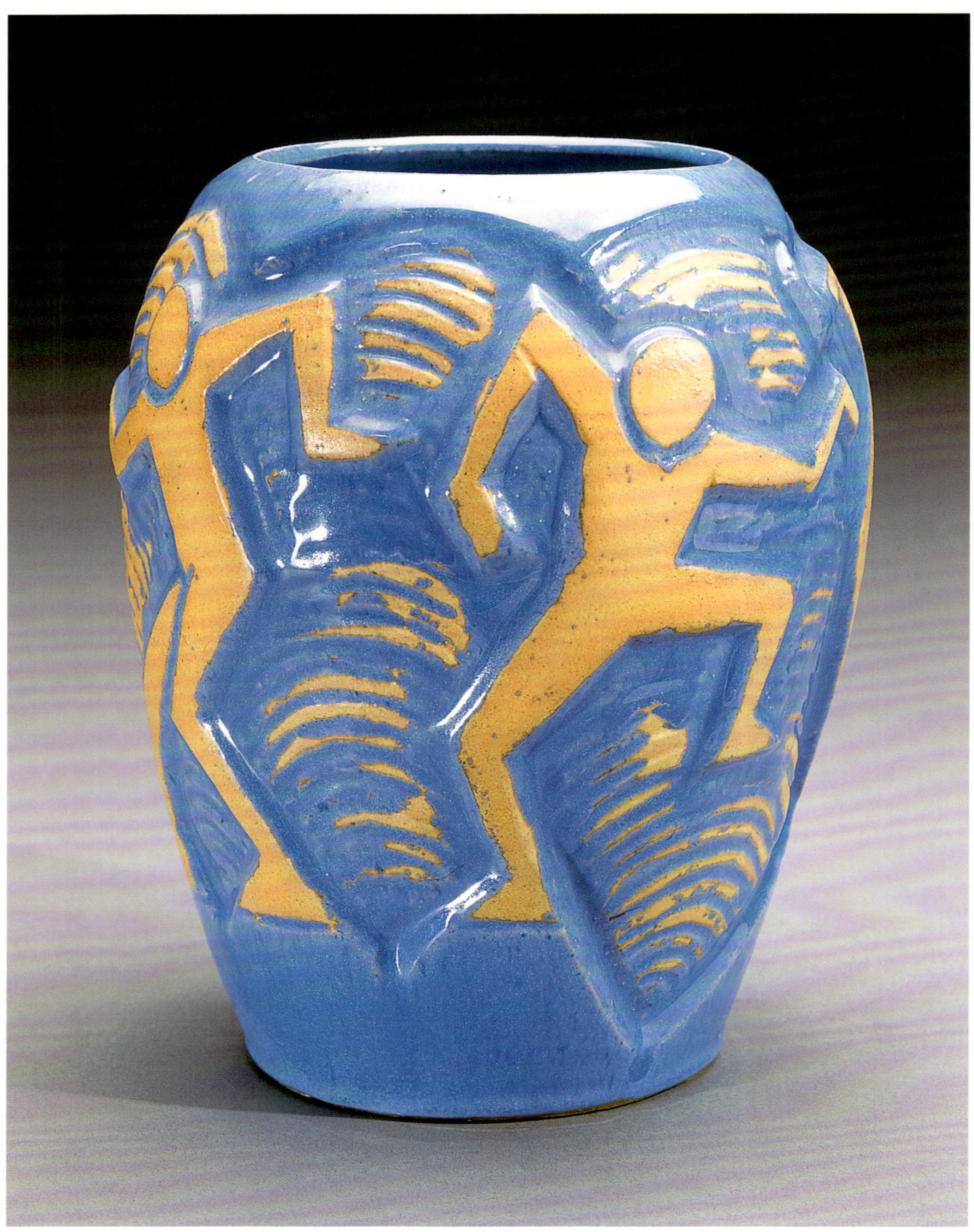

Dancing Man Vase, ca. 1931

Ceramic, 7½ x 6¼ x 6¼ in.
Louise Lehman Collection
Thrown by Peter Anderson, decorated by Walter Anderson

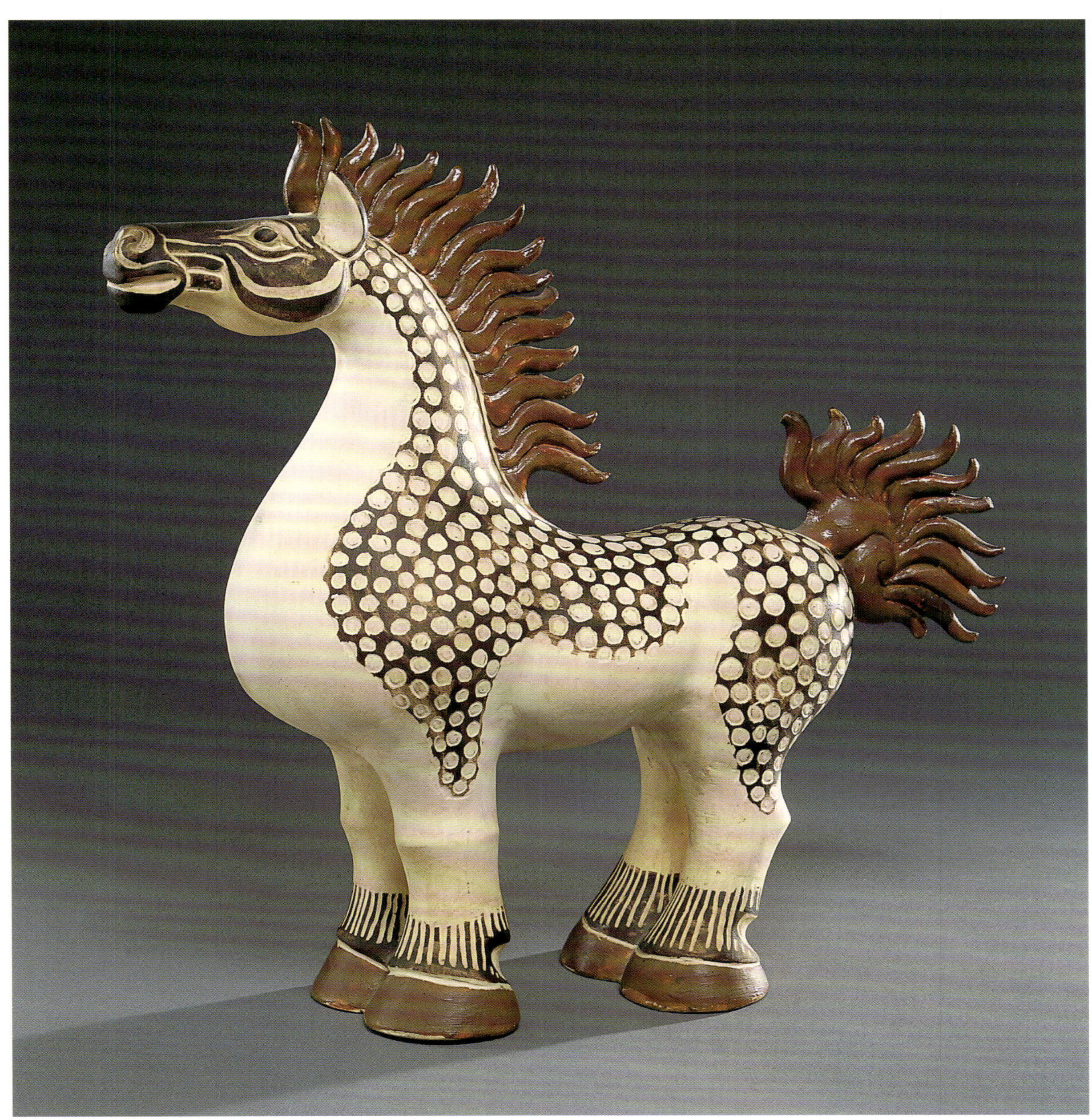

Chesty Horse, ca. 1935

Ceramic, 13½ x 4½ x 14 in.
Louise Lehman Collection
Anderson's horse is reminiscent of the bronze horses made during the Han dynasty (206 B.C.–A.D. 220) and paintings done during the Tang dynasty (618–906) in China.

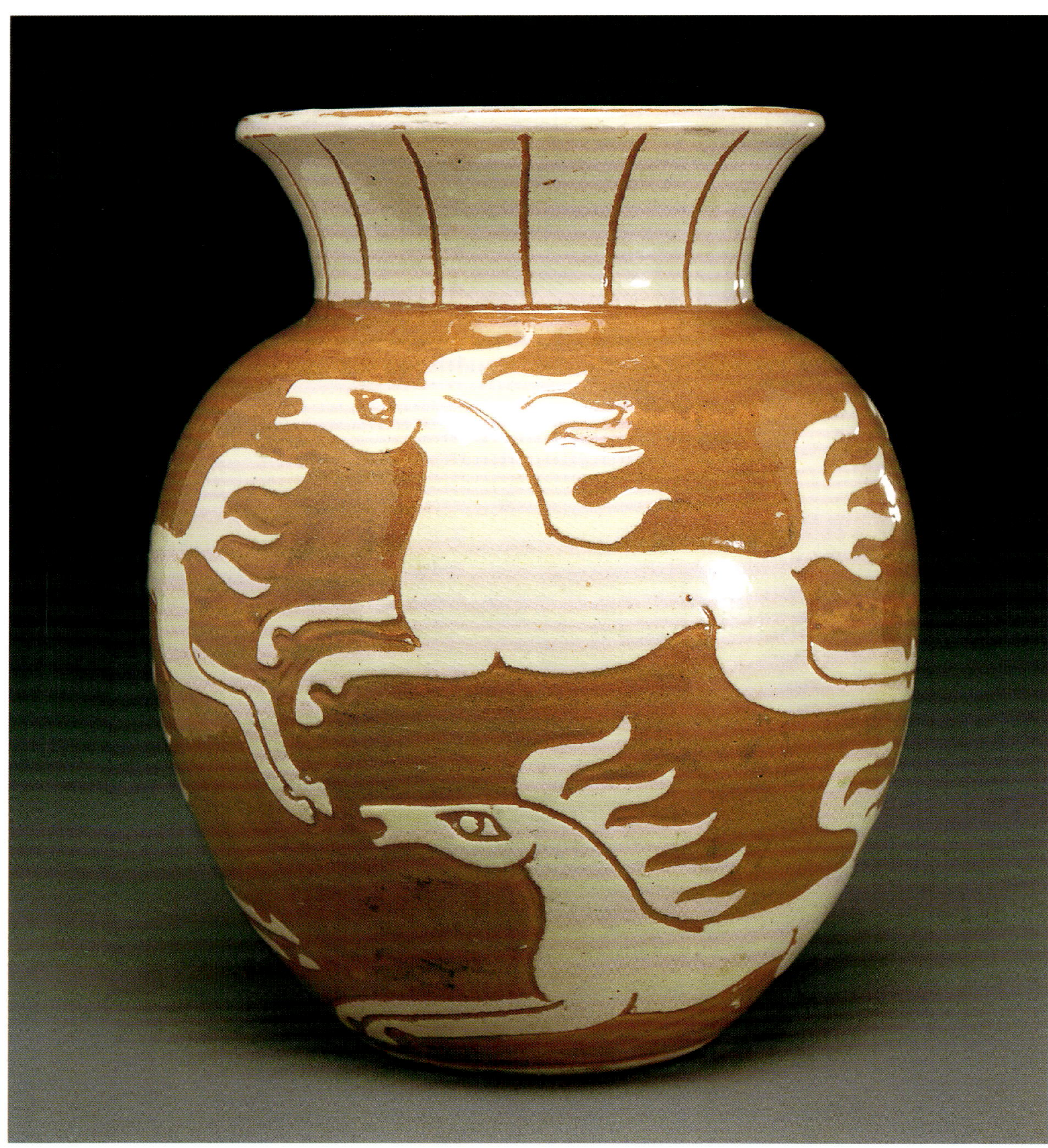

Horse Design Vase, ca. 1935

Ceramic, 8 x 6½ x 6½ in.
Louise Lehman Collection
Thrown by Peter Anderson, sgraffito decoration by Walter Anderson

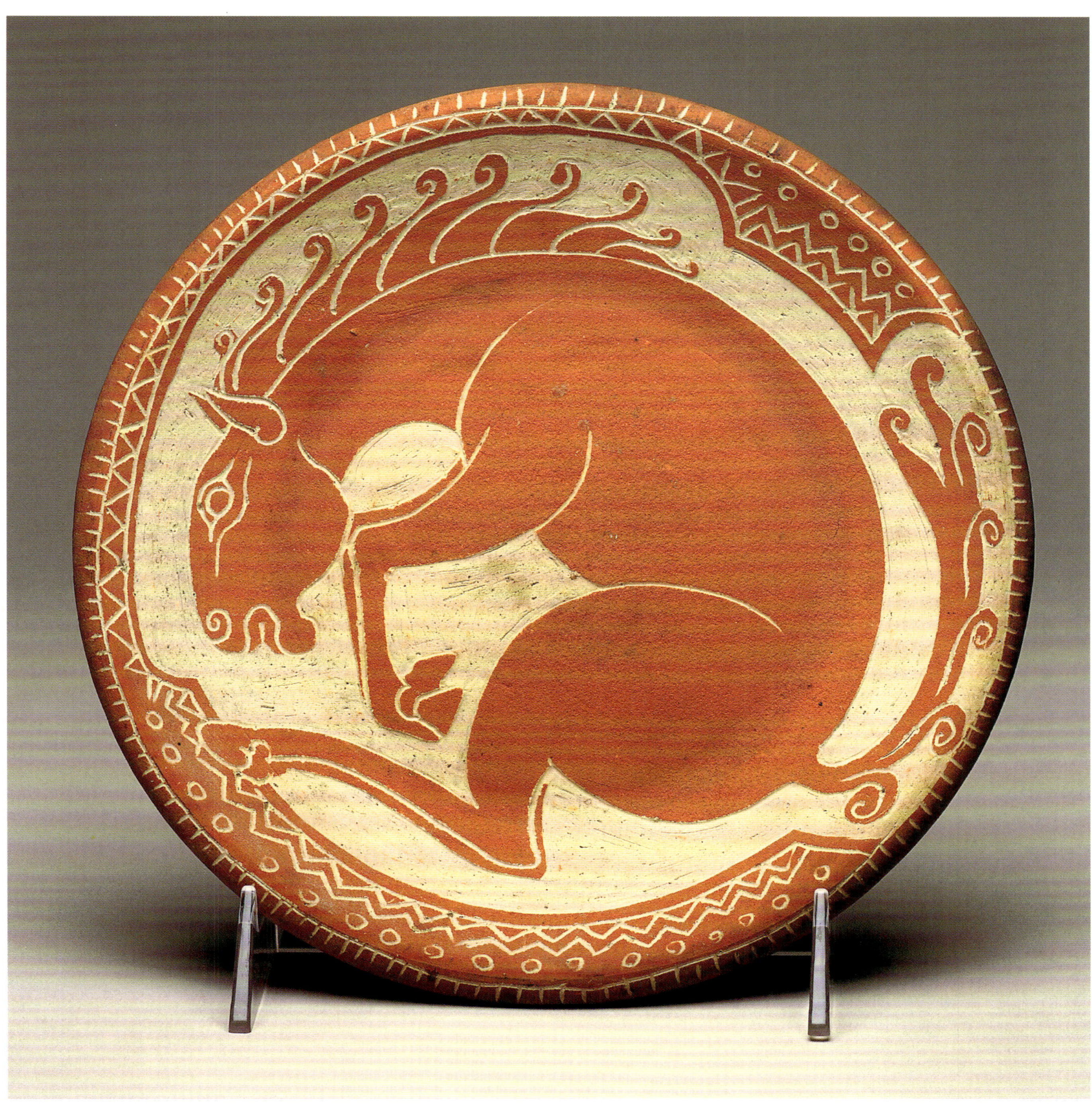

Horse Plate, ca. 1935

Ceramic, 8½ x 8½ x 1¾ in.
Marjorie Anderson Ashley
Thrown by Peter Anderson, sgraffito decoration by Walter Anderson

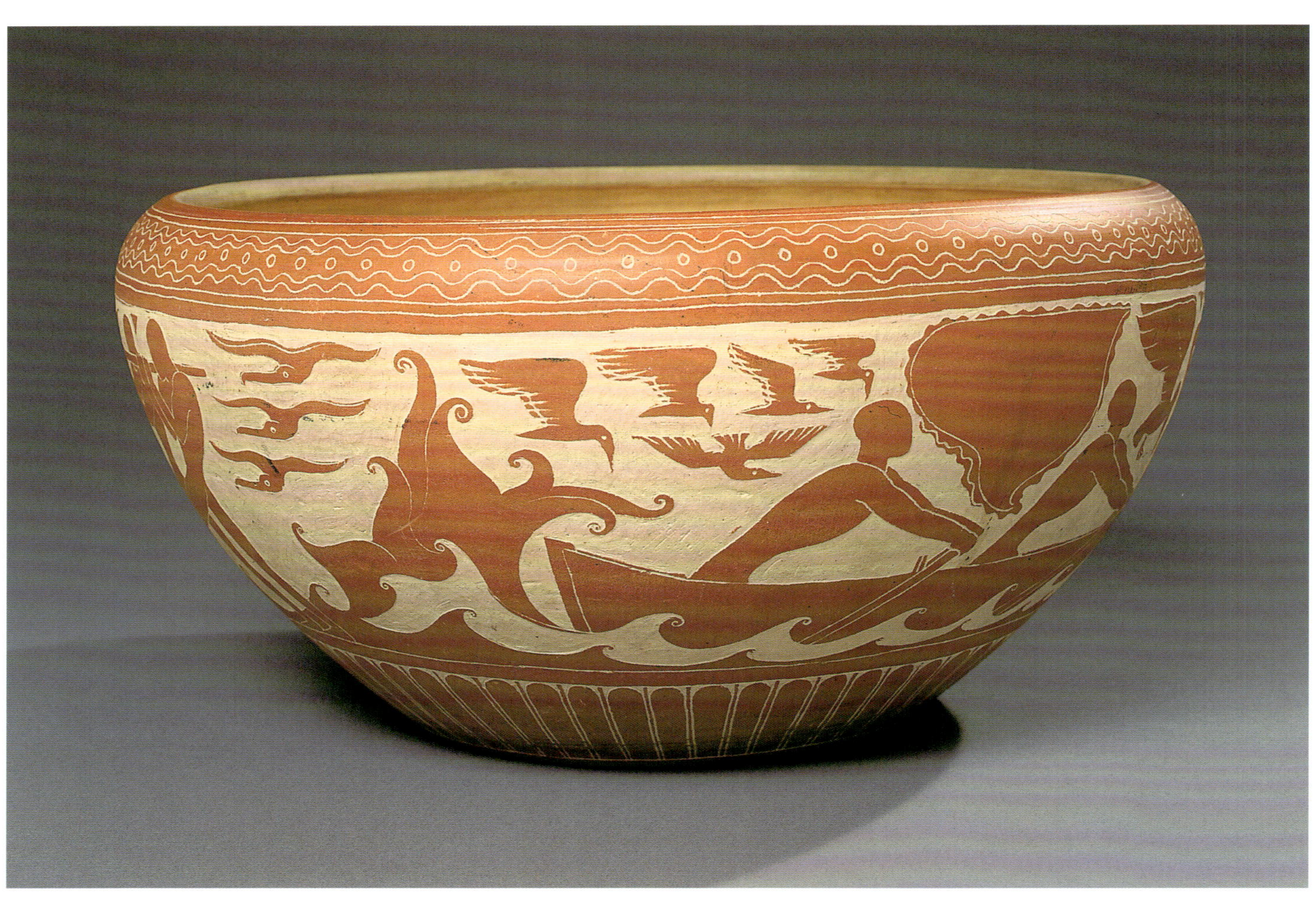

Harvesting the Sea Bowl, ca. 1934

Ceramic, 7½ x 14½ x 14½ in.
The Family of Walter Anderson
Thrown by Peter Anderson, sgraffito decoration by Walter Anderson

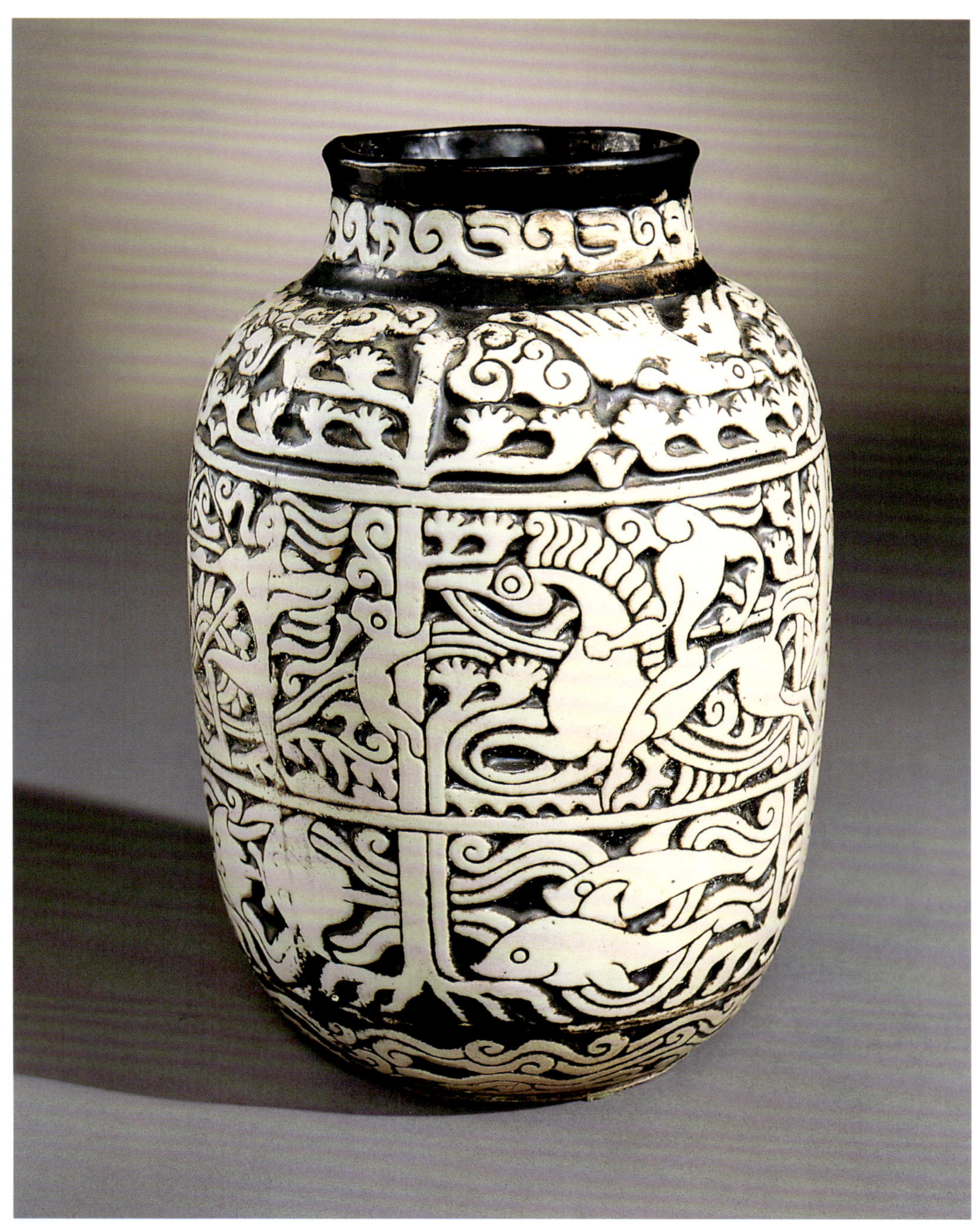

Sea, Earth and Sky Vase, ca. 1934

Ceramic, 12 x 7 x 7 in.
Walter Anderson Museum of Art, 95.4.1
Gift of Mr. and Mrs. Gerald Maples, dedicated to Frances Wynn Maples
Thrown by Peter Anderson, decoration by Walter Anderson
This piece is reminiscent of Minoan figures, dolphins, and sea life at the Knossos palace site.

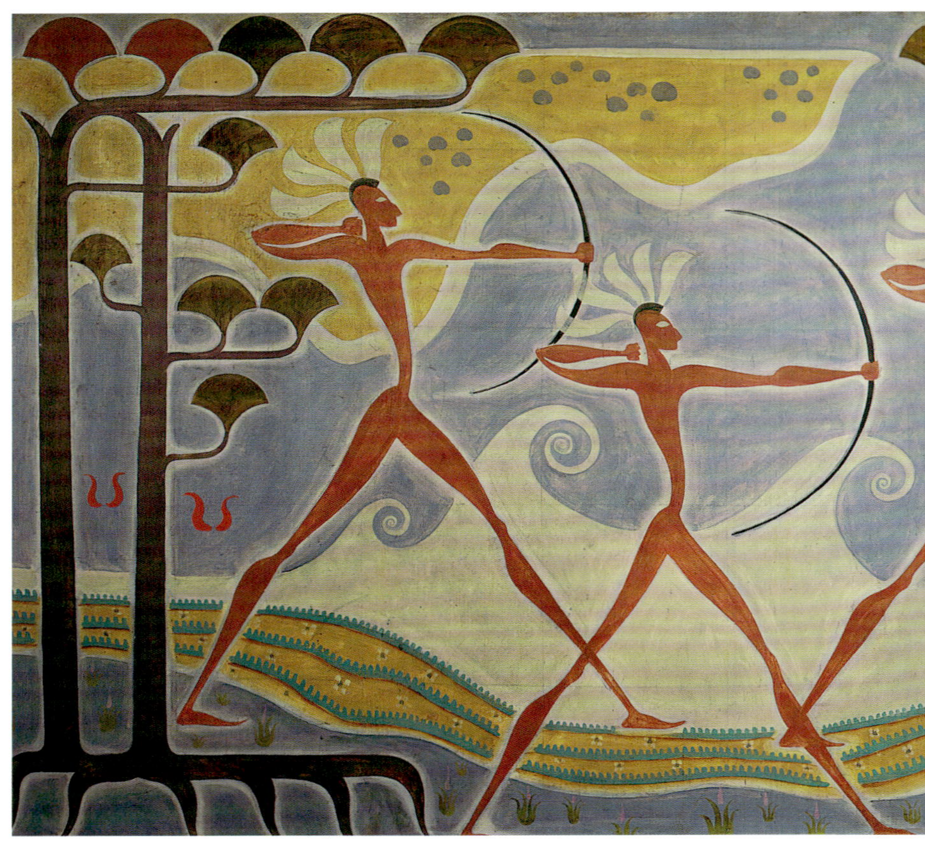

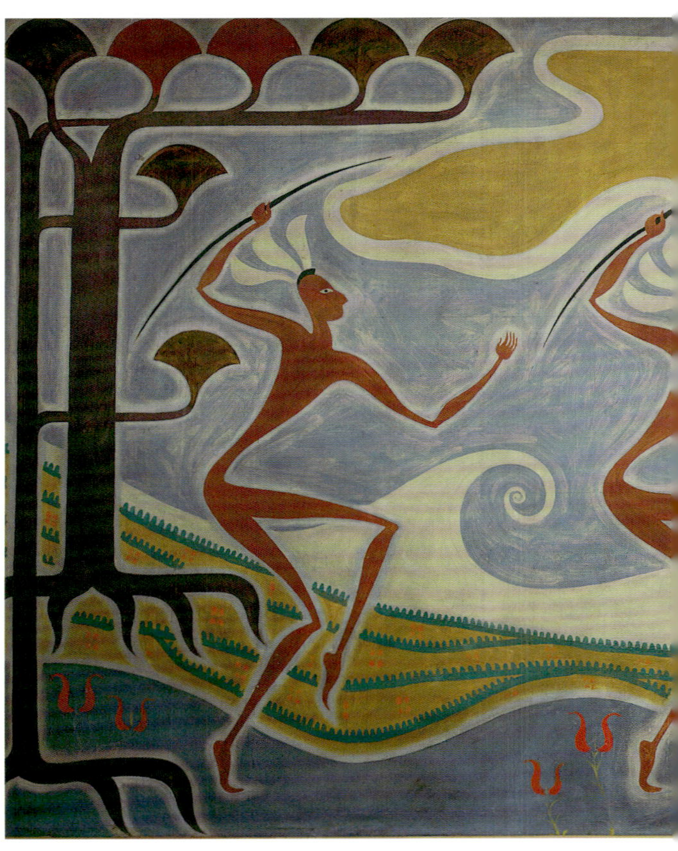

Ocean Springs: Past and Present (The Chase), 1934

Oil on canvas, 55 x 168 in.
Walter Anderson Museum of Art
Anderson received a commission from the Public Works of Art Project to paint a series of six murals, which he entitled *Ocean Springs: Past and Present*, for the Ocean Springs High School.

Ocean Springs: Past and Present (Bringing the Deer Home), 1934

Oil on canvas, 55 x 168 in.
Walter Anderson Museum of Art

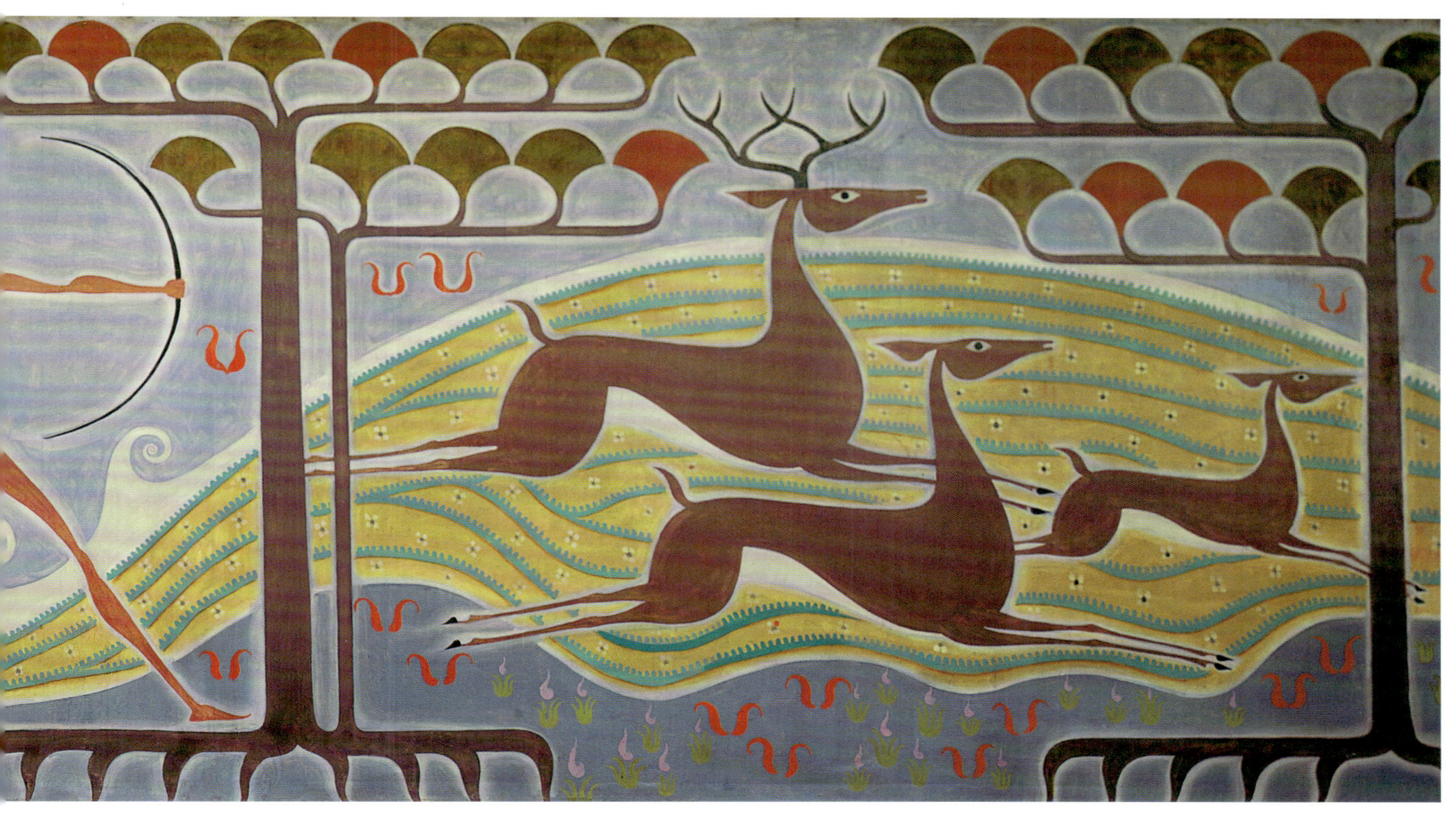

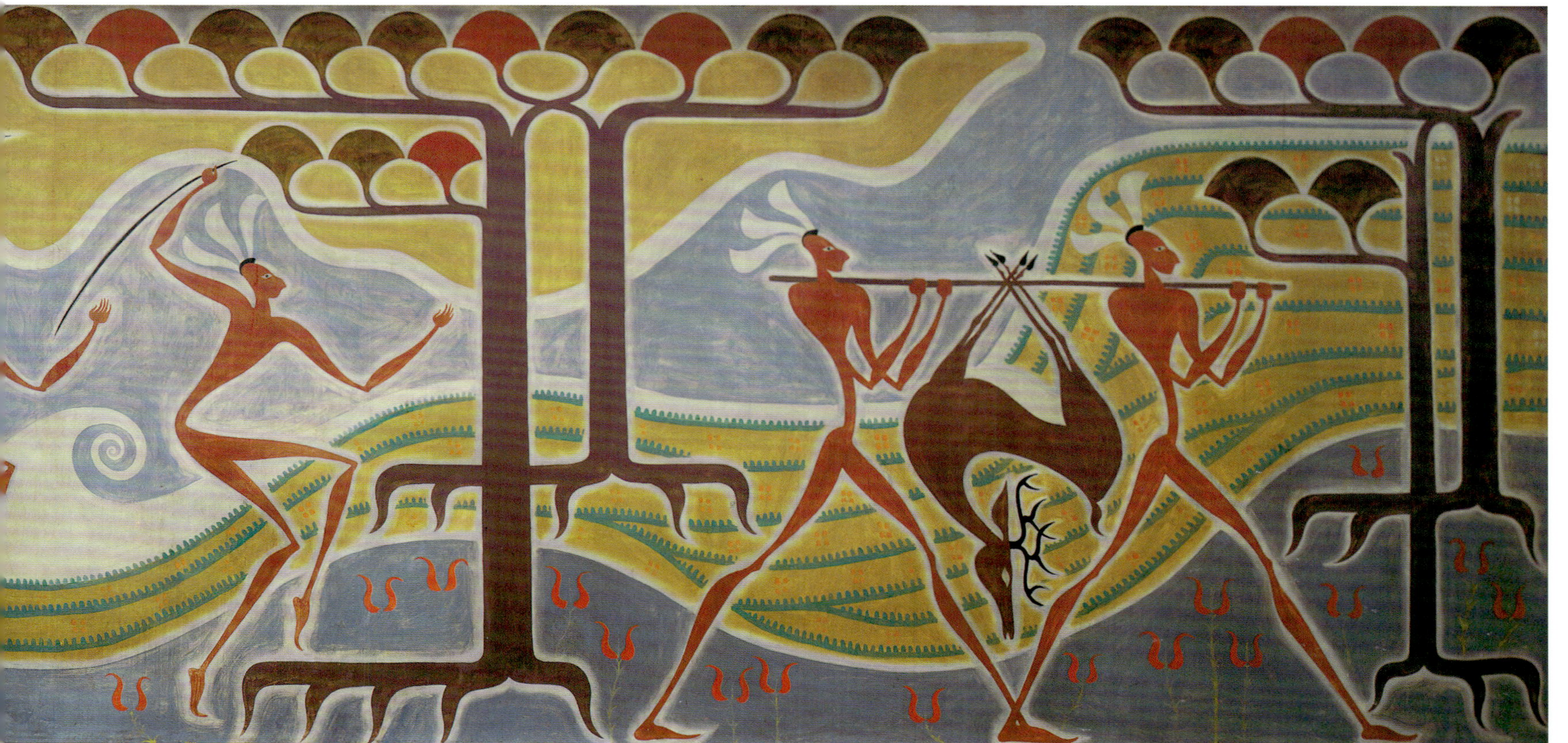

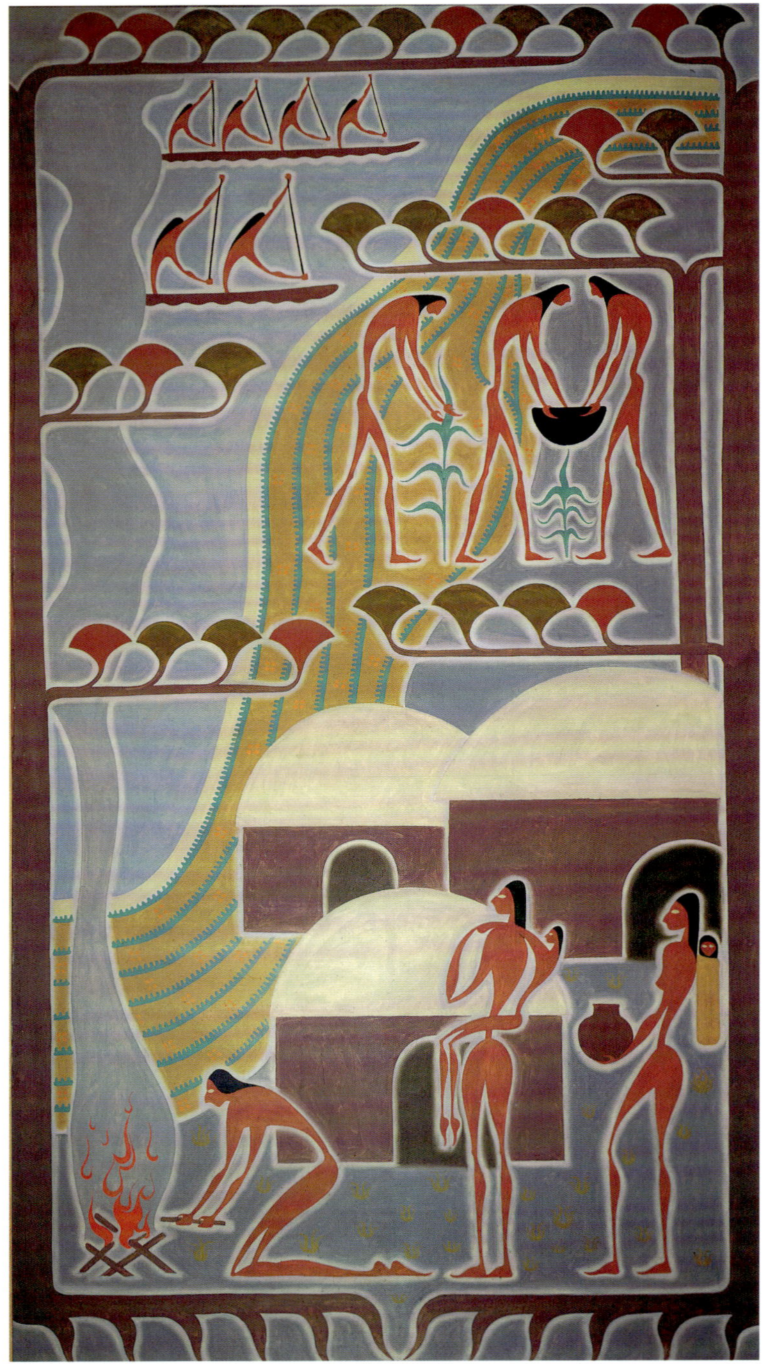

Ocean Springs: Past and Present (Feast in Camp), 1934

Oil on canvas, 132 x 72 in.
Walter Anderson Museum of Art
This vertical work was placed to the left of the auditorium stage; the coastline connected with the placement of the two horizontal murals on the side wall.

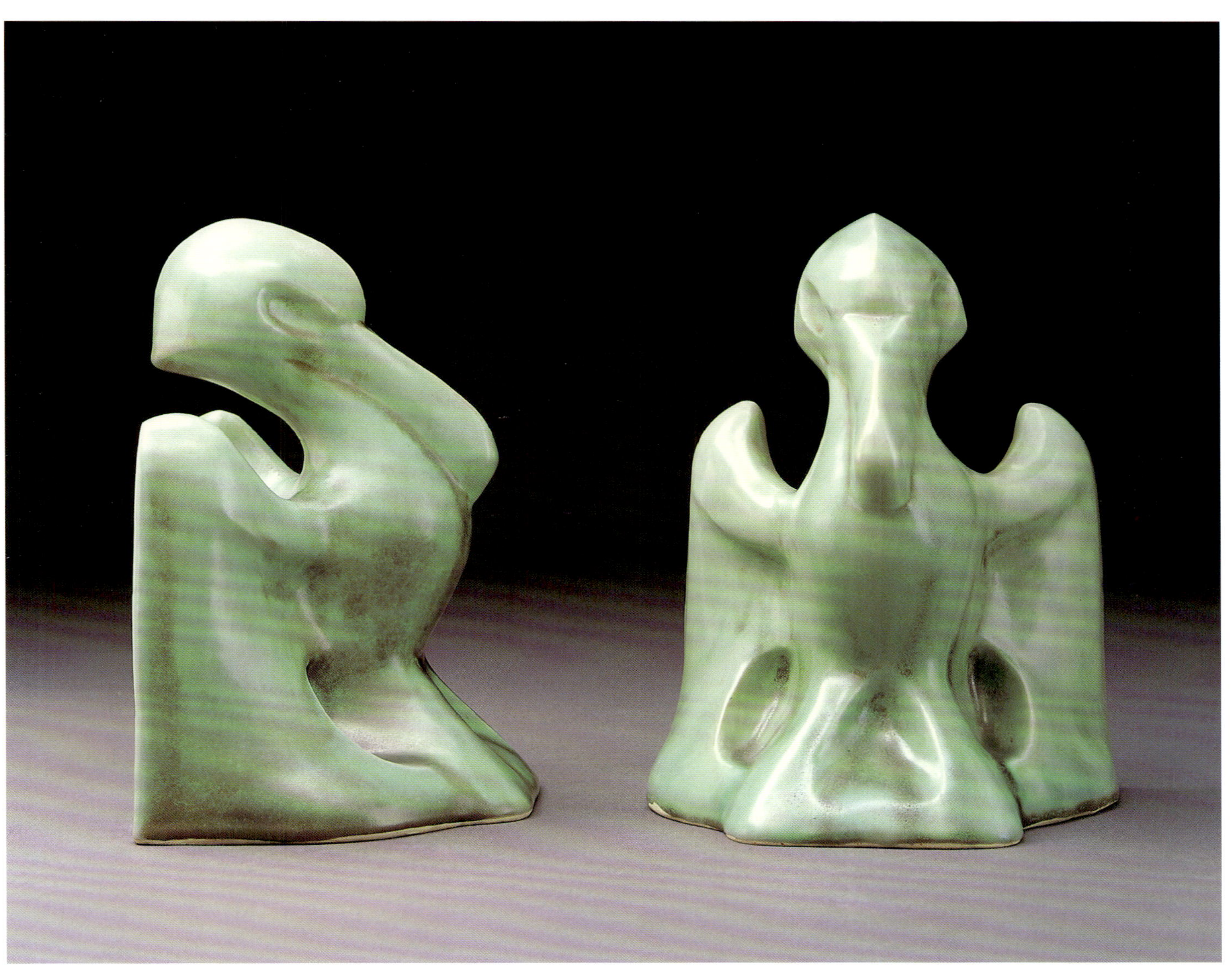

Pelican Bookends, ca. 1928

Ceramic, 8½ x 5½ x 5½ in. each
Walter Anderson Museum of Art, 01.1.2a and b

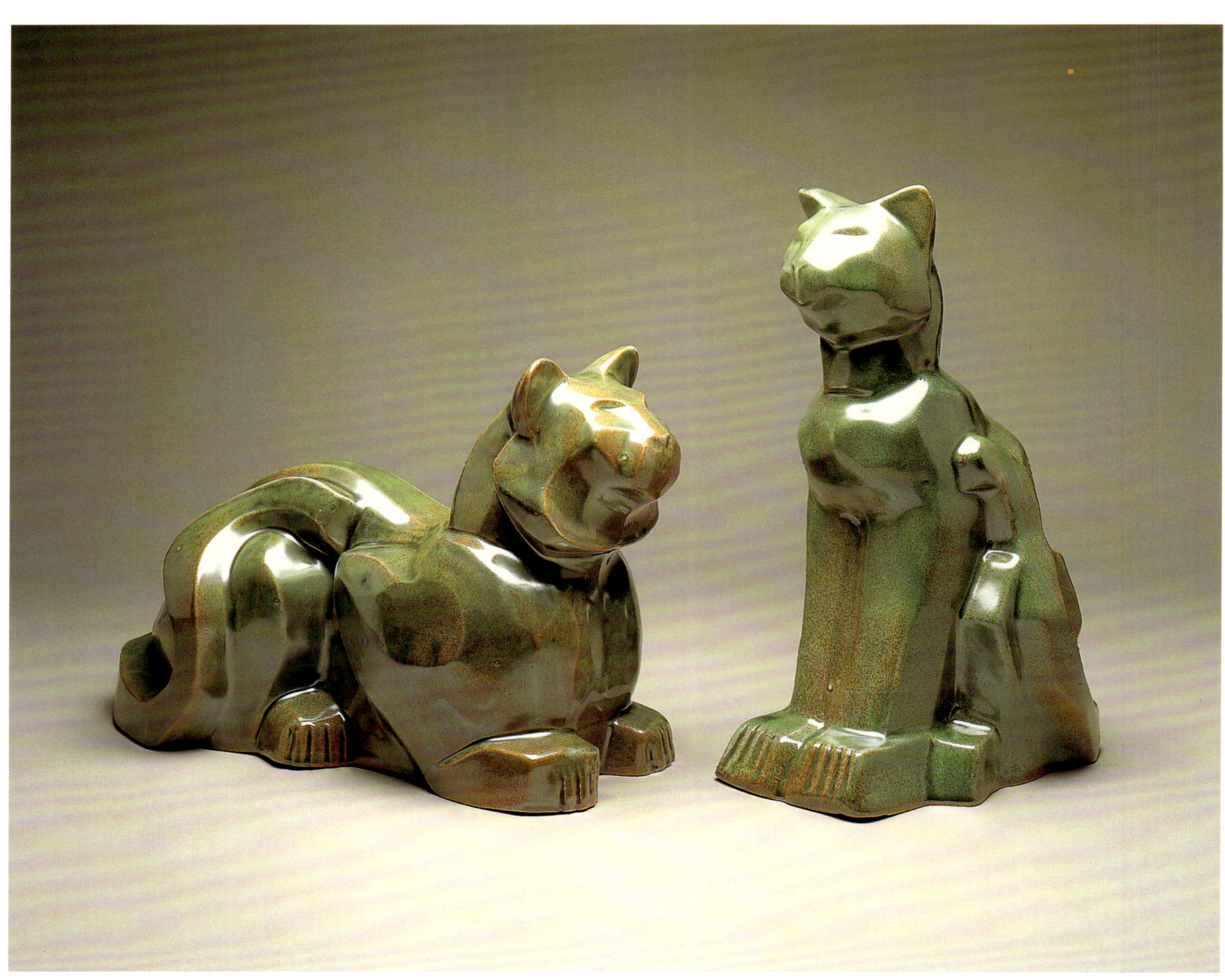

Resting and Sitting Geometric Cats, 1928

Ceramic, resting cat 8½ x 12 x 6½ in., sitting cat 12 x 7½ x 6 in.
The Family of Walter Anderson

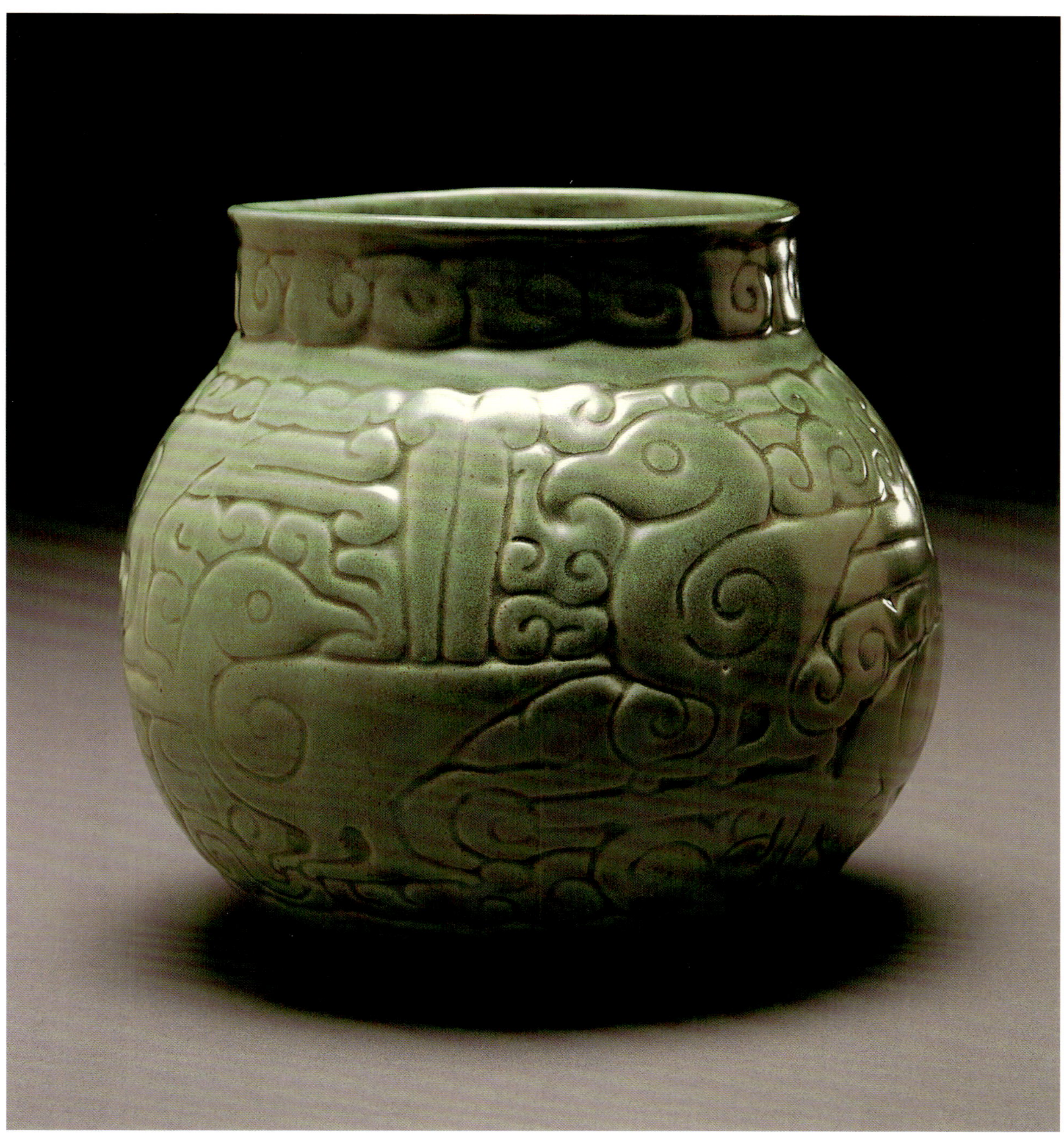

Tern Motif Vase, ca. 1935

Ceramic, 7½ x 7 x 7 in.
The Family of Walter Anderson
Thrown by Peter Anderson, decorated by Walter Anderson
Posthumous cast, 1995

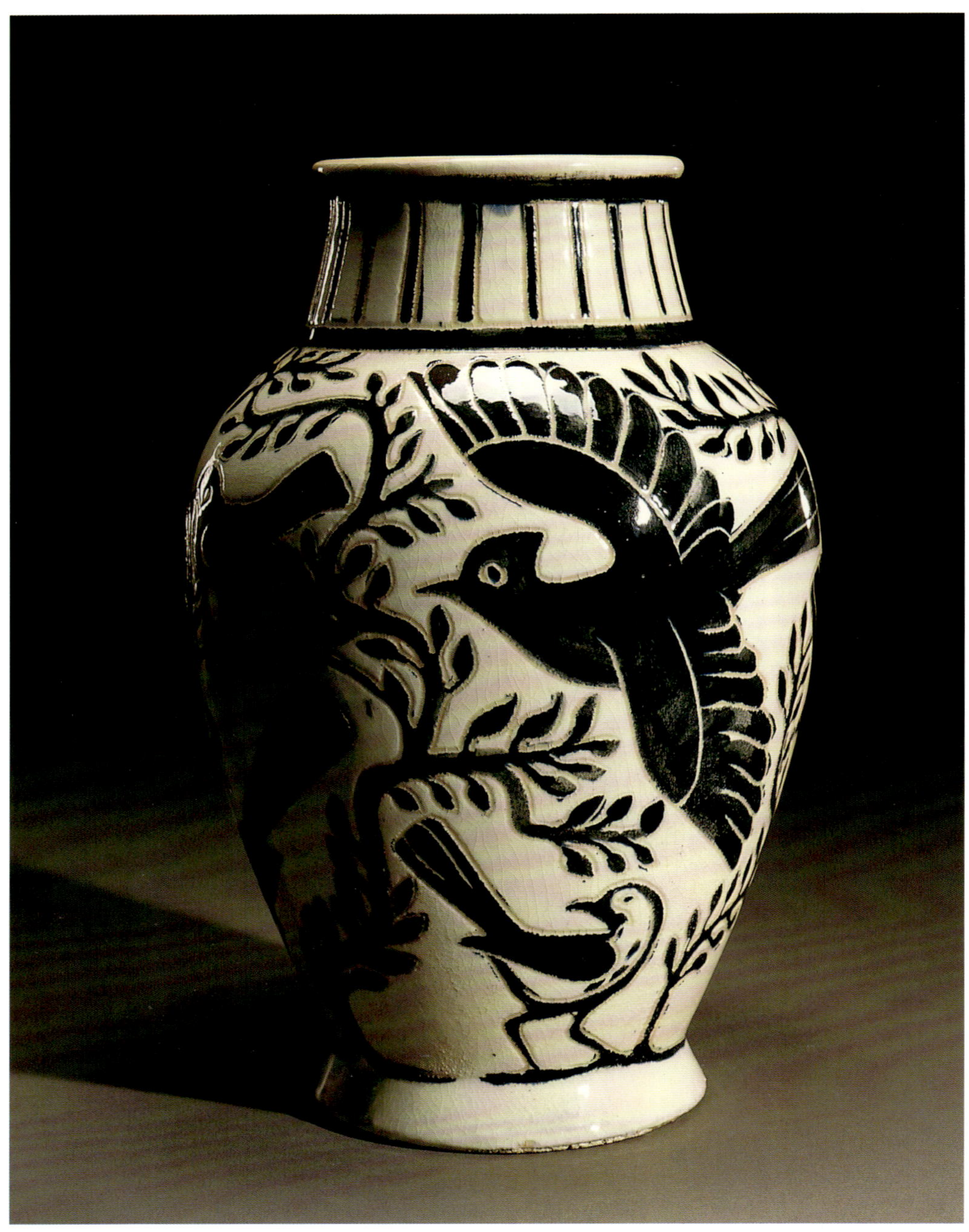

Black Birds and Vine Vase, ca. 1935

Ceramic, 12½ x 7½ x 7½ in.
Walter Anderson Museum of Art, 91.8.2
Gift of the Family of James McConnell Anderson
Thrown by Peter Anderson, decorated by Walter Anderson

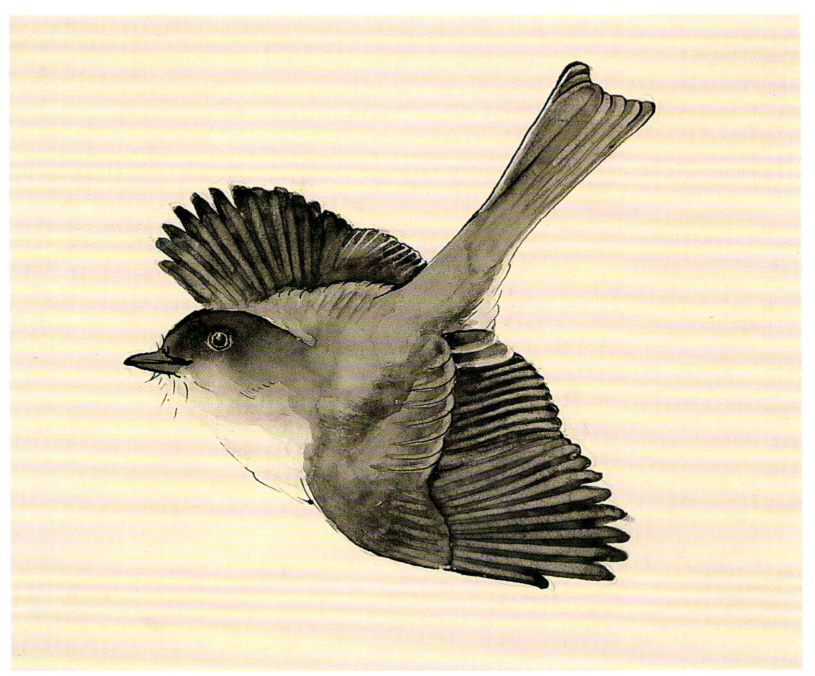

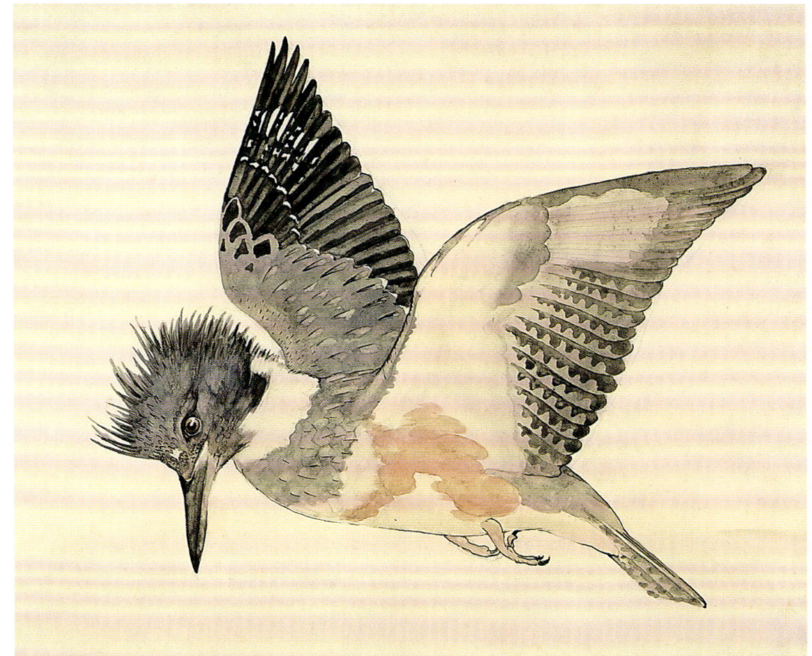

Chimney Swift, 1934

Watercolor and ink on paper, 8¾ x 11 in.
The Family of Walter Anderson

Kingfisher, 1934 (right)

Watercolor and ink on paper, 11 x 17½ in.
The Family of Walter Anderson
These birds are from a series of sixteen watercolors Anderson drew for a proposed book on the birds of the Southeast, suggested by Baltimore pediatrician Edwards Park, a friend of the family.

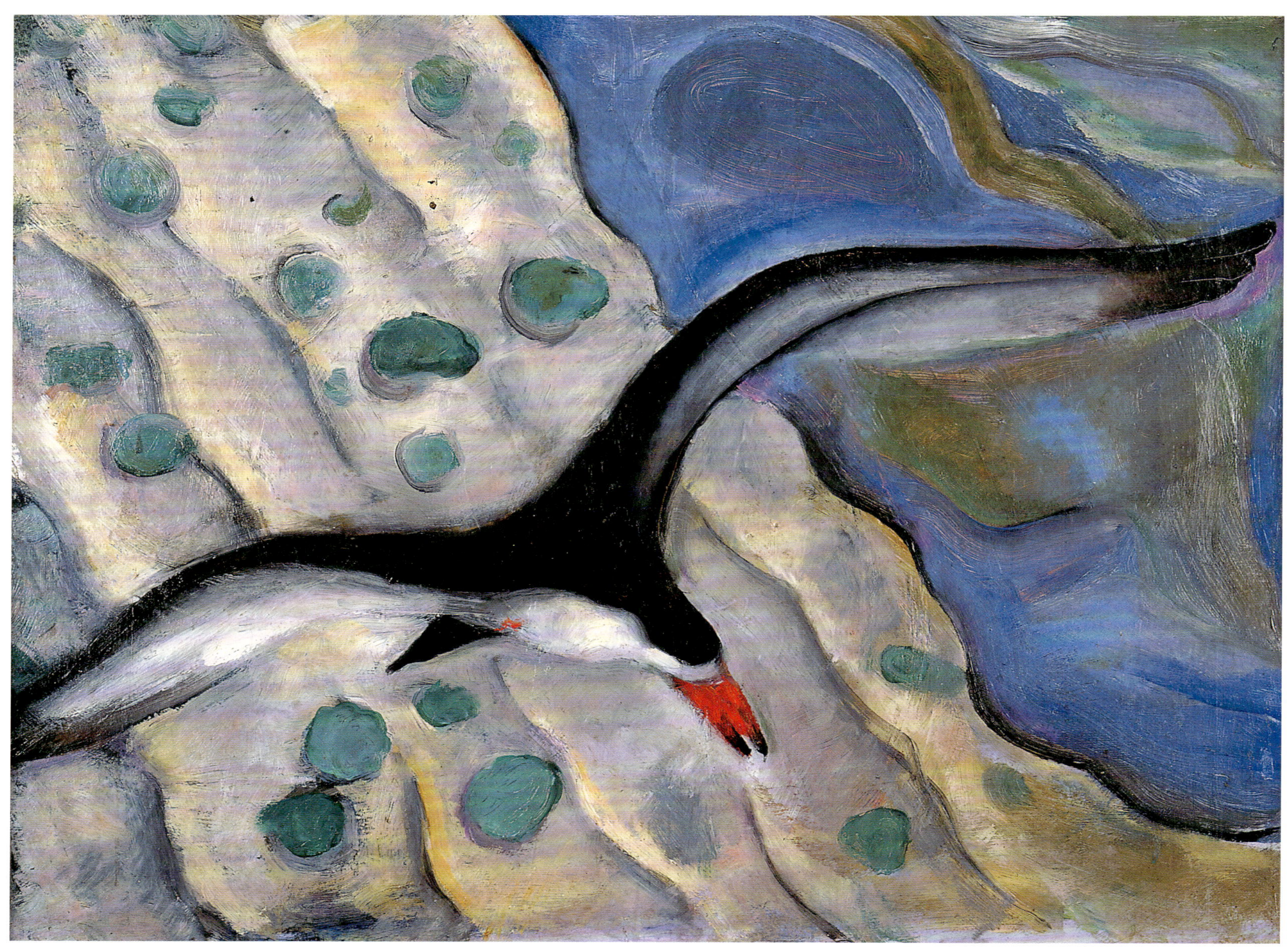

Black Skimmer, 1934

Oil on wood, 18 x 25 in.
The Family of Walter Anderson
Locally known as the "shearwater," the Black Skimmer is the bird for which Peter Anderson named Shearwater Pottery.

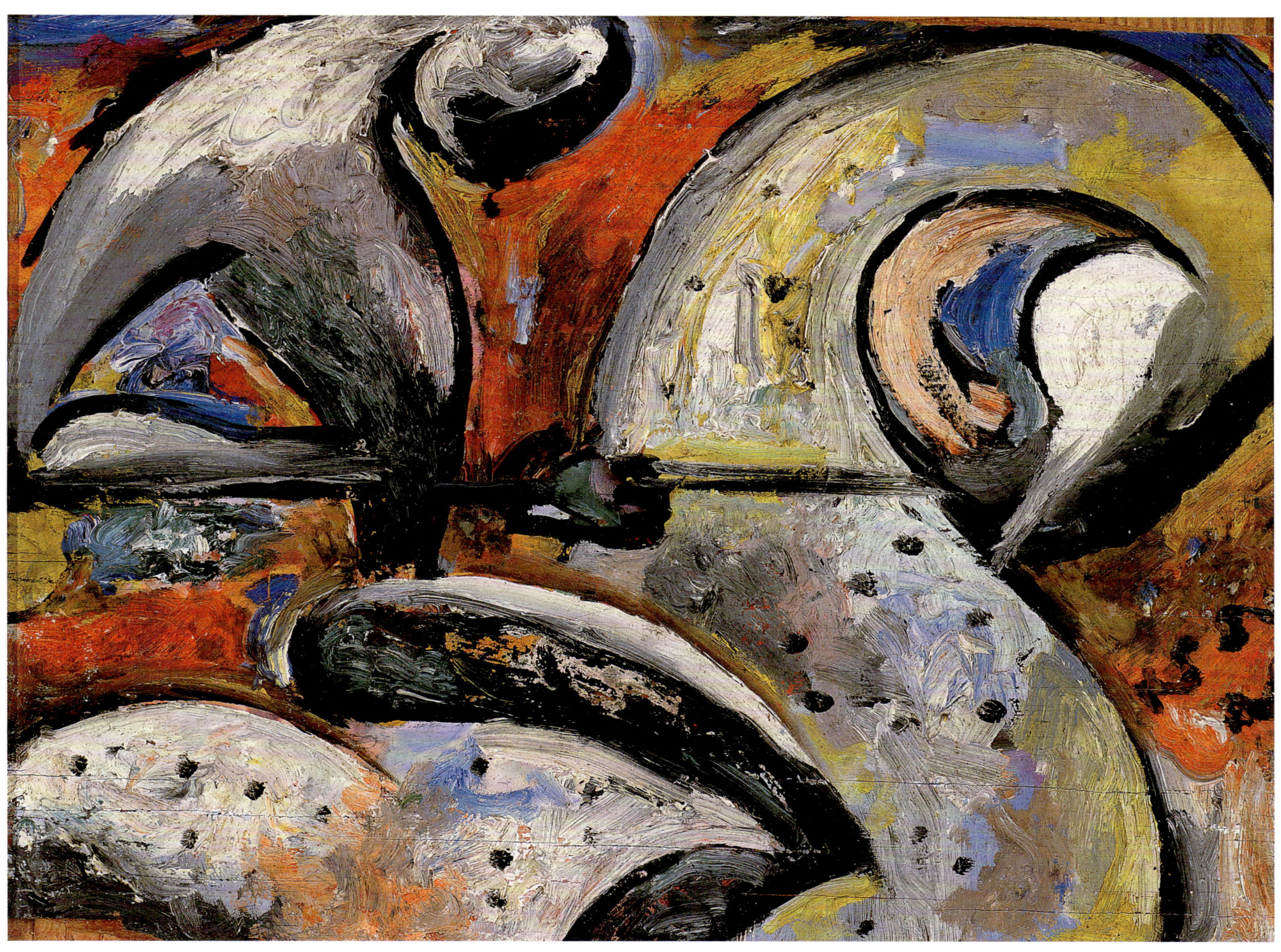

Man on Horse, 1934

Oil on wood, 16½ x 21 in.
The Family of Walter Anderson

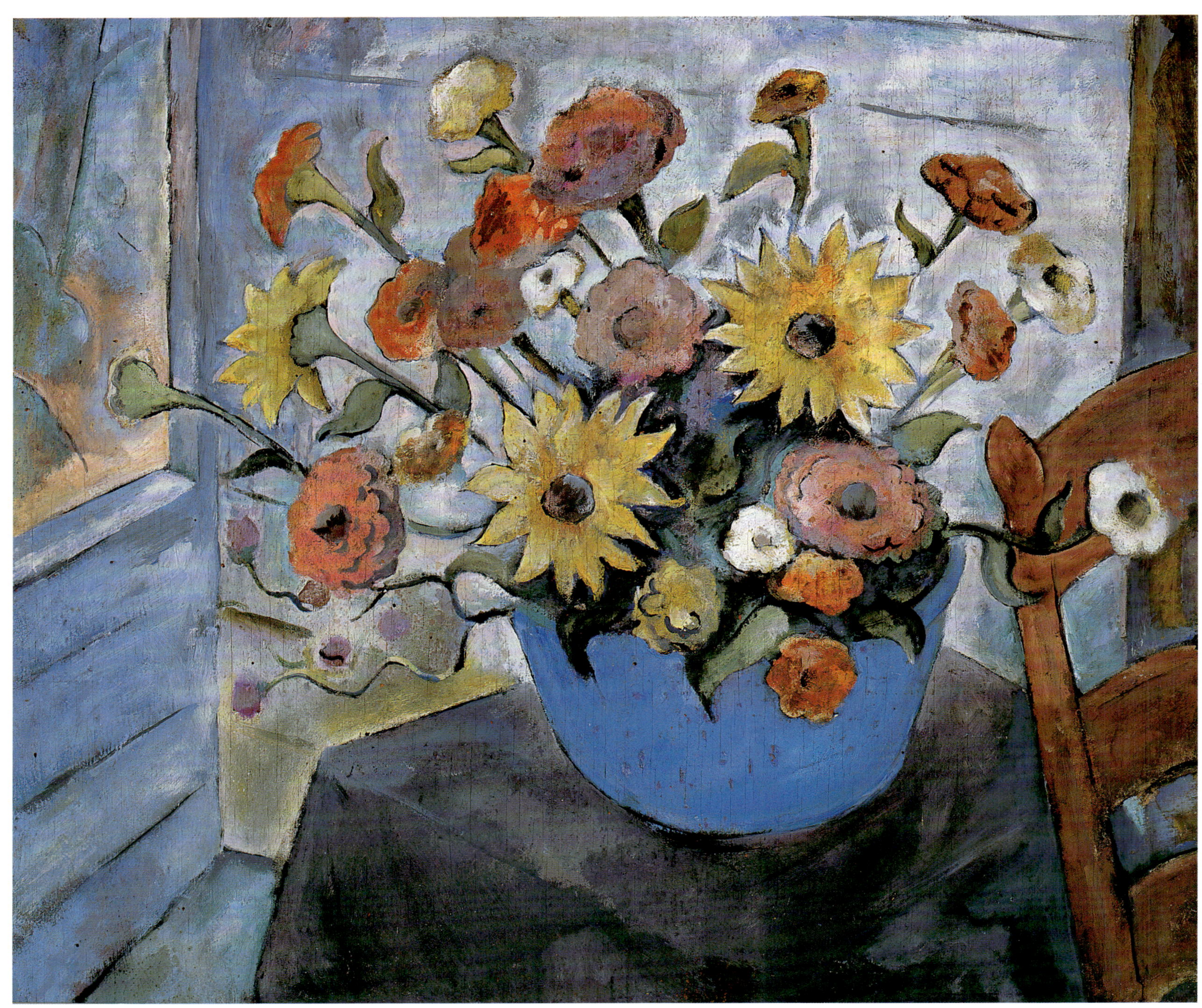

Zinnias, 1934

Oil on wood, 20 x 30 in.
The Family of Walter Anderson

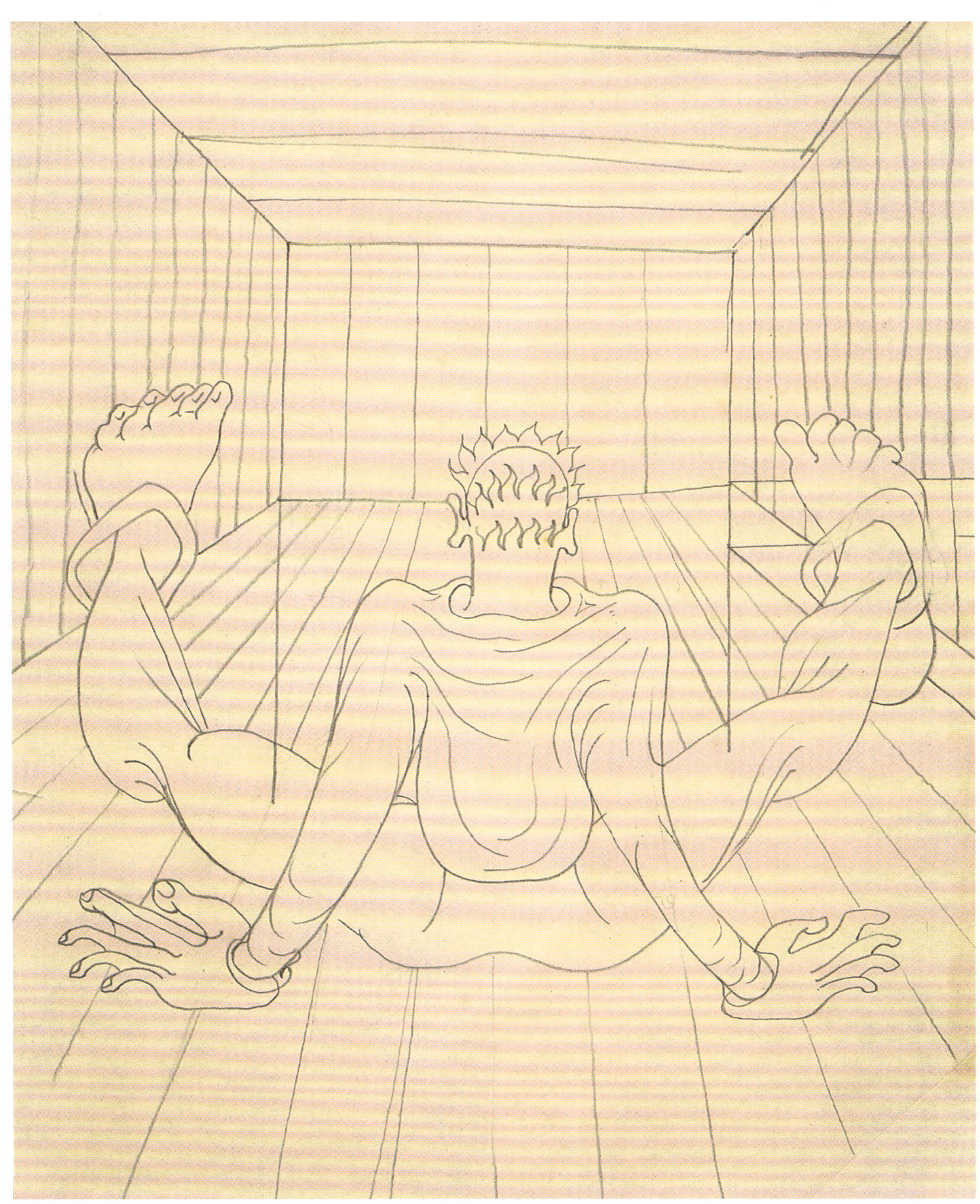

Alienado, ca. 1940

Pencil on paper, 11 x 8½ in.
The Family of Walter Anderson
In 1937, Walter Anderson was hospitalized at Henry Phipps Psychiatric Clinic at Johns Hopkins University in Baltimore. He was released sixteen months later and for a short time was able to rejoin his family. However, over the next two years, he was hospitalized three more times, finally coming home for good in the spring of 1940.

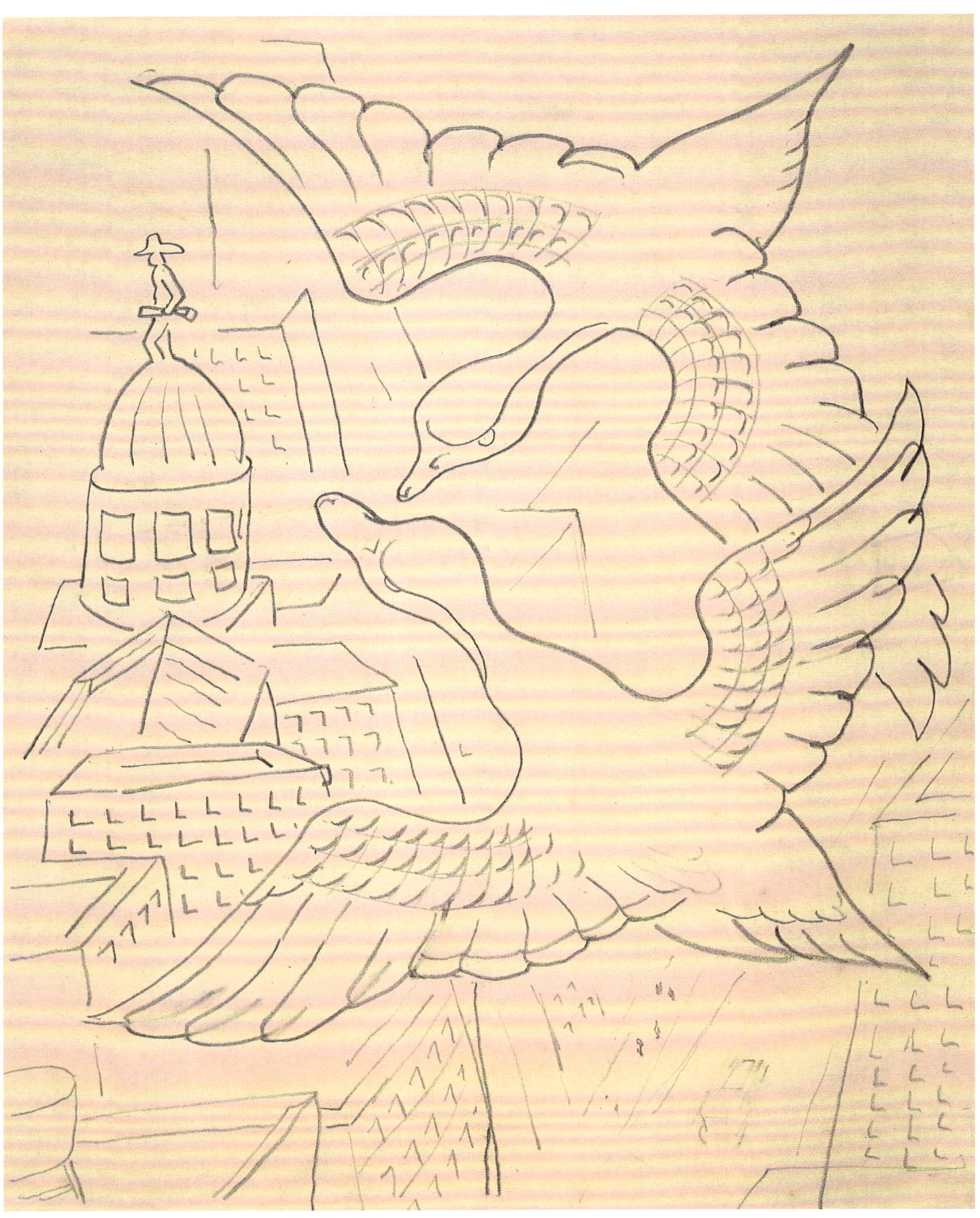

Ducks over Philadelphia, ca. 1939

Pencil on paper, 11 x 8½ in.
The Family of Walter Anderson
William Penn poses as a hunter on the top of City Hall, Philadelphia.

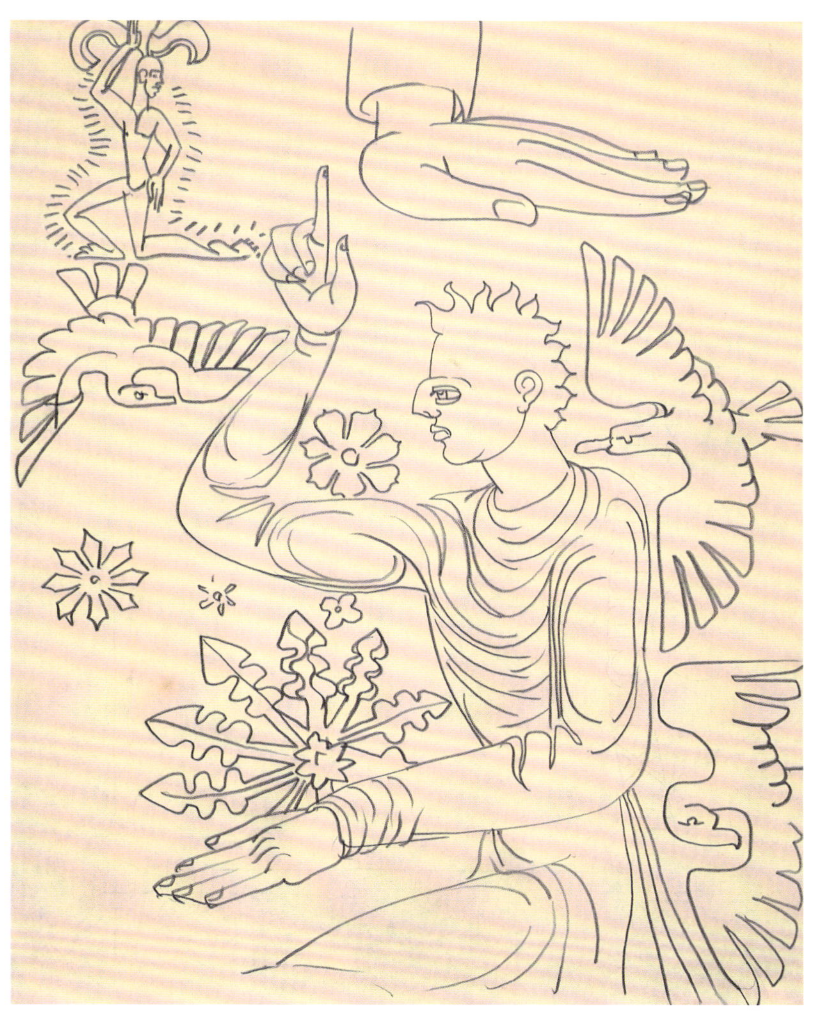

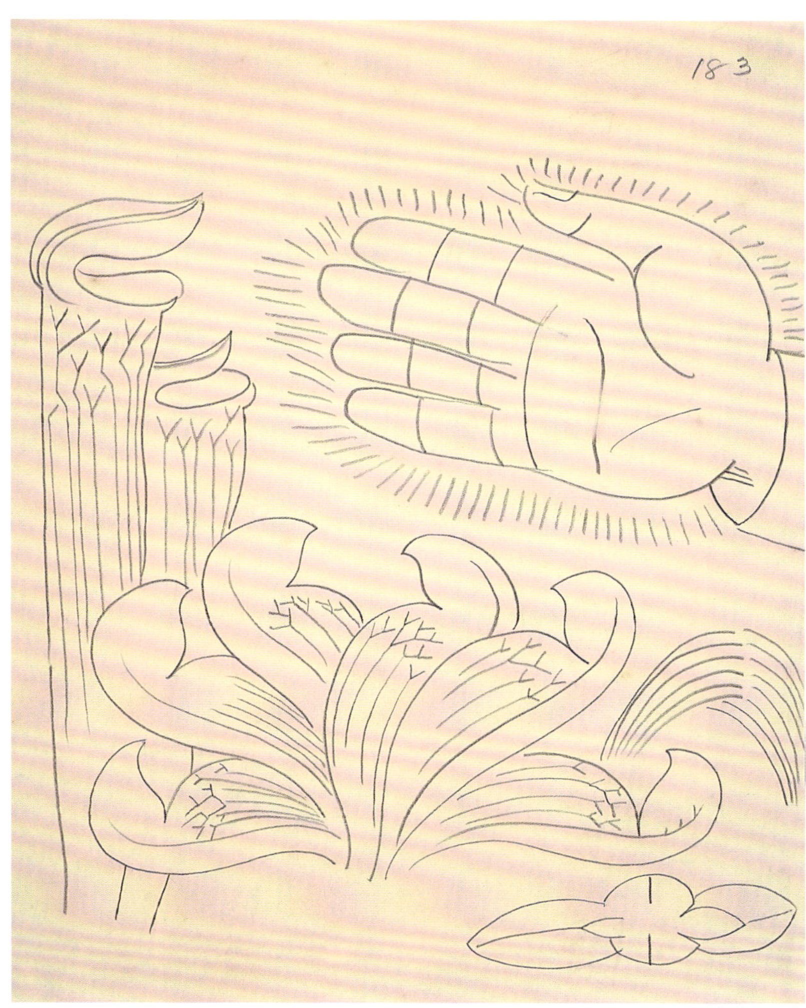

Man and Birds, ca. 1939

Pencil on paper, 11 x 8½ in.
The Family of Walter Anderson

Hand and Plants, ca. 1939

Pencil on paper, 11 x 8½ in.
The Family of Walter Anderson
Cryptic drawings from 1939 to 1940 show Anderson's interest in Buddhism and in the Hindu epic *The Ramayana*.

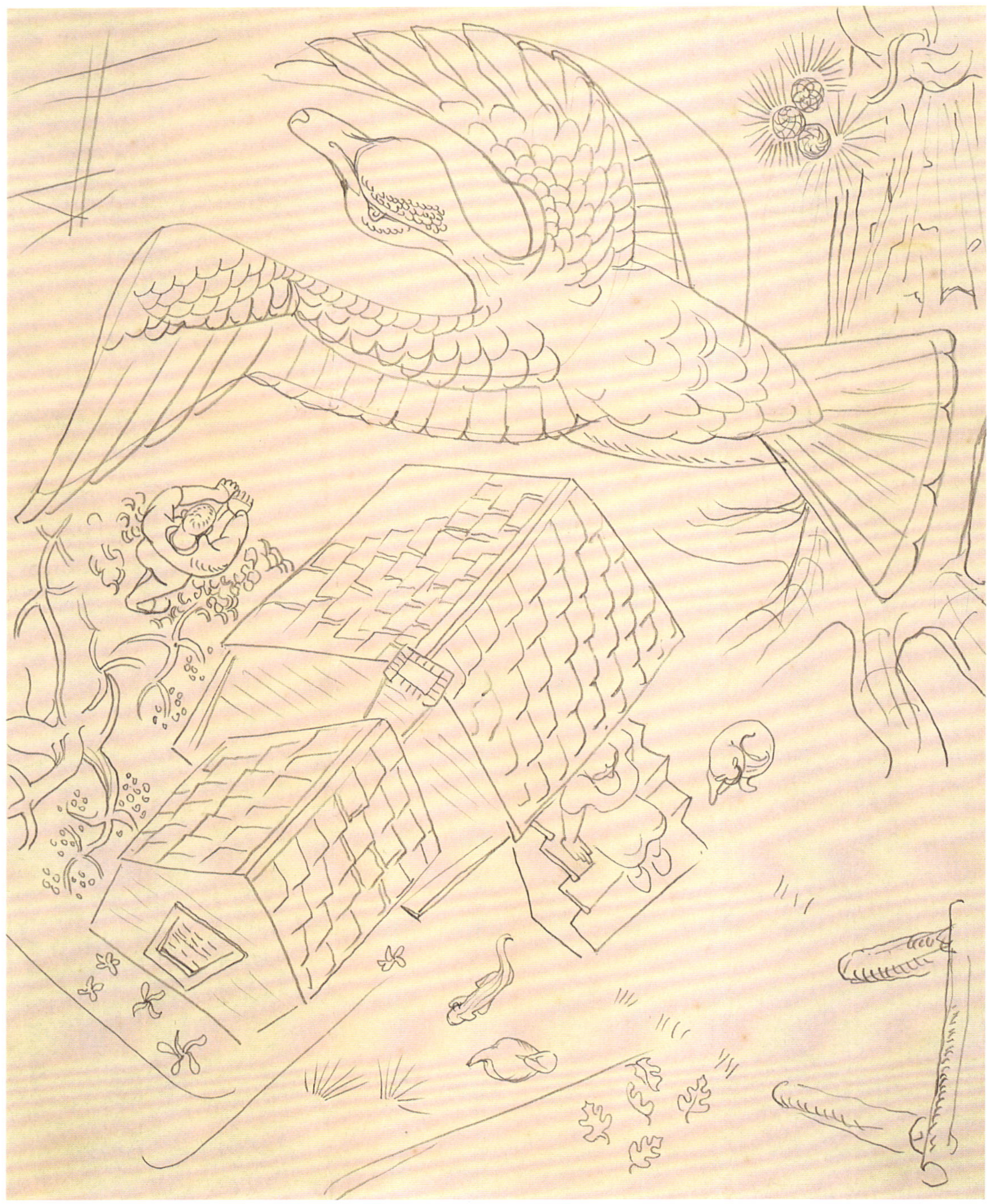

Birds Eye View, 1940

Pencil on paper, 11 x 8½ in.
The Family of Walter Anderson
Illustration drawn on the back of a letter written from the Mississippi State Hospital at Whitfield in January 1940.

January 31,

Dear Cissy,

Your letter came to day and I was charmed to get it another way of saying I was very glad. and excited to hear the name of those little birds we saw when it was so cold. Would that I was at home. they say the French have no name for home. I see some reason for it. It dosn't make them like it less any way

Will you be moveing back or ~~are~~ are you staying at the barn. I'm sending some hooked rugs some day this week. I hope you like them.

Which do you like best trees with leaves or trees without leaves, The is both and stop asking foolish questions.

The other side is supposed to be a duck flying over our house. probably a dog—is so you won't hear it quack.

All the houses are in a half dressed state the snow is almost gone. and ~~took s~~ have a mangy look. a Holstien look. I should have said. Its a Jersey look that I sucome to.. makes me want to do and be with brush and pencil.

How does one become a spectator and at the same time retain ones pants? I can't stop they keep on coming. You need not answer.

My formula for drawing its a secret.

We drove to Vicksburg not so long ago and came home just at sunset lots of color coming and going. I don't think you and I properly appreciated Vicksburg maybe we will go there again someday. I don't remember a bridge- There's

Letter to Sissy, 1940

Pencil on paper, 11 x 8½ in.
The Family of Walter Anderson

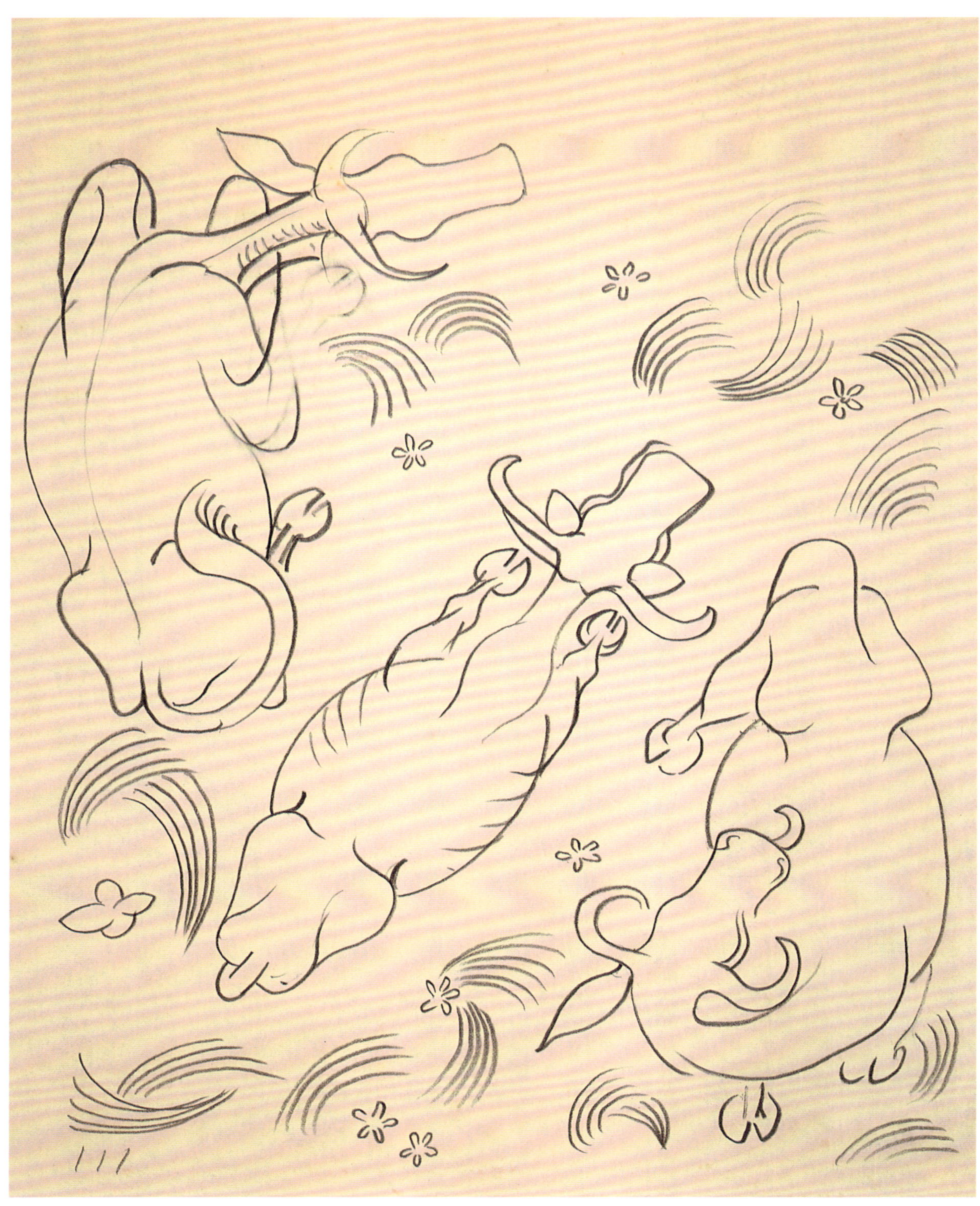

Cows from Above, ca. 1940

Pencil on paper, 11 x 8½ in.
The Family of Walter Anderson

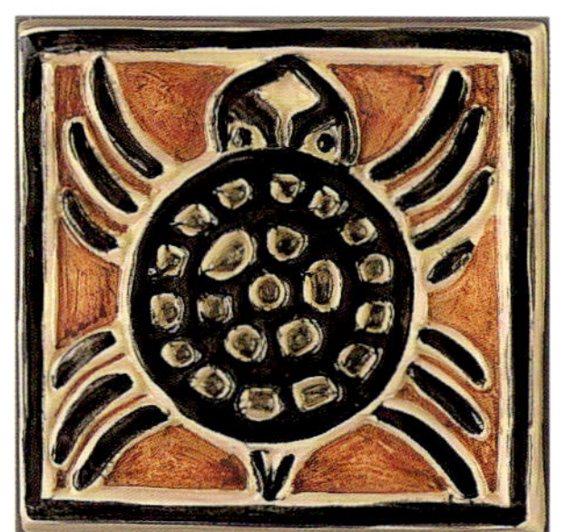

WAR YEARS AT OLDFIELDS: 1940–1945

After receiving treatment at the Henry Phipps Psychiatric Clinic at Johns Hopkins University in Baltimore, the Sheppard and Enoch Pratt Hospital in Towson, Maryland, and the Mississippi State Hospital at Whitfield, Walter Anderson settled with his family and Sissy's ailing father at Oldfields, the Grinstead family homestead in Gautier. Here he began one of his happiest, most productive periods, a time of renewal and healing, of playing with his children, exploring the fields, marshes, and pinelands, and observing plants and insects. Freed from the routines of the pottery, he had time to draw, paint, and make block prints, to illustrate some of his favorite books, to produce toys, puppet plays, and stories for the children, and to build his own kiln and fire a new series of figurines. He kept the house stocked with firewood, built a rental cottage, and celebrated the passing of the seasons and daily hours in a series of watercolors and lyrical "calendar drawings" which capture seasonal phenomena and record events in his daily life. His earliest watercolors at Oldfields use primary colors and repetitive design in a manner reminiscent of ancient hieratic presentation. One of his favorite books during those years was *A Method for Creative Design* by the Mexican theorist Adolfo Best-Maugard, a work which reduces all of art to seven basic motifs: zigzag, half-circle, circle, straight line, s-curve, wavy line, and spiral. Anderson combined these motifs—found in both art and nature—in every conceivable way.

At night he read—and "visualized"—Milton, Dante, Goethe, Homer, Ossian, and the great epics of voyage and discovery, myth and legend. Drawing rapidly as he read—the book to his left and a dip pen in his right hand—he made ninety-nine drawings of Shakespeare's *Hamlet* alone, and over two thousand of Cervantes's *Don Quixote*. The finished drawings fell to the floor around the dining room table, to be collected the next morning by Sissy. For him, reading was a process of visualization, during which he "realized" scenes latent in the text.

At Oldfields, he also created a number of murals (compositions ranging over several sheets of paper), including series devoted to barnyard animals, the garden, plowing, and the plants that grew in the cutover lands, the boggy places created by lumbermen as they felled the pine savannahs. In 1945, the flower garden he had designed and planted bloomed profusely with zinnias—his favorite flower—as well as with sunflowers and tithonia, known for its brilliant vermilion. Like the garden, his watercolors burst into a broad palette of ever-brighter color.

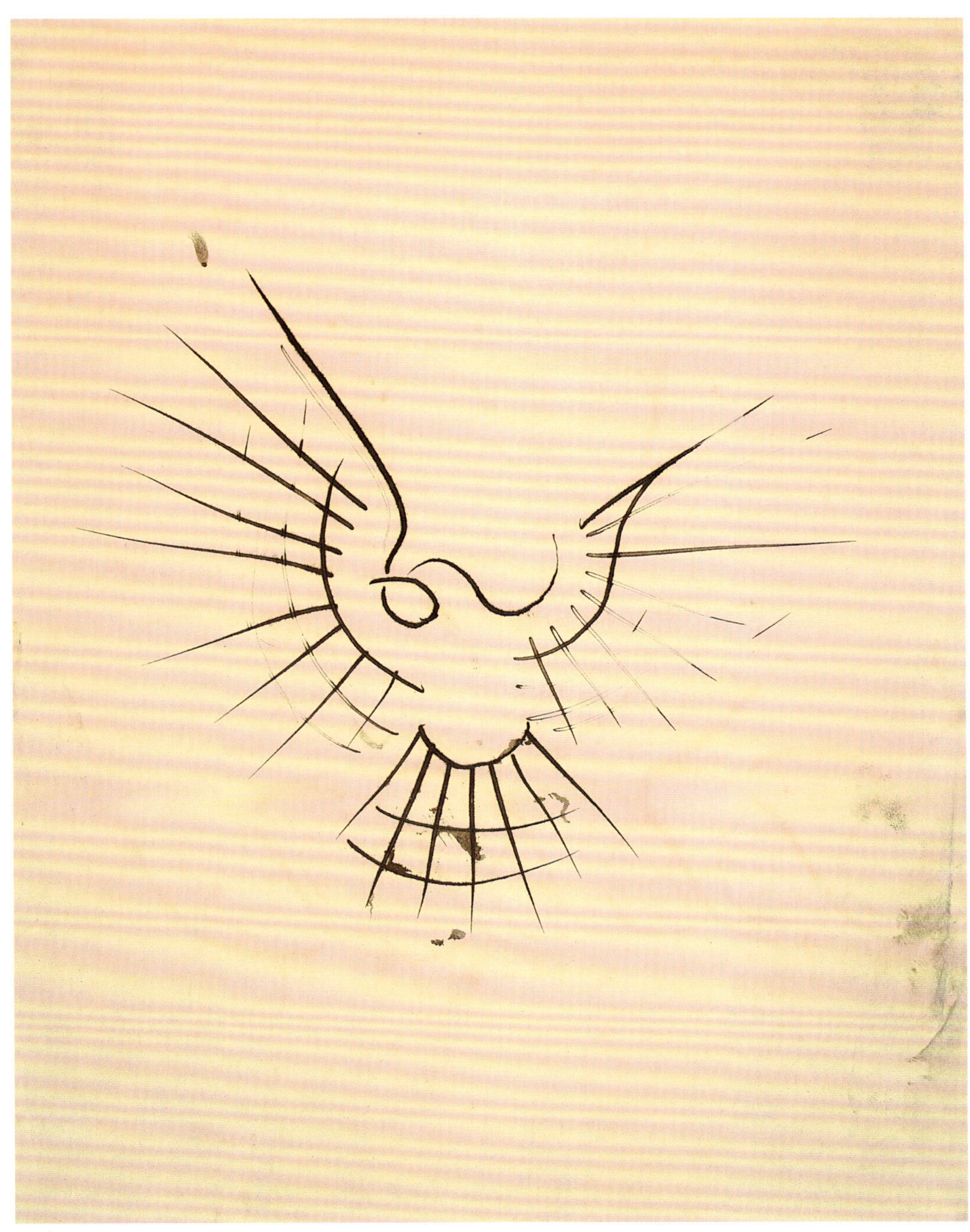

Tern, ca. 1942

Ink on paper, 11 x 8½ in.
Walter Anderson Museum of Art, 91.4.1
Gift of The Family of Walter Anderson in memory of Sandy Ashley
This is suggestive of an archetypal bird rather than a specific one; Anderson often reduced a subject to a few lines to capture its essence.

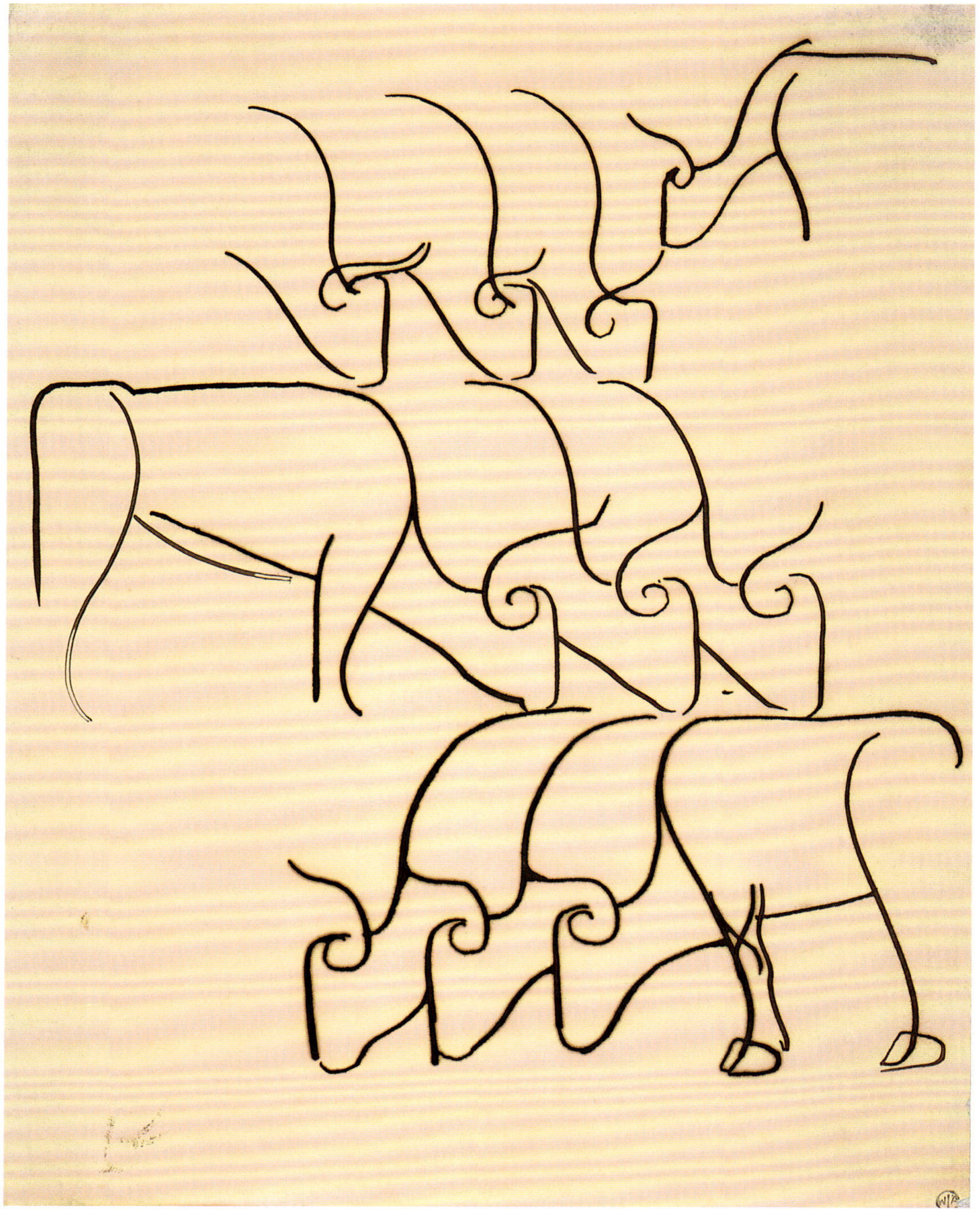

Cows, ca. 1942

Ink on paper, 11 x 8½ in.
The Family of Walter Anderson

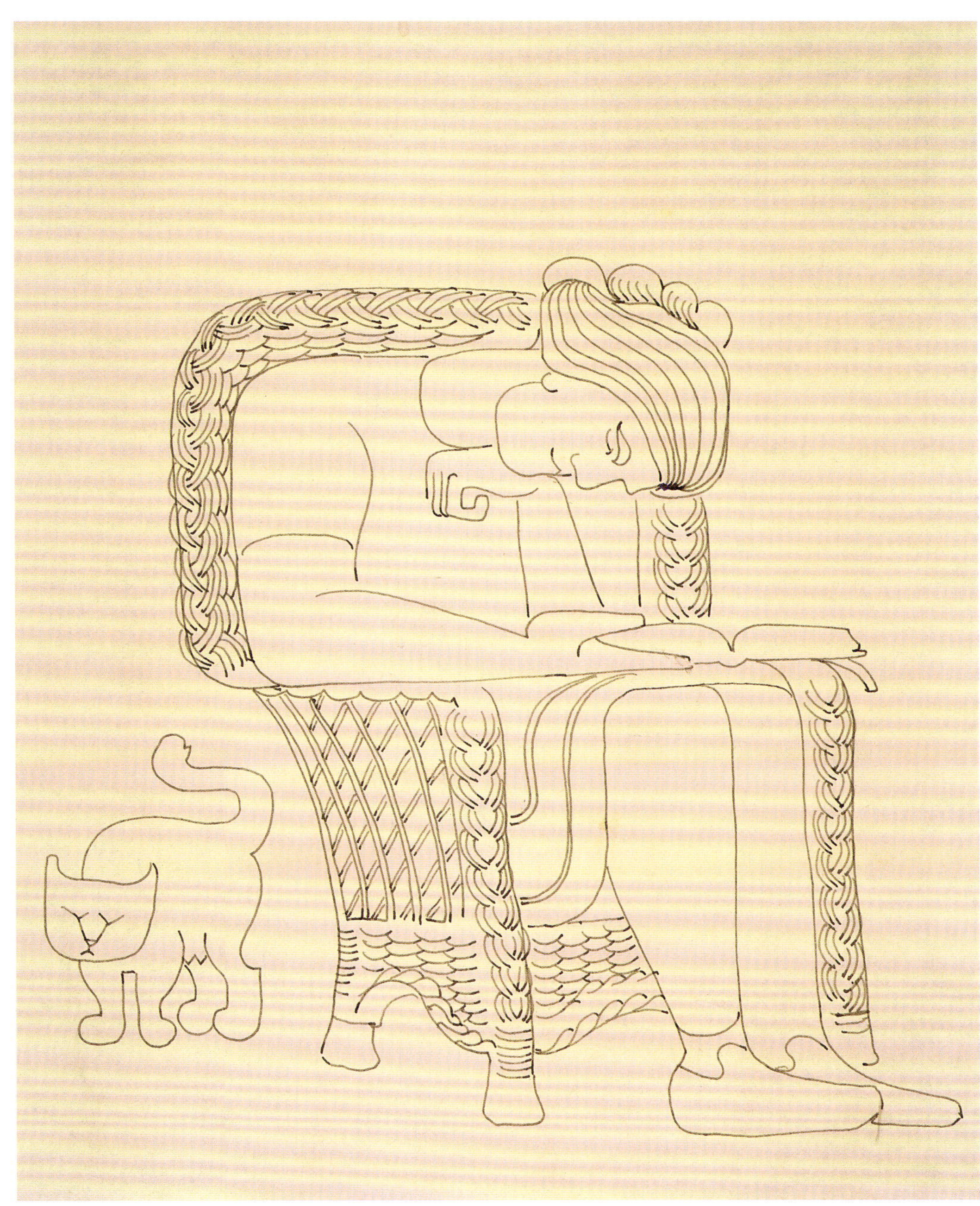

Sissy Reading, ca. 1942

Pencil on paper, 11 x 8½ in.
The Family of Walter Anderson
The bent composition recalls similar designs in German Expressionism.

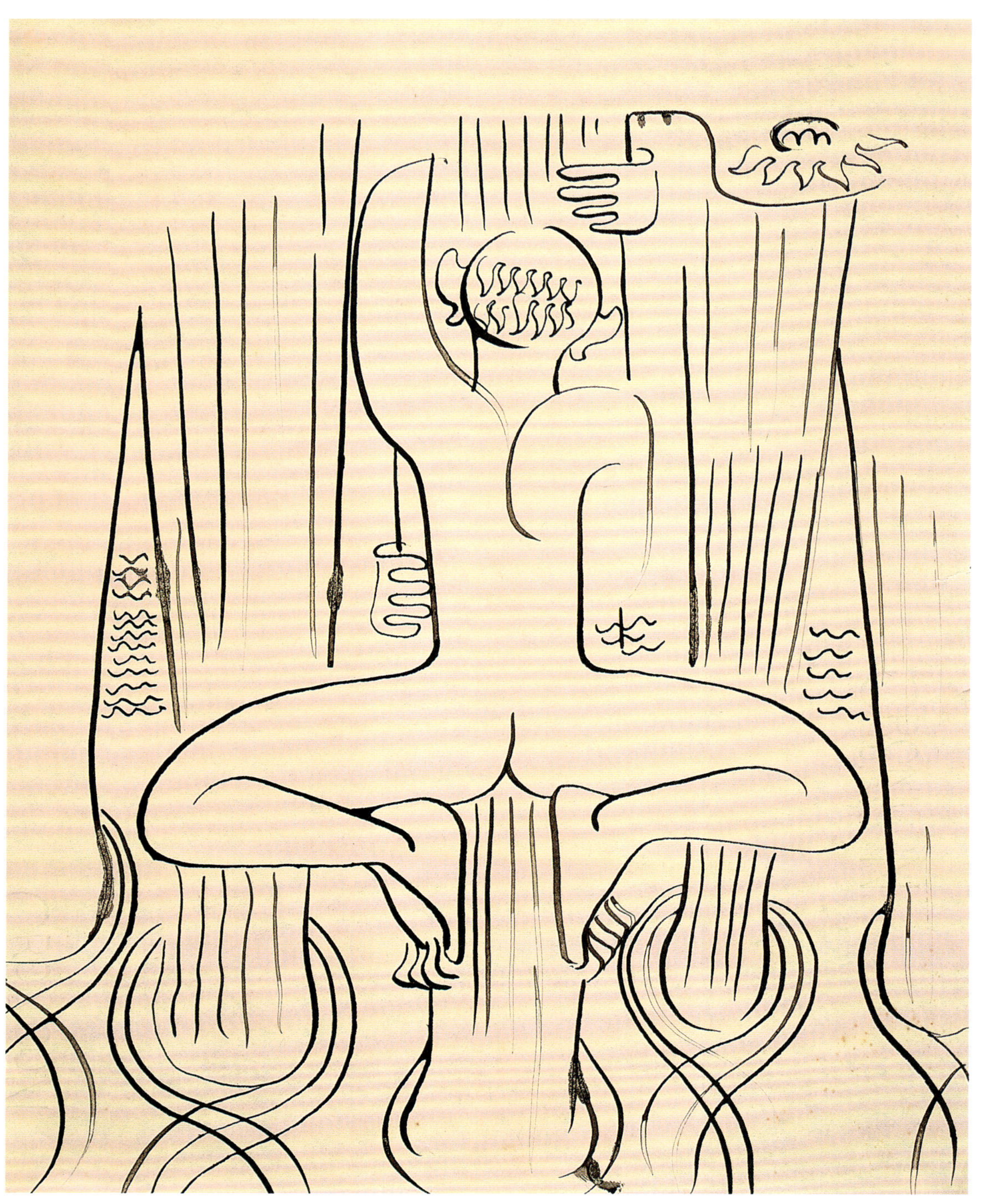

Finding a Nest, ca. 1942

Ink on paper, 11 x 8½ in.
The Family of Walter Anderson

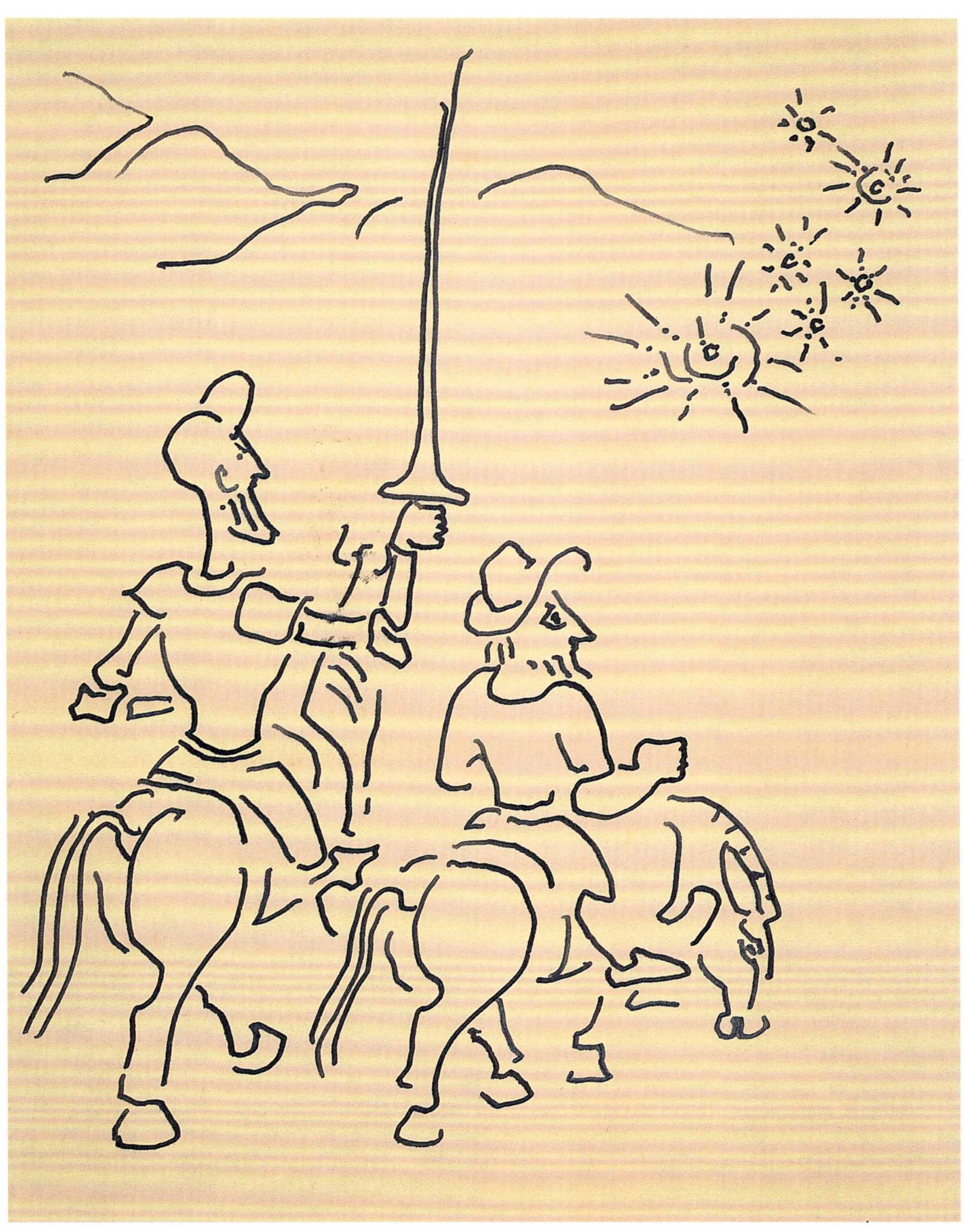

Don Quixote and Sancho Panza, ca. 1941

Ink on paper, 11 x 8½ in.
The Family of Walter Anderson
One of more than two thousand ink drawings referring to Anderson's favorite book. Around 1940, Anderson began to study Spanish so that he could read Miguel de Cervantes's novel in the original and also translate a history of art—*Summa Artis*—by the Spaniard José Pijoan.

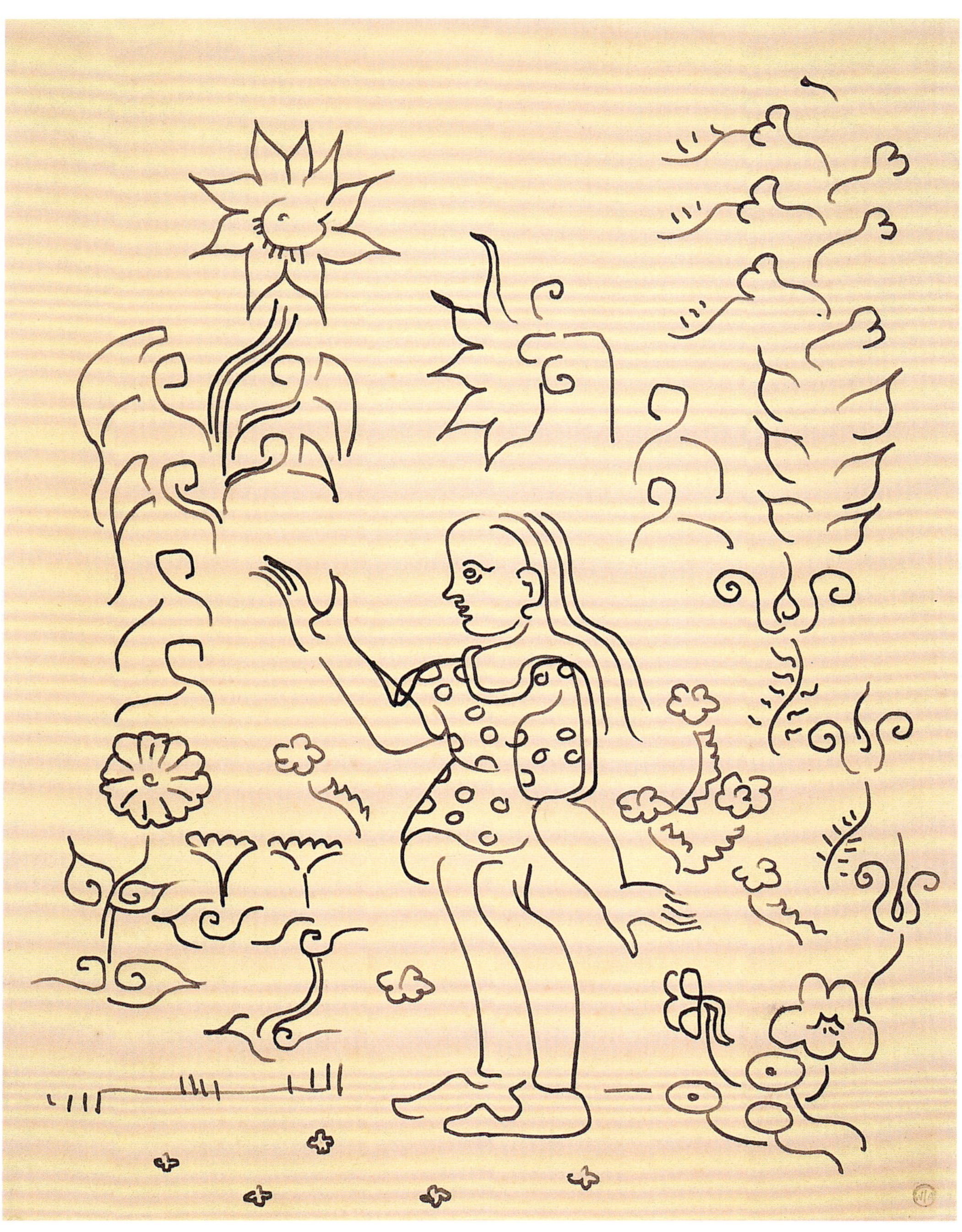

Alice in a Garden, ca. 1941

Ink on paper, 11 x 8½ in.
The Family of Walter Anderson
One of a hundred drawings illustrating *Alice in Wonderland*. The flowers were those found in his own garden and in the woods at Oldfields.

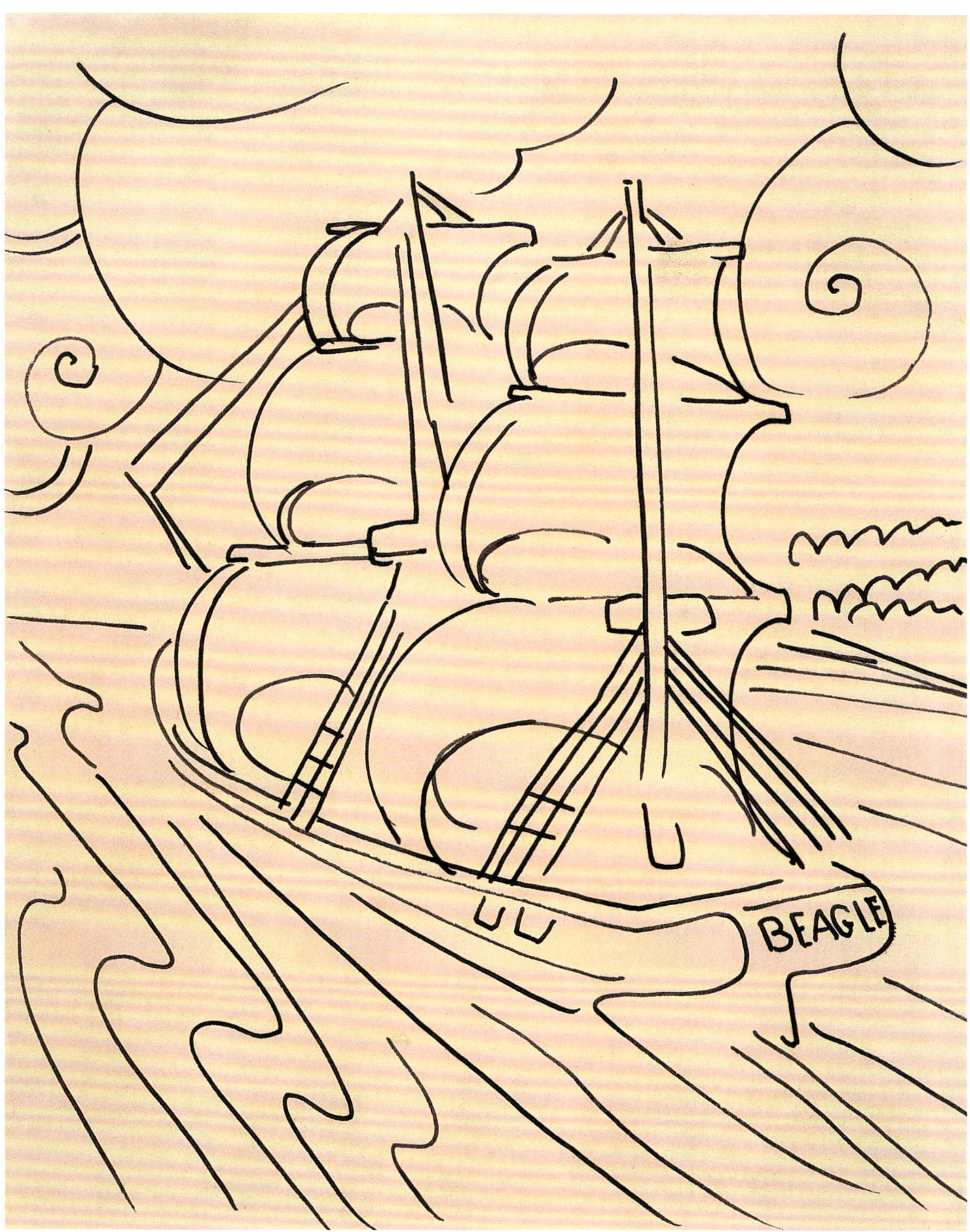

The Beagle, ca. 1941

Ink on paper, 11 x 8½ in.
The Family of Walter Anderson
Anderson did 740 drawings related to *The Voyage of the Beagle* by Charles Darwin.

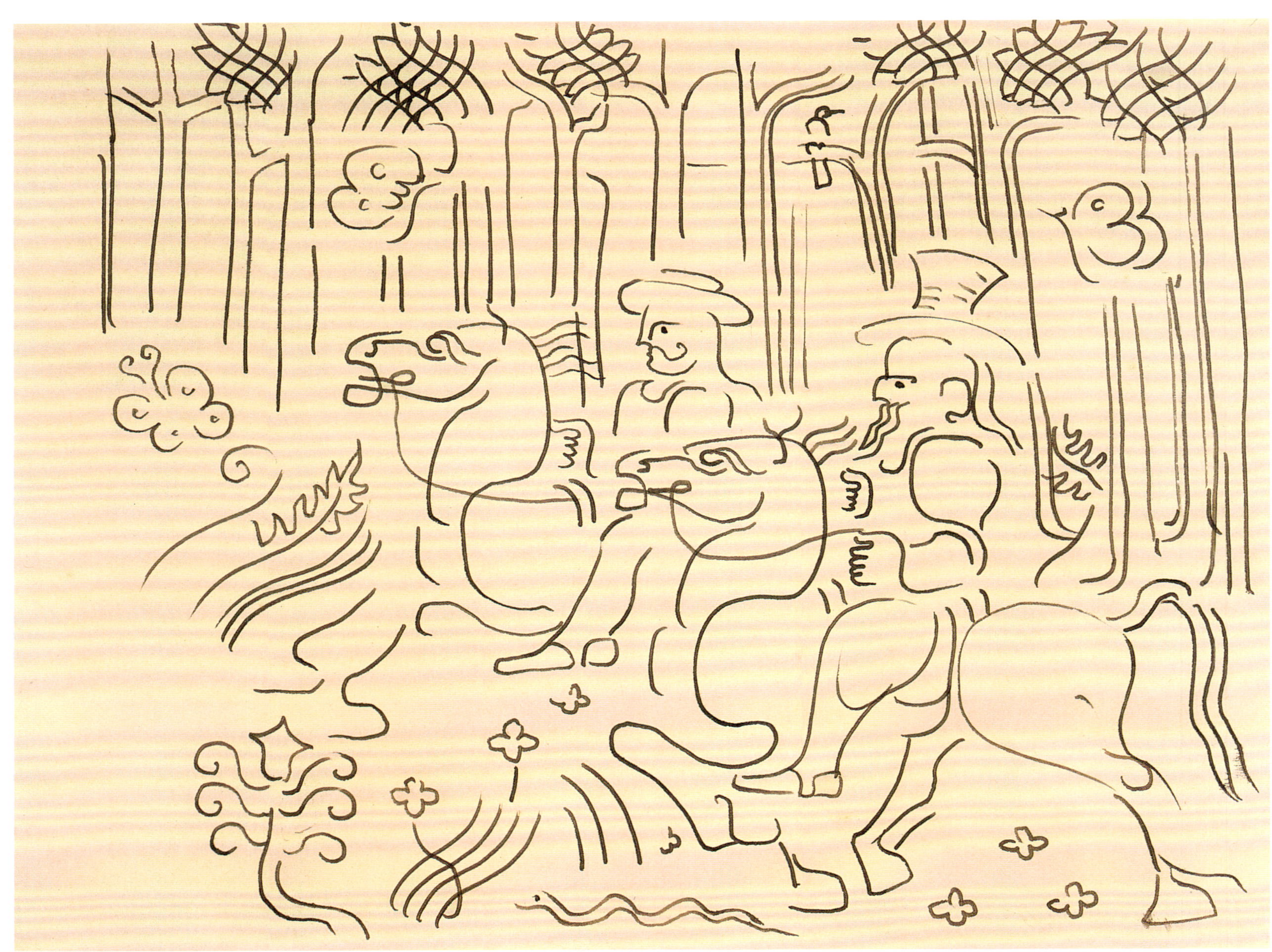

Darwin and Companion, ca. 1941

Ink on paper, 8½ x 11 in.
The Family of Walter Anderson

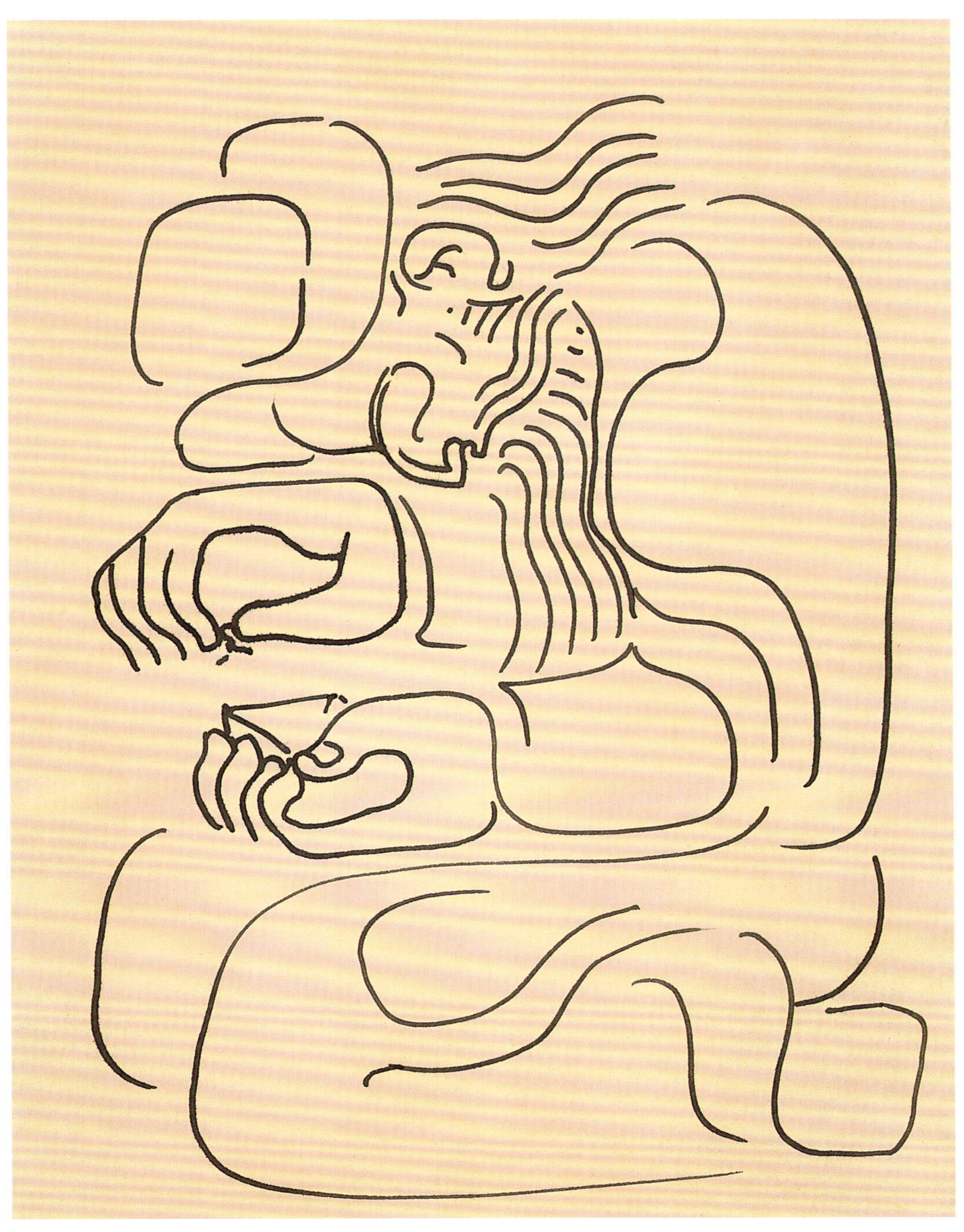

Darwin Entomologizing in the Galapagos, ca. 1941

Ink on paper, 11 x 8½ in.
The Family of Walter Anderson

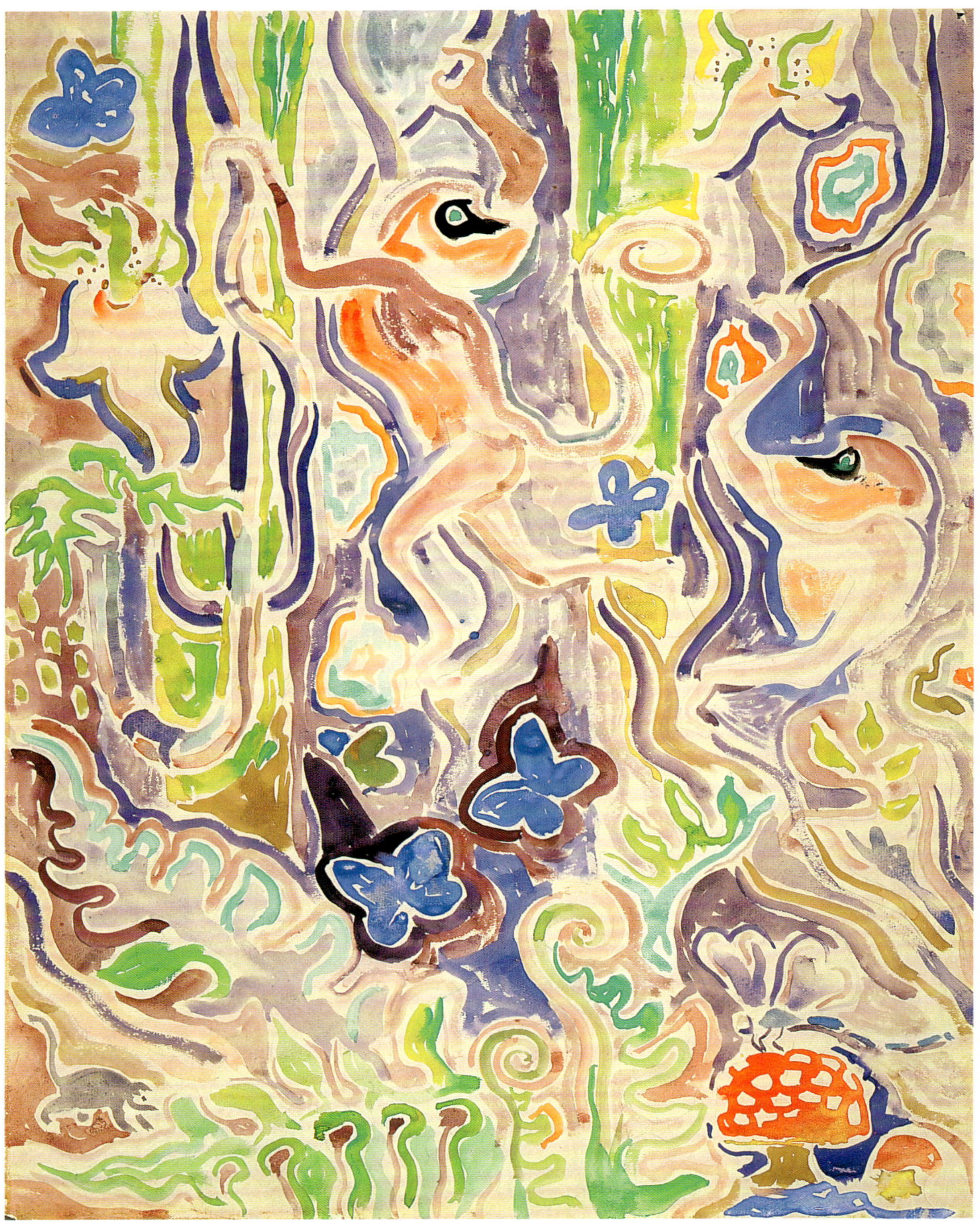

The Darwinian Jungle, 1945

Watercolor on paper, 25 x 19 in.
The Family of Walter Anderson

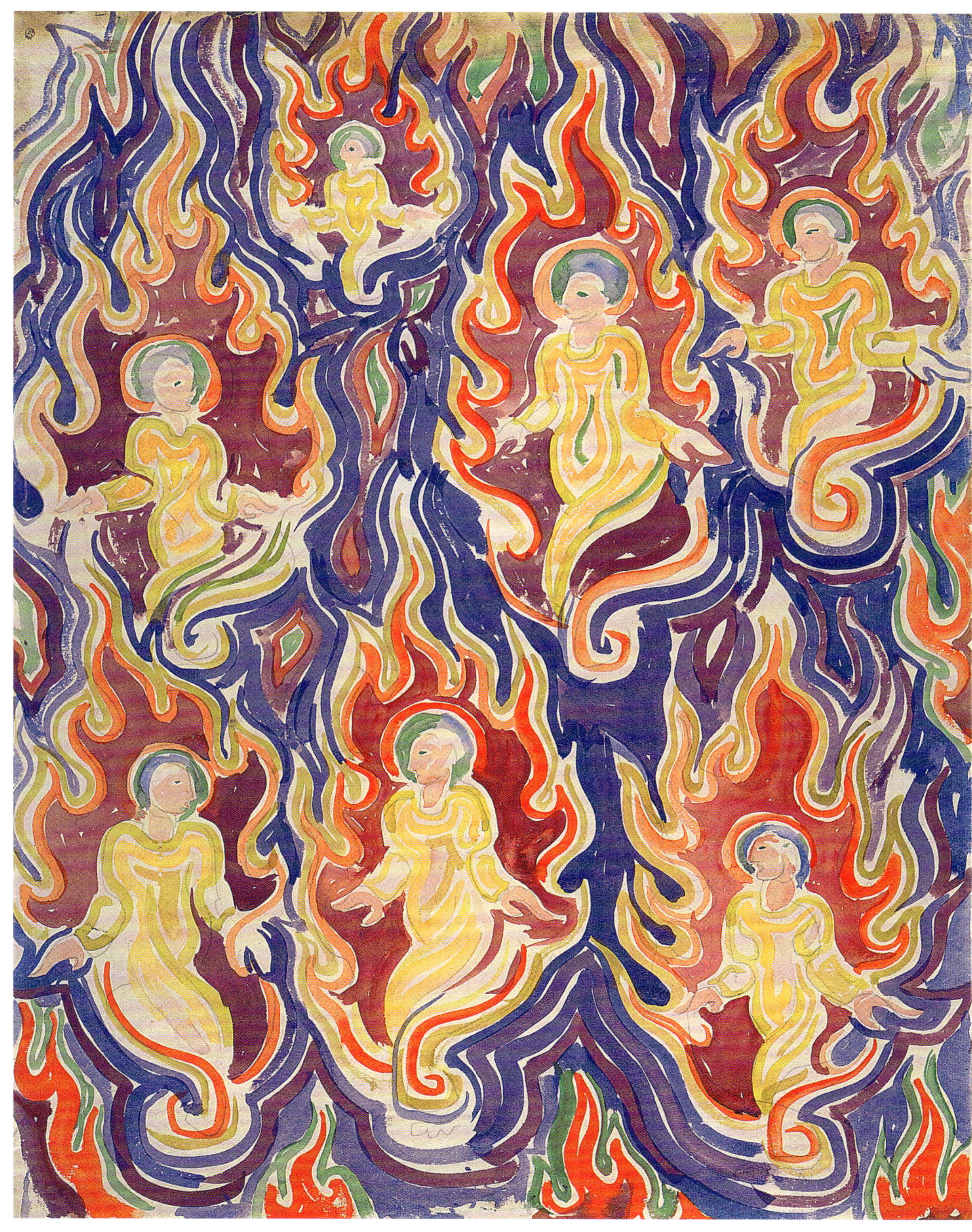

Flaming Angels, ca. 1945

Watercolor on paper, 25 x 19 in.
Walter Anderson Museum of Art, 96.1.1
Gift of The Family of Walter Anderson in memory of Amelia Grinstead Stebly
Anderson used watercolor, ink, and crayon in a series of illustrations for Milton's *Paradise Lost*.

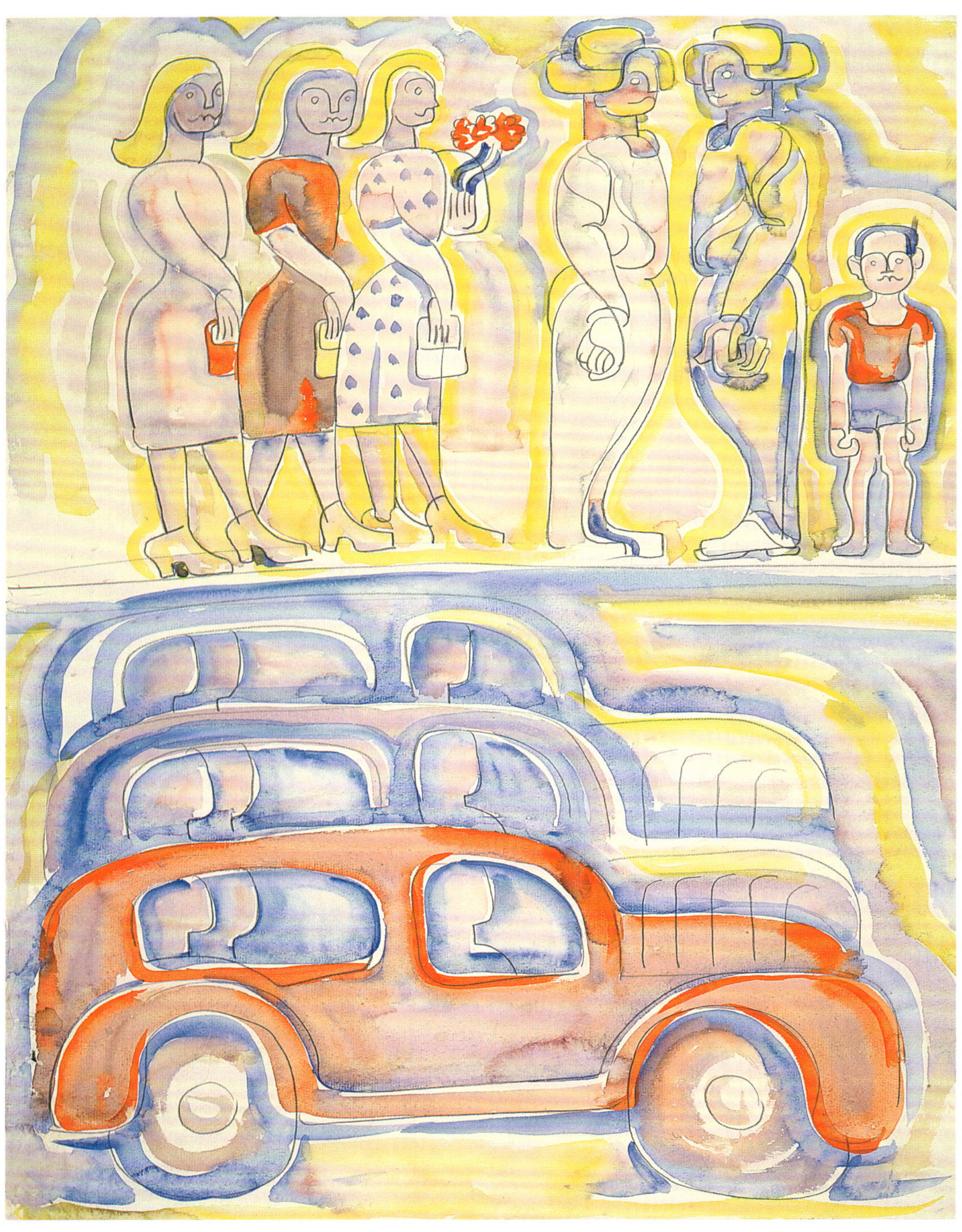

People and Cars, 1943

Watercolor on paper, 25 x 19 in.
Walter Anderson Museum of Art, 84.5.1
Anderson's trips to New Orleans in 1943 resulted in many ink drawings, which were later made into watercolors back at Oldfields.

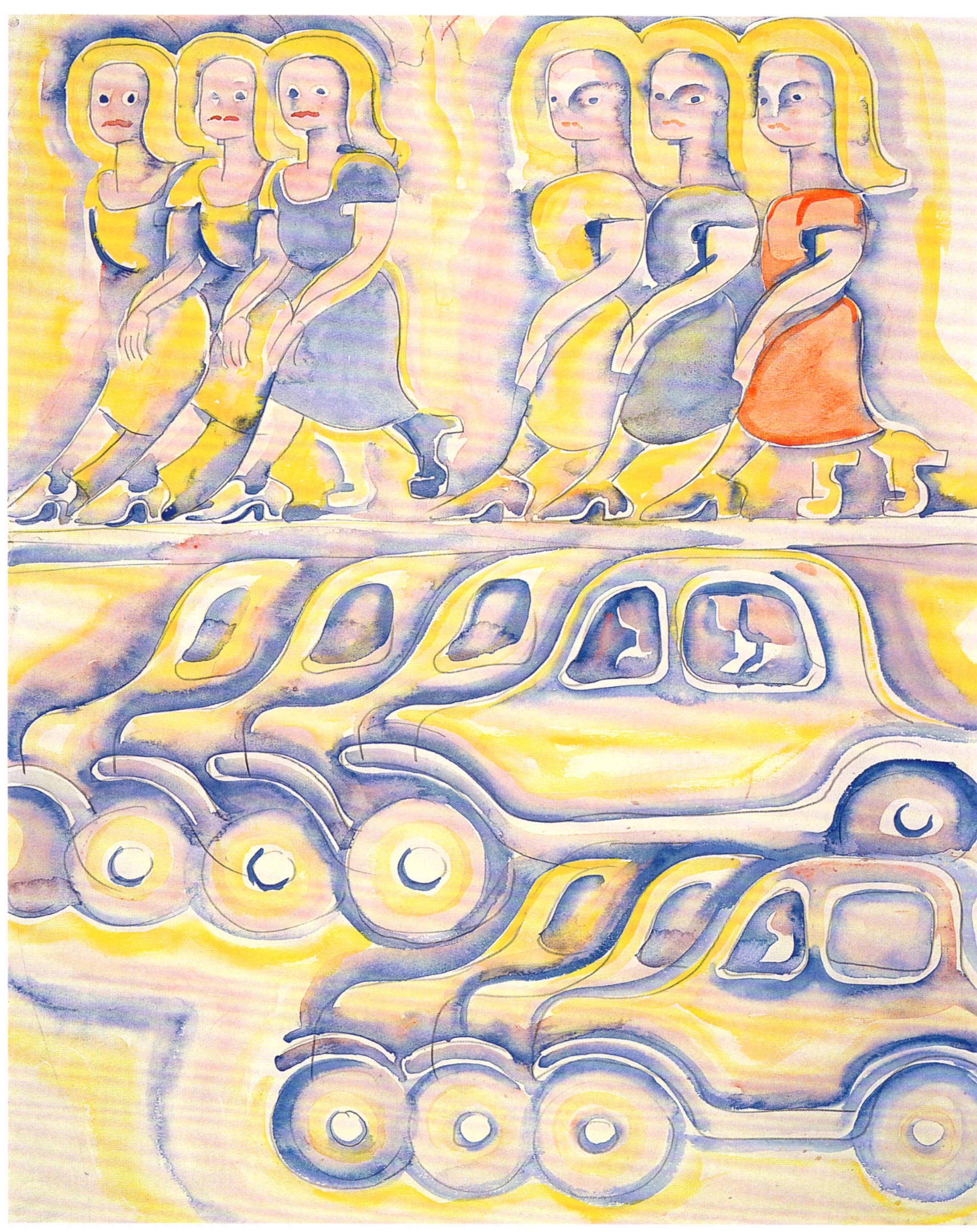

Woman and Cars, 1943

Watercolor on paper, 25 x 19 in.
Walter Anderson Museum of Art, 84.5.2

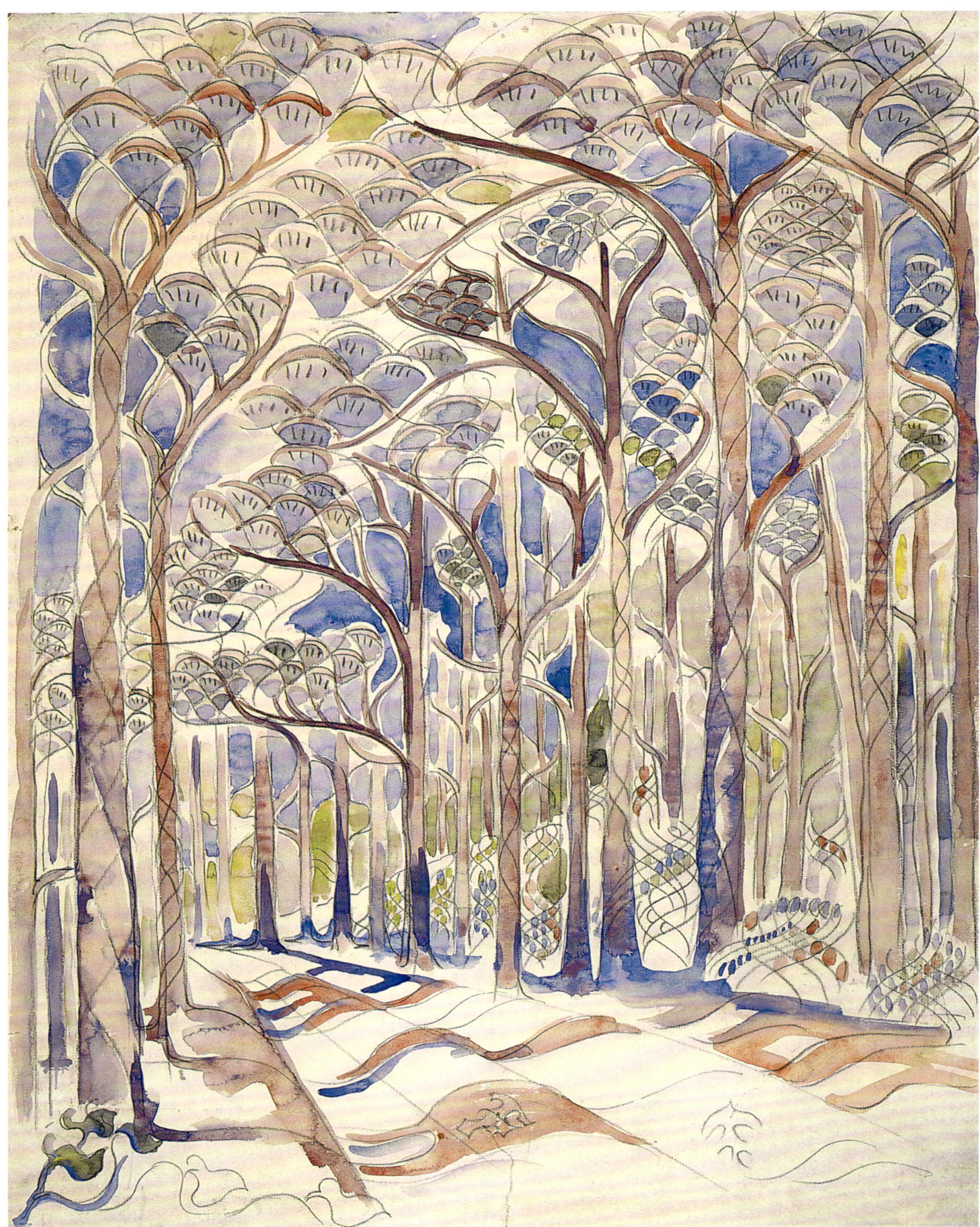

Road to Oldfields, ca. 1943

Watercolor on paper, 25 x 19 in.
Walter Anderson Museum of Art, 89.3.1
Anderson made several drawings and watercolors of the long road leading from the paved county highway to the plantation home.

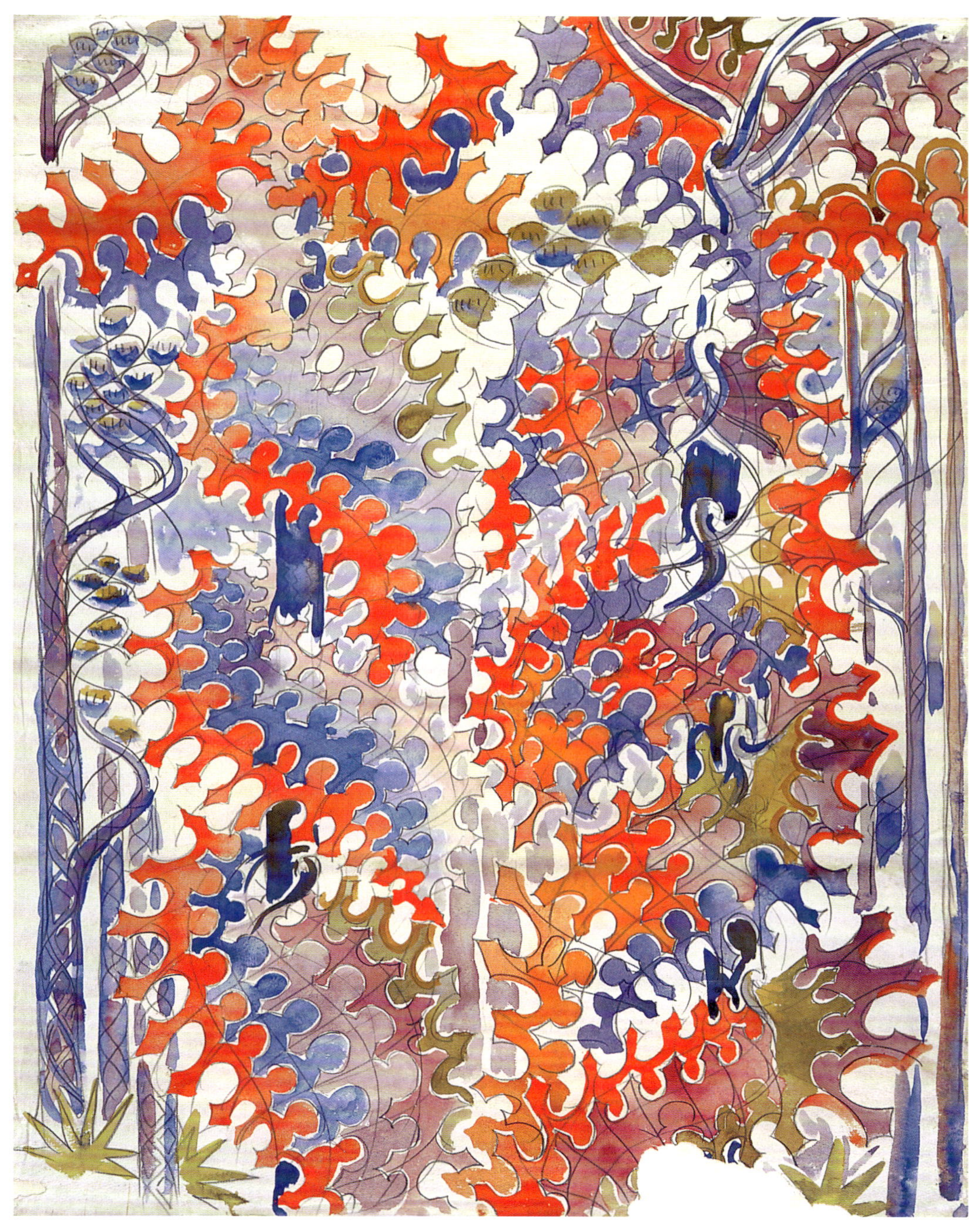

Fall Woods, ca. 1943

Watercolor on paper, 25 x 19 in.
Walter Anderson Museum of Art, 97.2.1

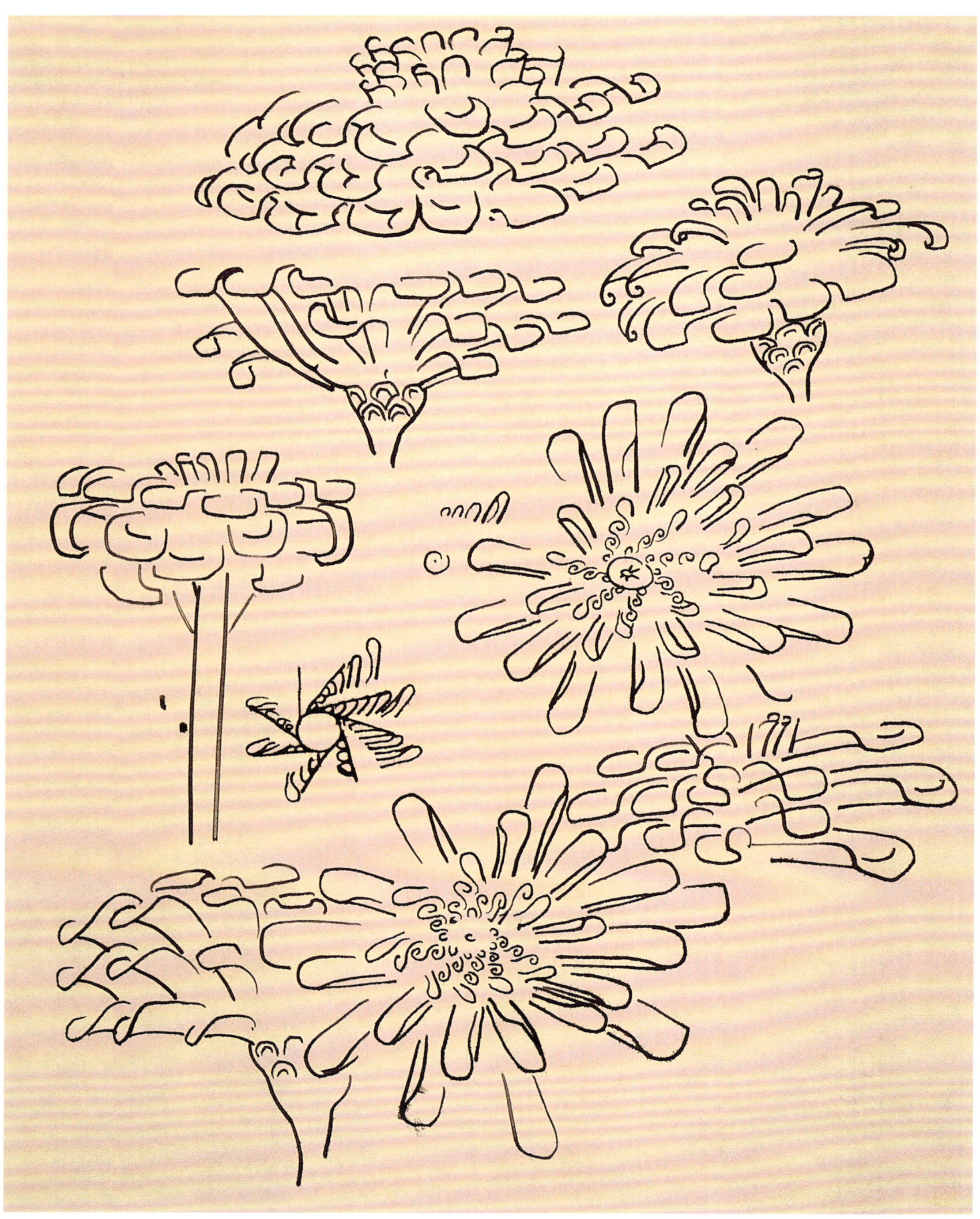

Zinnia, ca. 1943

Ink on paper, 11 x 8½ in.
Walter Anderson Museum of Art, 92.1.2

Oh, Zinnias,
Most explosive and illuminating
Of flowers,
Summation of all flowers,
Essence of excentric form
Essence of concentric form!
—Walter Anderson

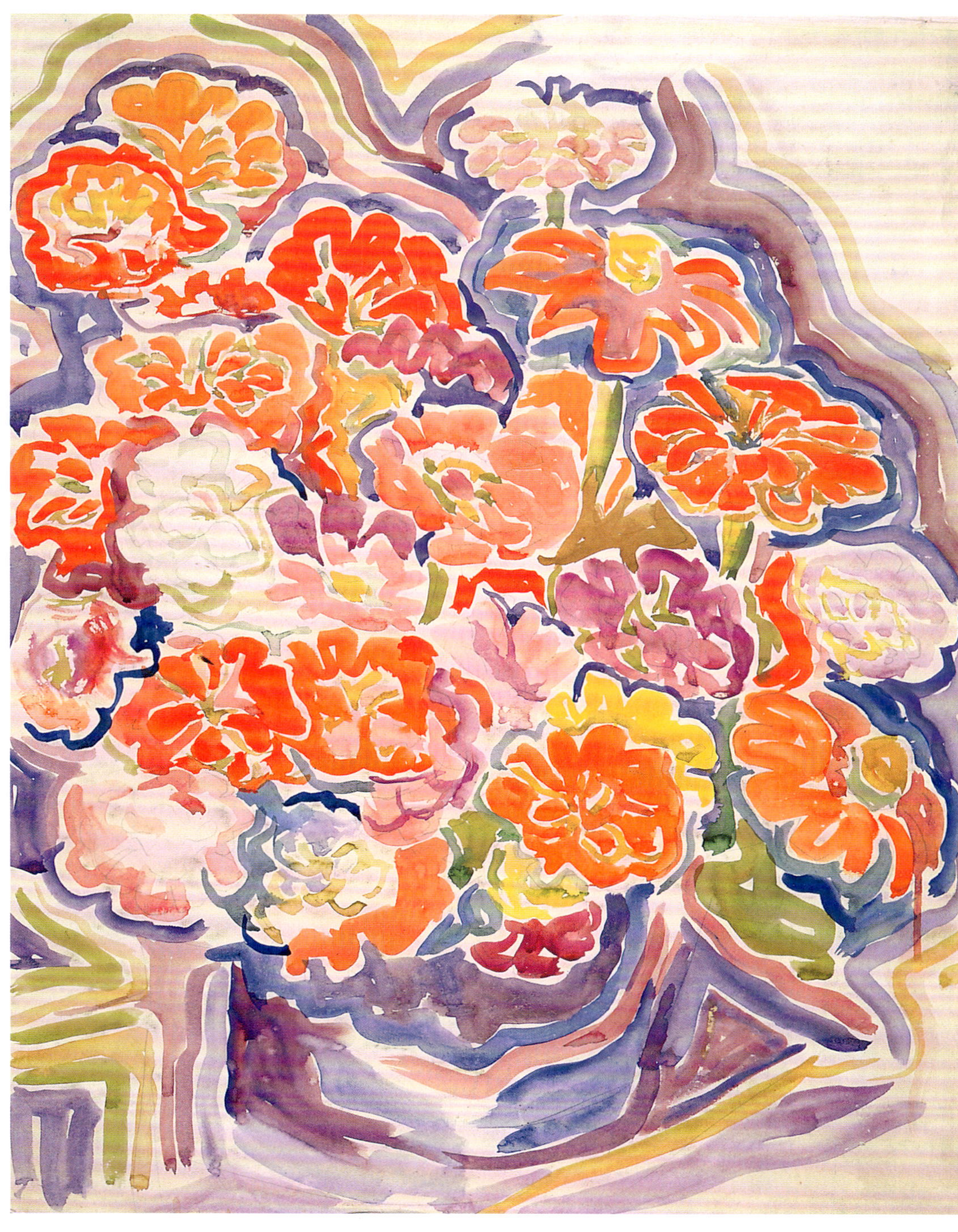

Zinnias, ca. 1945

Watercolor on paper, 25 x 19 in.
The Family of Walter Anderson

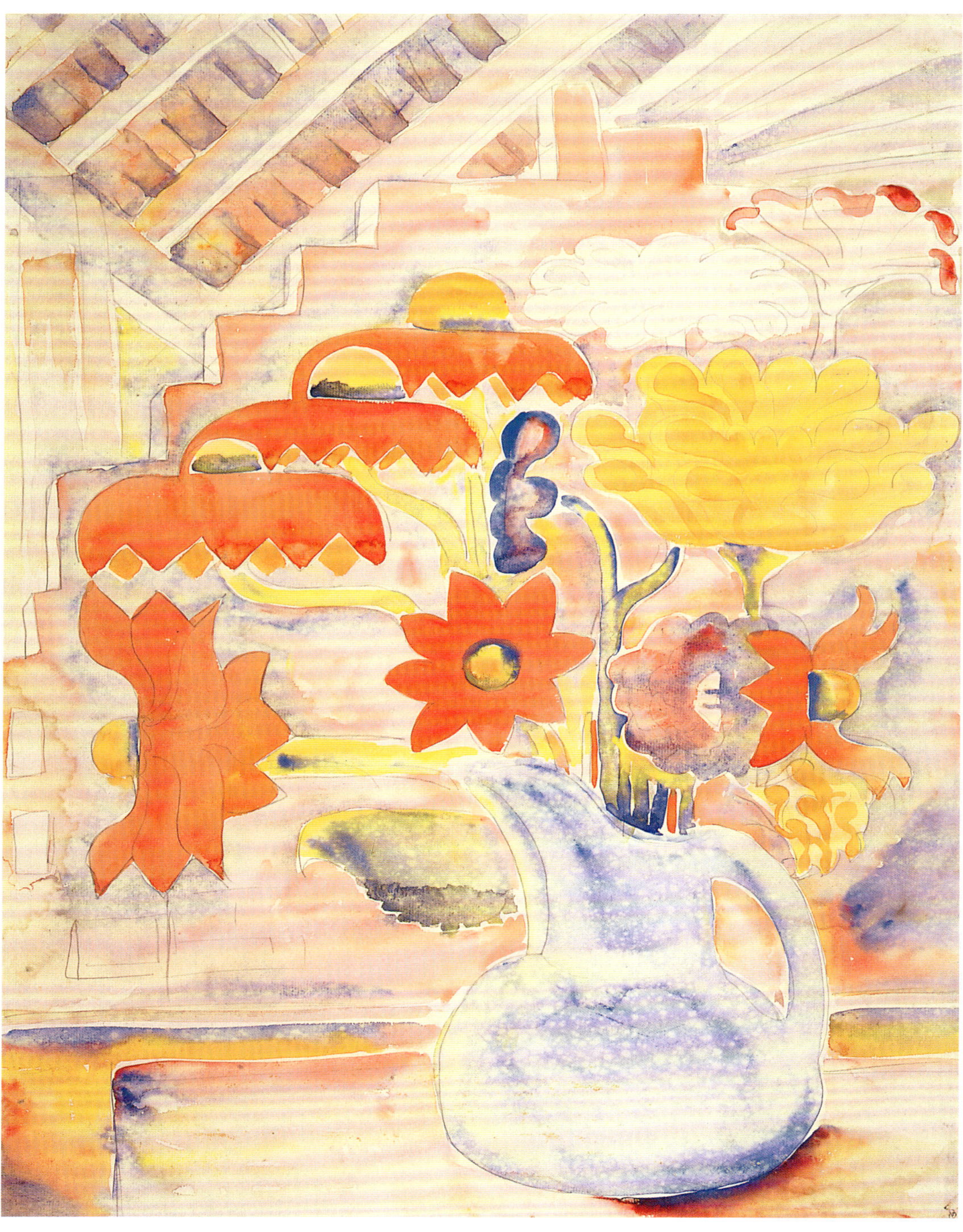

Zinnias and Tithonias, 1945

Watercolor on paper, 25 x 19 in.
The Family of Walter Anderson
Zinnias and tithonias in a Shearwater vase painted in the attic at Oldfields. Note the pre-Columbian pyramid effect of the chimney masonry. Anderson read about early Indian civilizations in Central and South America and discussed them with Tulane archaeologist Franz Blom.

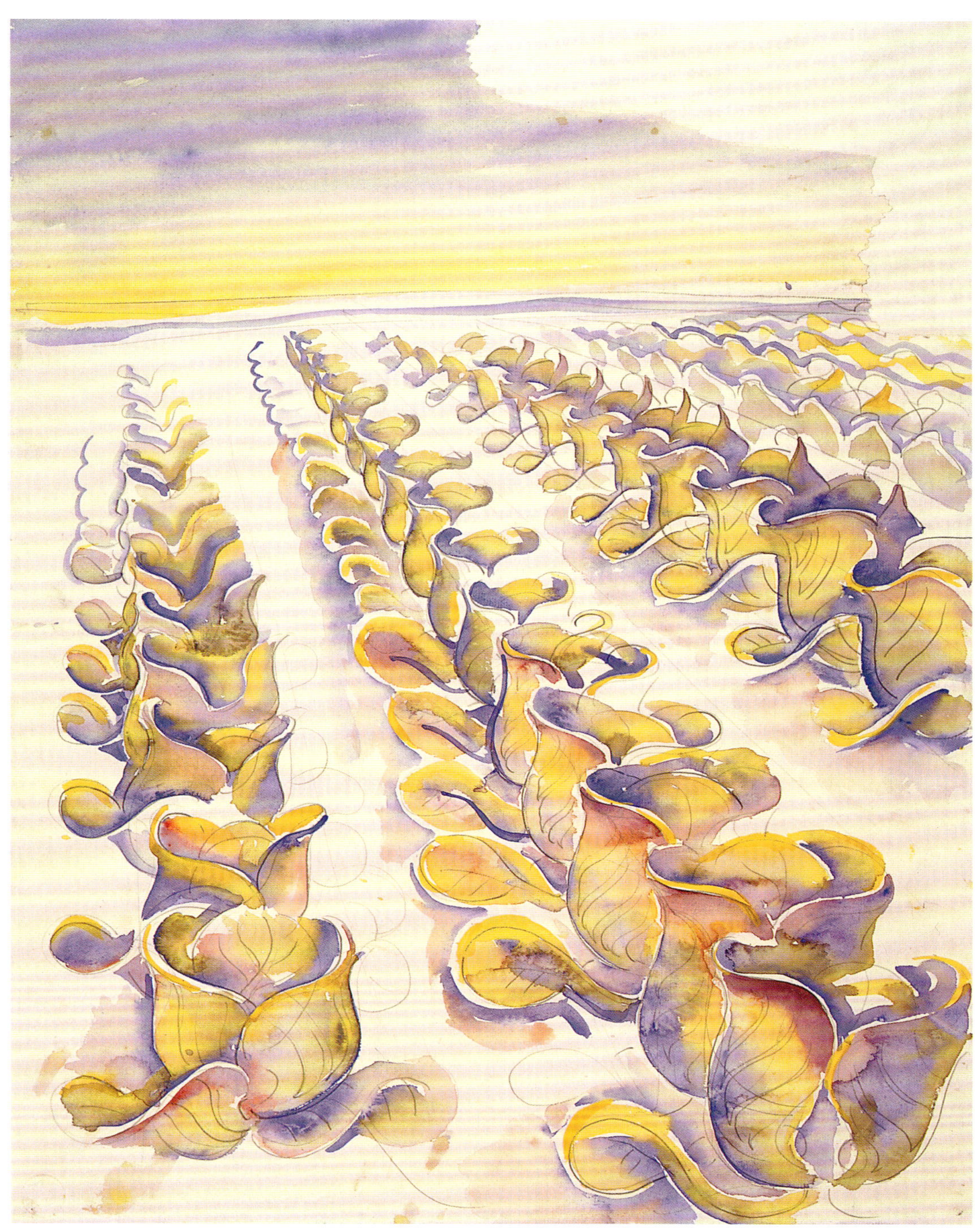

Cabbage Rows, 1943

Watercolor on paper, 25 x 19 in.
The Family of Walter Anderson

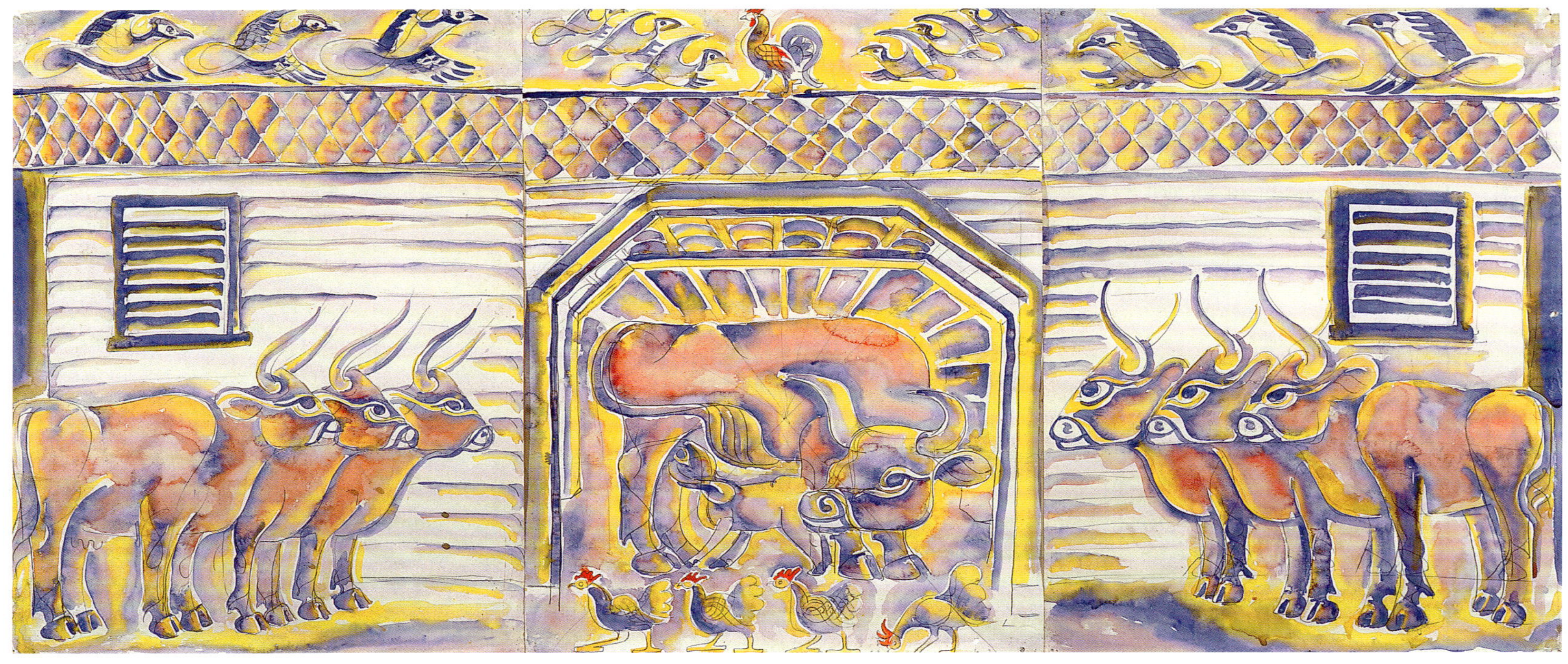

Barnyard Nativity, 1943

Watercolor on paper, 3 separate sheets, each 25 x 19 in.
The Family of Walter Anderson

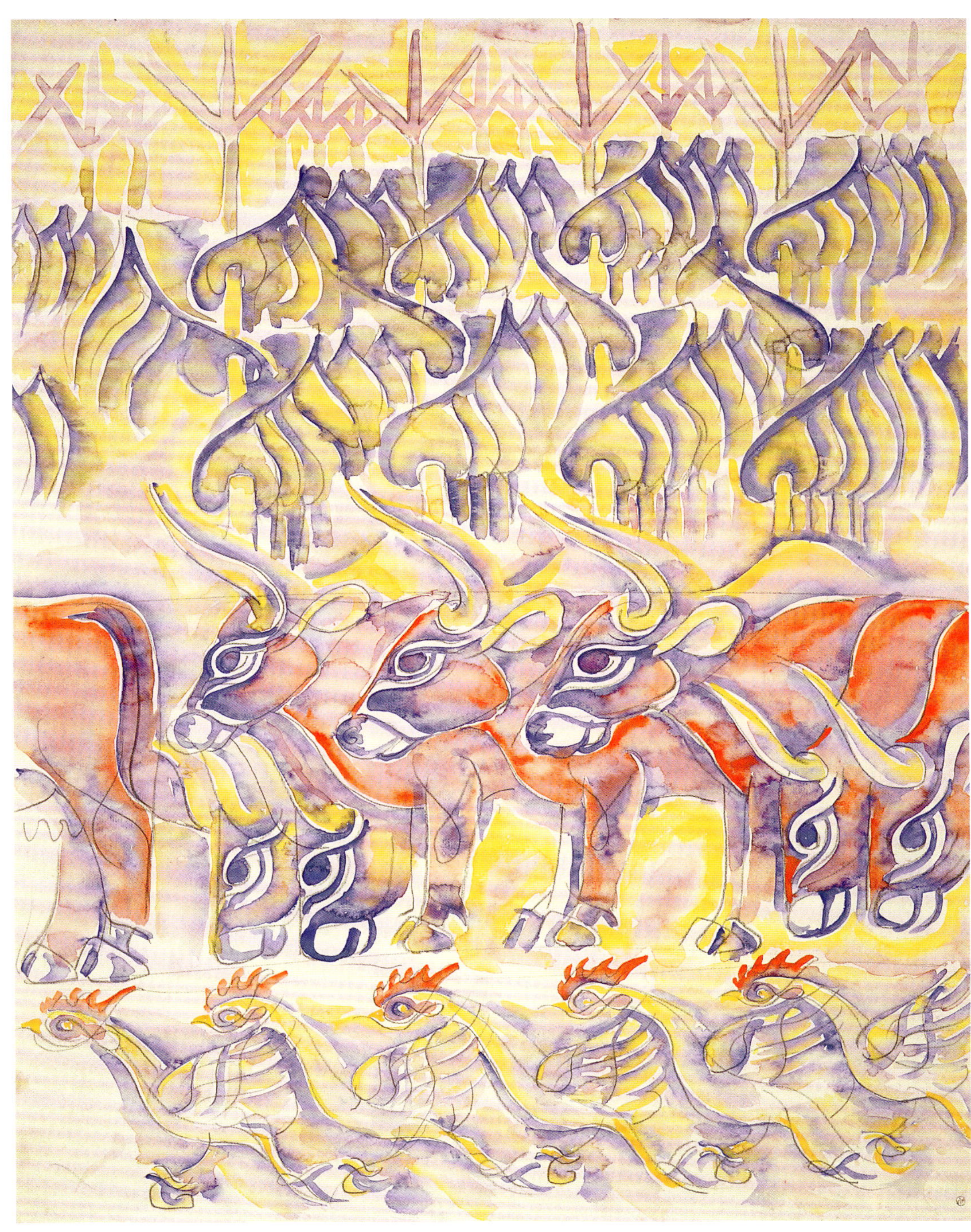

Chickens, Cows and Cornrows, 1943

Watercolor on paper, 25 x 19 in.
The Family of Walter Anderson

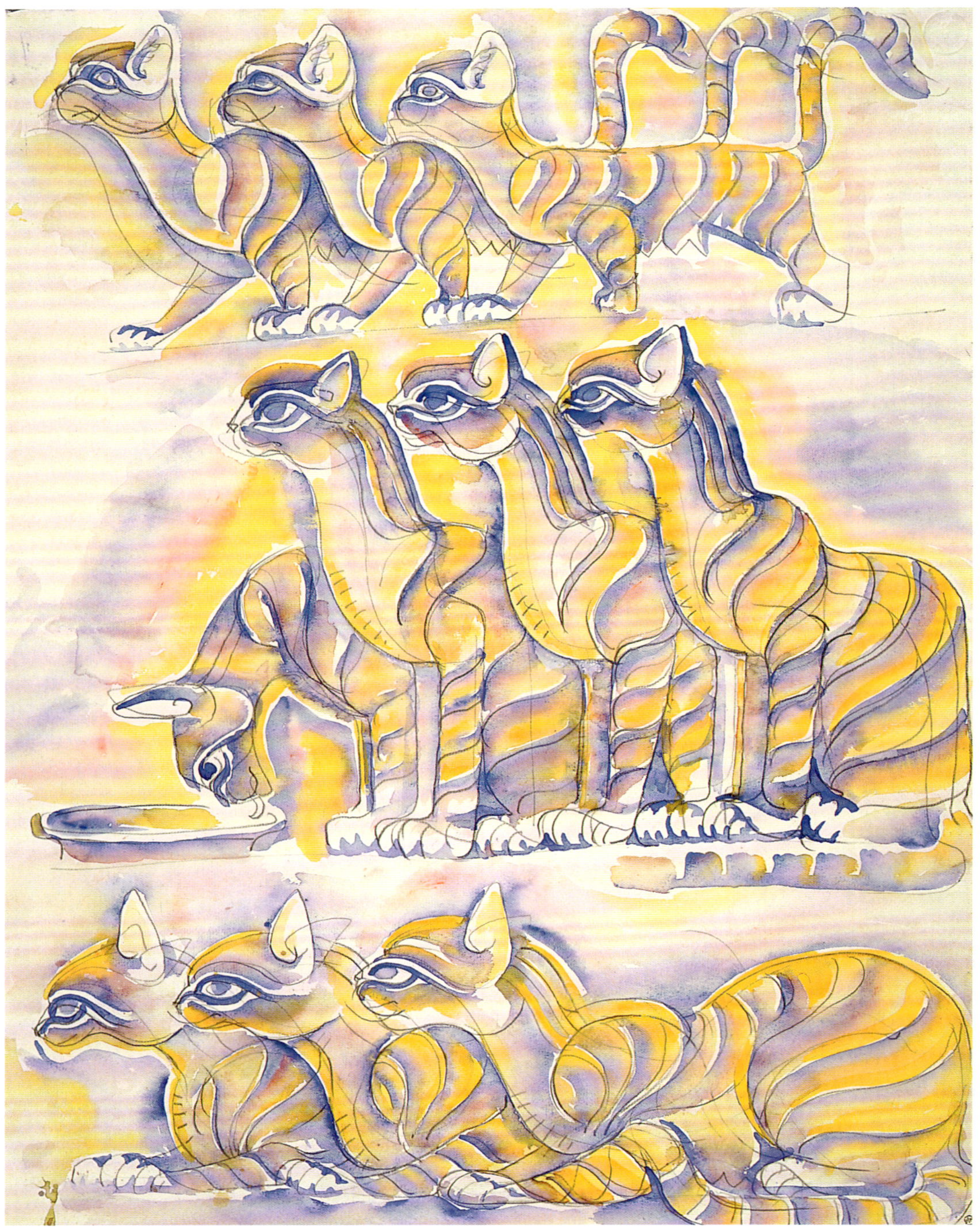

Cats, 1943

Watercolor on paper, 25 x 19 in.
The Family of Walter Anderson

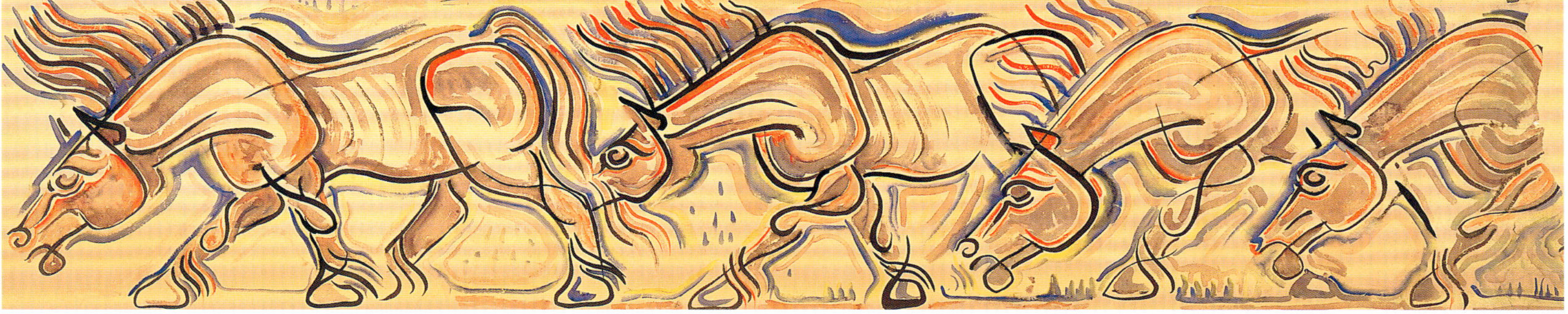

Four Horses, 1945

Watercolor on paper, 19 x 102 in.
Walter Anderson Museum of Art, 02.1.5
One of the watercolor paintings done on the back of wallpaper and found in 1987 in an old trunk at Shearwater Pottery; they were done at the same time as the large linoleum block prints.

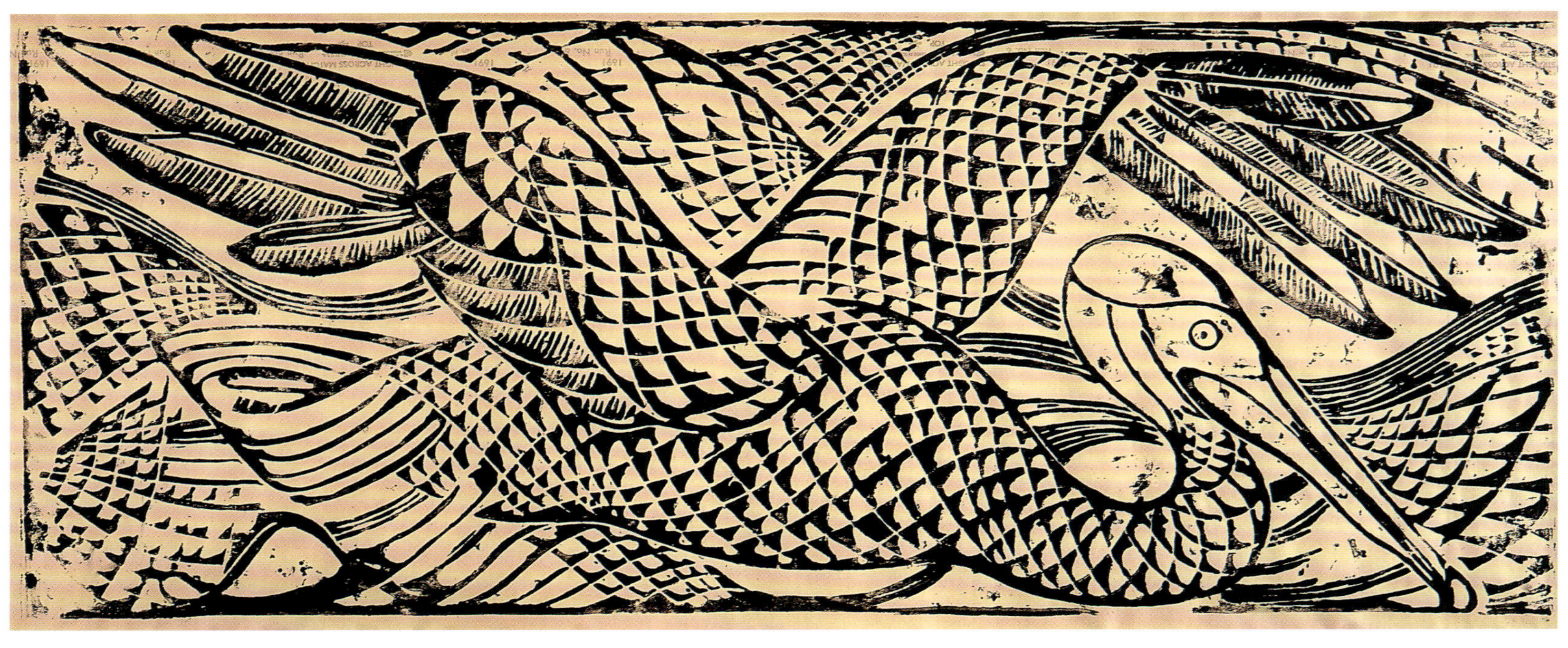

Horizontal Pelican, 1945

Linocut on paper, 21 x 61 in.
Walter Anderson Museum of Art, 94.1.1
Gift of Mr. and Mrs. Dick Schumacher

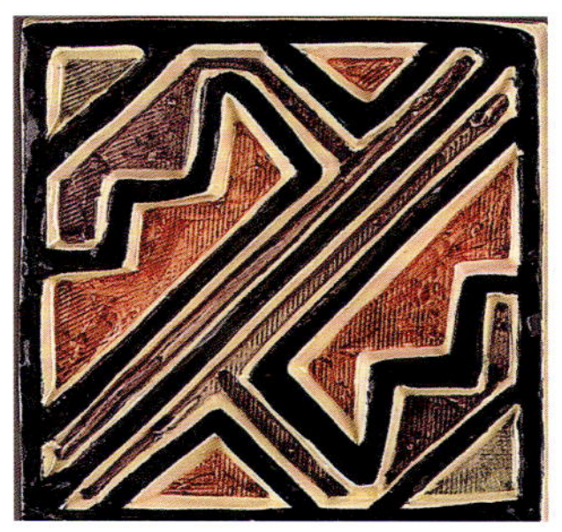

LINOLEUM BLOCK PRINTS AND TRAVEL: 1945–1950

Transforming the Oldfields attic into a studio, Anderson bought rolls of surplus linoleum and wallpaper and made huge prints, most of them twenty inches wide and six feet long, but some twelve feet. He hoped these prints—he called the horizontal ones "overmantels" and the vertical ones "scrolls"—would provide inexpensive art to ordinary people, especially for their children's rooms, replacing the mass-produced pieces that one could find at the local five-and-ten. Over three hundred large-scale prints were produced from 1945 to 1949, the first body of oversized prints made by an American artist. Their subjects were drawn from phenomena typical of the coast: birds and animals, pine trees and pelicans, the clouds and waves of the Mississippi Sound.

By the end of 1945, in hopes of finding a "common language of forms" for modern art, he began working on fairy tales—first in large tempera paintings, and then in a series of huge linoleum block prints based on fairy tales from around the world. He used a pipe filled with sand to press the paper onto the inked design, and colored them by hand, working so rapidly that he did not pause to print one block before carving the next. When the fairy-tale block prints were exhibited at the Brooklyn Museum in 1949, he wrote to the curator that they were offered as "an alternative to the atom bomb, in a series of explosions so identified with the life of man that they stimulate without destroying." Many of the block prints were shown the following year—along with watercolors and woodcarvings—in a traveling exhibition sponsored by the American Association of University Women, which opened at the Brooks Memorial Art Gallery in Memphis.

Rather than visit the Brooklyn Museum show, Anderson chose to travel to China, in hopes of seeing the murals of Tibet. In a logbook written on that trip, he describes endless waits in train stations, rickshaw rides, camping under the eaves of houses, and the loss of his passport, money, and possessions, stolen one night by a group of soldiers. He had flown to Hong Kong, made his way to Chongqing (Chungking) and then to Chengdu (still the entrance to Tibet from the east), and walked westward for two or three days before the incident forced him to return. In Hong Kong, as he waited for a new passport and a cable from his mother, he did watercolors of sea creatures—crabs and lobsters—which mark another new approach to color and texture.

In interesting logbooks, he recorded not only the China trip but also a trip to Costa Rica and long excursions by bicycle to draw the landscapes, flora, and fauna of Texas, Florida, North Carolina, and Tennessee; to see the paintings of one of his old teachers in Philadelphia; and to draw the city scenes of New Orleans. He camped in the open air or in some convenient shelter when it rained, and ate sporadically, enjoying his freedom and intimacy with nature. Travel and "writing up the log" were two constants of his life.

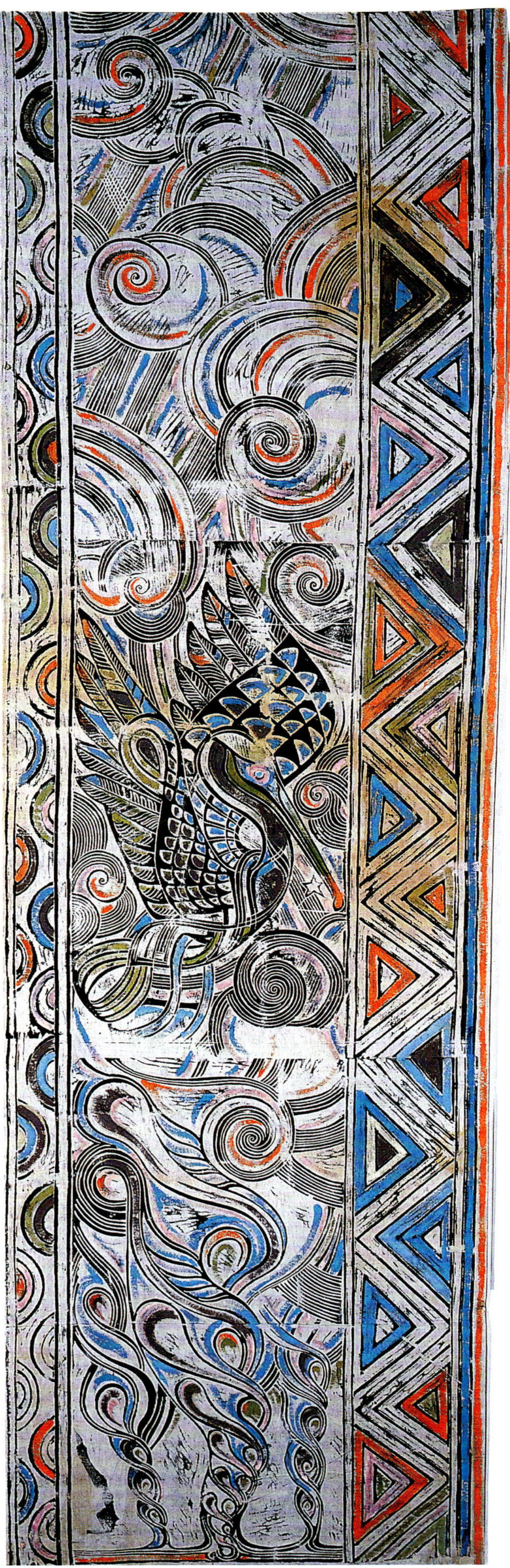

Clouds, Pelican and Waterspout, 1945

Linocut on fabric, 110 x 19 in.
The Family of Walter Anderson
Printed and painted by Walter Anderson

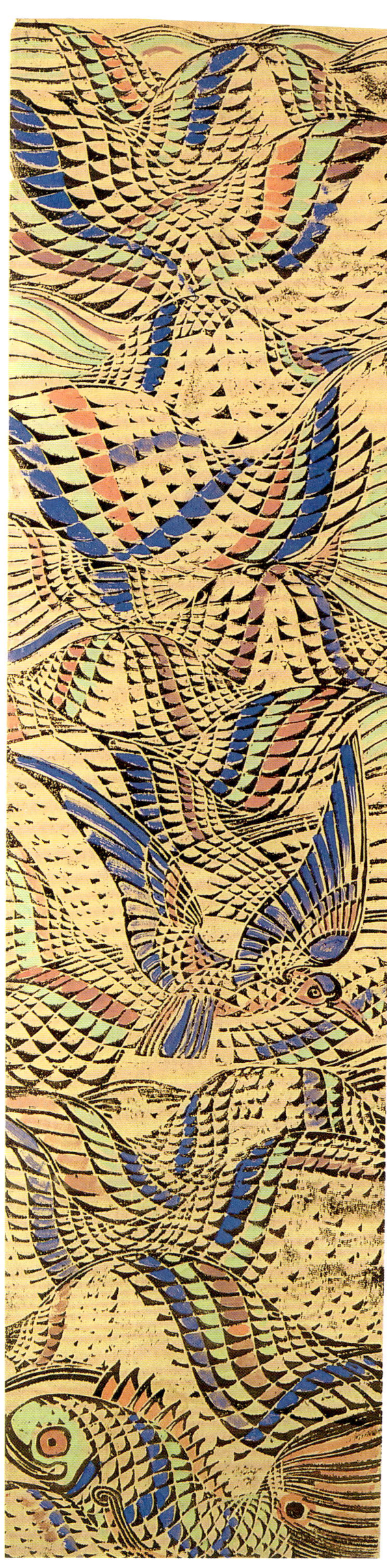

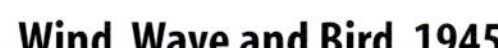

Wind, Wave and Bird, 1945

Linocut on paper, 76 x 18 in.
The Family of Walter Anderson
Printed and painted by Walter Anderson

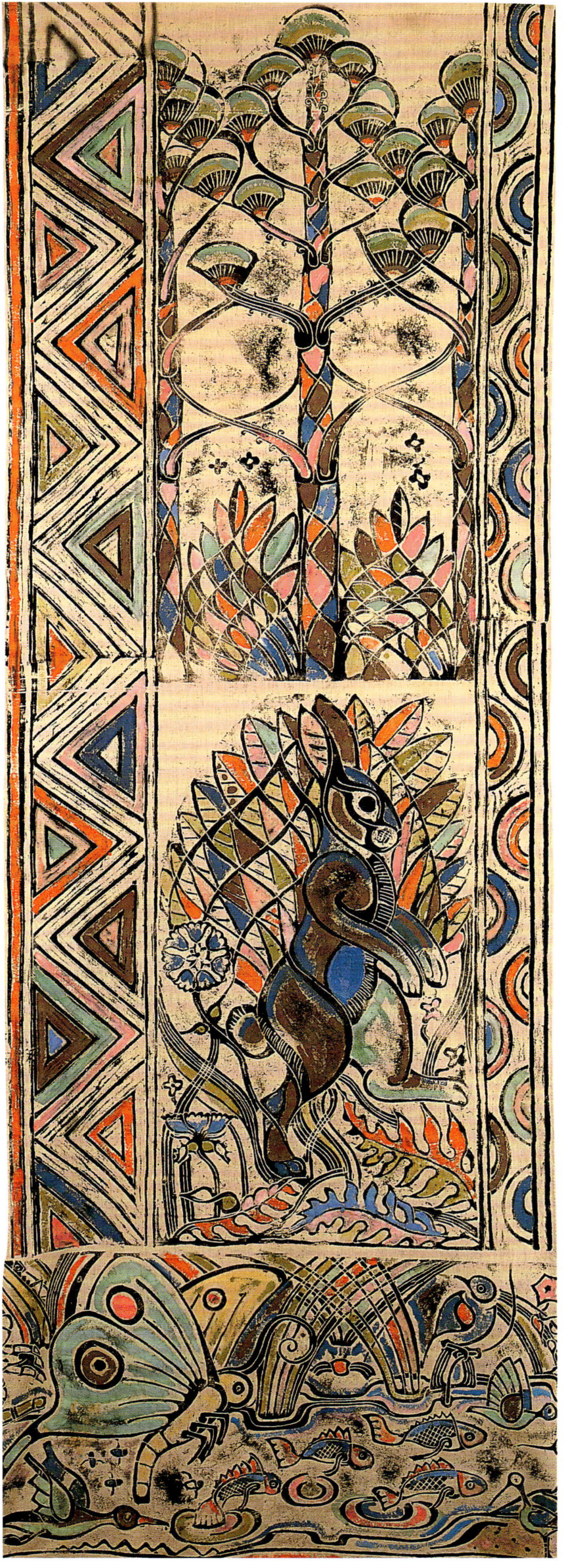

Buck Rabbit, 1945

Linocut on fabric, 120 x 35 in.
The Family of Walter Anderson
Printed and painted by Walter Anderson

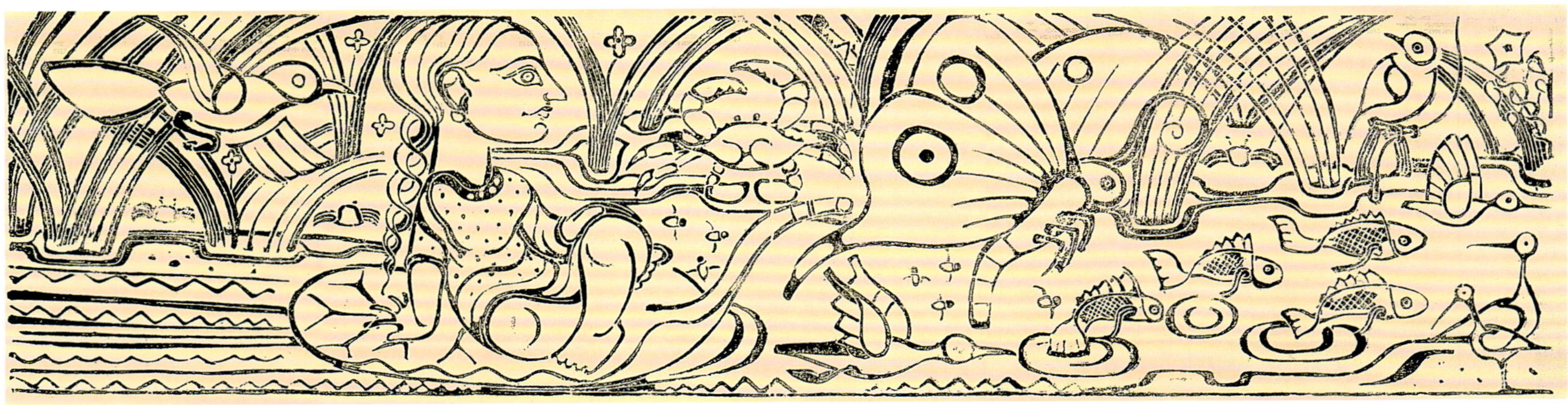

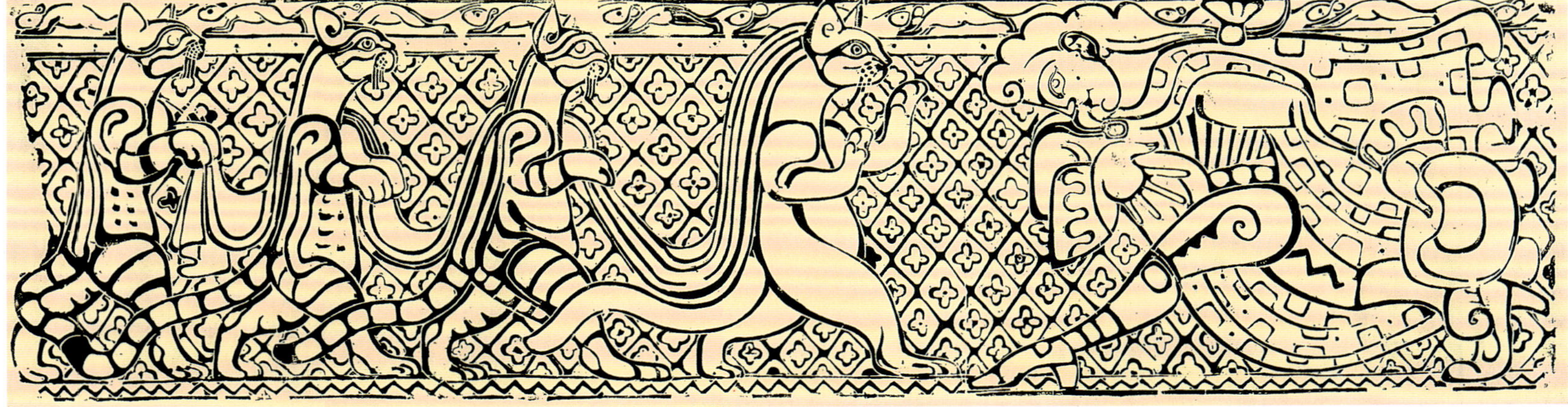

Thumbelina, 1945

Linocut on paper, 24 x 61 in.
The Walter Anderson Museum of Art, 94.3.1
From a series of images illustrating fairy tales from all over the world.
This tale is by Hans Christian Andersen.

Wedding of the Cat Princess, 1946

Linocut on paper, 19 x 74 in.
Joan Gilley Collection
From *The White Cat* by Madame D'Aulnoy

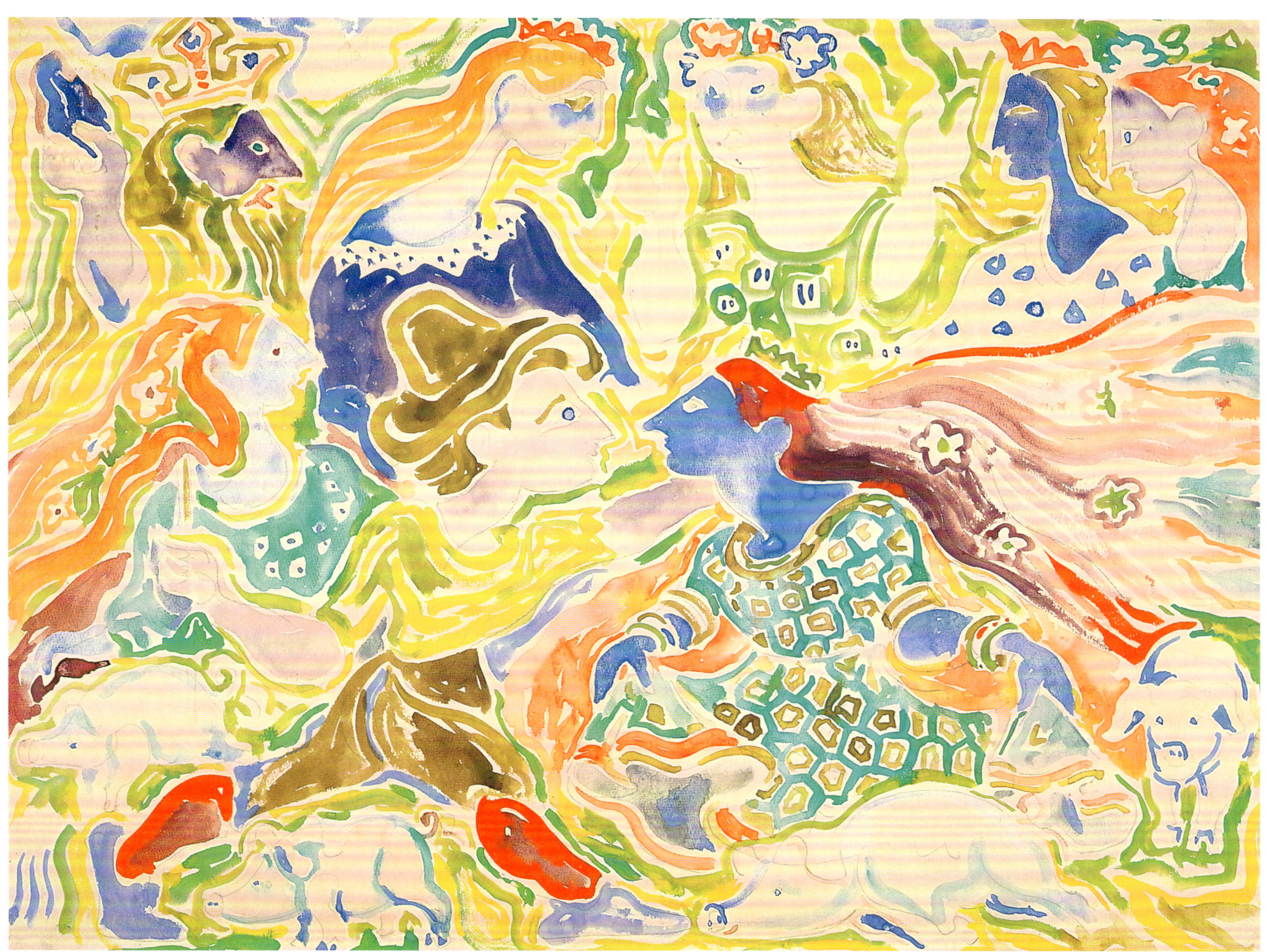

The Princess and the Swineherd, 1945

Watercolor on paper, 25 x 19 in.
The Family of Walter Anderson
From Hans Christian Andersen's tale "The Swineherd"

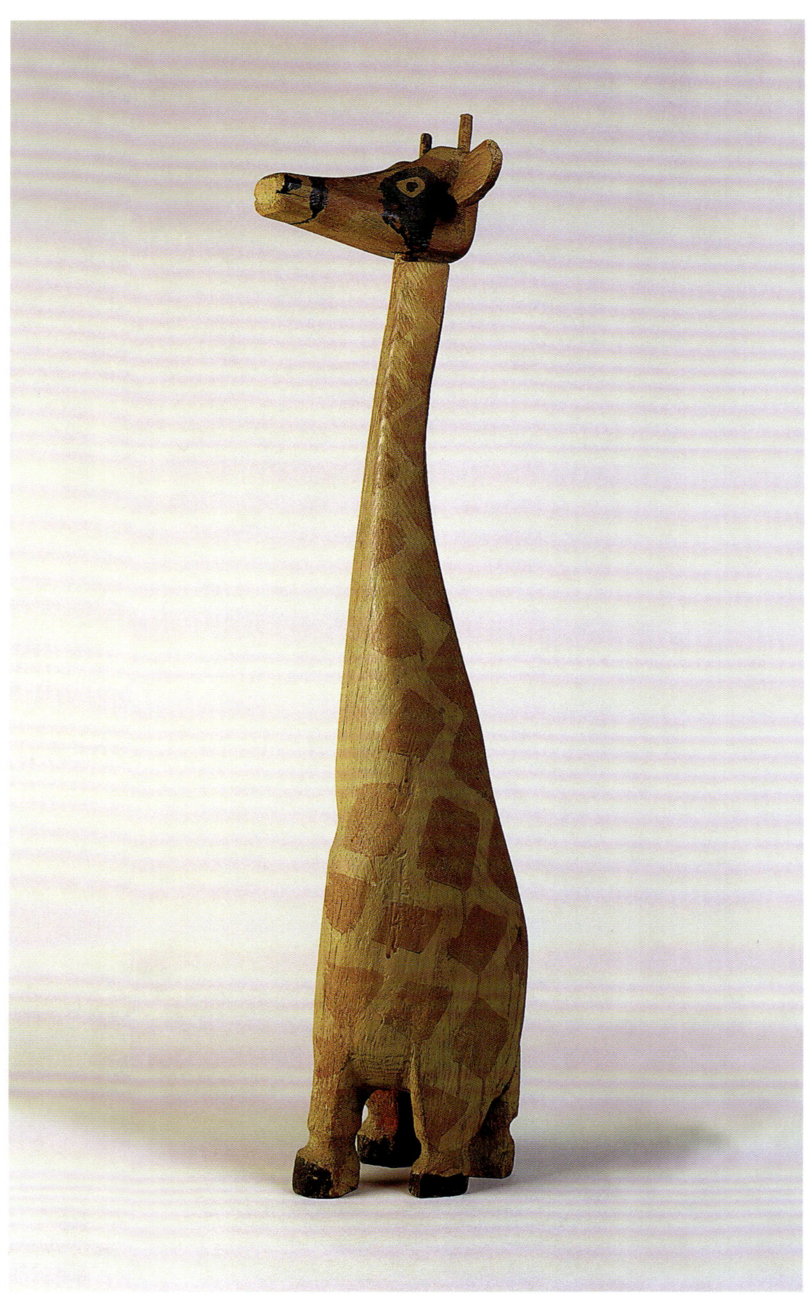

Giraffe, 1948

Oak, 33 x 5 x 6 in.
Louise Lehman Collection

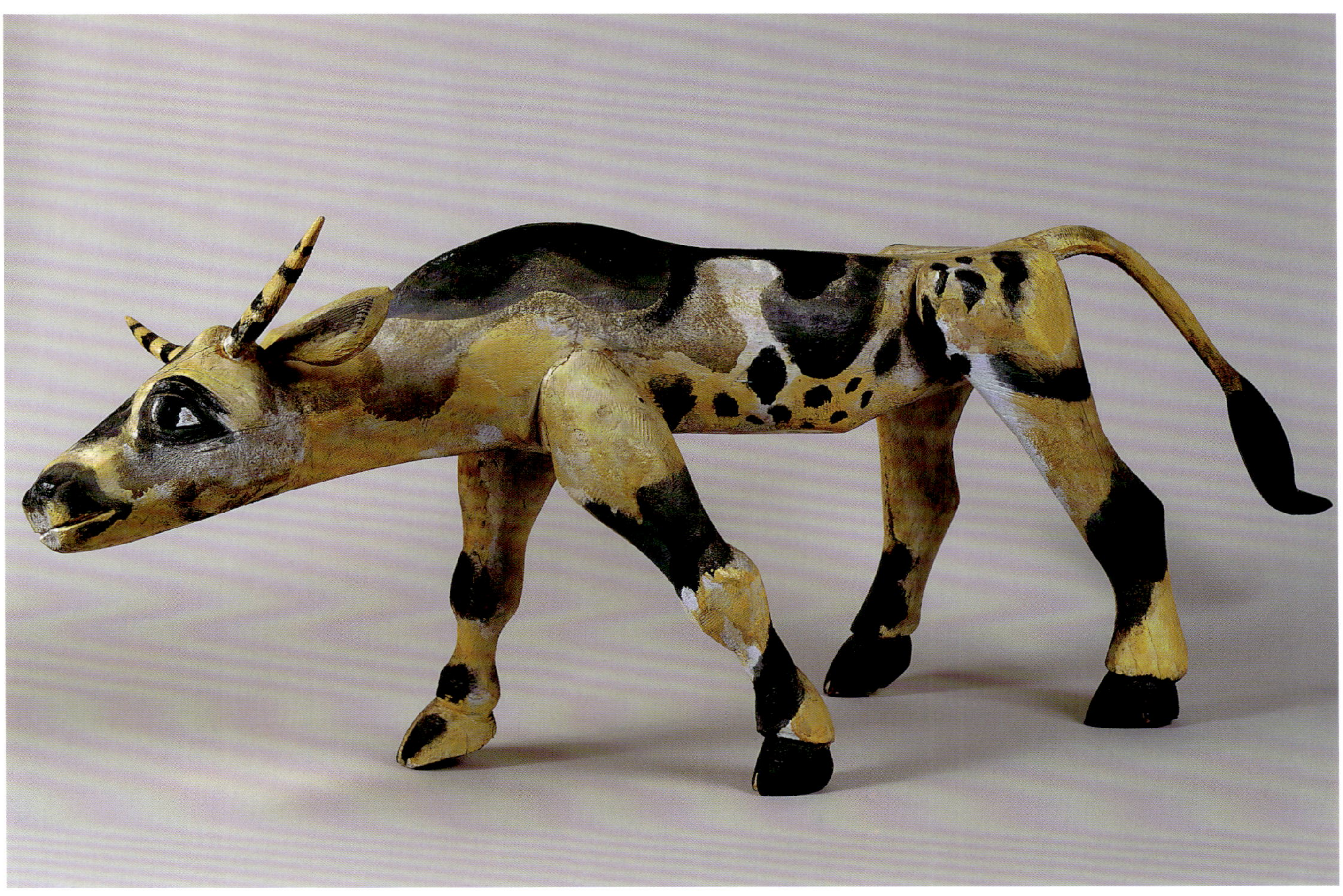

Cow, 1948

Oak, 19 x 49 x 13 in.
Louise Lehman Collection
In 1948–1949 Anderson carved numerous animals, some of which were exhibited at the Brooklyn Museum. These works were carved from an oak tree that fell during a hurricane in 1947.

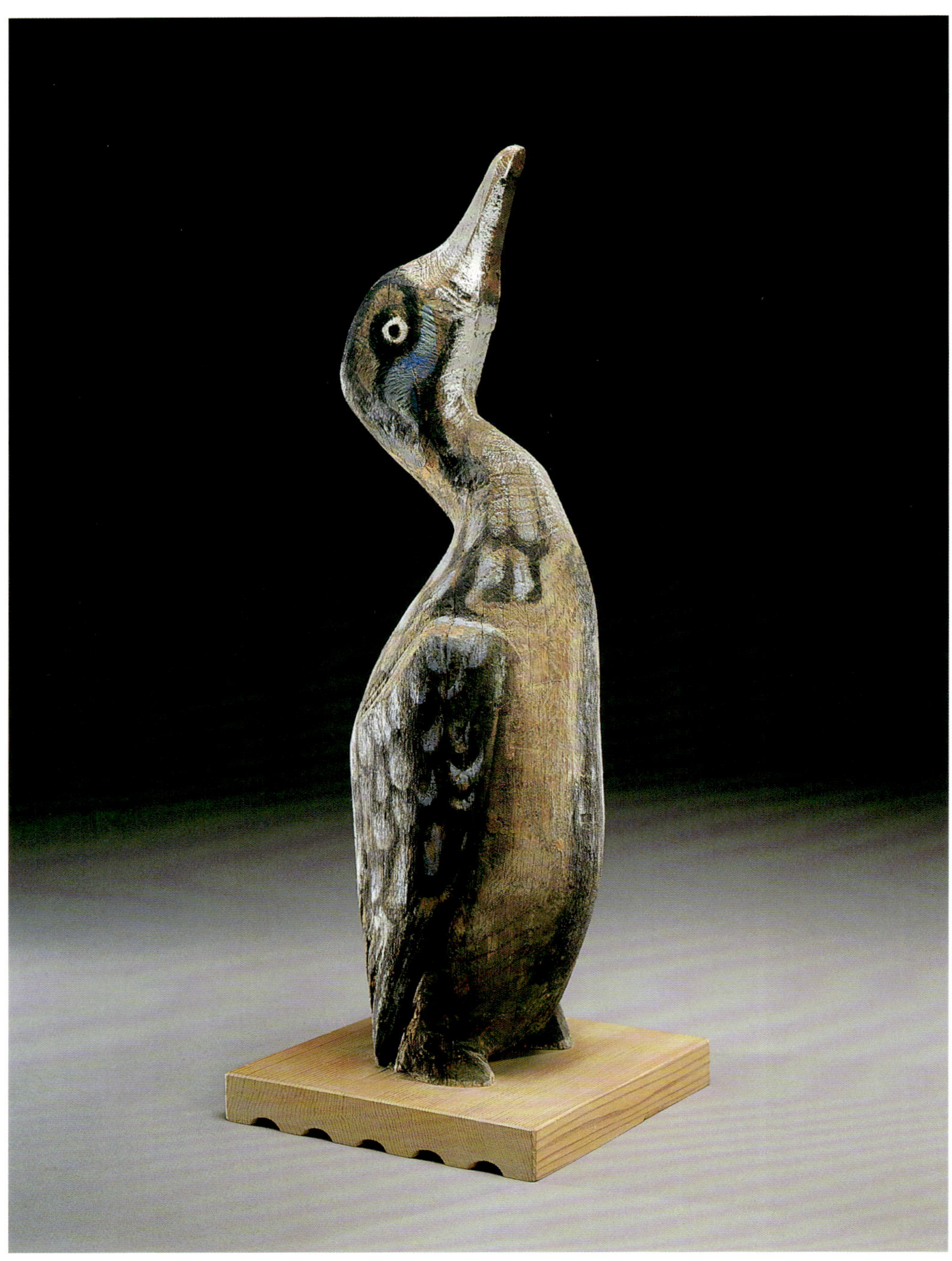

Cormorant, 1947

Oak, 19 x 5 x 5 in.
Louise Lehman Collection

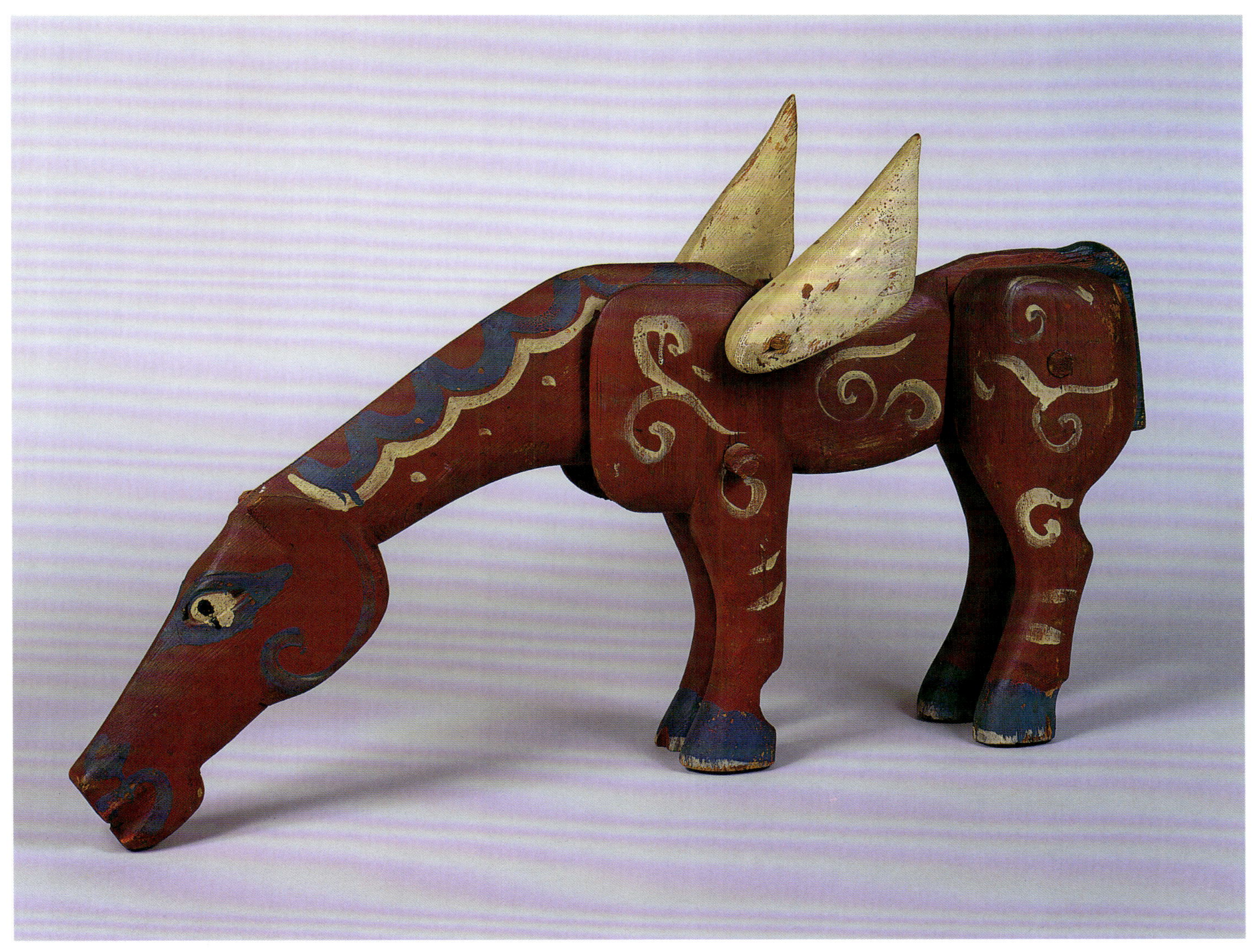

Pegasus, 1948

Oak, 15 x 29 x 7 in.
Louise Lehman Collection

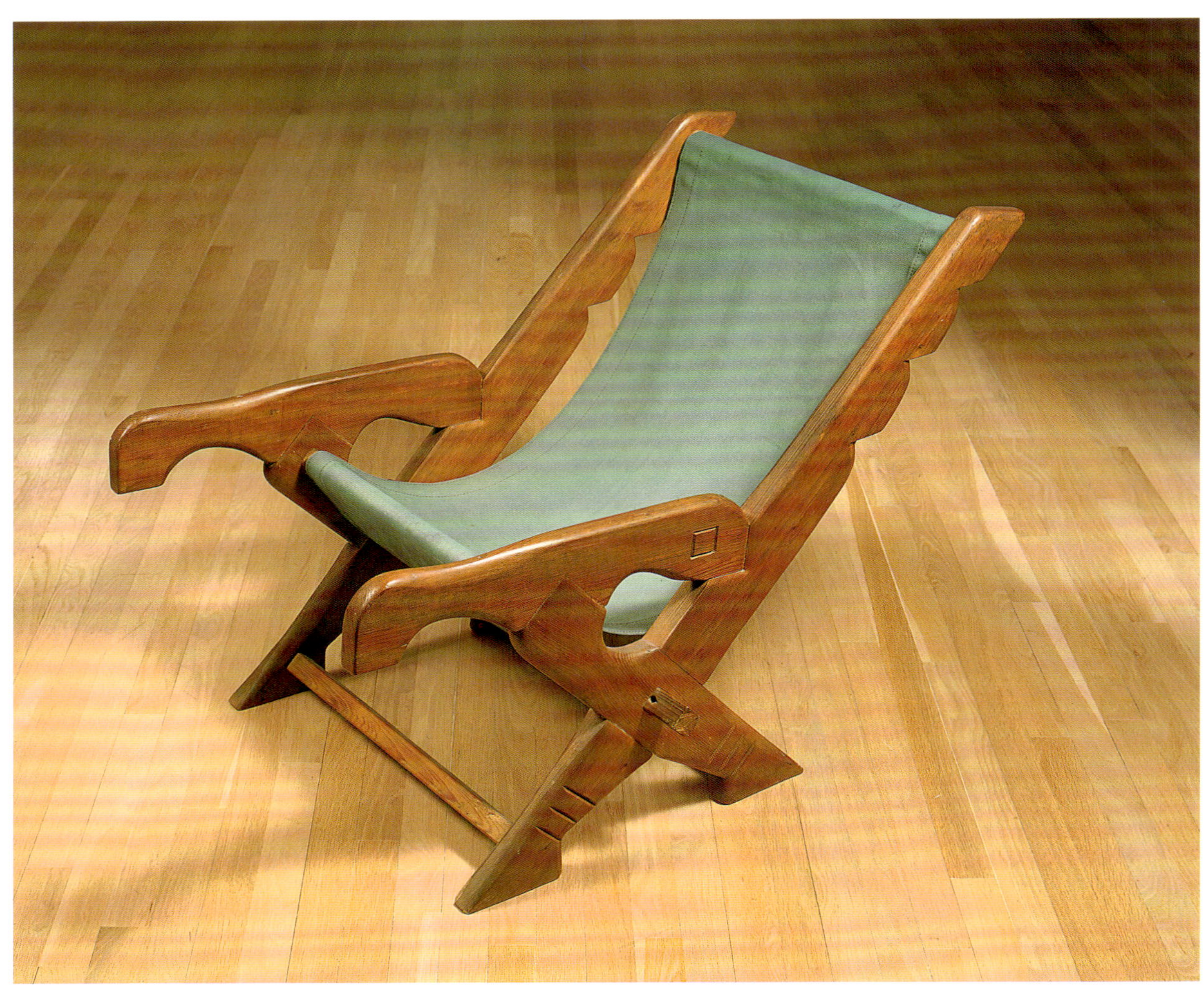

Pelican Chair, ca. 1950

Stained cypress, 30 x 24 x 41 in.
The Family of Walter Anderson

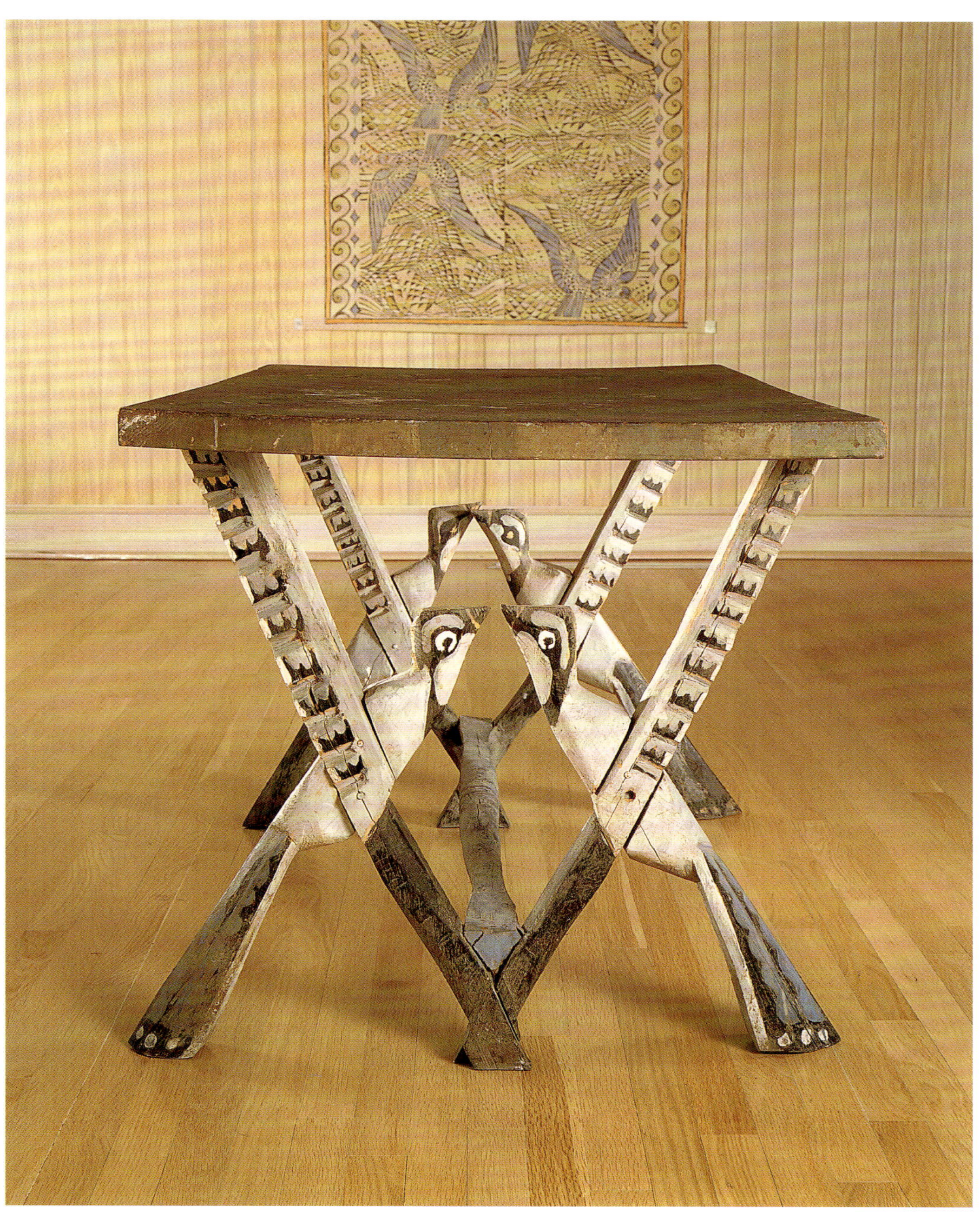

Blue Jay Table, ca. 1955

Cypress and oak, 21 x 29 x 59 in.
Walter Anderson Museum of Art, 94.19.1

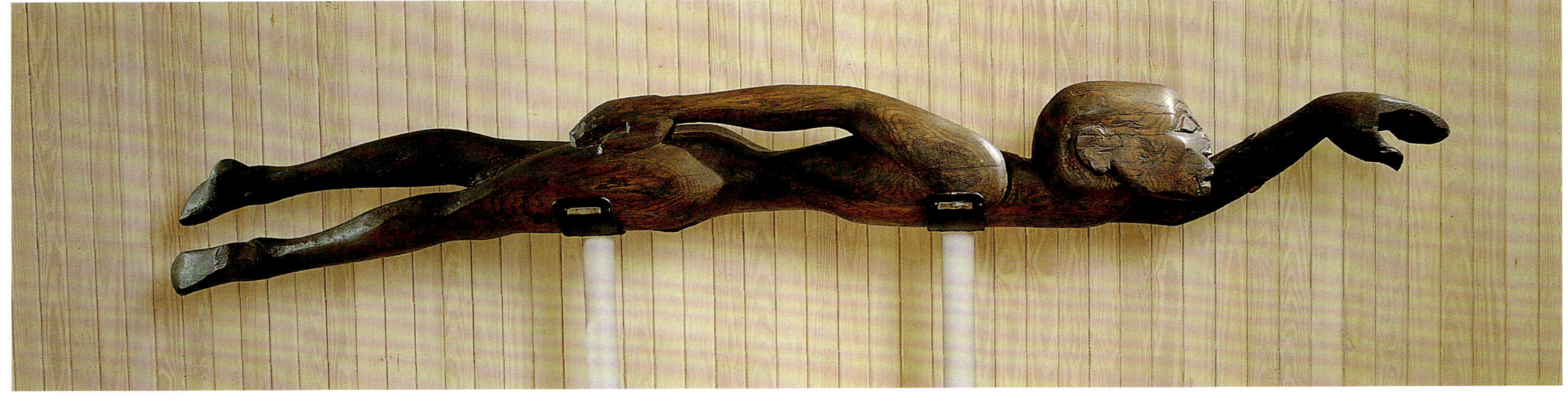

Swimmer, 1948

Oak, 14 x 11 x 120 in.
The Family of Walter Anderson
This piece was also carved from the oak tree that fell in the 1947 hurricane.

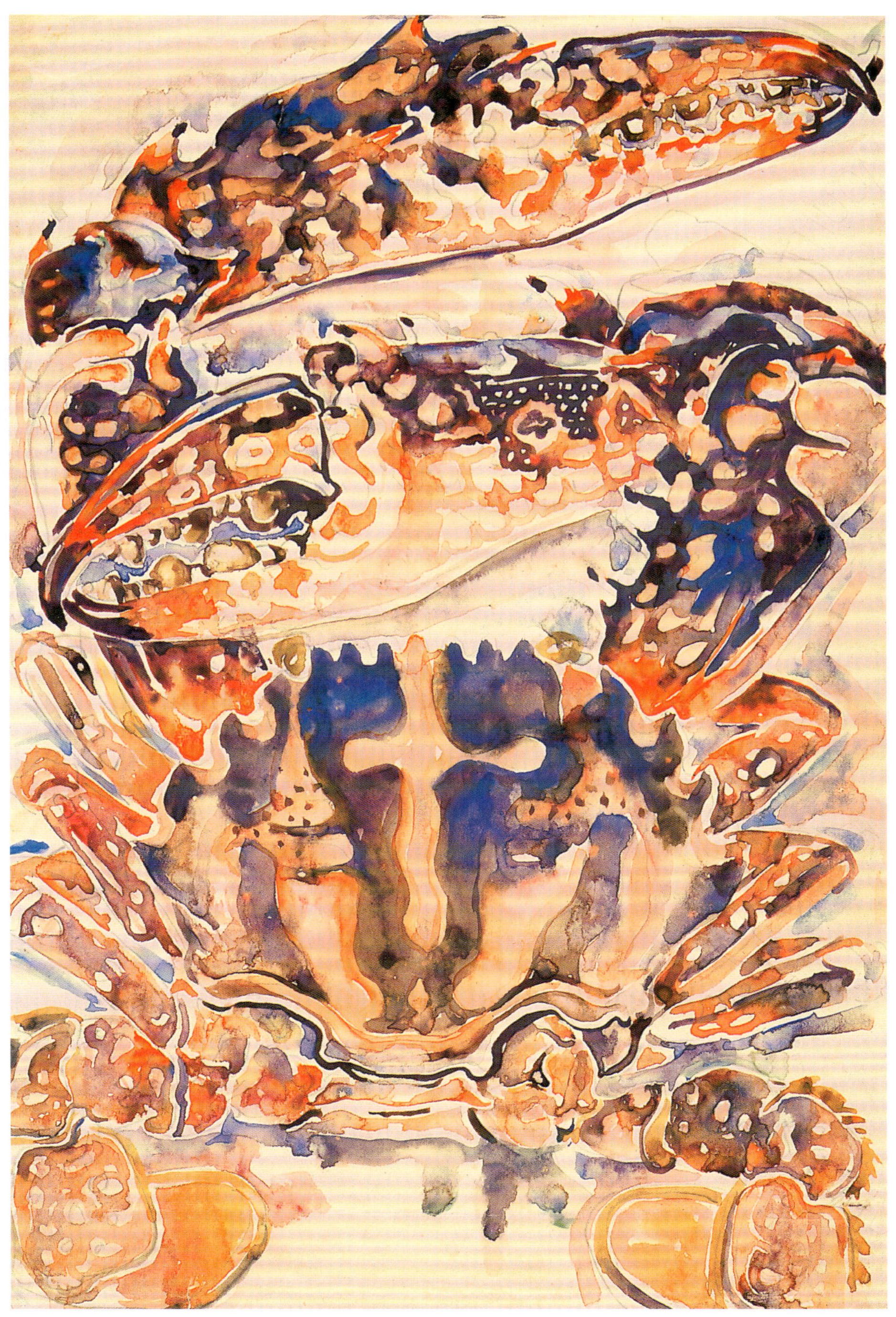

Chinese Crab, 1949

Watercolor on paper, 13 x 8½ in.
The Family of Walter Anderson

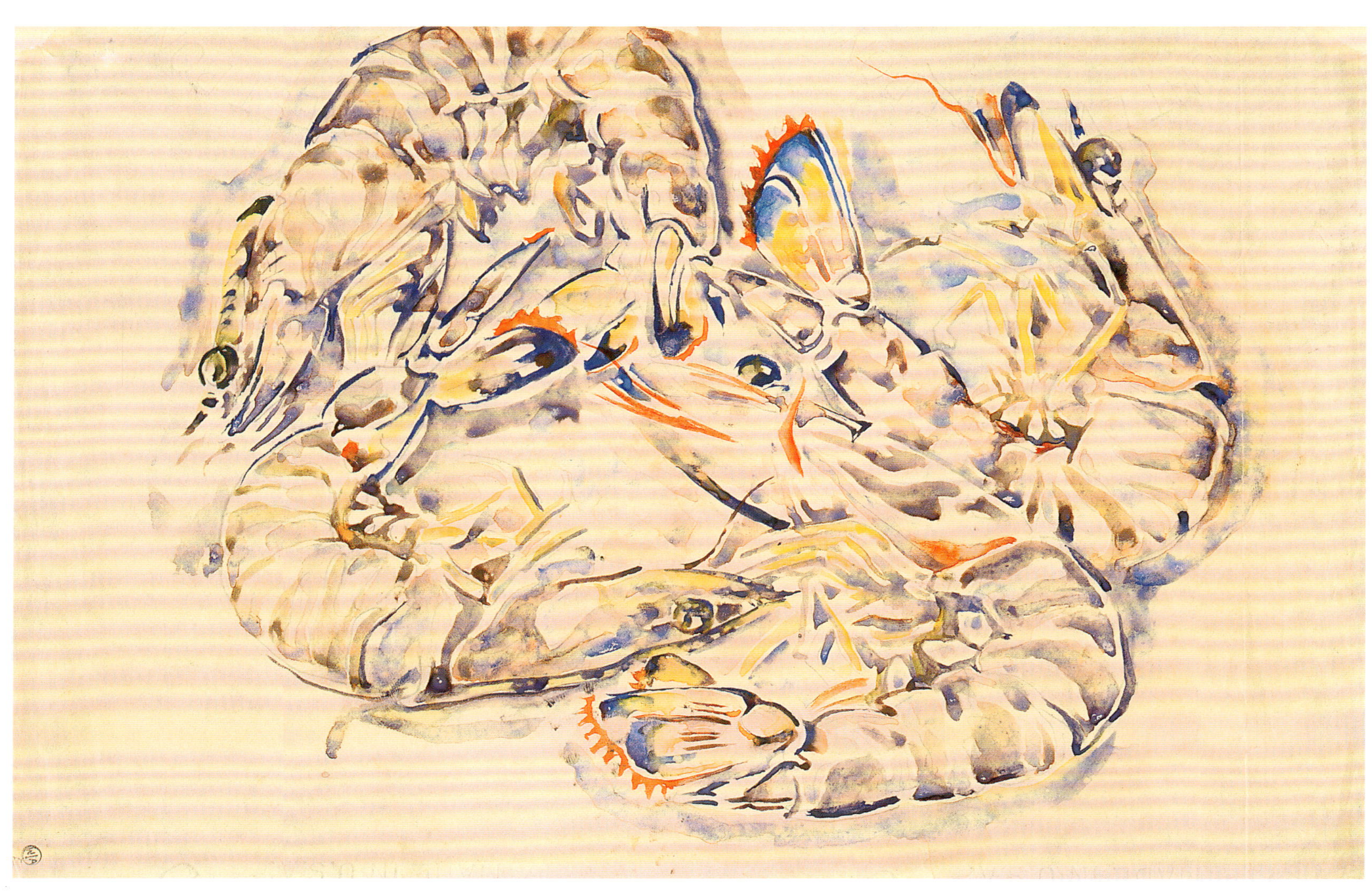

Chinese Shrimp, 1949

Watercolor on paper, 8½ x 13 in.
The Family of Walter Anderson

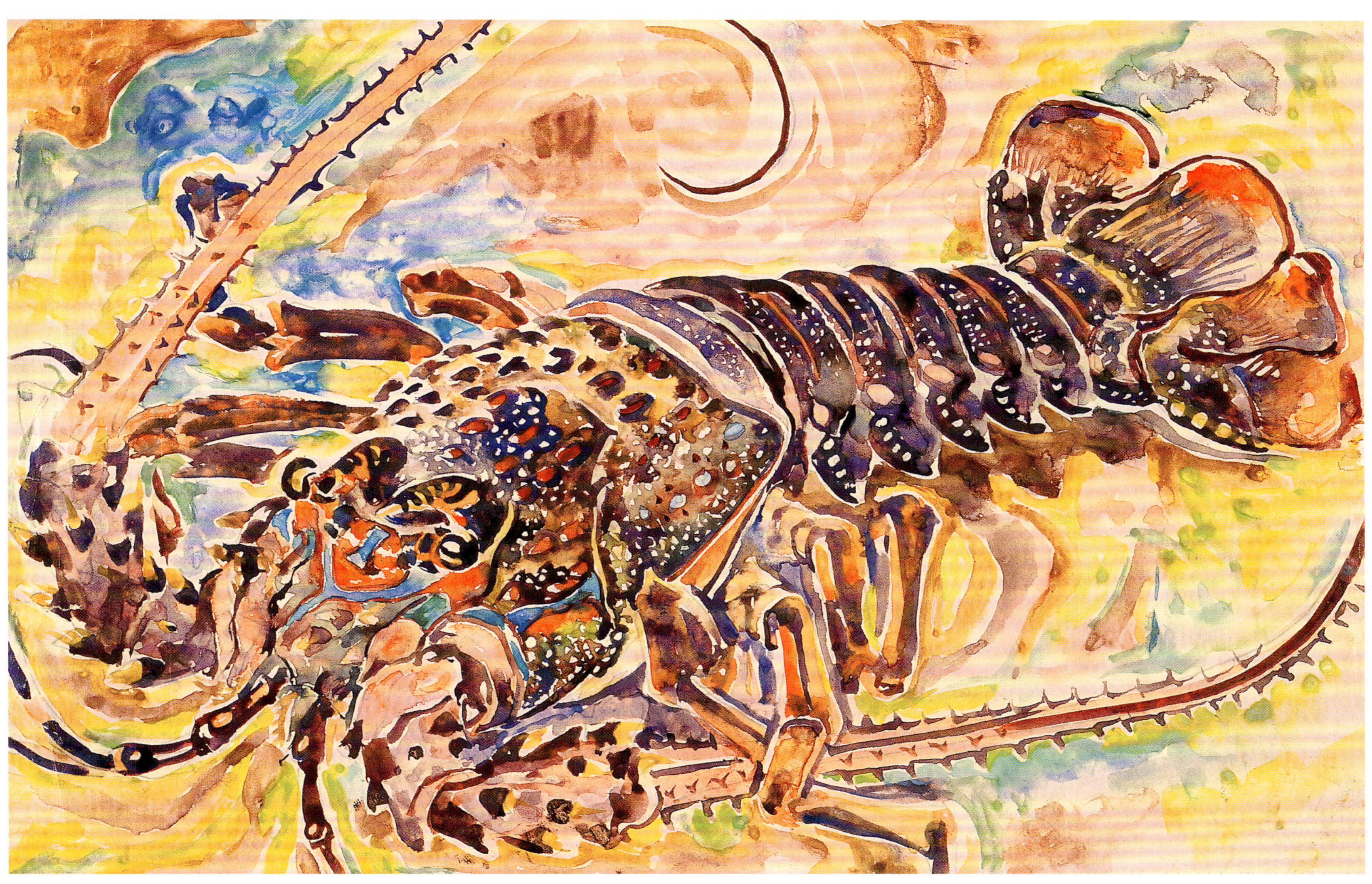

Chinese Lobster, 1949

Watercolor on paper, 8½ x 13 in.
The Family of Walter Anderson

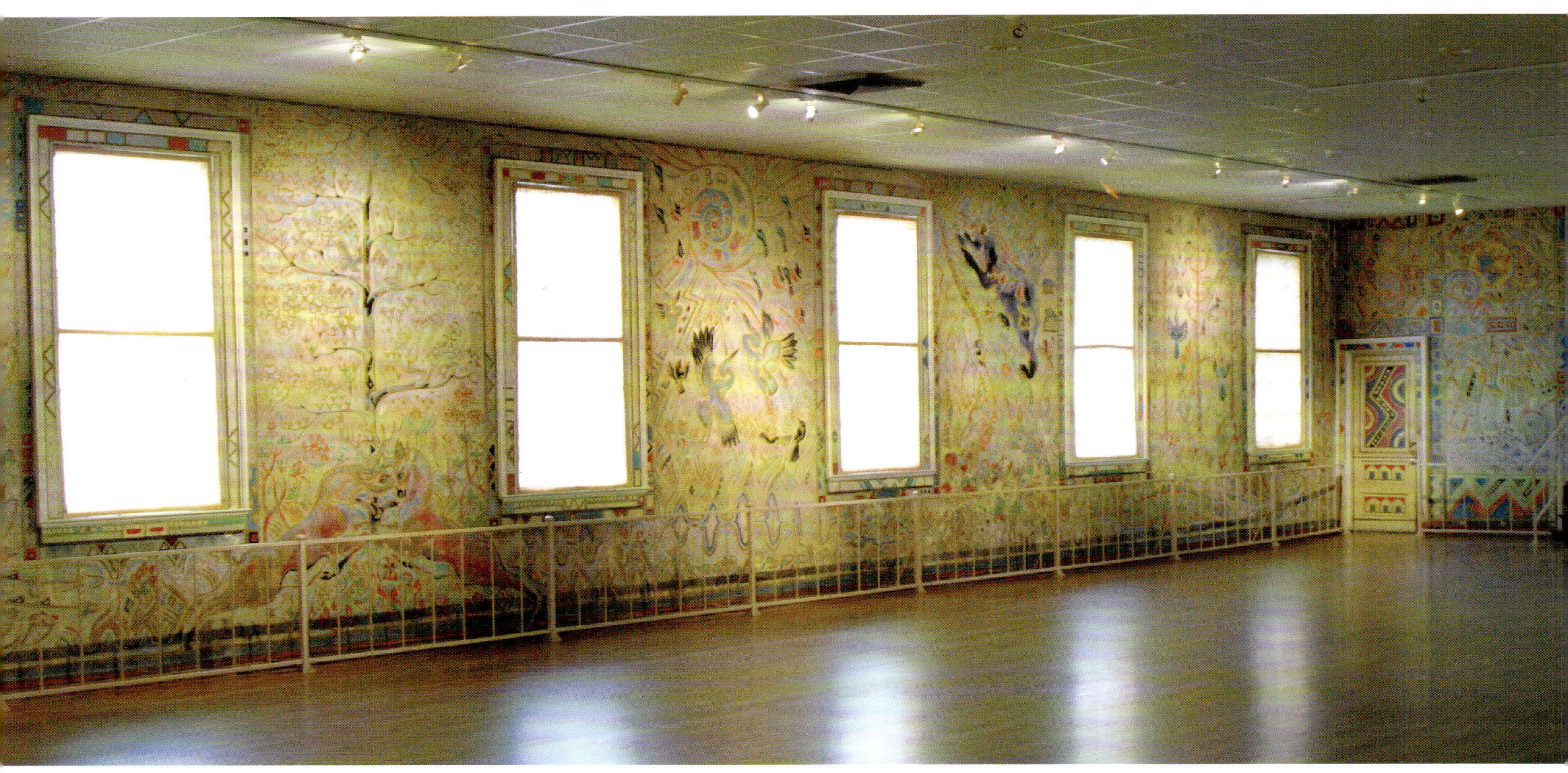

Panoramic view of the Community Center, Ocean Springs, Mississippi

Built 1950, murals painted 1951–1952

12 ft. x 42 ft. 6 in. x 84 ft. 6 in.
North Wall (l to r): *Mars, Jupiter, Saturn, Uranus*
East Wall (far right): *The Sun*
Community Center Mural
Oil and tempera on stucco
The City of Ocean Springs, Mississippi

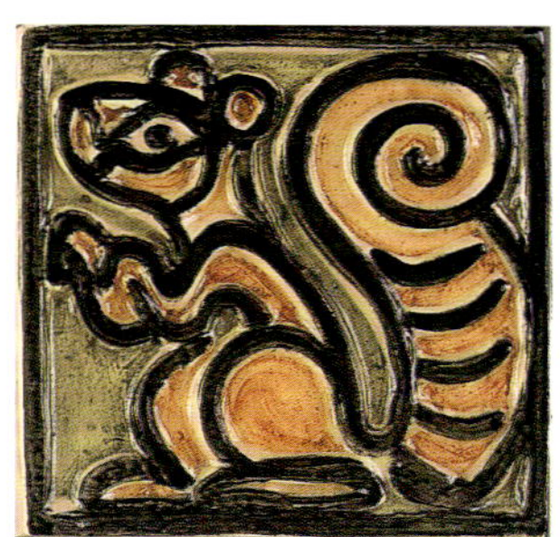

MURALS AND STILL LIFES: 1950–1960

In 1951, the town of Ocean Springs built a new Community Center for civic and private events. The three thousand square feet of cinder-block wall were unpainted, and Anderson—who had thought a great deal about the artist's obligation to society and society's to the artist—offered to create a mural for the fee of one dollar. After considering the possibilities of fresco, he decided to use oil paint provided by the city, and applied it directly to the stucco surface, achieving a fresco-like effect. The mural celebrated the history and natural environment of the town of Ocean Springs and of the spot where Biloxi Bay enters the Mississippi Sound. The mural on the south side of the large room portrays the Biloxi Indians with gifts, welcoming French soldiers, clergy, and the swashbuckling explorer Pierre Le Moyne, Sieur d'Iberville, who landed there in 1699. Anderson painted himself standing in a boat with the landing party. Pelicans, skimmers, and gulls and the skyline of Deer Island anchor the mural in a specific place.

Distracted by those who stopped to watch him paint, Anderson took to working at night, in dim light that hampered him in his efforts. After many months of labor, with the mural nearly complete, Anderson broke off work and secluded himself at his cottage. There, on the walls of a little room, he did a more personal mural, his vision of a day on the coast, from sunrise to night, based on Psalm 104, with its praise for the gift of light. If the Community Center mural had addressed history, the environment, and the cycle of the seasons, the Little Room was a hymn to creation. On the ceiling, Anderson painted the mystical zinnia, with its square, swirling petals, and he adorned the fireplace with a muse-like representation of the Mississippi River.

During this time of retreat, he also devoted much time to still life. "Painting still life," he once wrote, "is one way of paying the debt which we owe to the earth. All the beauty, all the form and our own inadequacy in expressing our gratitude is slightly satisfied by increasing our consciousness of the beauty of fruit, flowers, vegetables, the voluptuous return, gift of an austere mother to her children." He also sailed his skiff thirty-two miles out to the Chandeleur Islands to paint and to study the life of pelicans. For a brief time, he was treated for alcoholism at De Paul Sanitarium in New Orleans, and, while there, painted portraits of the staff and of fellow patients.

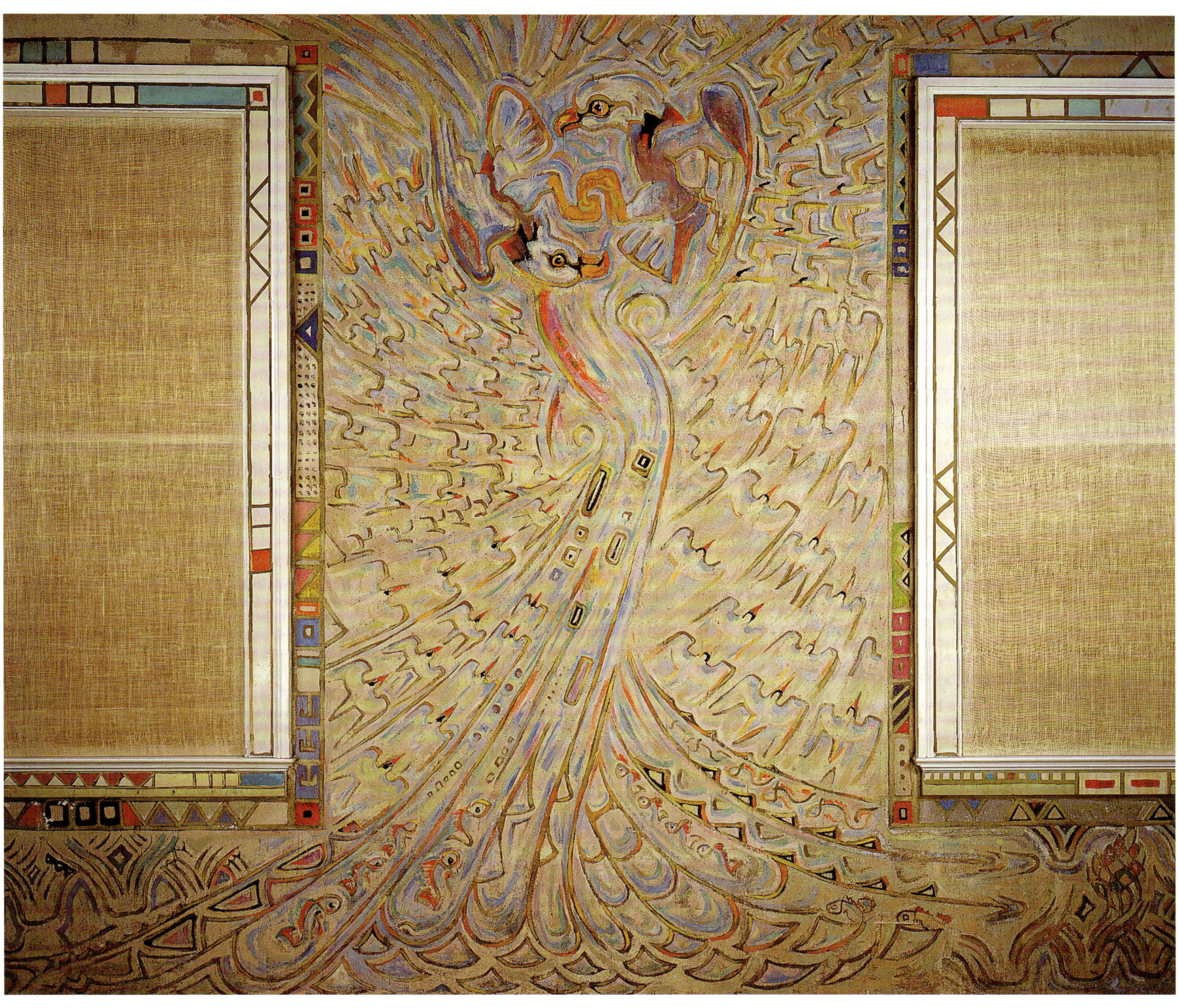

Venus Panel (north wall), 1951

Community Center Mural
Oil and tempera on stucco, 12 ft. H
The City of Ocean Springs, Mississippi
The eagles are inspired by Walt Whitman's poem "The Dalliance of the Eagles."

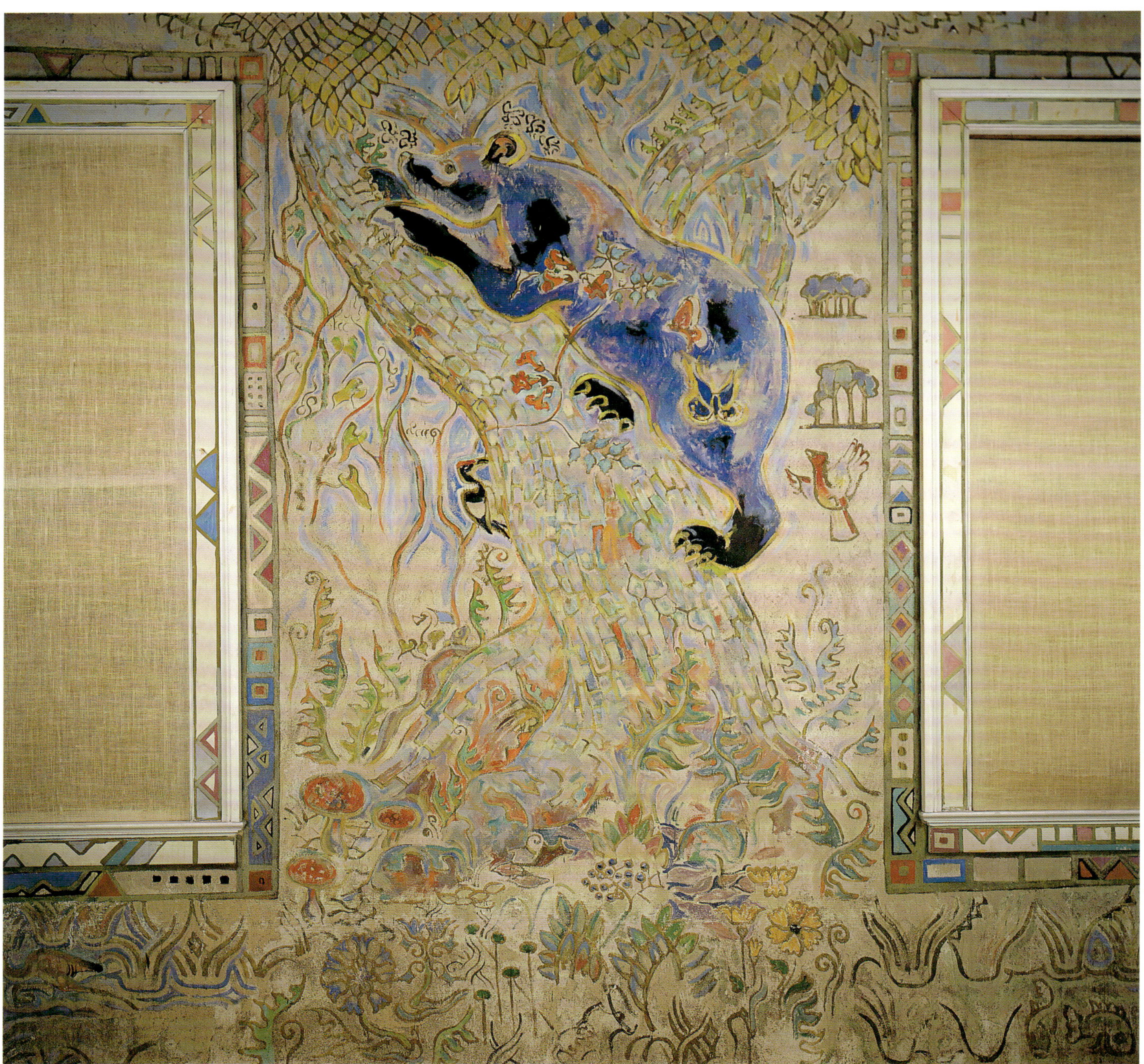

Saturn Panel (north wall), 1951

Community Center Mural
Oil and tempera on stucco, 12 ft. H
The City of Ocean Springs, Mississippi
Anderson explained that this scene alluded to Saturn devouring his children during the Golden Age.

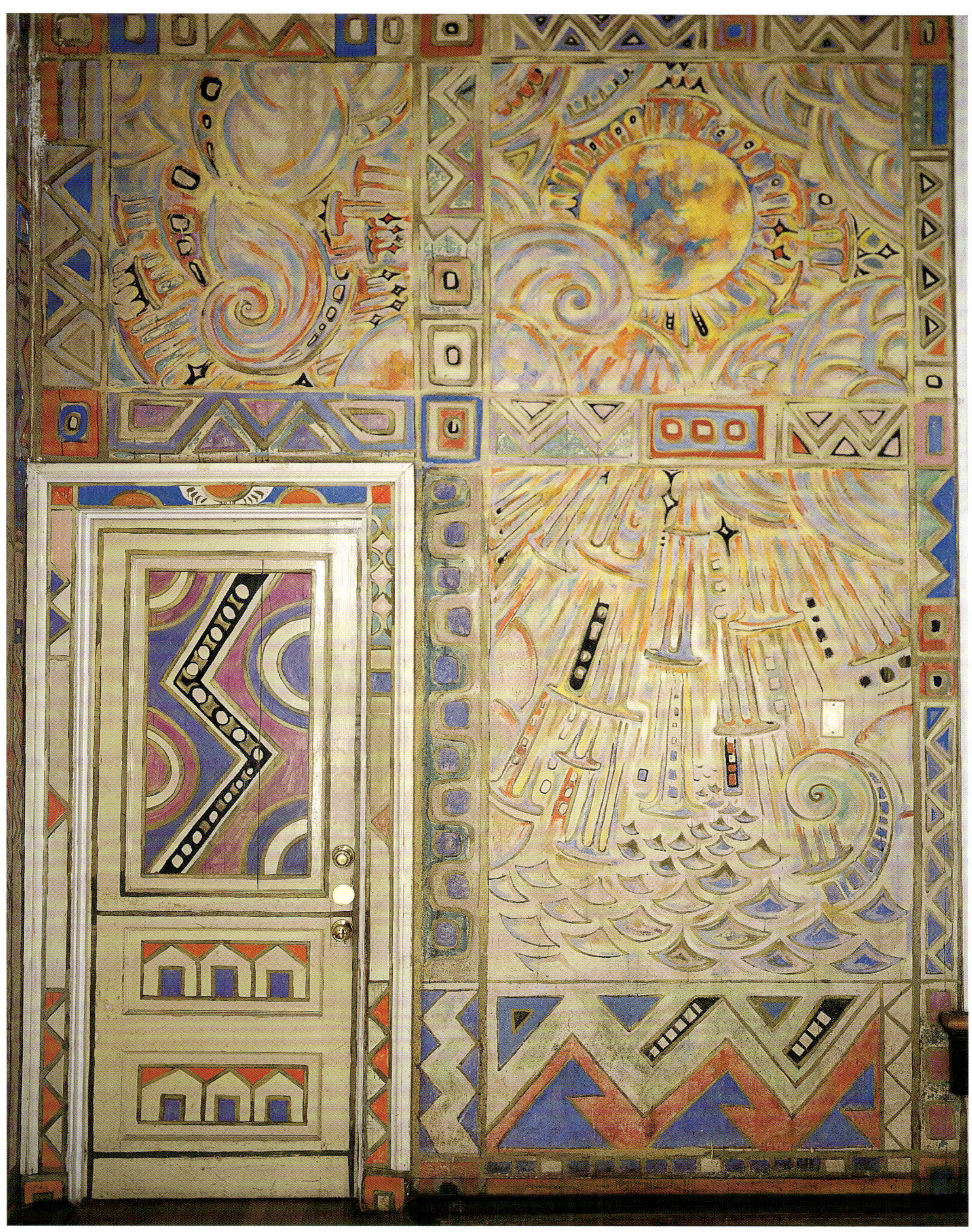

Sun (east wall), 1951

Community Center Mural
Oil and tempera on stucco, 12 ft. H
The City of Ocean Springs, Mississippi

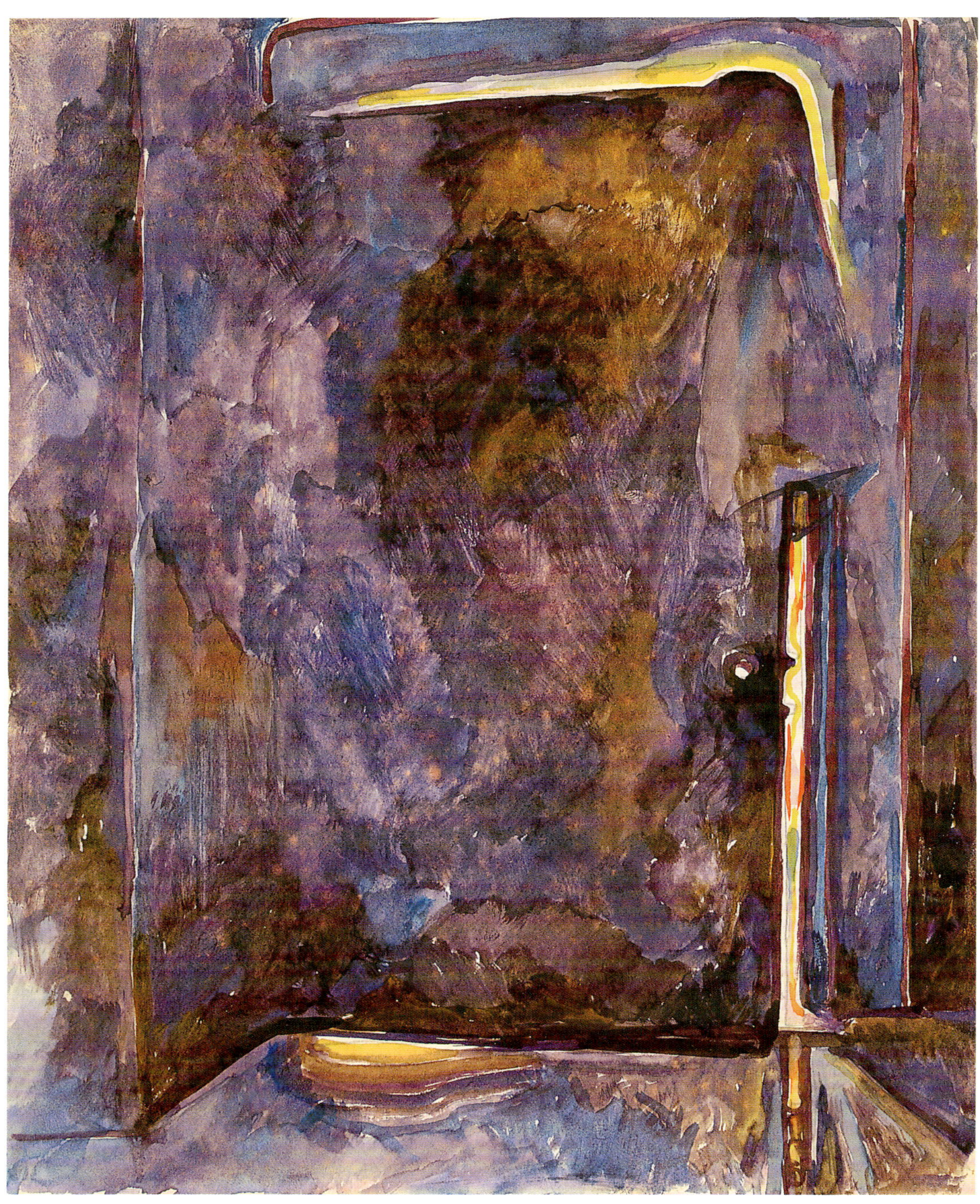

Door to the Little Room, 1953

Watercolor on paper, 11 x 8½ in.
The Family of Walter Anderson

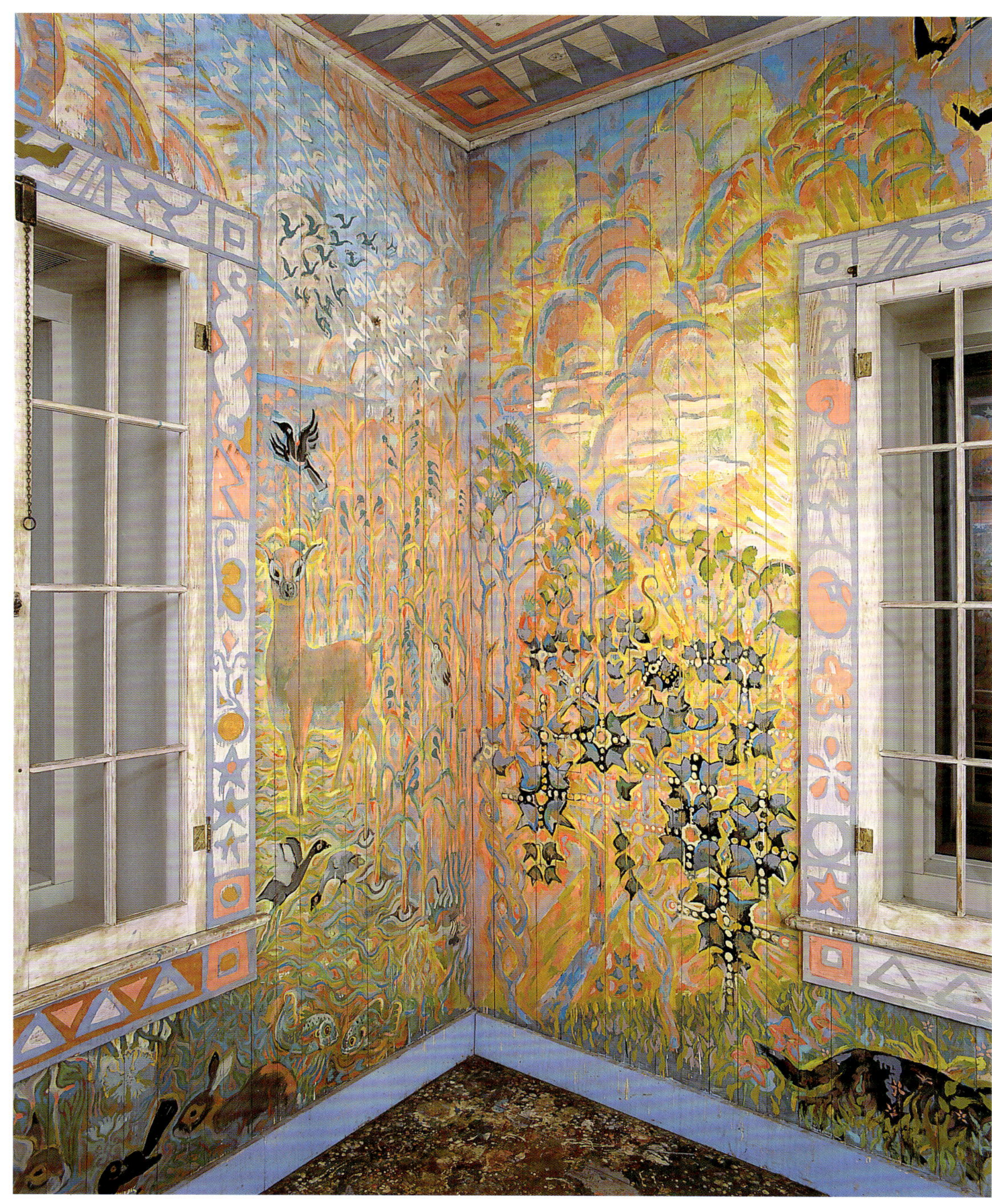

Little Room (southwest corner), 1951–1953

Oil on wood, 10 x 11 ft.
Walter Anderson Museum of Art

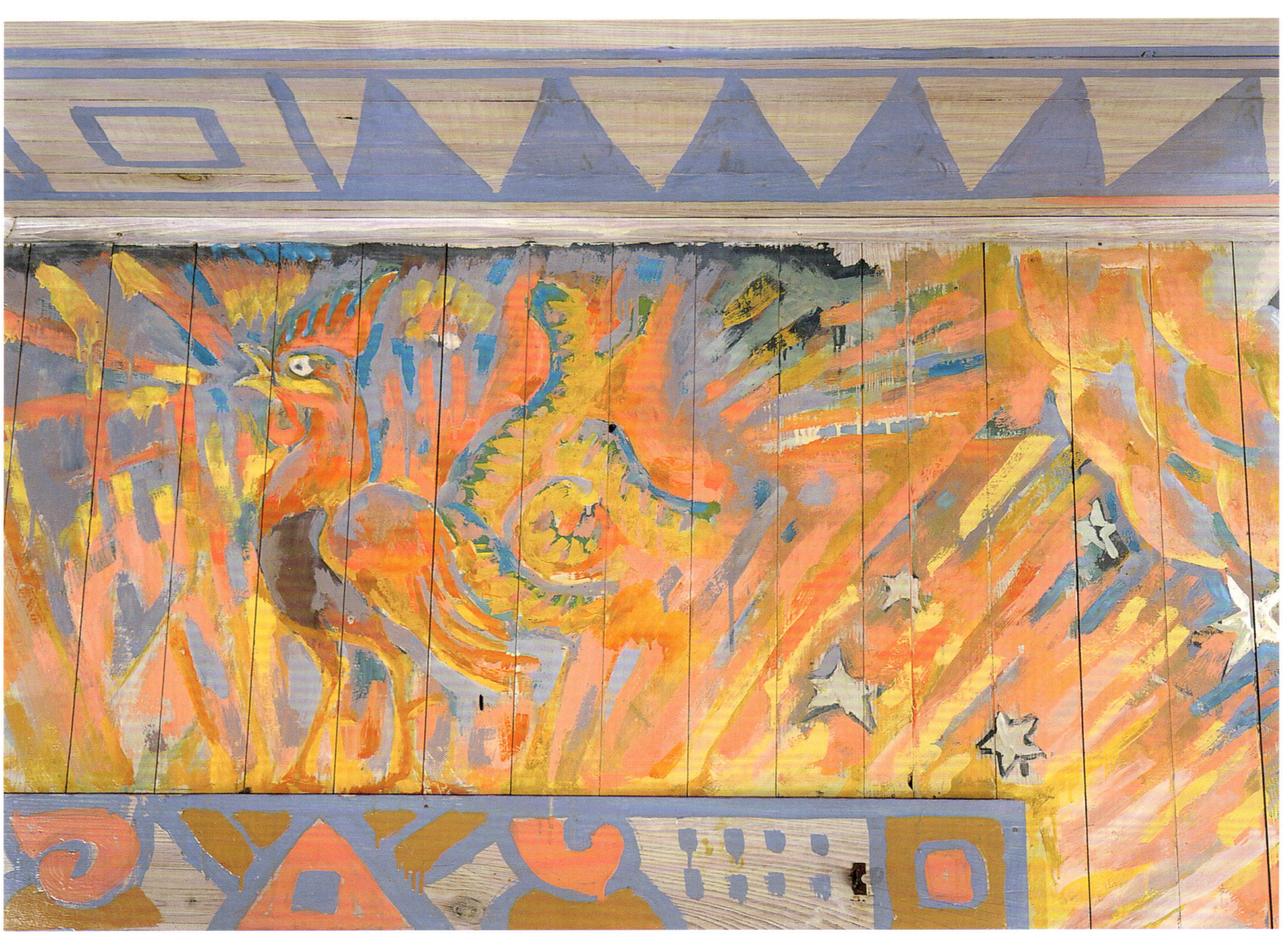

Little Room (detail from the east wall), 1951–1953

Oil on wood, east wall 10 x 11 ft.
Walter Anderson Museum of Art

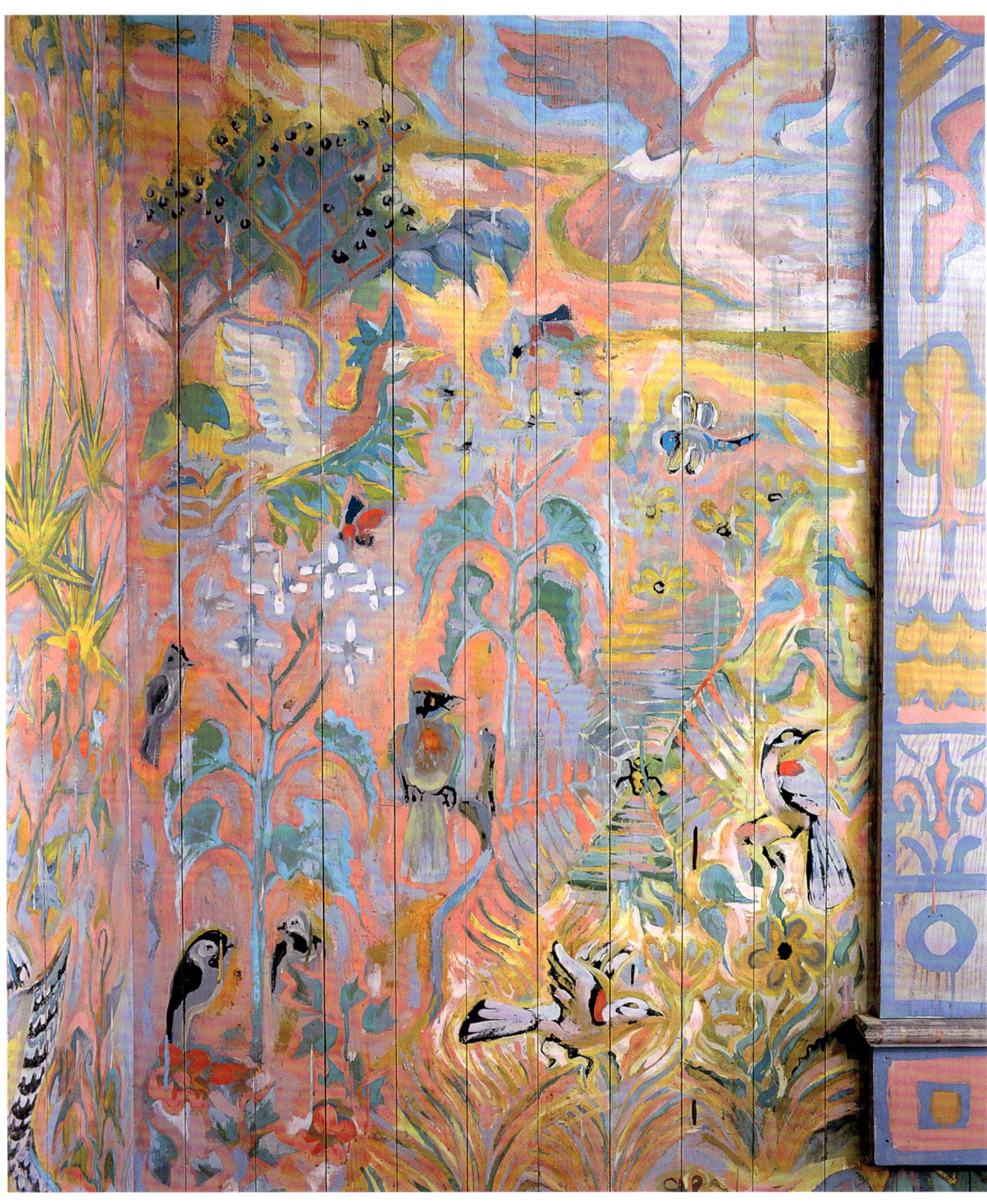

Little Room (detail from the south wall), 1951–1953

Oil on wood, south wall 10 x 13 ft.
Walter Anderson Museum of Art

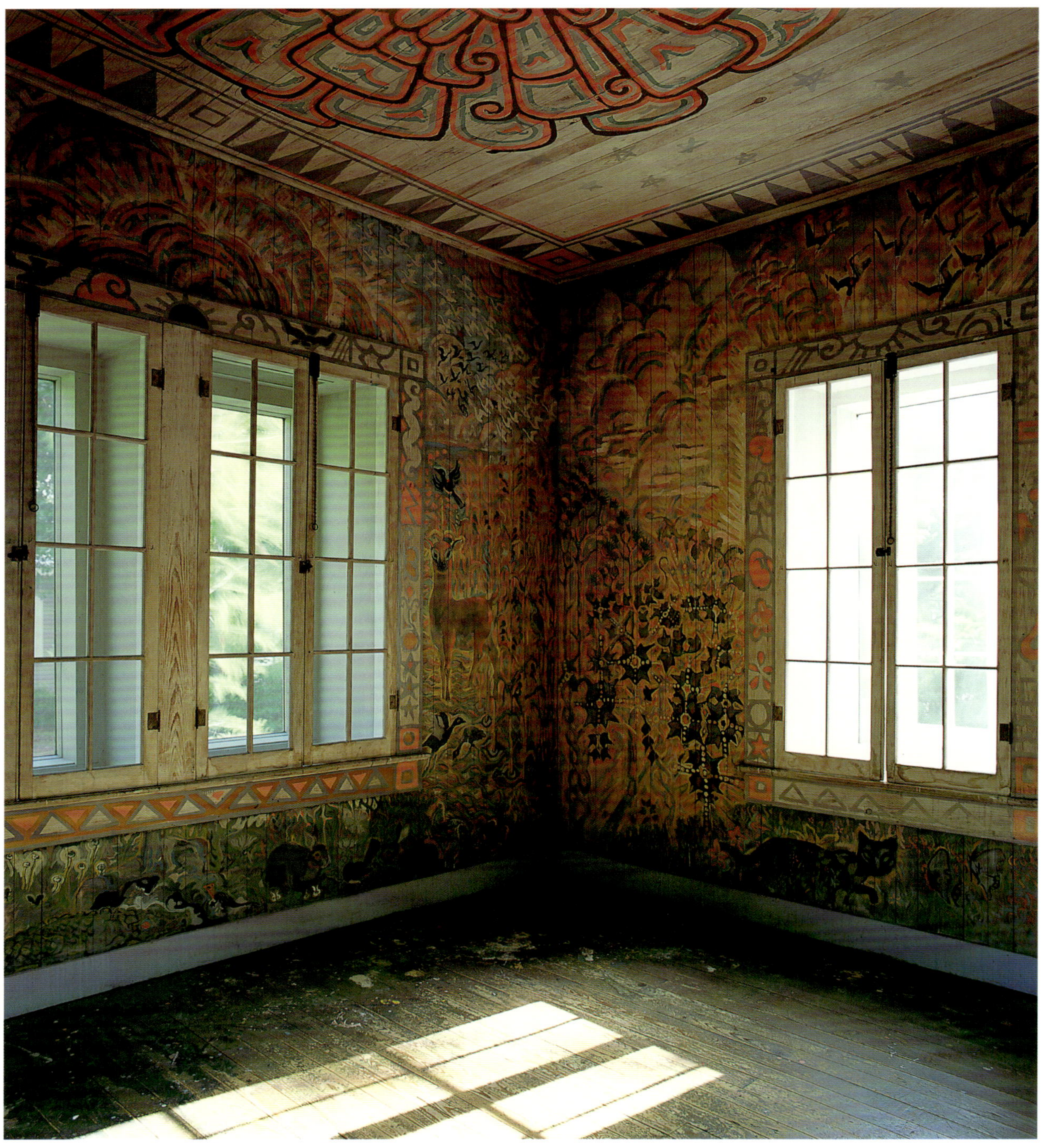

Little Room, 1951–1953

Oil on wood, 10 x 13 ft.
Walter Anderson Museum of Art

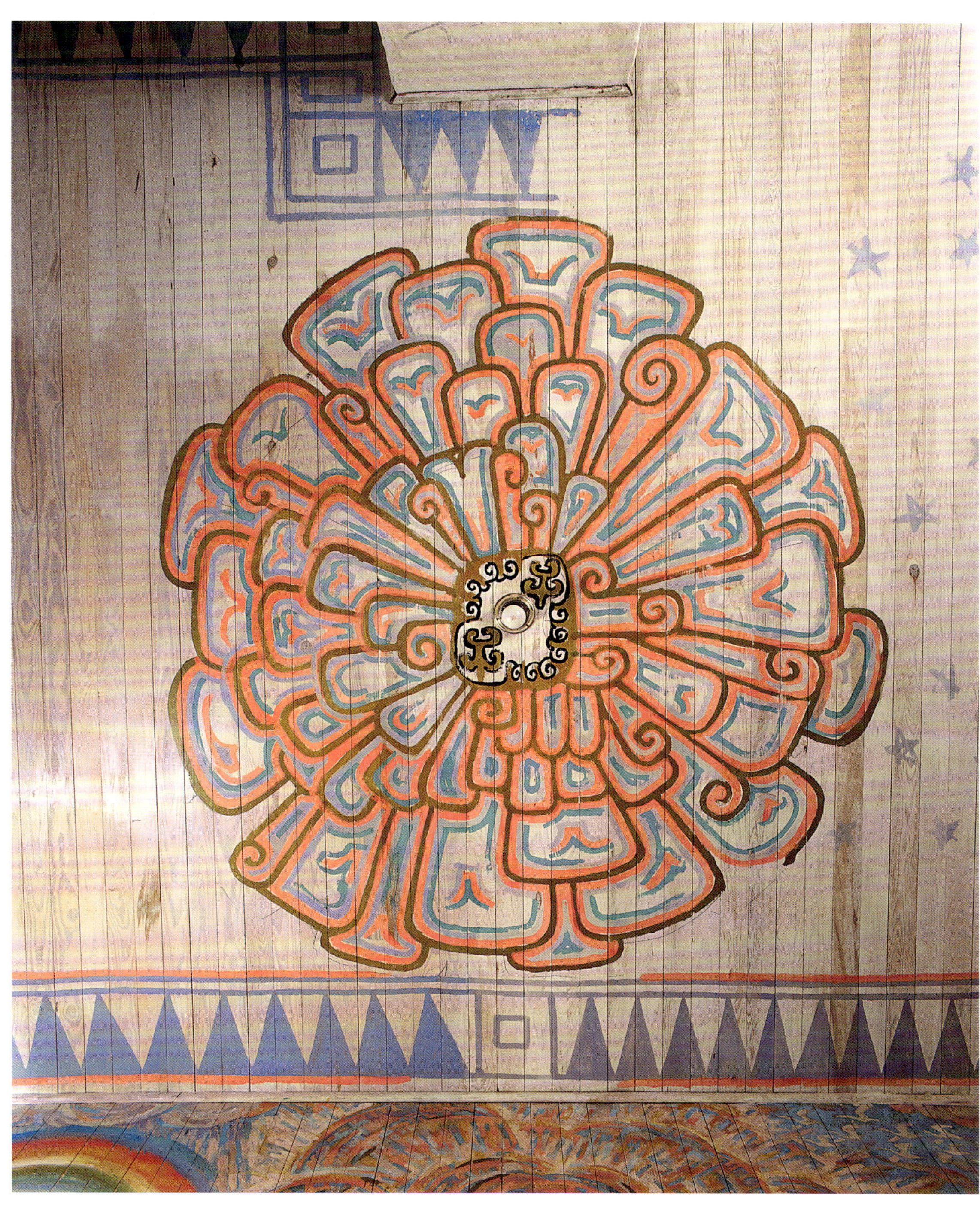

Little Room (ceiling), 1951–1953

Oil on wood, 11 x 13 ft.
Walter Anderson Museum of Art

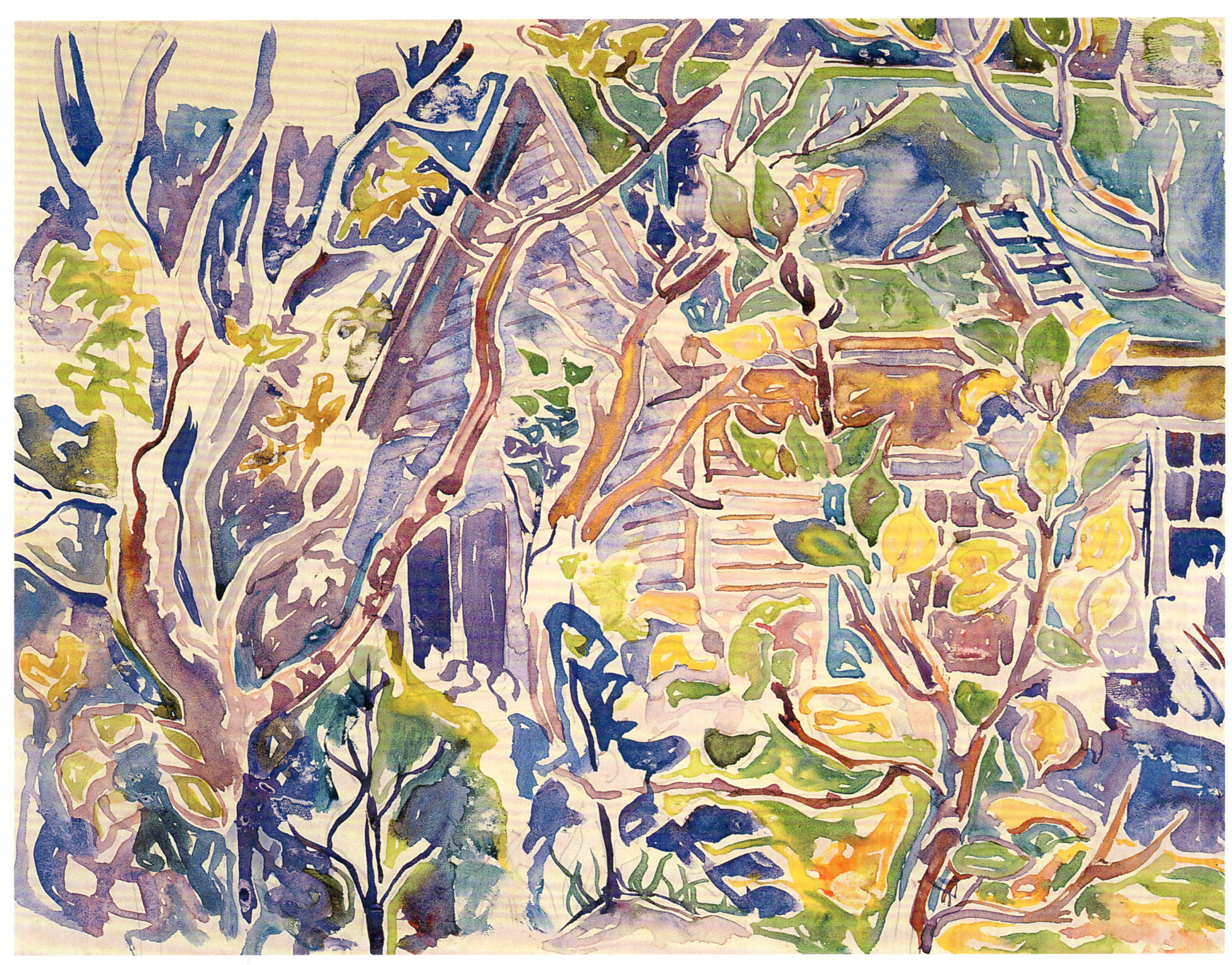

Cottage, 1948–1950

Watercolor on paper, 8½ x 11 in.
The Family of Walter Anderson

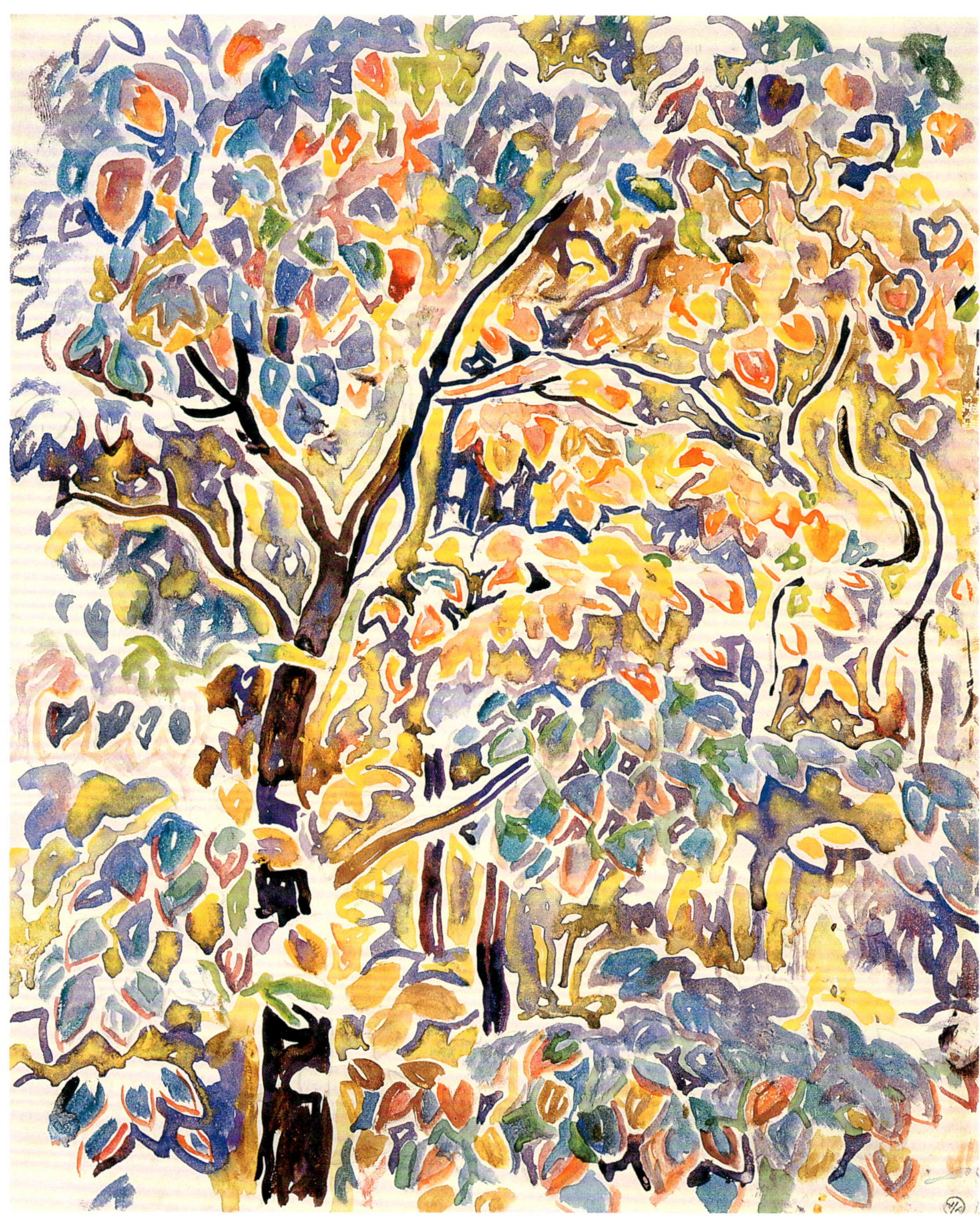

Woods, ca. 1960

Watercolor on paper, 11 x 8½ in.
Walter Anderson Museum of Art, 97.9.1

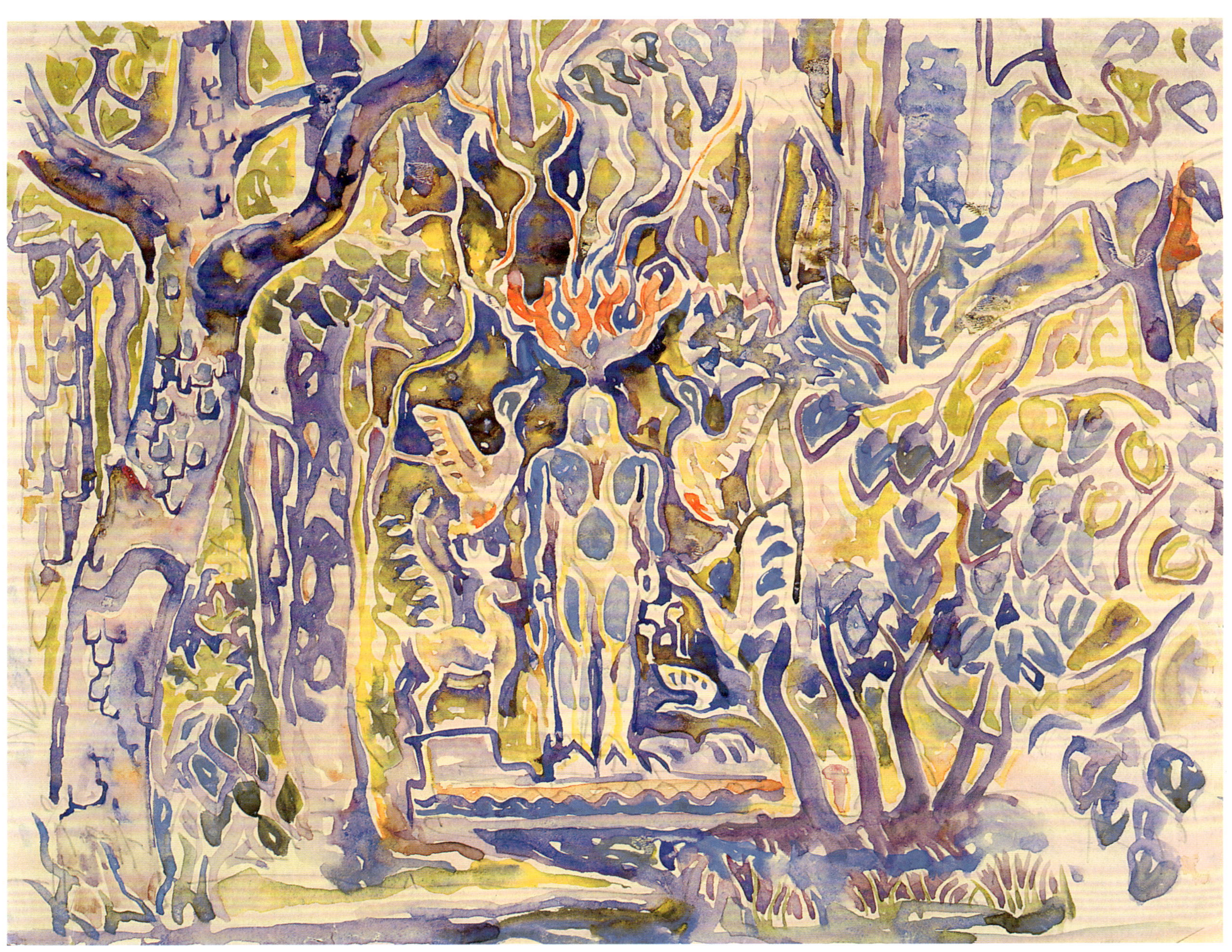

Father Mississippi, 1953

Watercolor on paper, 8½ x 11 in.
The Family of Walter Anderson

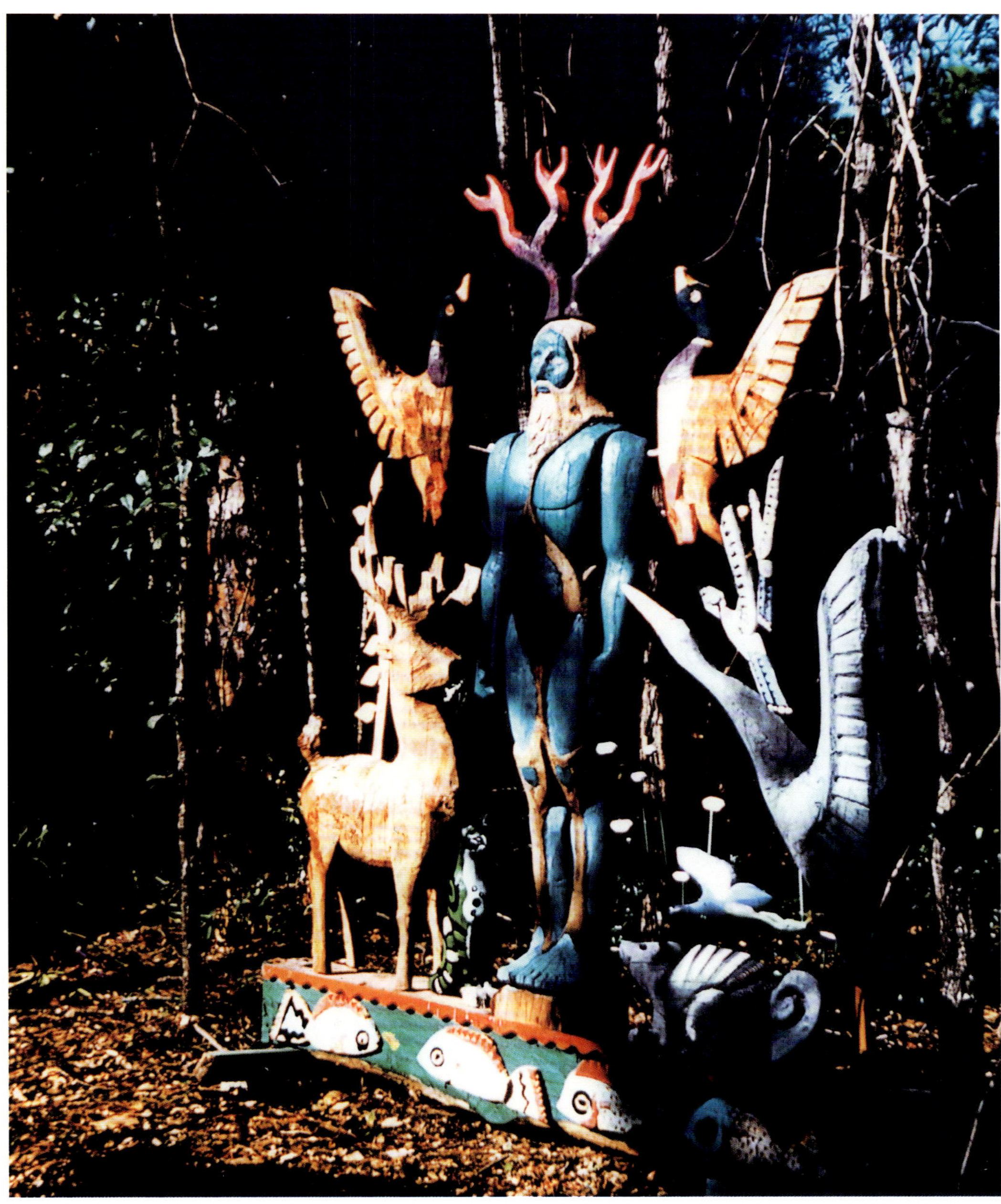

Father Mississippi, 1953

Painted wood, approx. 12 x 9 ft.
Photograph courtesy of The Family of Walter Anderson
The *Father Mississippi* group was carved from the oak tree that fell during the 1947 hurricane. The central river figure was about twelve feet tall and surrounded by the creatures and plants that lived on the river's banks, in its waters, and in the air above. The "antlers" were the tributaries of the river. Much of it weathered away over the next ten years, but it still attracted curious visitors until Anderson dismantled it.

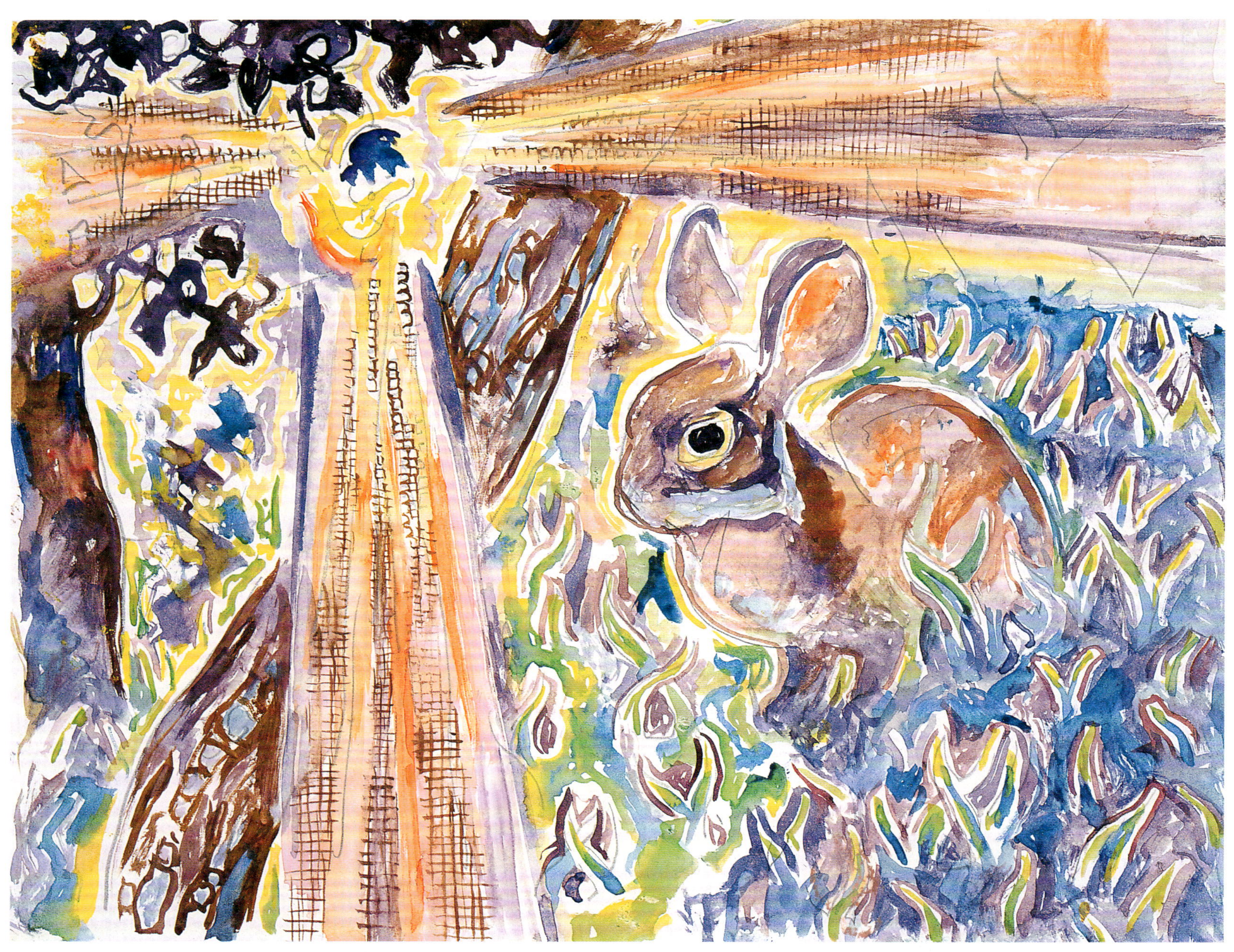

Rabbit with Crucifix Light Rays, ca. 1955

Watercolor on paper, 8½ x 11 in.
The Family of Walter Anderson

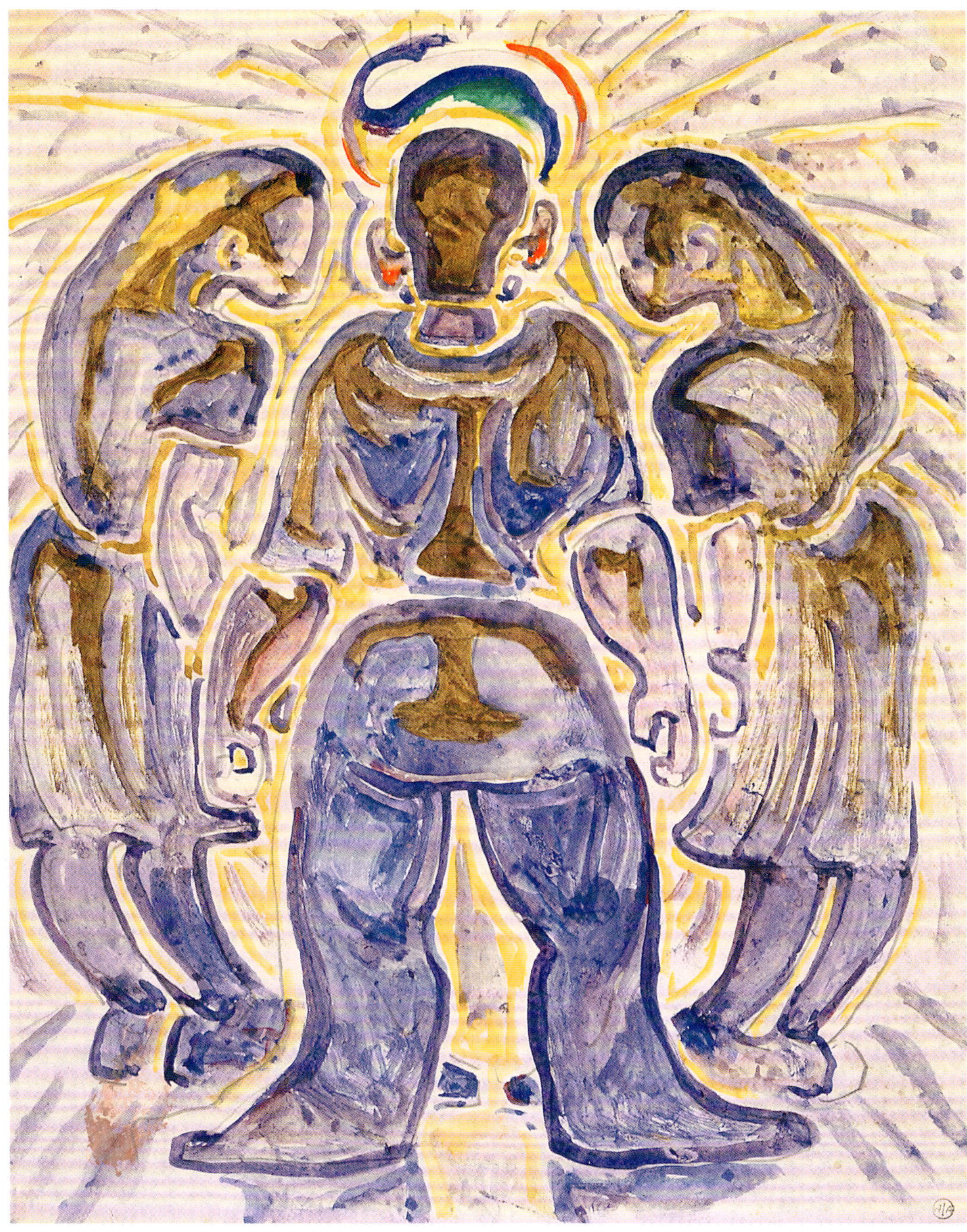

What Does He See?, ca. 1960

Watercolor on paper, 11 x 8½ in.
The Family of Walter Anderson
Anderson used the yin yang symbol in the murals as well as in this enigmatic painting.

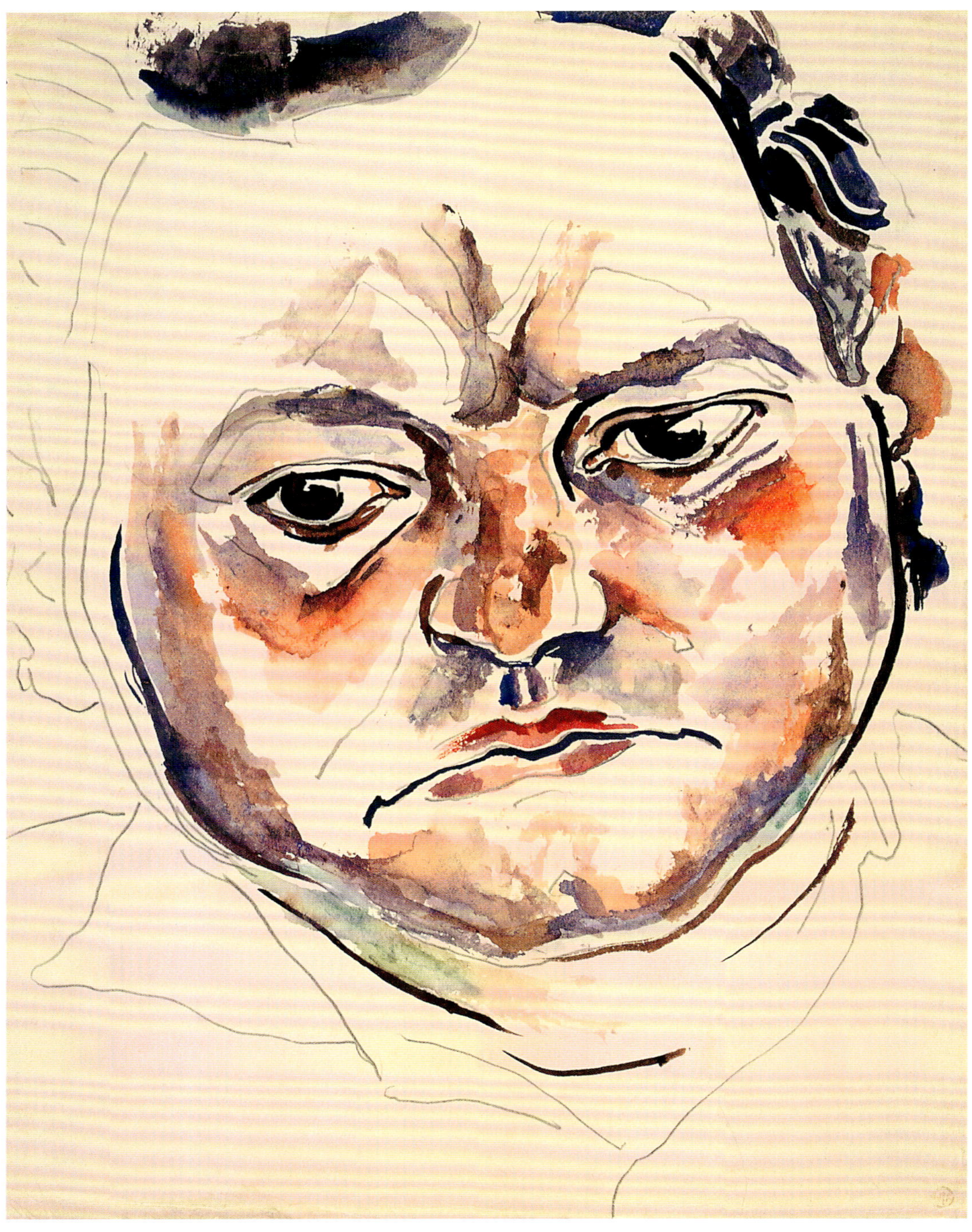

Mr. Le Blanc, 1955

Watercolor on paper, 11 x 8½ in.
Walter Anderson Museum of Art, 99.2.1
Anderson painted fellow patients at De Paul Sanitarium, New Orleans, with tender compassion, writing in his journal, "So soon as man shall see light in another man, he shall possess light himself."

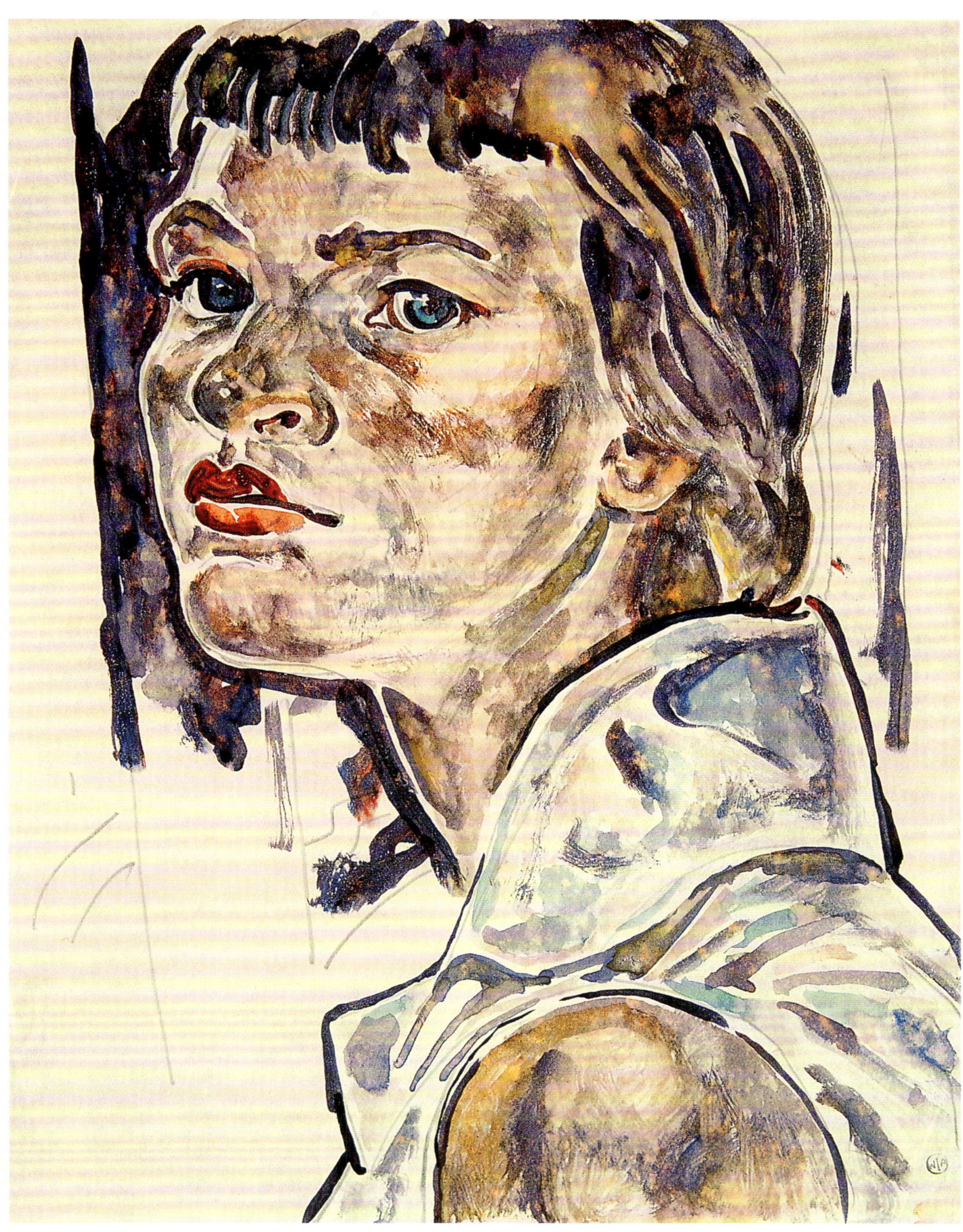

Portrait of Young Woman, ca. 1950

Watercolor on paper, 11 x 8½ in.
Walter Anderson Museum of Art, 75.1.1

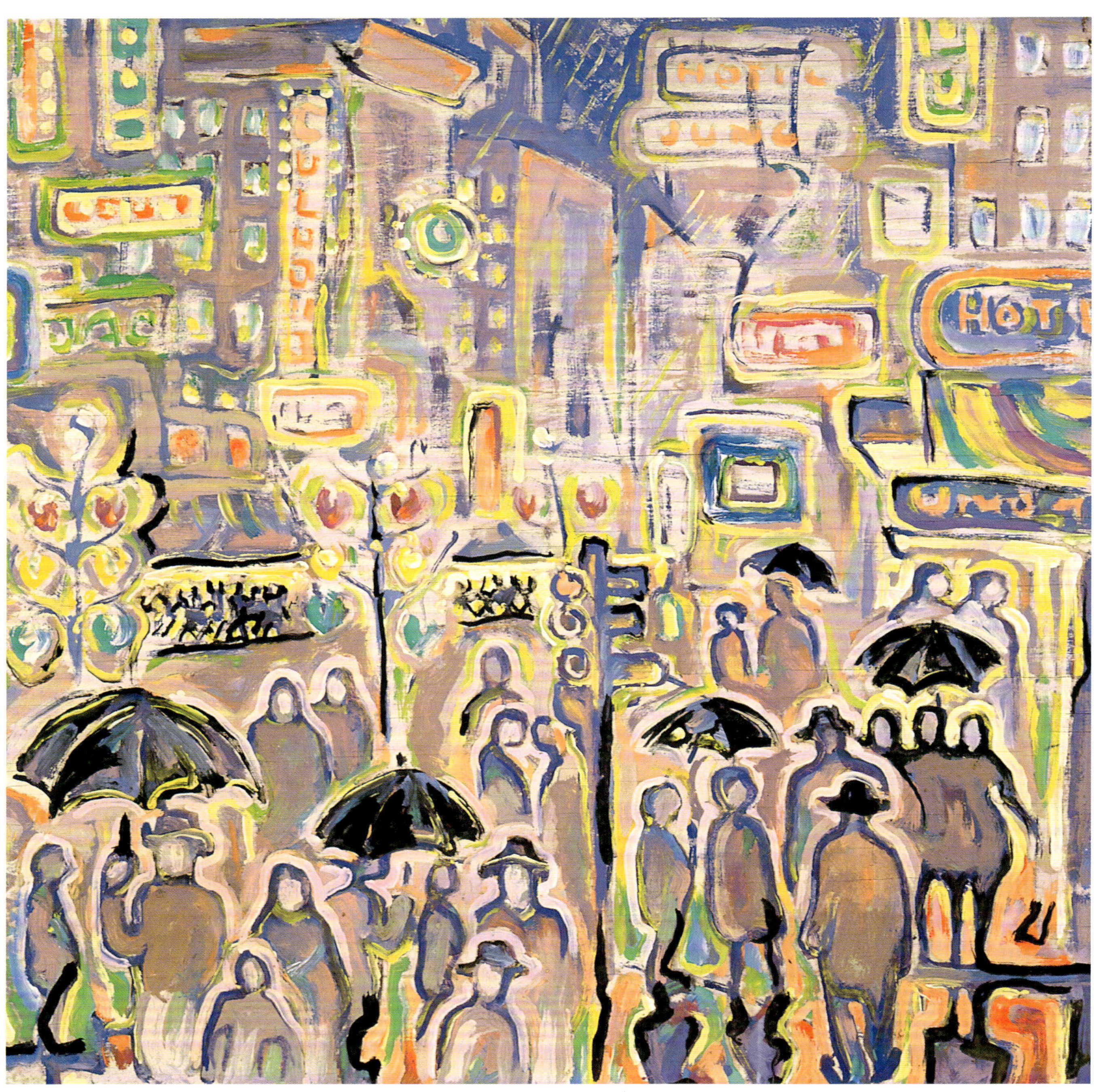

New Orleans Street Scene, 1962

Oil on wood, 29 x 29 in.
The Family of Walter Anderson
One of the few oil paintings done during the latter part of Anderson's life, this one shows a rainy evening on Canal Street during Mardi Gras.

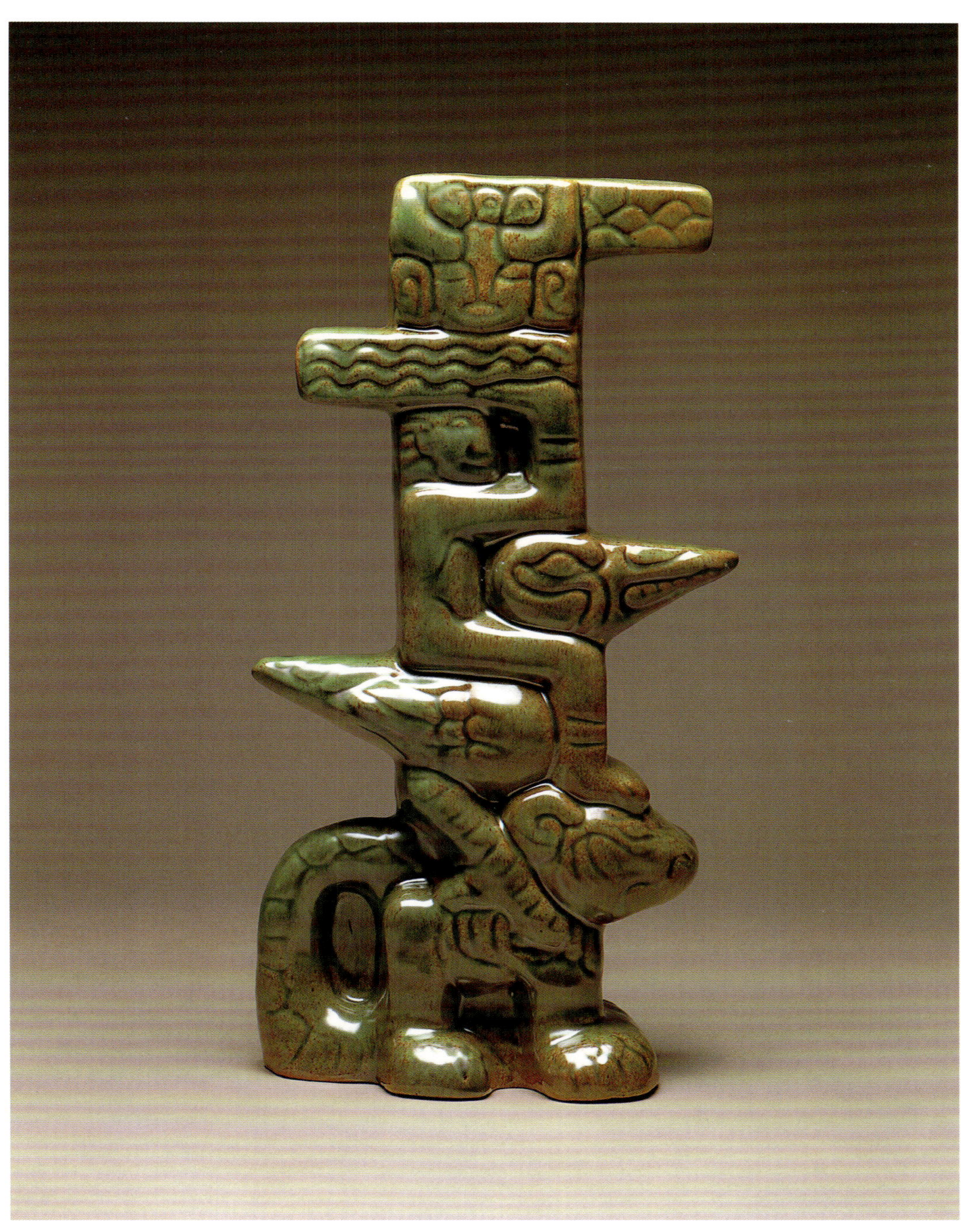

Totem Lamp Base, ca. 1950

Ceramic, 12½ x 7 x 4 in.
Walter Anderson Museum of Art, 94.5.1
This lamp base, reminiscent of the stacked totem forms of the ancient Americans, probably illustrates a myth or folktale.

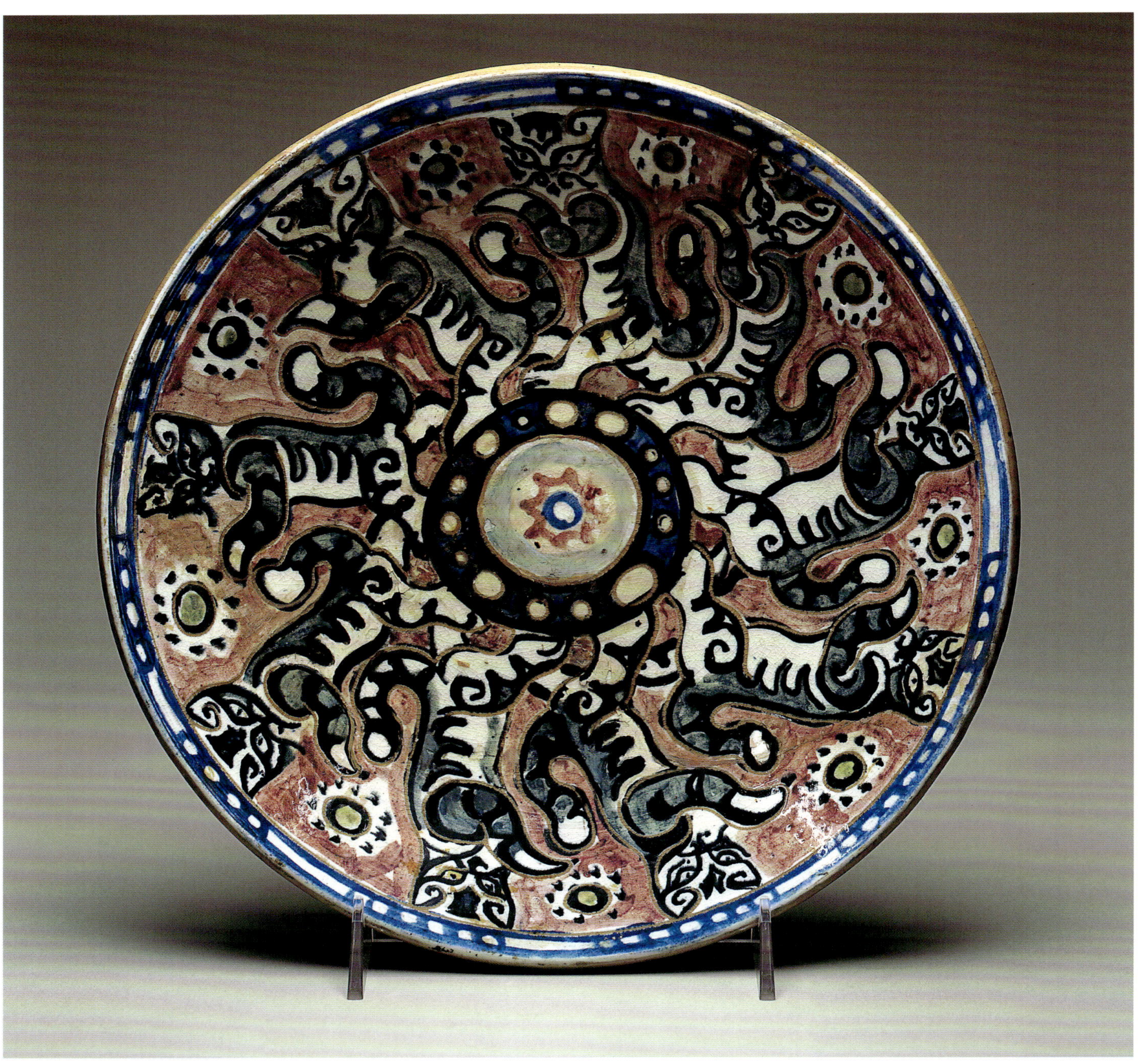

Walking Cats Plate, 1955

Ceramic, 8½ x 8½ x 1½ in.
The Family of Walter Anderson
Thrown by Peter Anderson, decorated by Walter Anderson

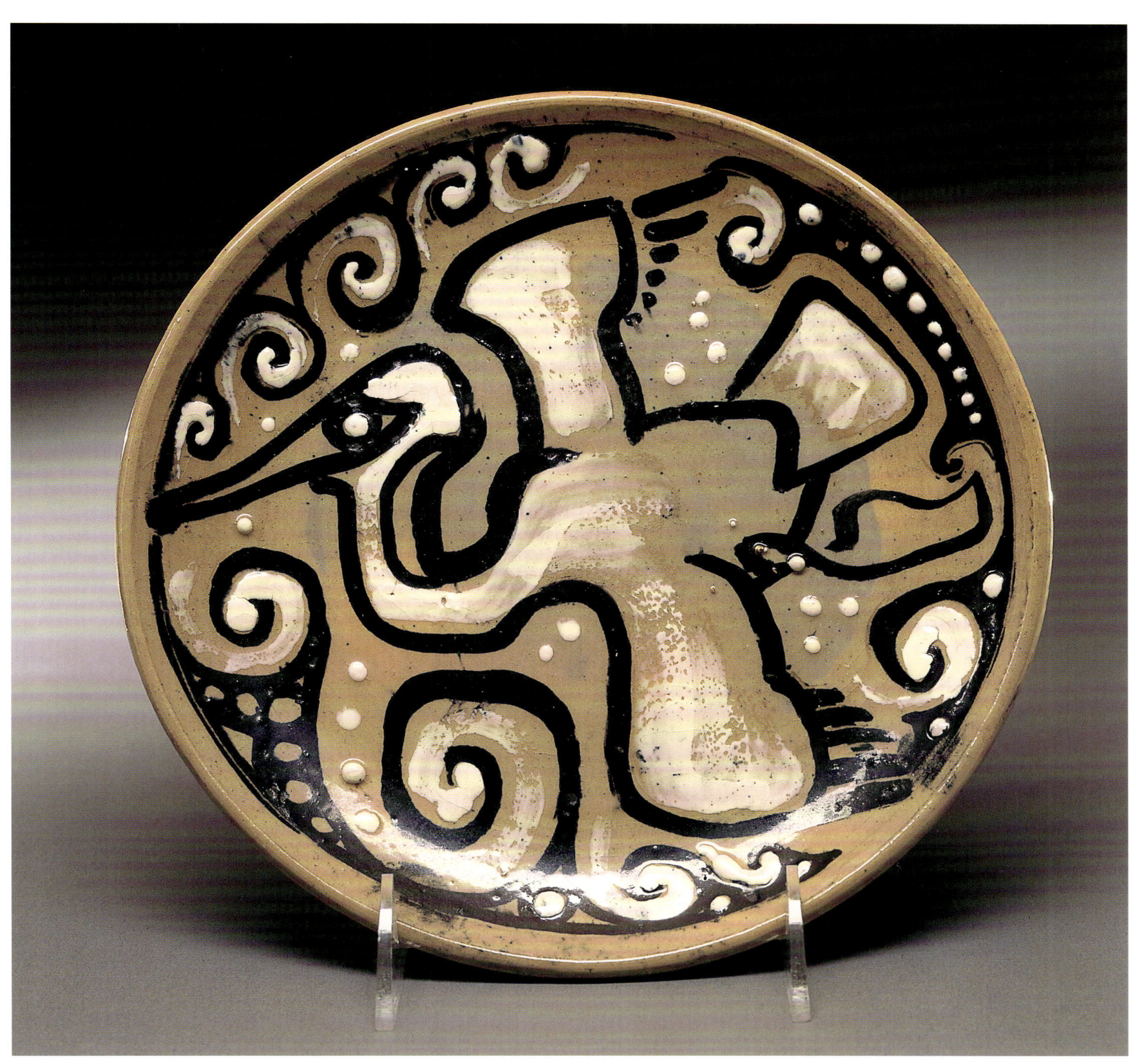

Pelican Plate, ca. 1950

Ceramic, 8 x 8 x 1½ in.
Walter Anderson Museum of Art, 98.12.5
Thrown by Peter Anderson, decorated by Walter Anderson

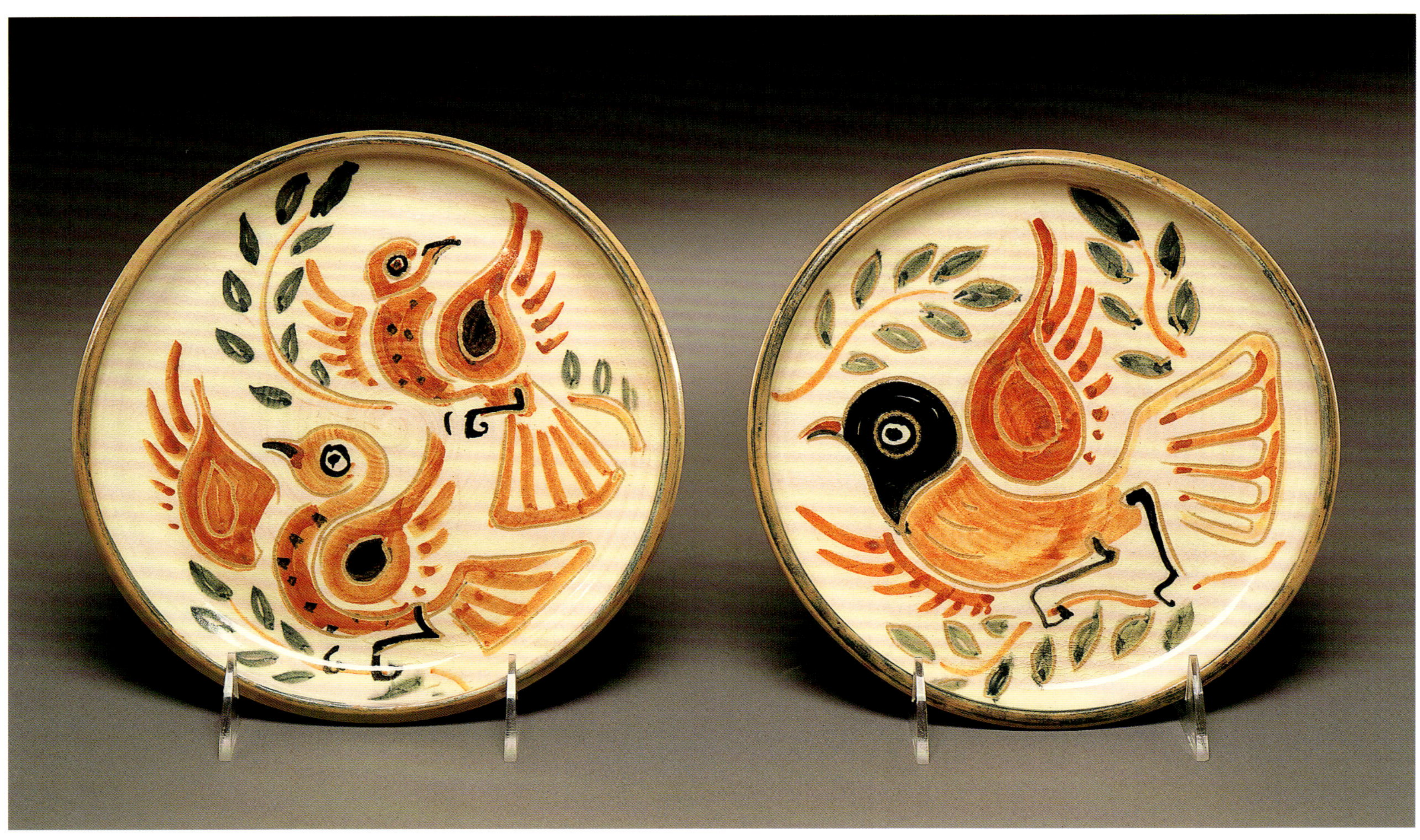

Two Brown Thrashers Plate ca. 1955

Rufus Sided Towhee Plate, ca. 1955

Ceramic, each 8 x 8 x 1½ in.
Louise Lehman Collection
Thrown by Peter Anderson, decorated by Walter Anderson

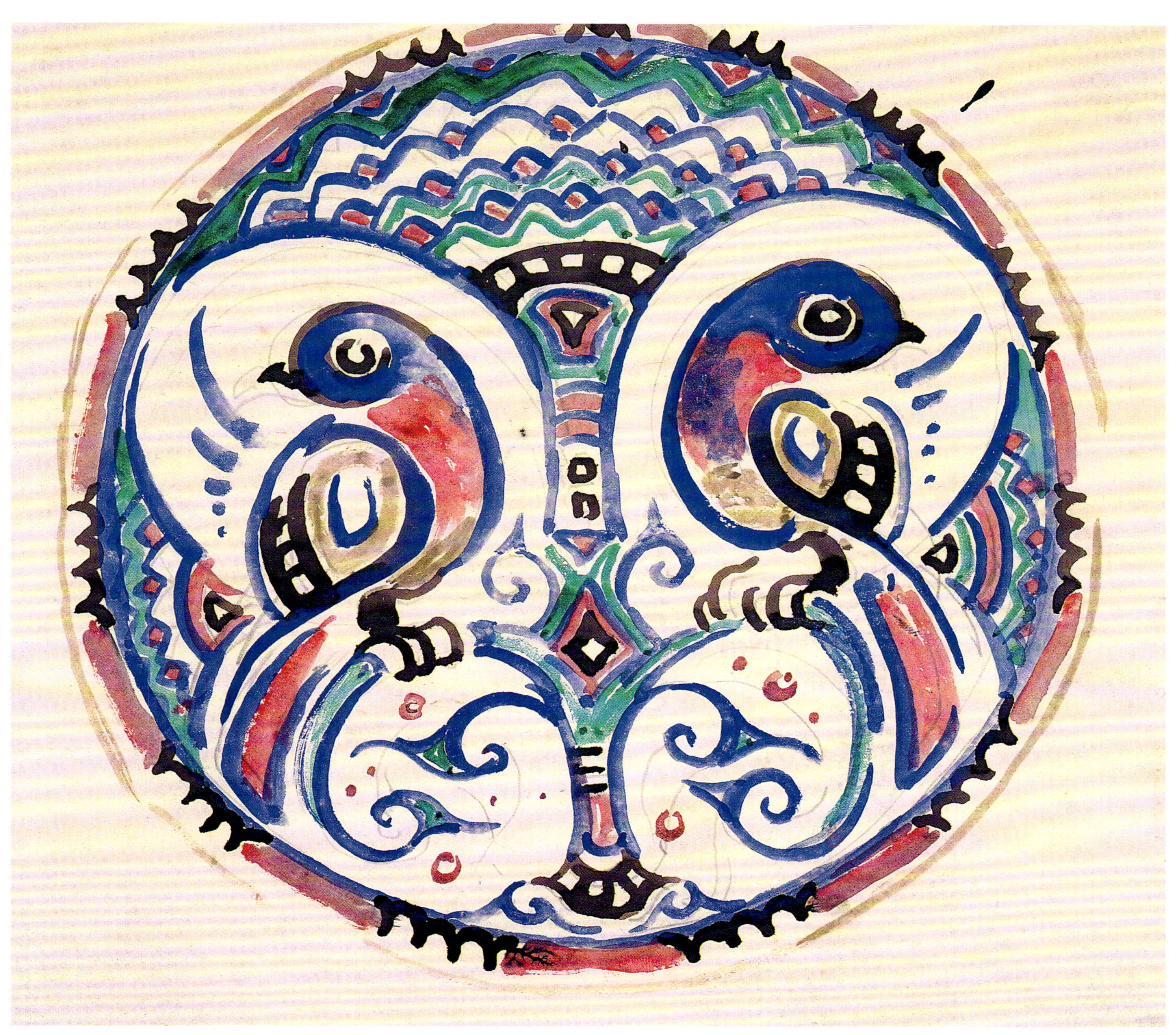

Design for Tree of Life Bird Plate, ca. 1955

Watercolor on paper, 8½ x 11 in.
The Family of Walter Anderson

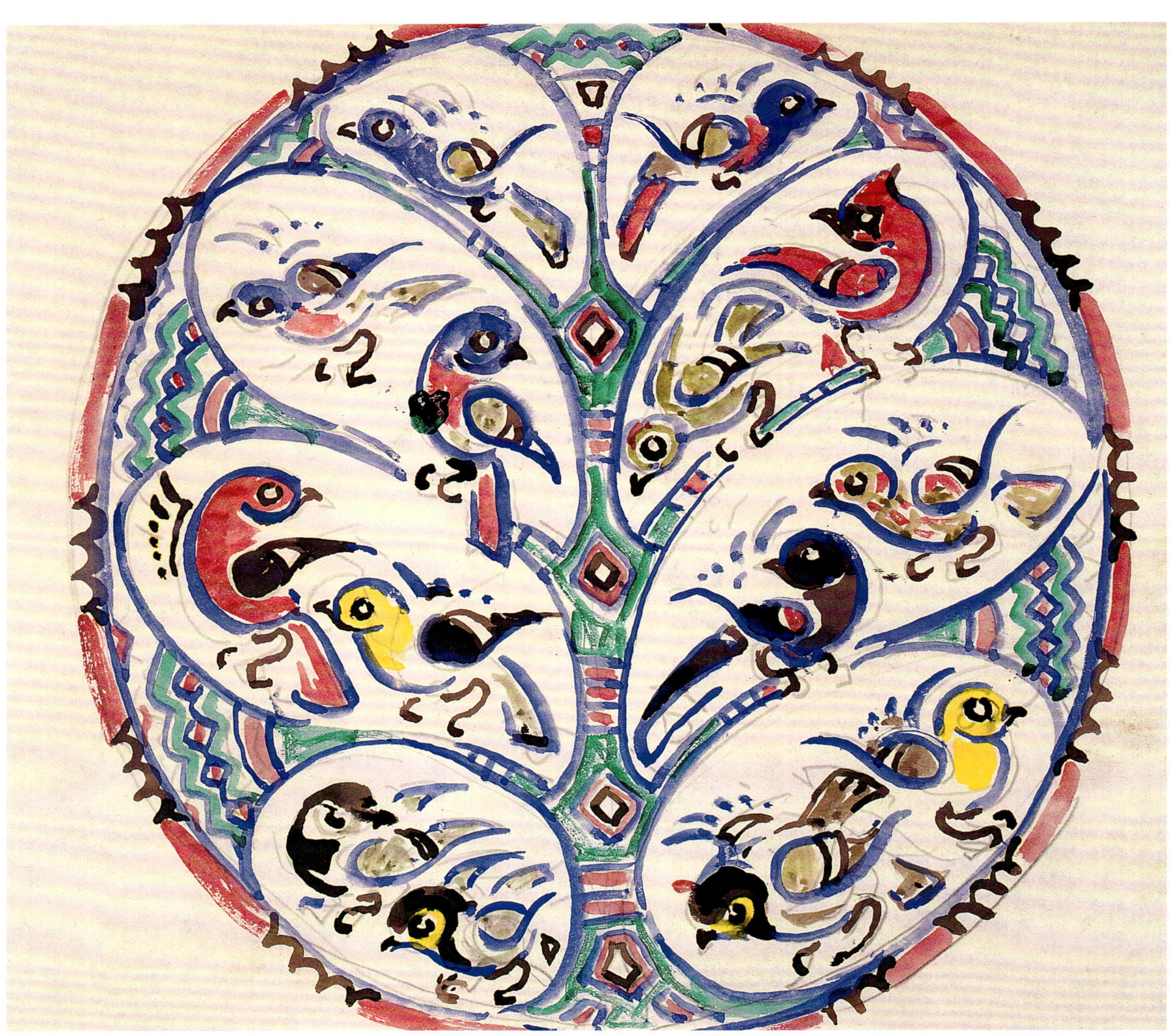

Design for Tree of Life with Birds Plate, ca. 1955

Watercolor on paper, 8½ x 11 in.
The Family of Walter Anderson
This tree of life celebrates the spring bird migration on the Gulf Coast as well as the classical seven-branched tree.

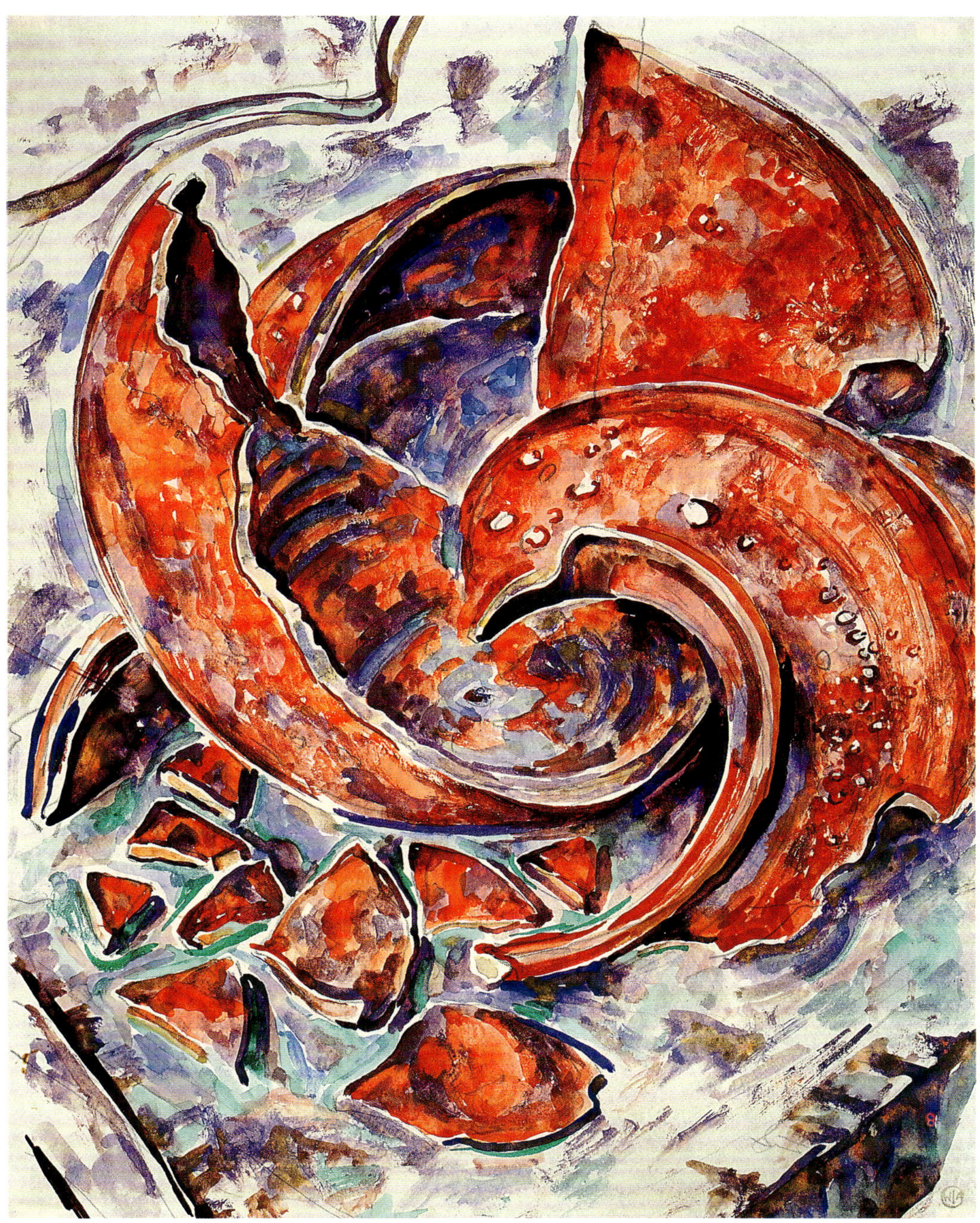

Broken Red Pot, 1960

Watercolor on paper, 11 x 8½ in.
Walter Anderson Museum of Art, 97.3.1
Along with the murals, the watercolors of the 1950s and 1960s are the artworks on which Anderson's reputation has rested since his death. Copper red was an expensive and difficult glaze. This work's careful execution probably constitutes an apology and a tribute to his brother the potter because he, Walter, had broken the vase.

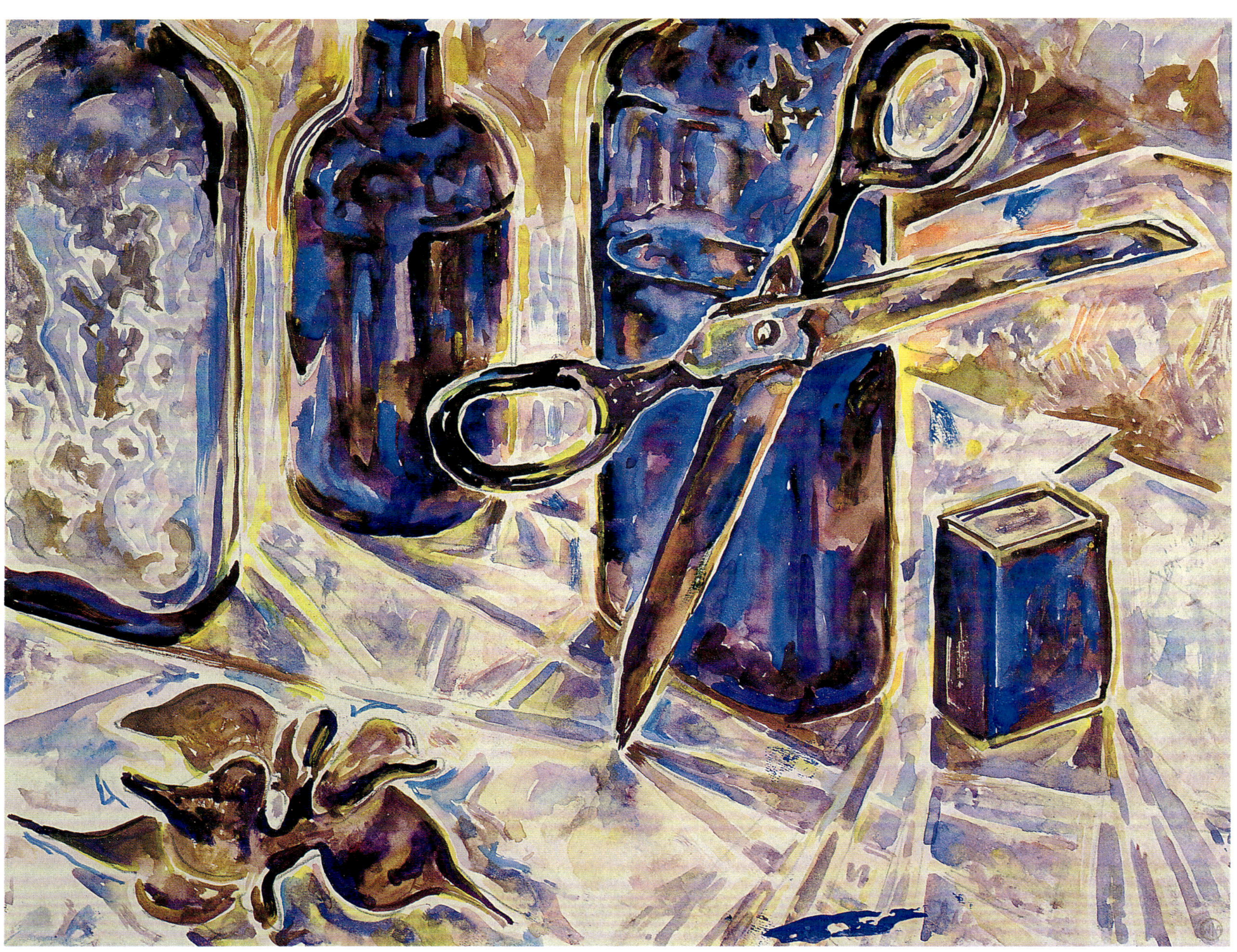

Scissors and Bottles, ca. 1950

Watercolor on paper, 8½ x 11 in.
Walter Anderson Museum of Art, 00.2.1

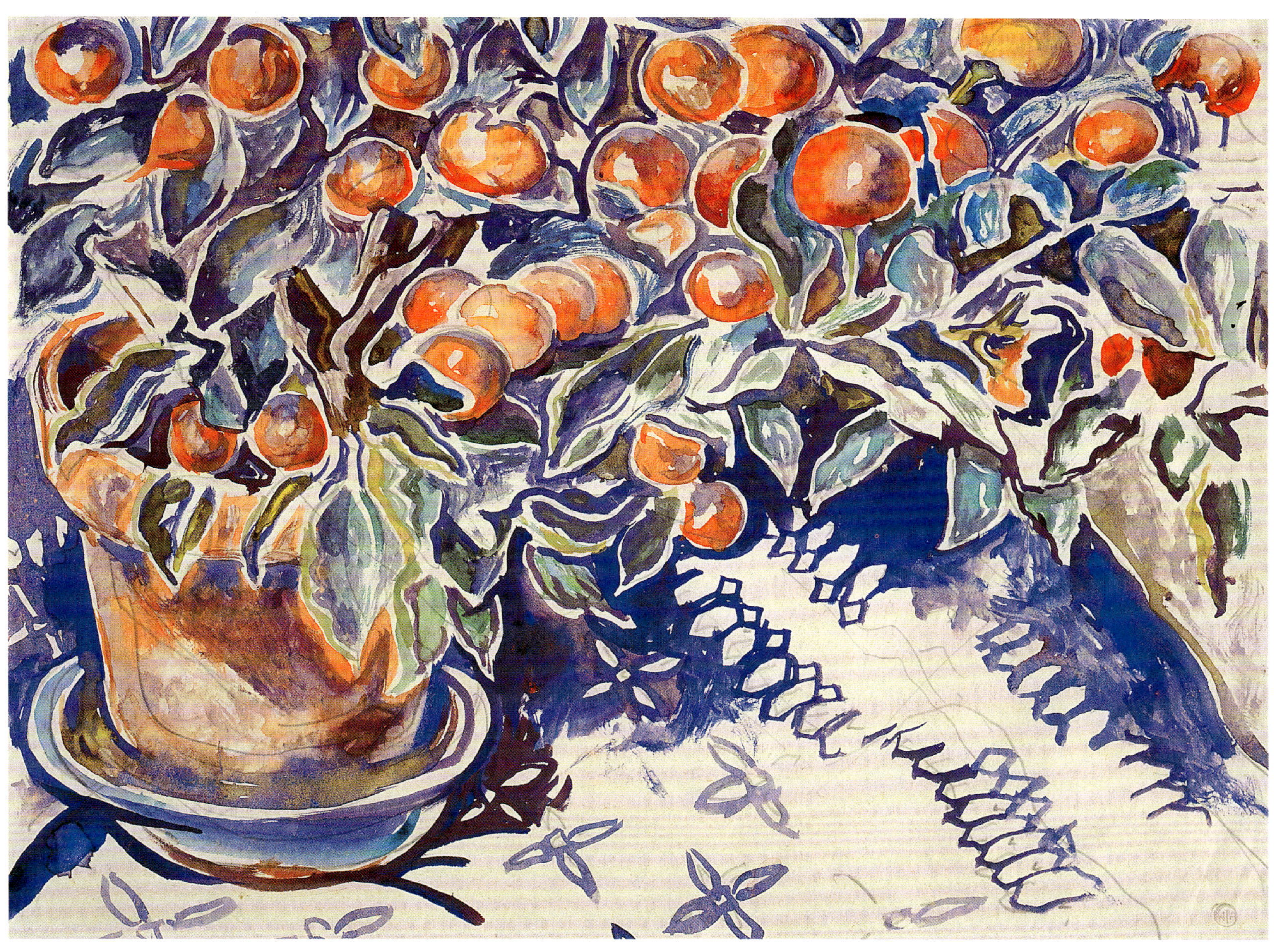

Jerusalem Cherry, ca. 1960

Watercolor on paper, 8½ x 11 in.
Walter Anderson Museum of Art, 00.1.1

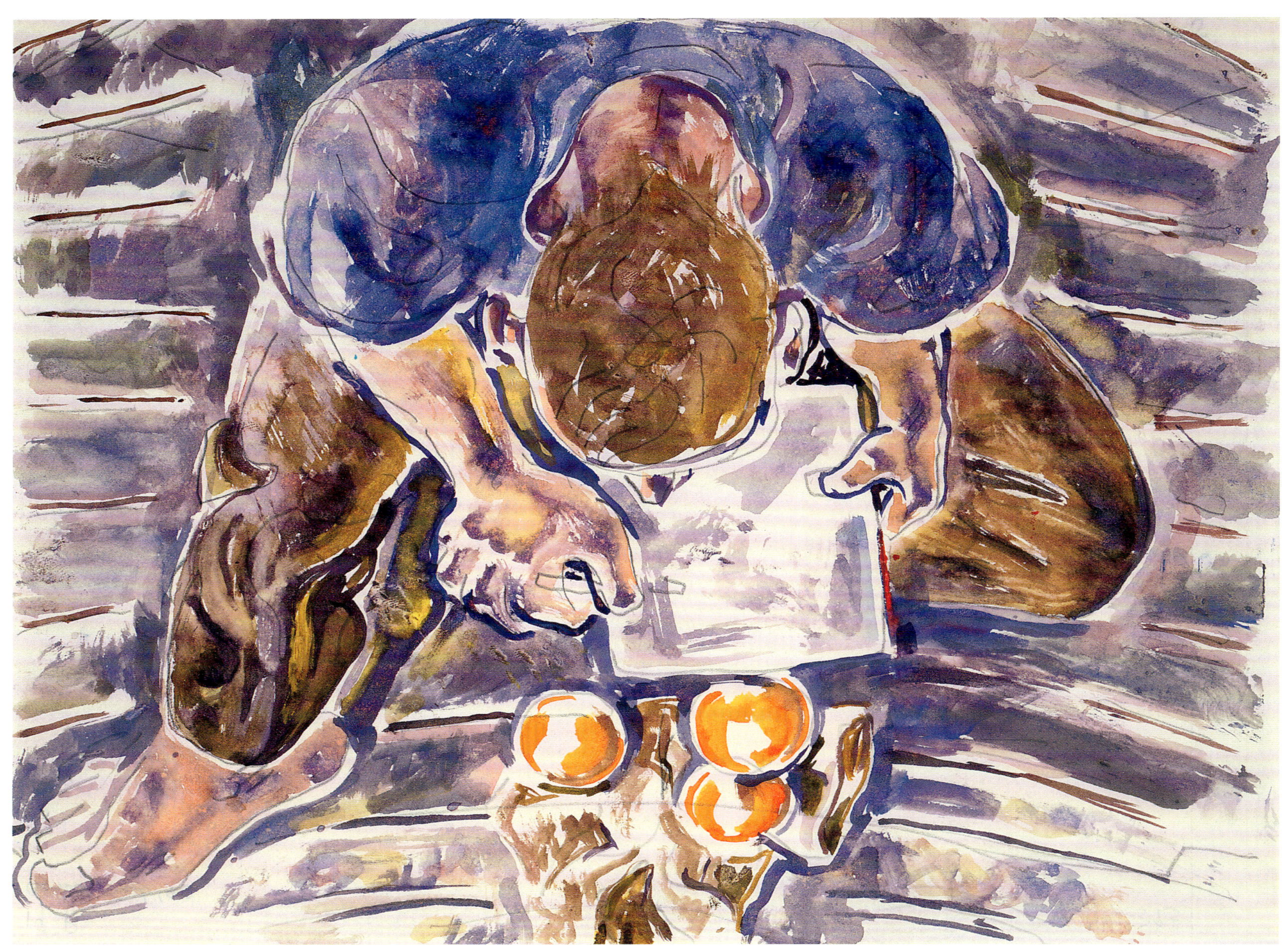

The Artist Painting Oranges, ca. 1952

Watercolor on paper, 8½ x 11 in.
The Family of Walter Anderson

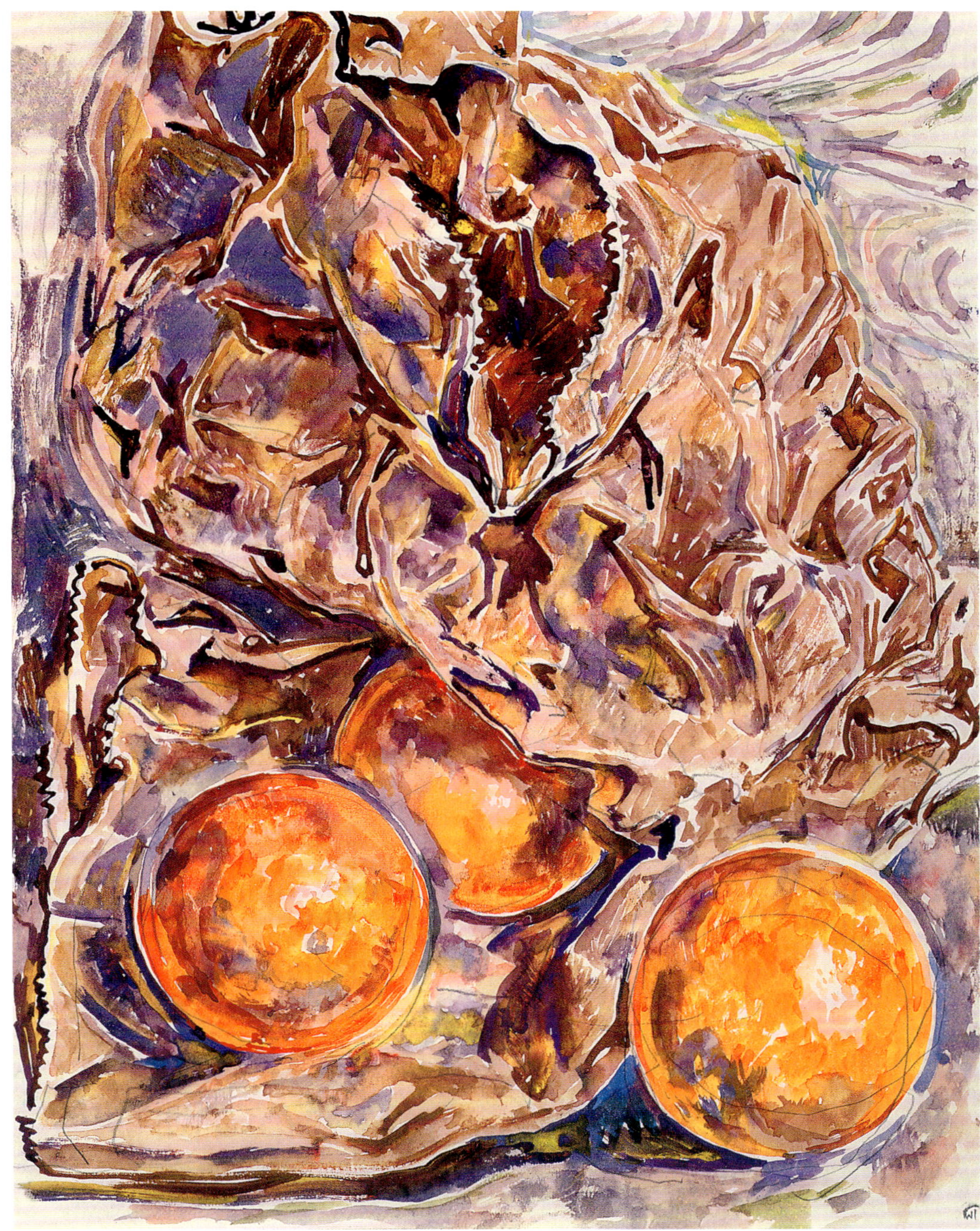

Oranges and Sack, ca. 1952

Watercolor on paper, 11 x 8½ in.
The Family of Walter Anderson

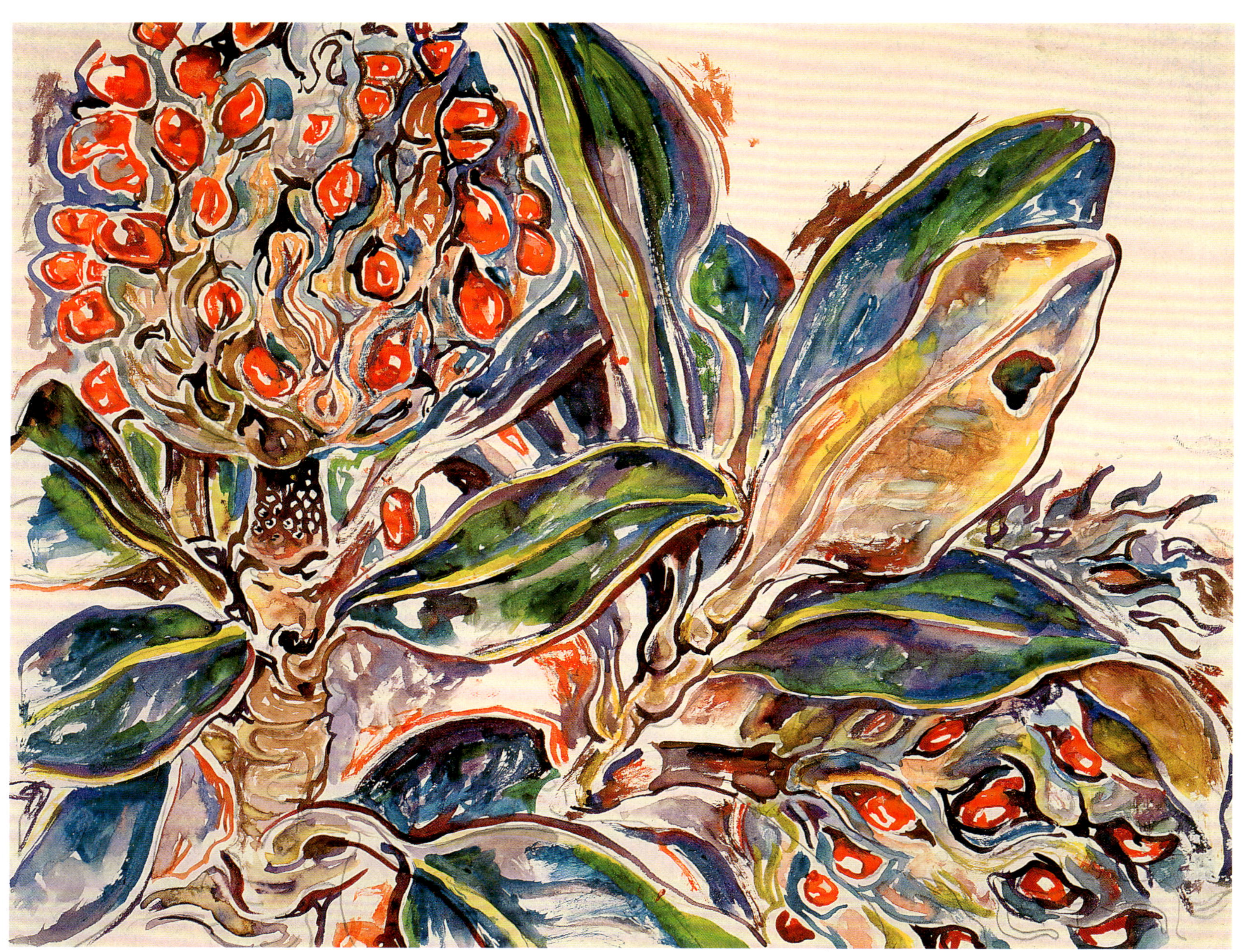

Magnolia Seed Pod, 1953

Watercolor on paper, 8½ x 11 in.
Walter Anderson Museum of Art, 75.1.5

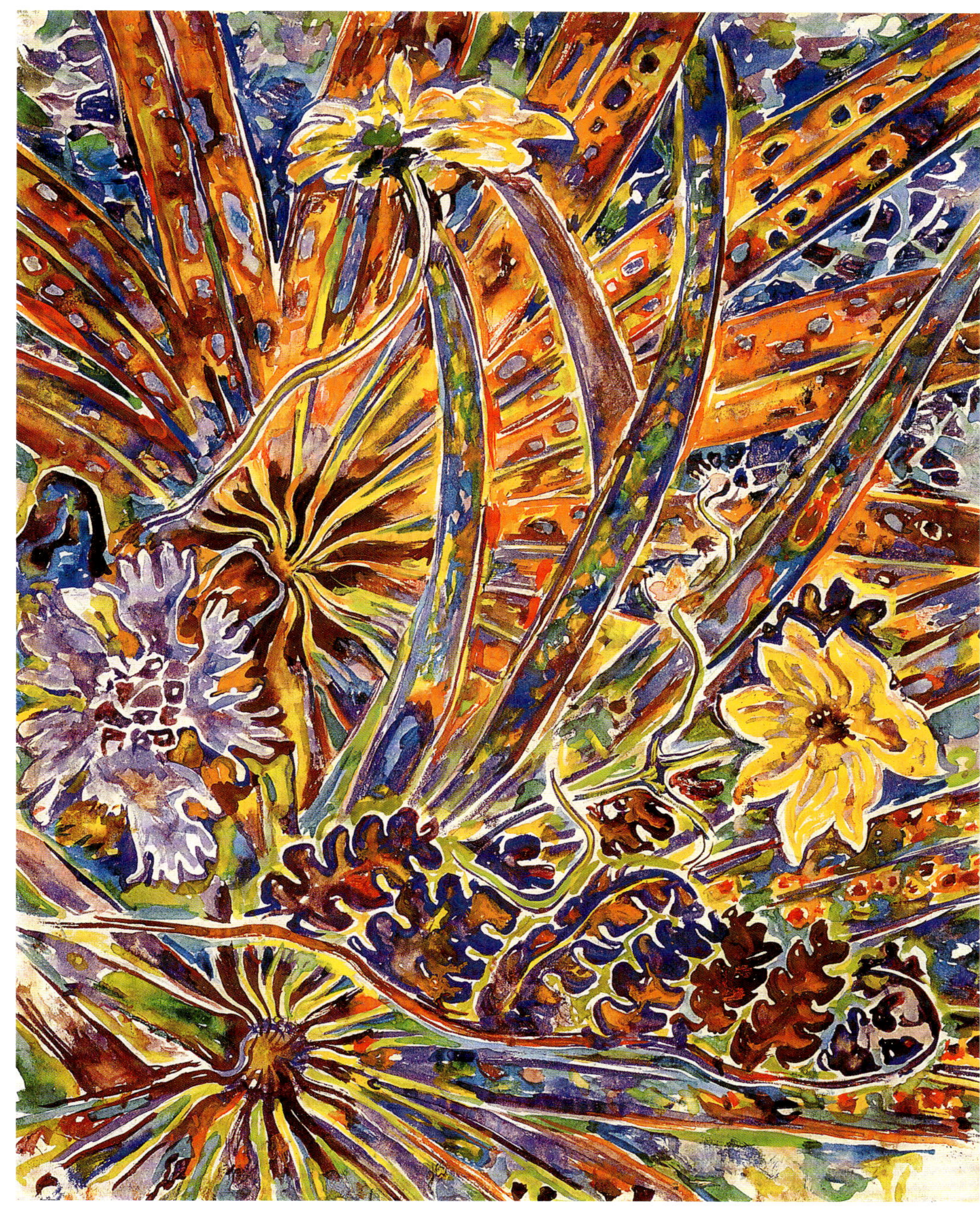

Palmetto with Flowers, ca. 1960

Watercolor on paper, 11 x 8½ in.
Walter Anderson Museum of Art, 00.3.1

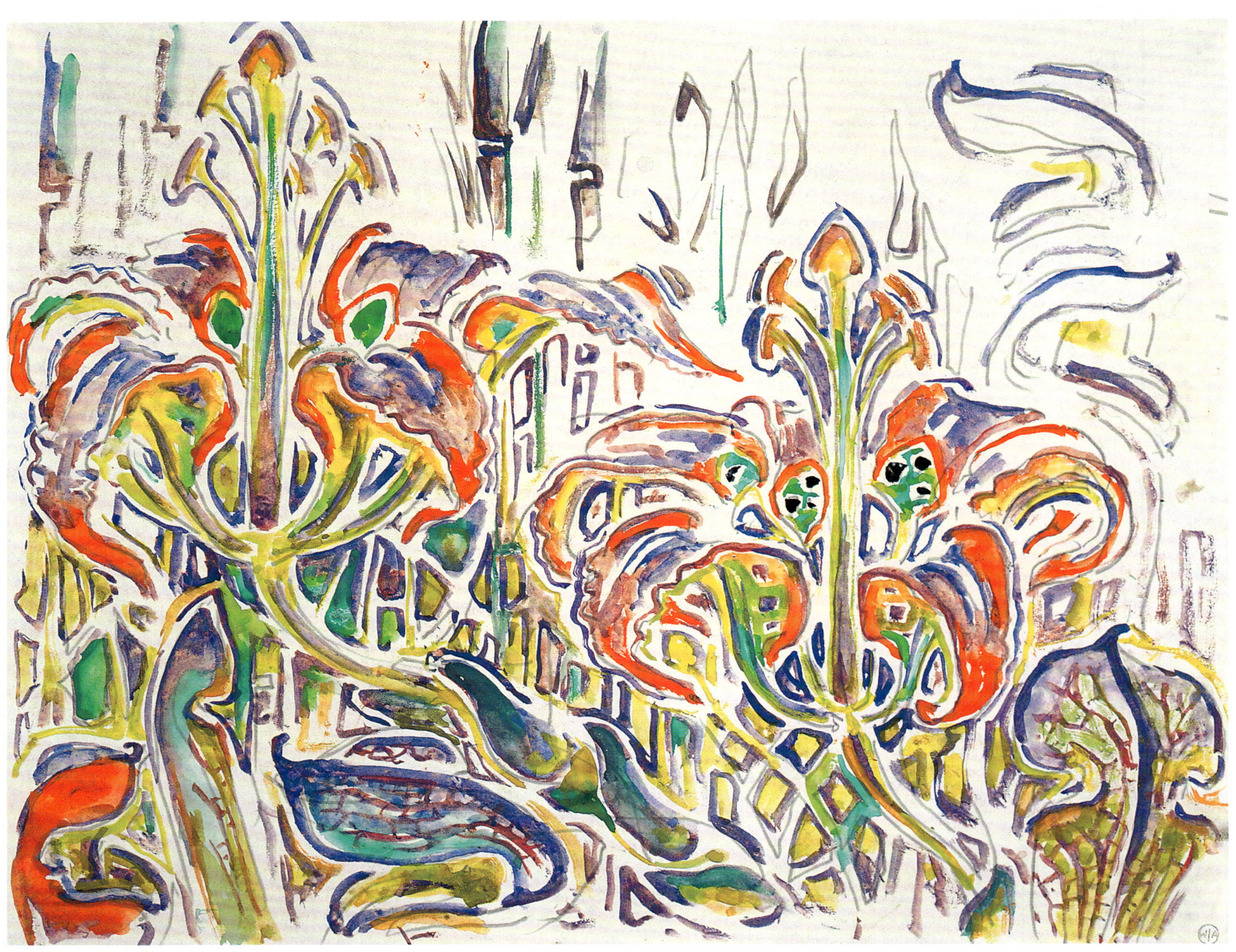

Red Wood Lilies, ca. 1955

Watercolor on paper, 8½ x 11 in.
The Family of Walter Anderson
Pine lilies were frequently referred to as "red wood lilies." Often stylized into flame-like touches of red in the 1934 murals, they were a constant motif throughout Anderson's work.

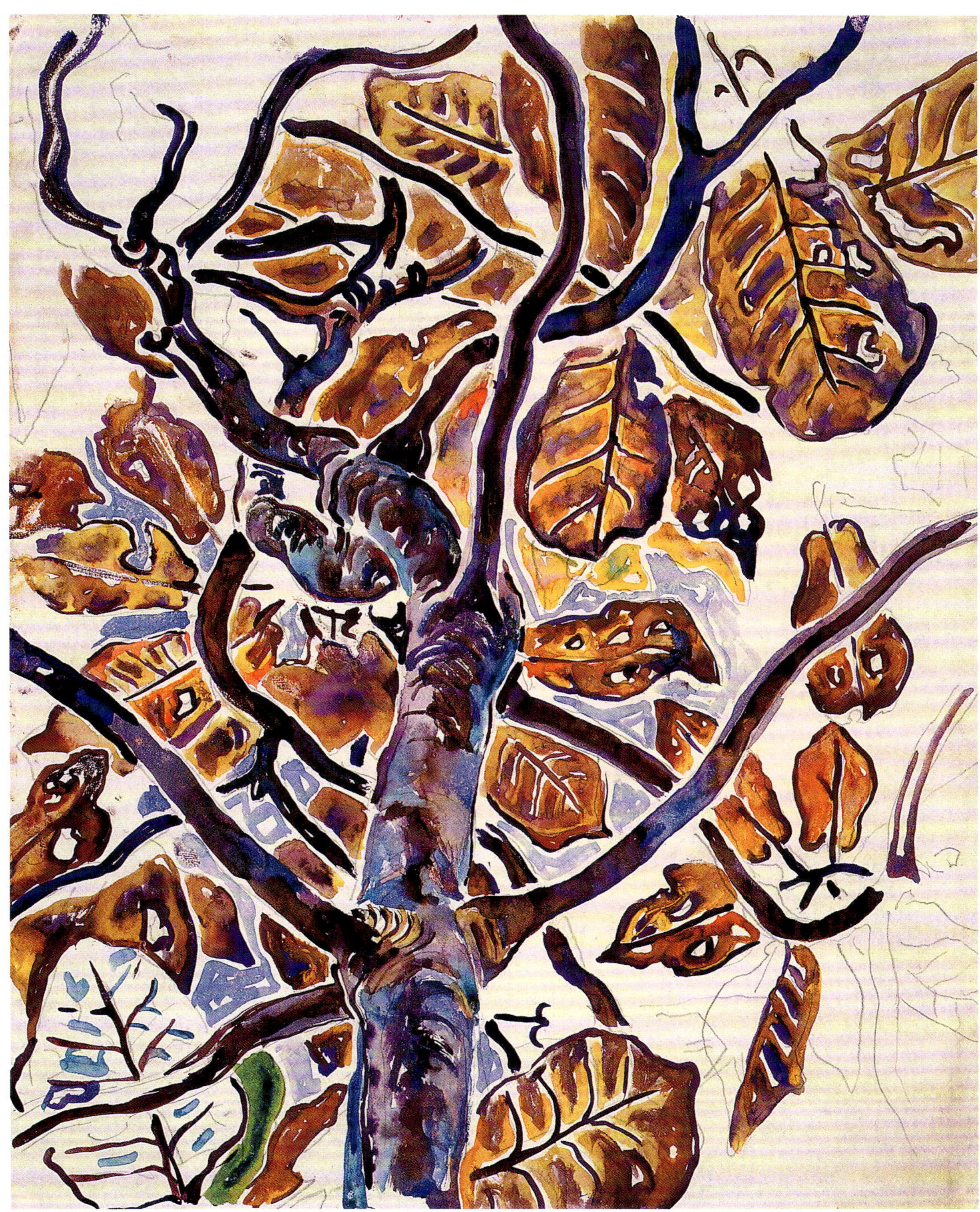

Broad Leaf Magnolia, ca. 1960

Watercolor on paper, 11 x 8½ in.
Walter Anderson Museum of Art, 97.9.1
The broadleaf magnolia has large leaves that are more delicate than those of the better-known *magnolia grandiflora*, and its blossoms can measure twelve inches across. Anderson planted one of these magnolias outside his cottage.

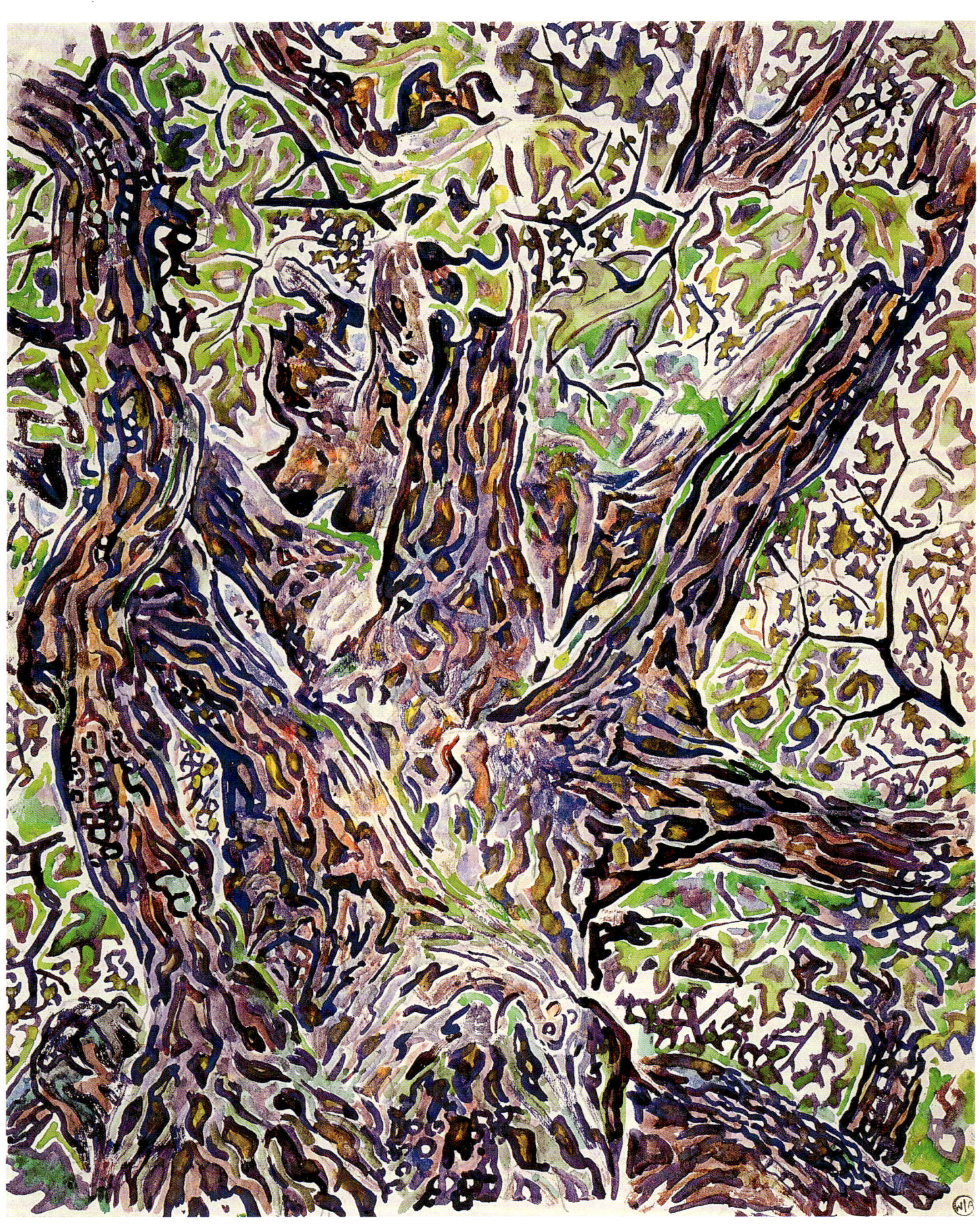

Red Oak with Squirrel, ca. 1955

Watercolor on paper, 11 x 8½ in.
The Family of Walter Anderson

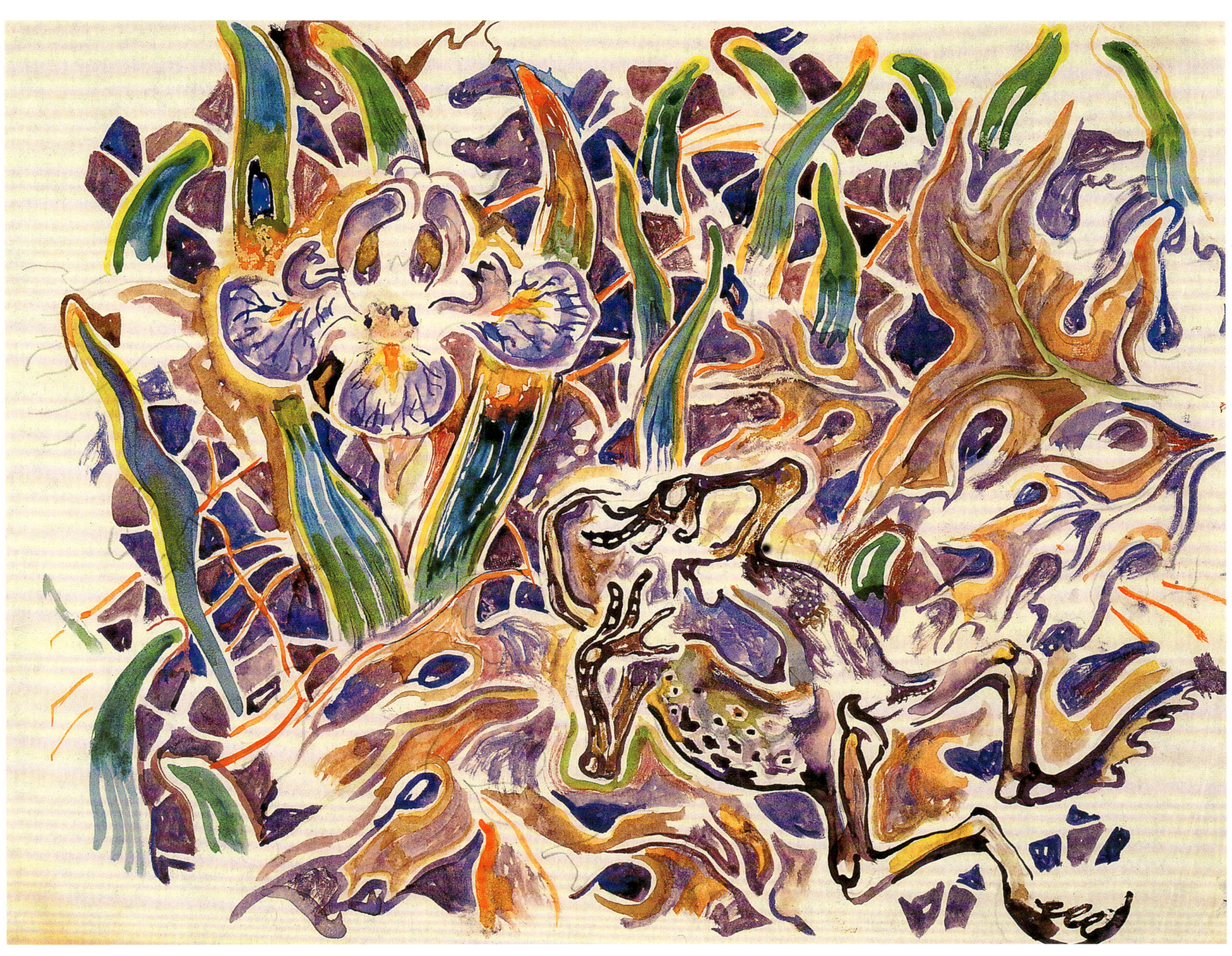

Frog with Iris, ca. 1960

Watercolor on paper, 8½ x 11 in.
Walter Anderson Museum of Art, 97.1.2

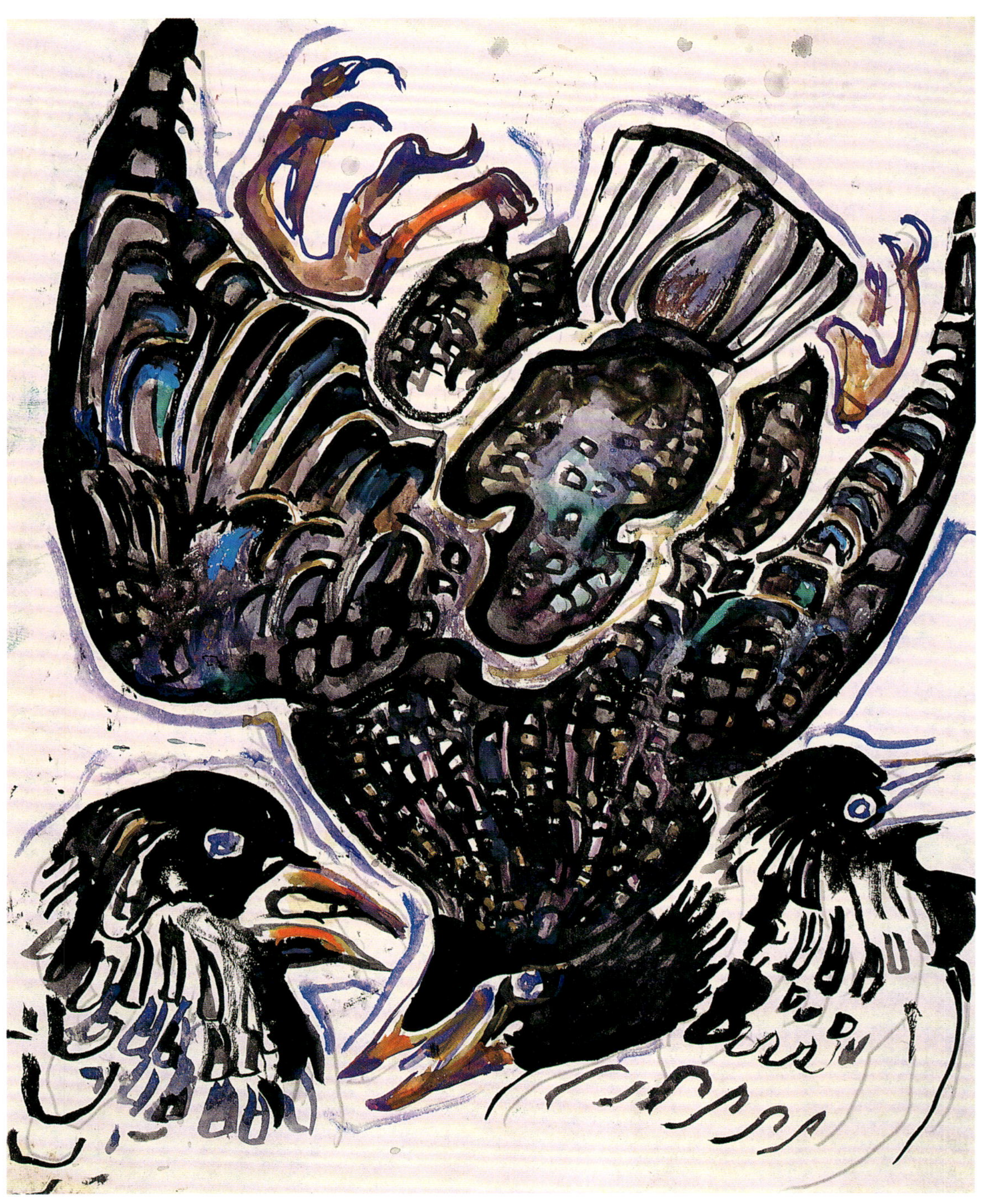

Dead Starling, ca. 1960

Watercolor on paper, 11 x 8½ in.
The Family of Walter Anderson

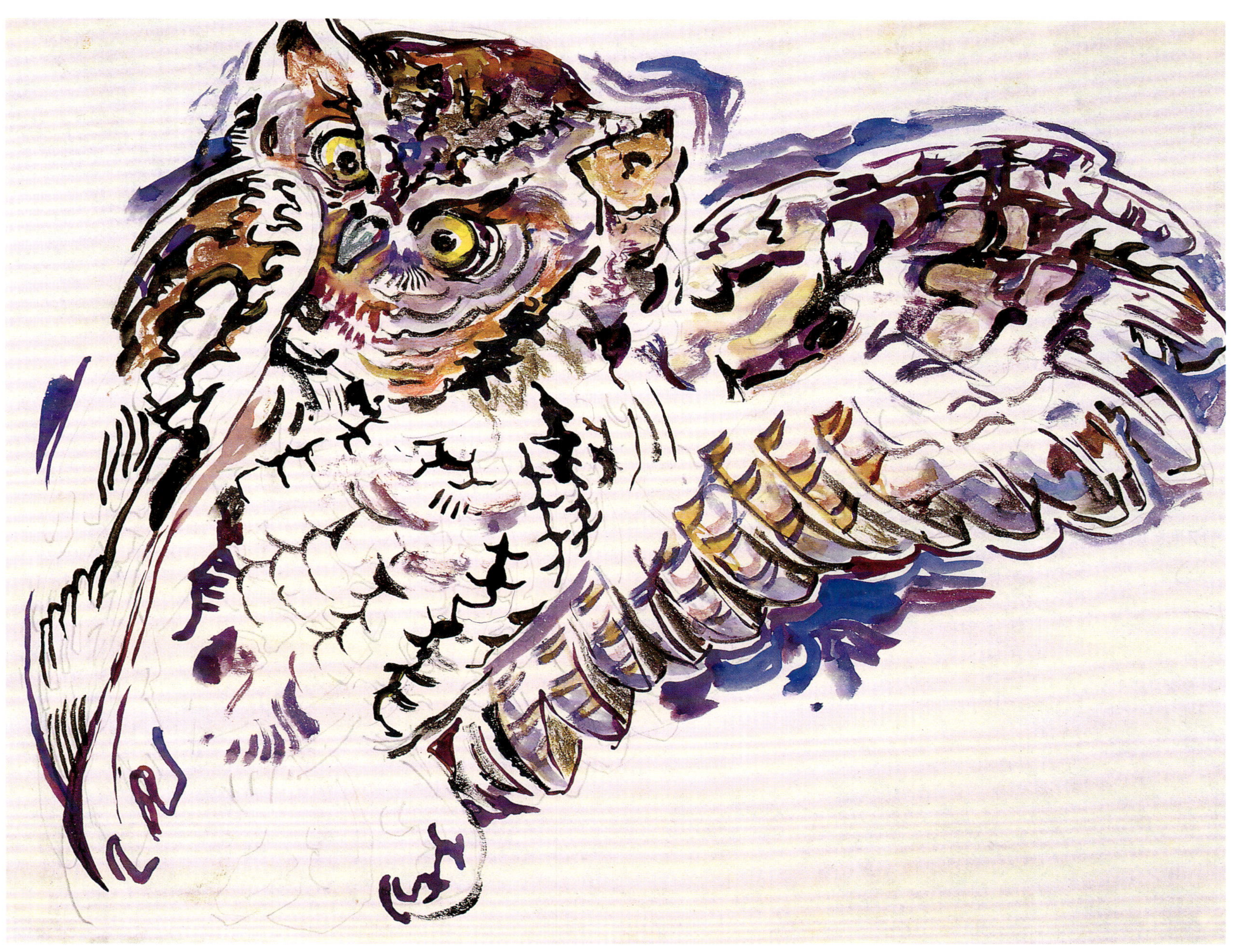

Owl, ca. 1960

Watercolor on paper, 8½ x 11 in.
Walter Anderson Museum of Art, 97.1.1

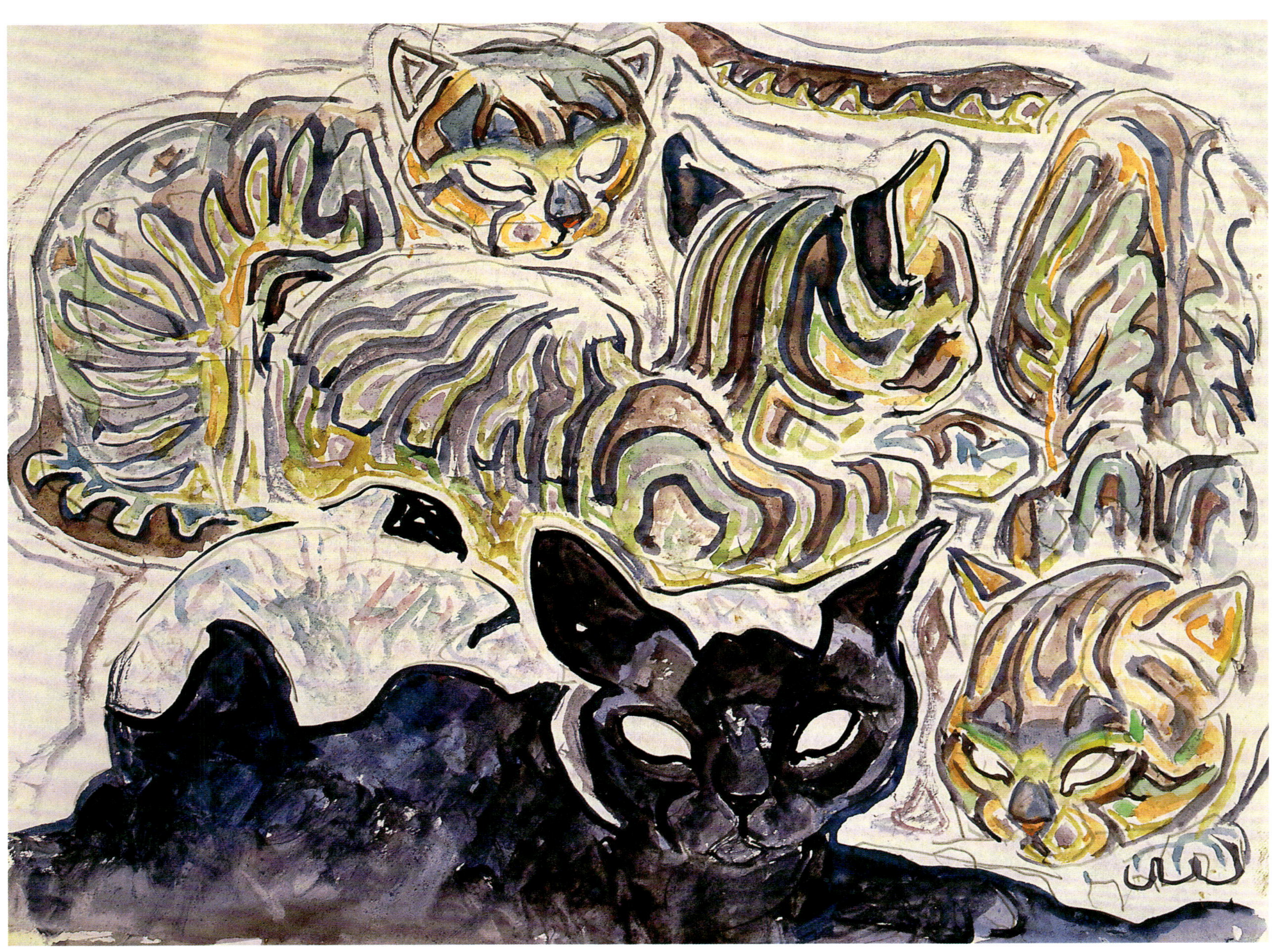

Cats, ca. 1955

Watercolor on paper, 8½ x 11 in.
Walter Anderson Museum of Art, 88.1.3
Anderson noted that the visual world around him contained "an embarrassment of riches." Cats and kittens were abundant at the Shearwater compound and were the source of many compositions.

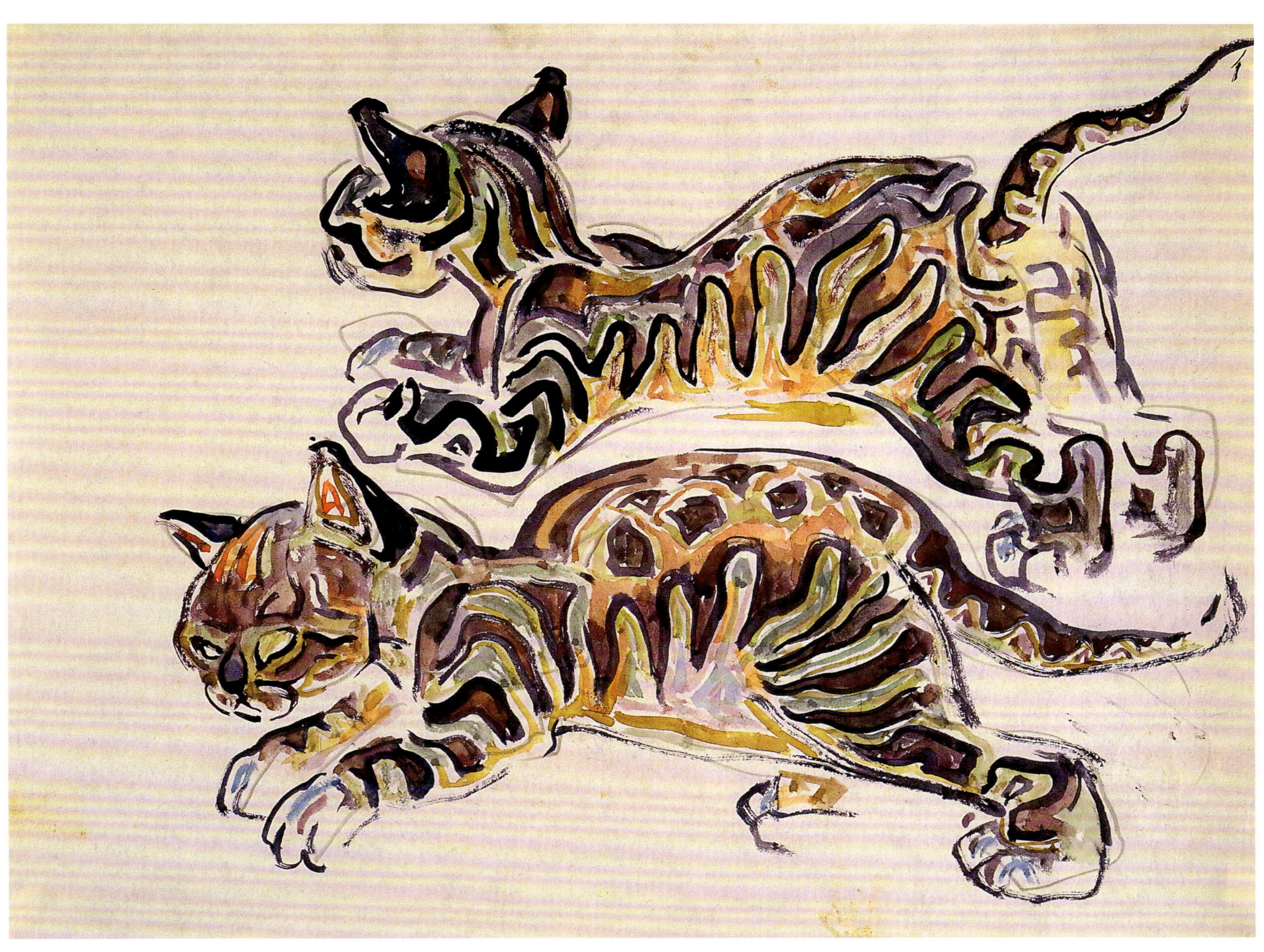

Two Kittens Pouncing, ca. 1955

Watercolor on paper, 8½ x 11 in.
Walter Anderson Museum of Art, 93.1.6
Gift of the Knight Foundation

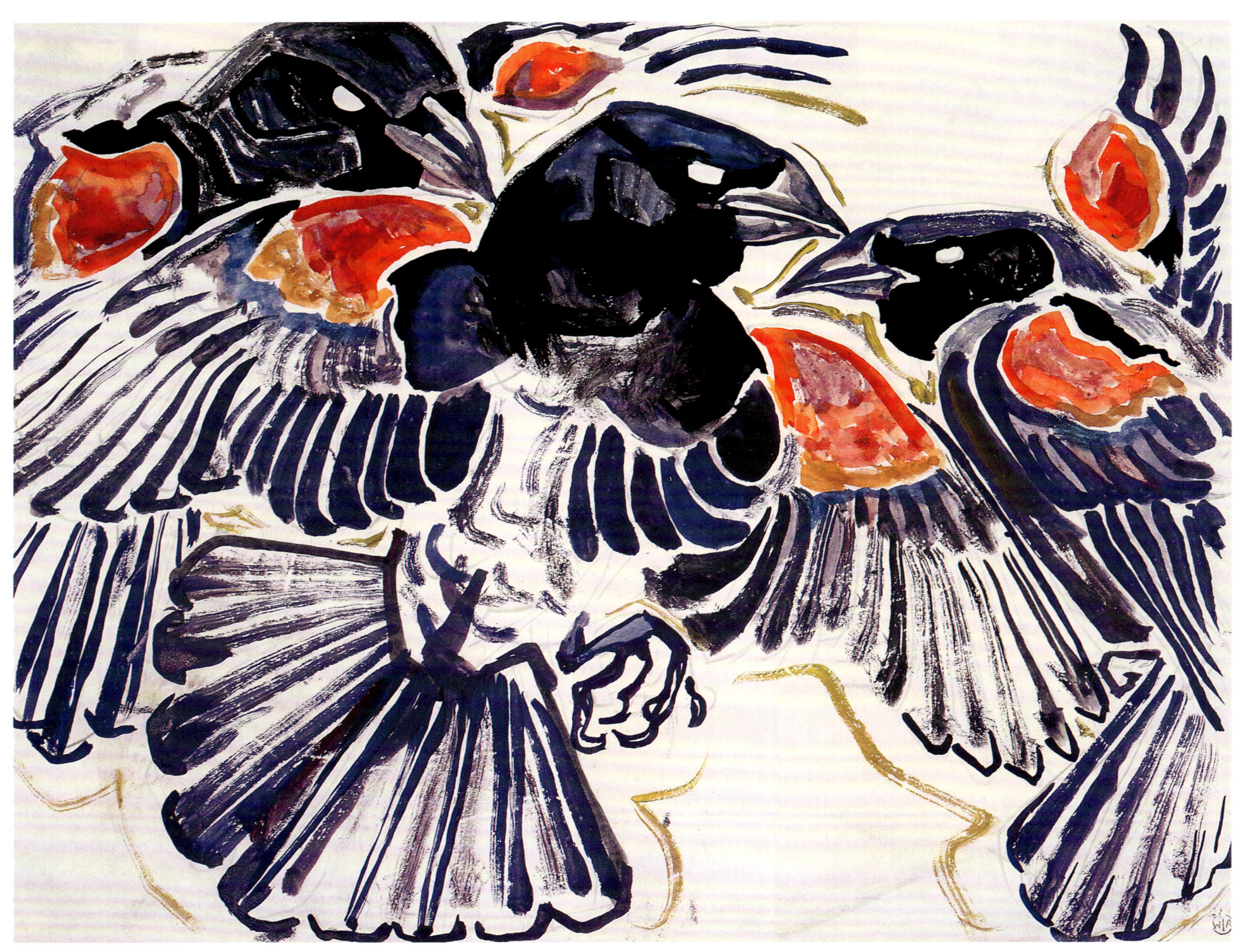

Redwings, ca. 1960

Watercolor on paper, 8½ x 11 in.
Walter Anderson Museum of Art, 87.1.2

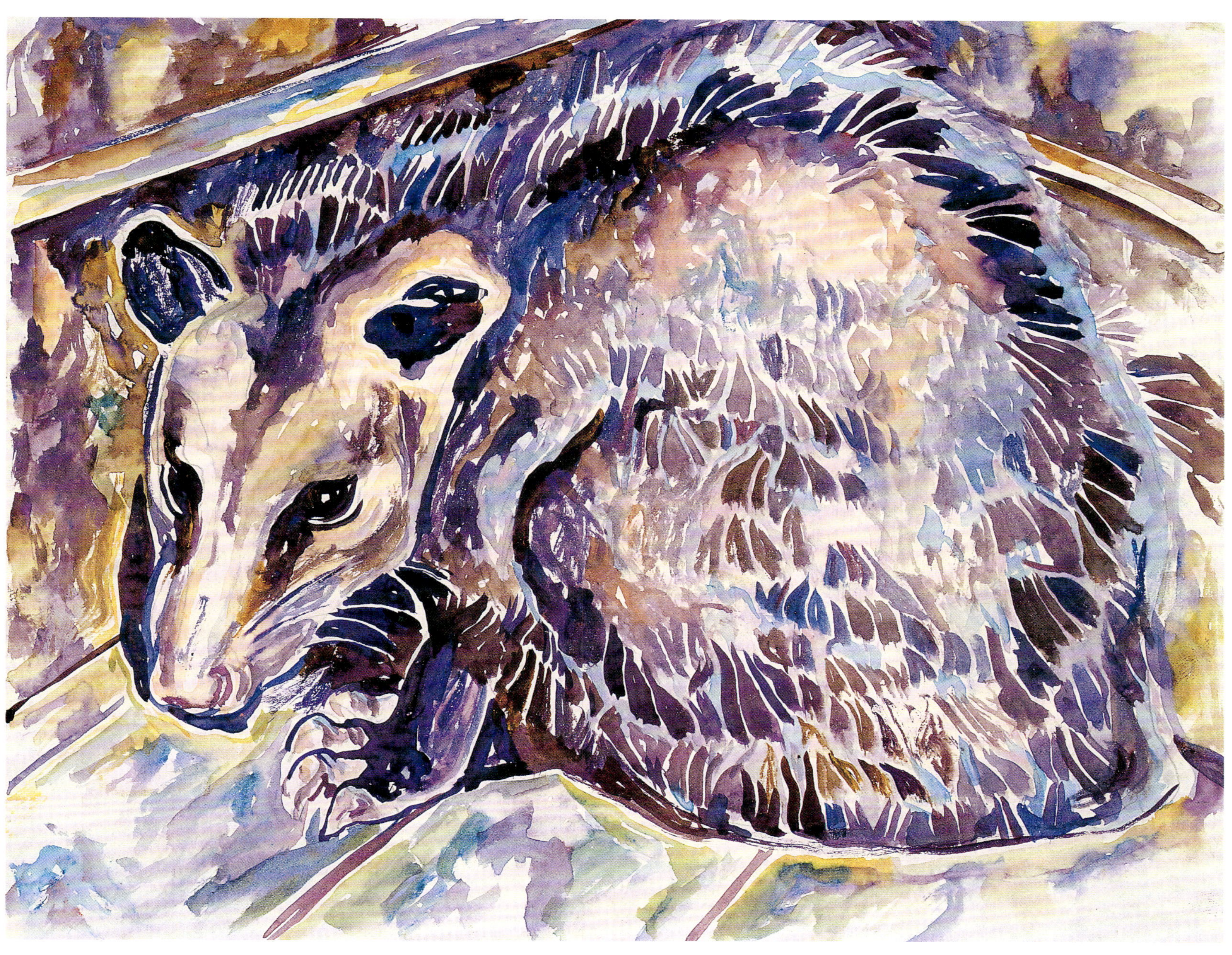

Opossum, ca. 1955

Watercolor on paper, 8½ x 11 in.
The Family of Walter Anderson

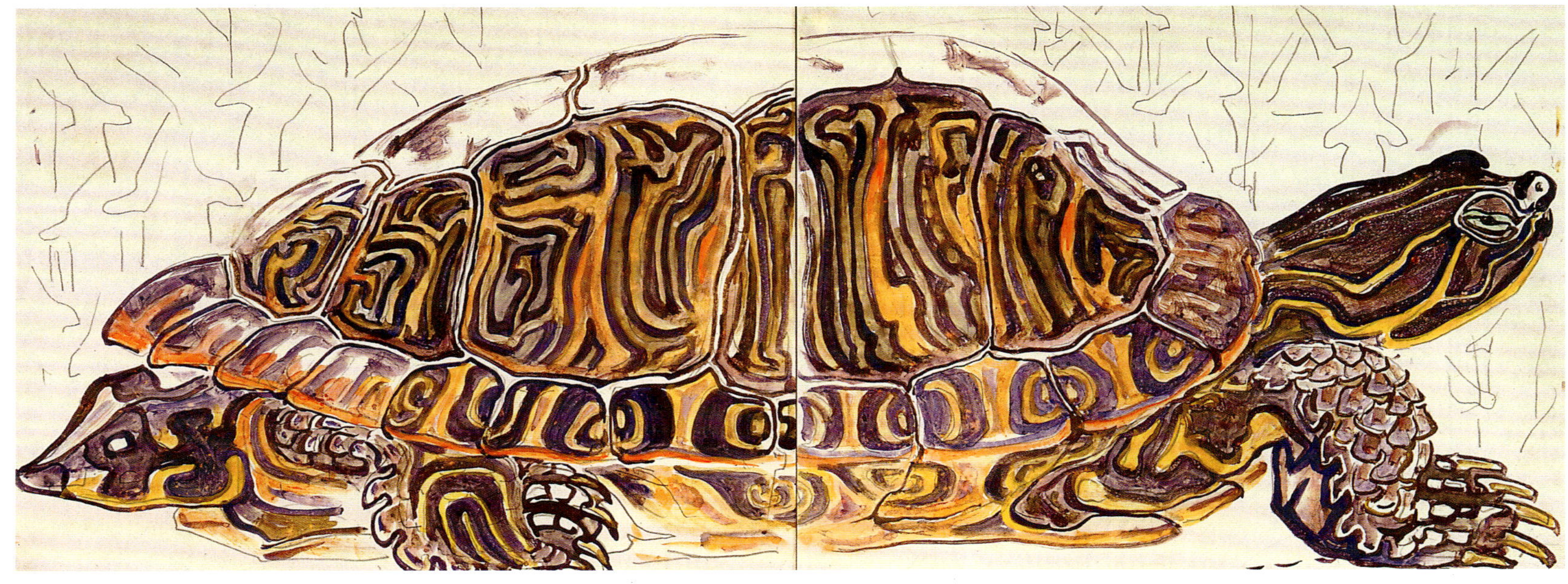

Turtle, ca. 1945

Watercolor on paper, two sheets, each 8½ x 11 in.
The Family of Walter Anderson
The turtle—its worlds, its complex beauty of form and color, its symbolism, and its relation to the whole—was an endless source of interest to Anderson. He often placed sheets of typing paper together to extend his composition.

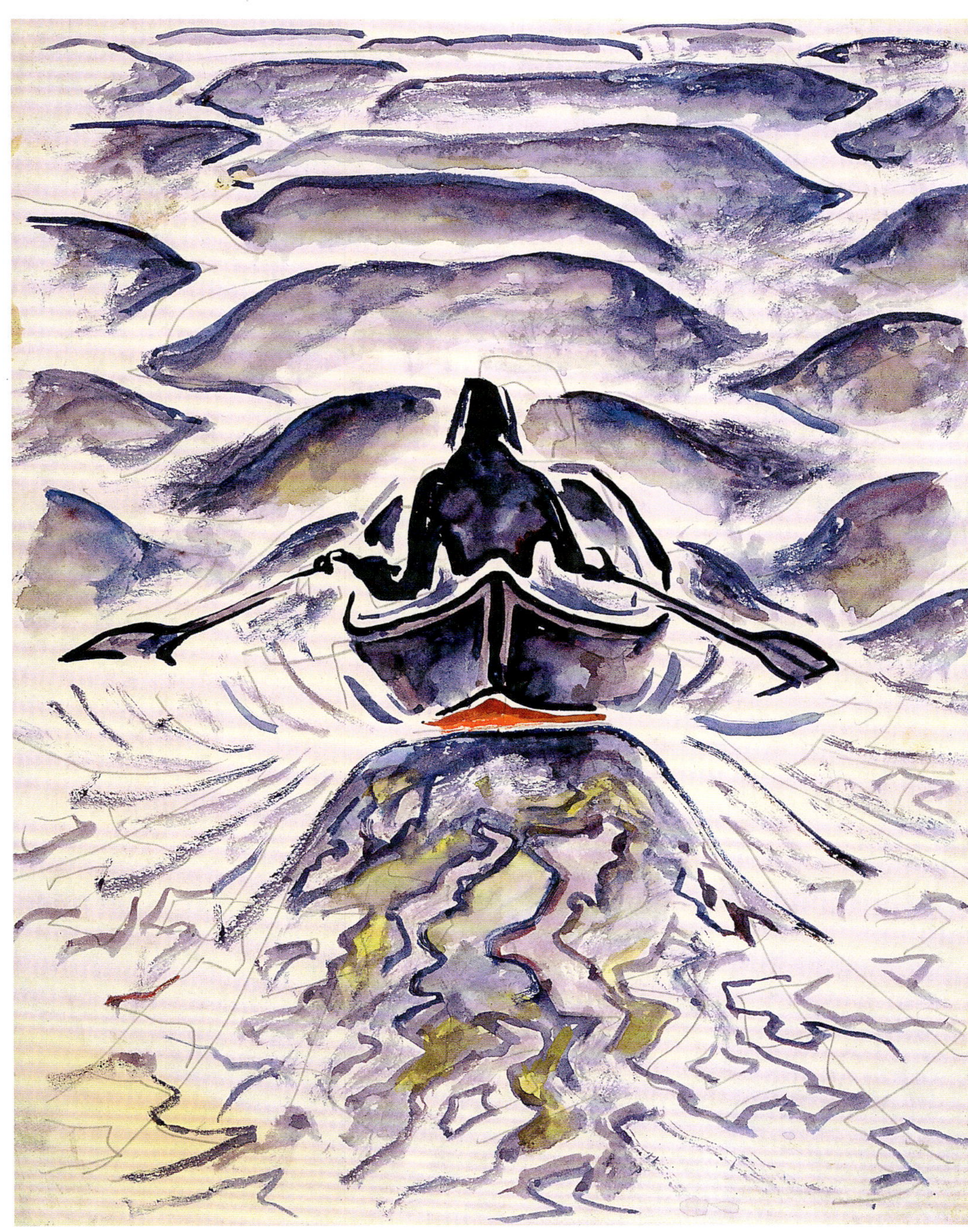

The Artist in His Boat, ca. 1960

Watercolor on paper, 11 x 8½ in.
The Family of Walter Anderson
Anderson frequently saw himself as a character from classical literature when he was making a particularly difficult crossing to the island. Perhaps this work refers to Charon, who in Greek mythology ferried the souls of the deceased over the river Styx to Hades.

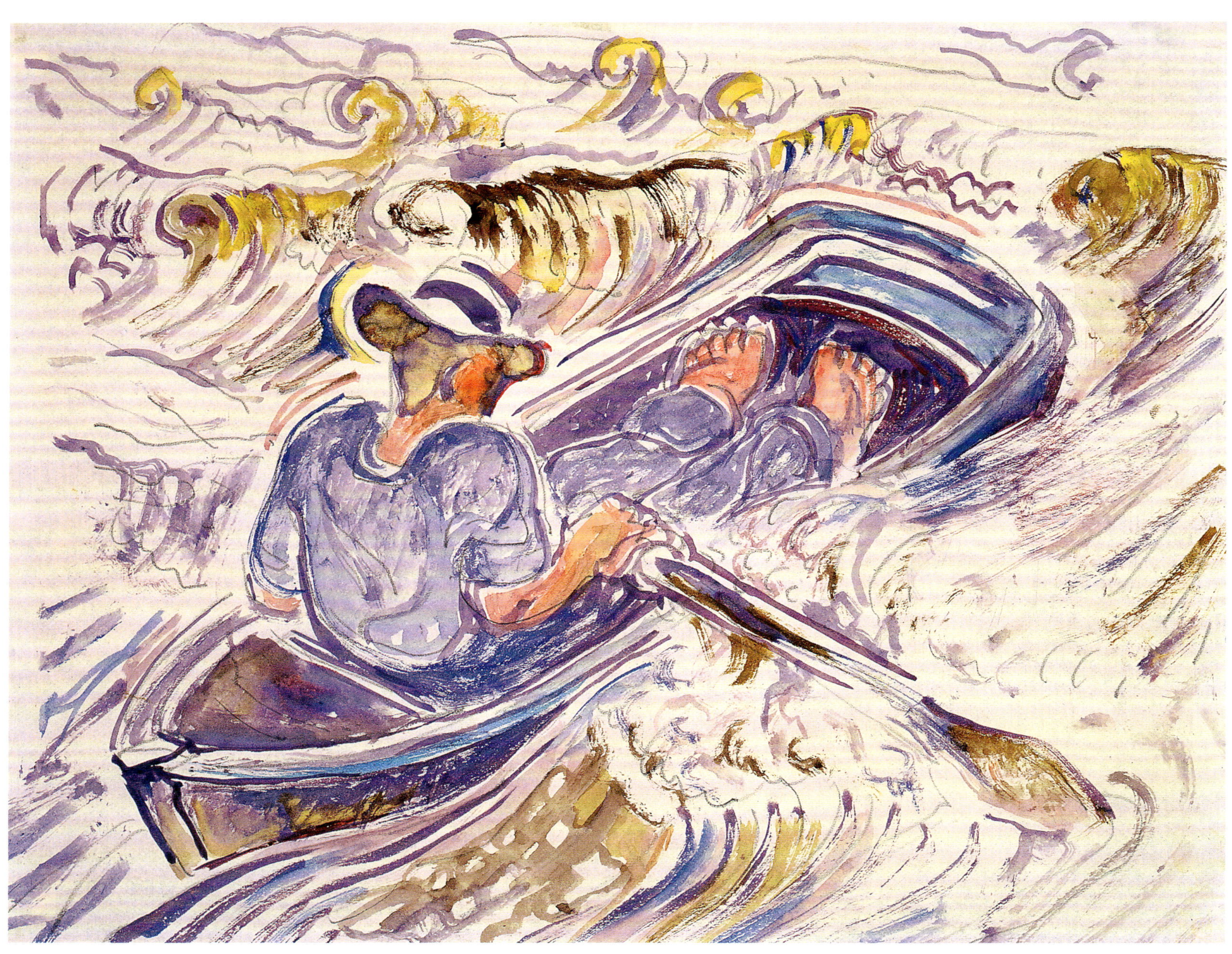

Walter Rowing His Boat, ca. 1955

Watercolor on paper, 8½ x 11 in.
The Family of Walter Anderson
Anderson wrote in his Horn Island logs, "I have at least five methods of propulsion—getting overboard and towing (in shallow water), getting overboard and shoving in deep water (this method requires a fair wind and if possible a fair tide), sailing—with the sail, or sailing with the umbrella—then the ordinary propulsion of oars, either rowing or pushing."

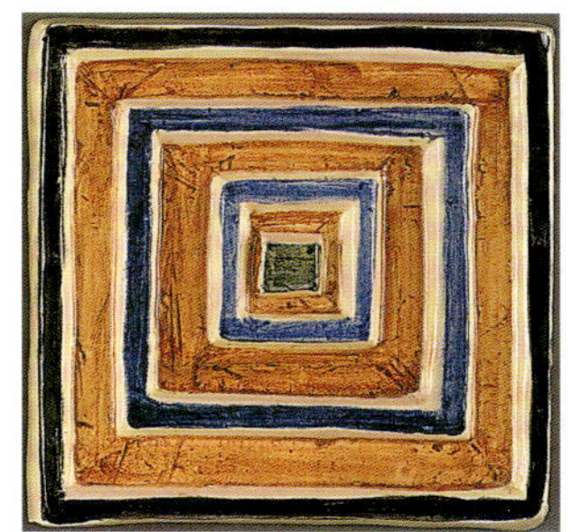

ISLAND YEARS: 1950–1965

During the last years of Anderson's life, he spent extended periods living and painting on the coastal barrier islands, particularly Horn Island, enduring harsh conditions and using his overturned boat for a shelter. Although he continued to work at Shearwater Pottery where he created new shapes and bolder, looser designs, he was more attracted than ever to the solitude and "infinite refreshment" of Horn Island, reaching the island in a series of boats, sailing, rowing, and paddling through the waters of the sound. Some crossings took more than a day, but the rewards were so great that he often felt like "Fortune's favorite child." He wrote, "Last night there was a beautiful sunset. One felt that it had been arranged with taste. So many sunsets seem to be simply wild explosions of color in order to stun people into a state of mute wonder. But this one had variety, vermilion red and purple together, and lilac and gold together against a heavenly clear green turquoise sky."

Despite a constant battle with the elements, Anderson did thousands of drawings and watercolors of the creatures of the sea, sand, and air. The island was not only an inexhaustible source of images but also the place that reflected most intensely the power and vulnerability of nature. His vision of the natural world was not a romantic, sentimental one, but an acceptance of nature's changing character, through all its forms and cycles. In more than eighty logbooks written on the island, he records moments of pure ecstasy: "It was an embarrassment of riches . . . a concentrated image that nothing could take from me." Horn Island provided him with the opportunity for "realization," an intense empathy with the subjects of his art: "The bird flies, and in that fraction of a fraction of a second man and the bird are real . . . and he, man, exists, and he is almost as wonderful as the thing he sees." In fleeting images of change and unity, his Horn Island watercolors capture moments when man and nature seem one, and the island itself becomes a symbol of our power and frailty.

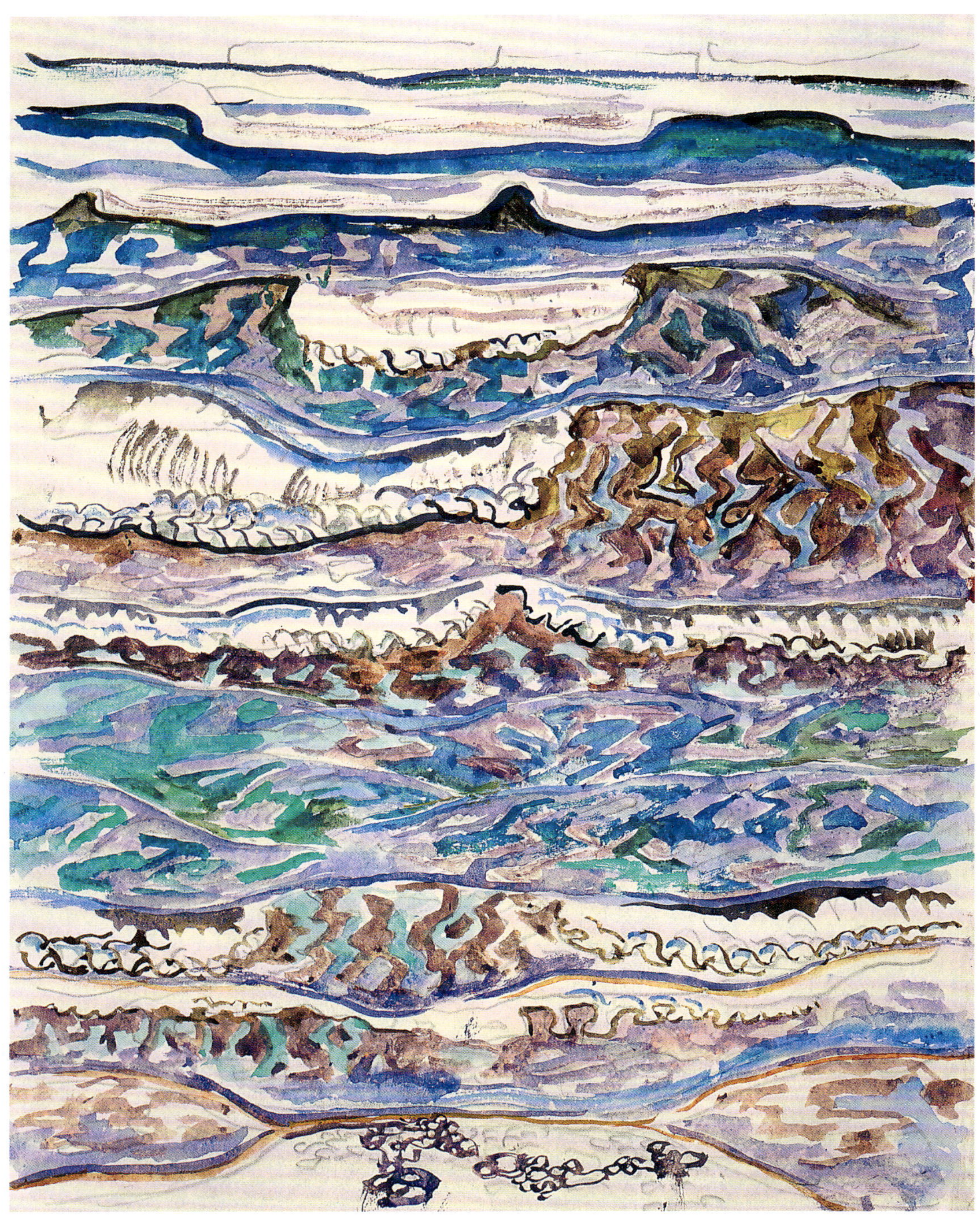

Waves, ca. 1960

Watercolor on paper, 11 x 8½ in.
The Family of Walter Anderson

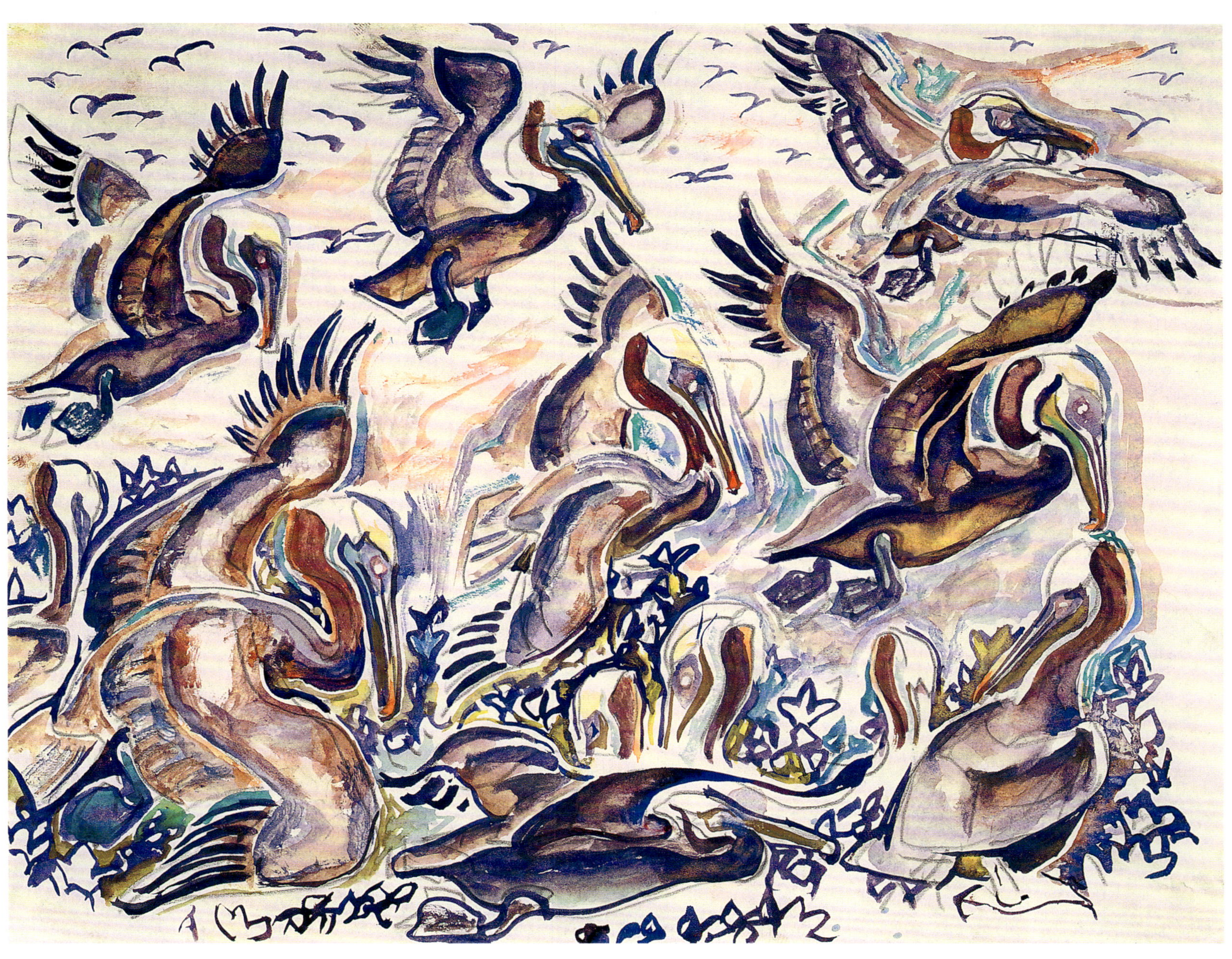

Flock of Pelicans on North Key, ca. 1952

Watercolor on paper, 8½ x 11 in.
The Family of Walter Anderson

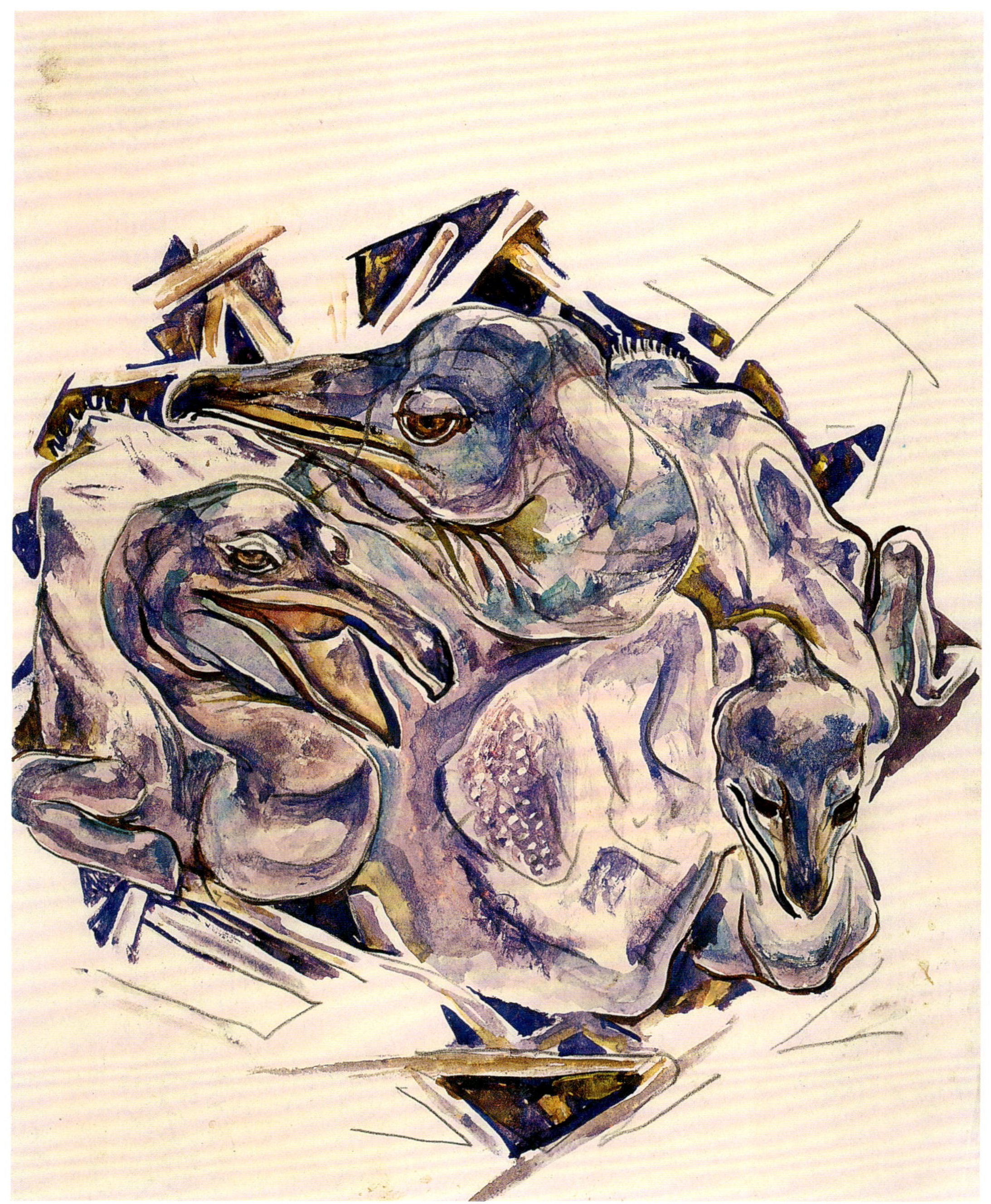

Young Pelicans, ca. 1950

Watercolor on paper, 11 x 8½ in.
The Family of Walter Anderson

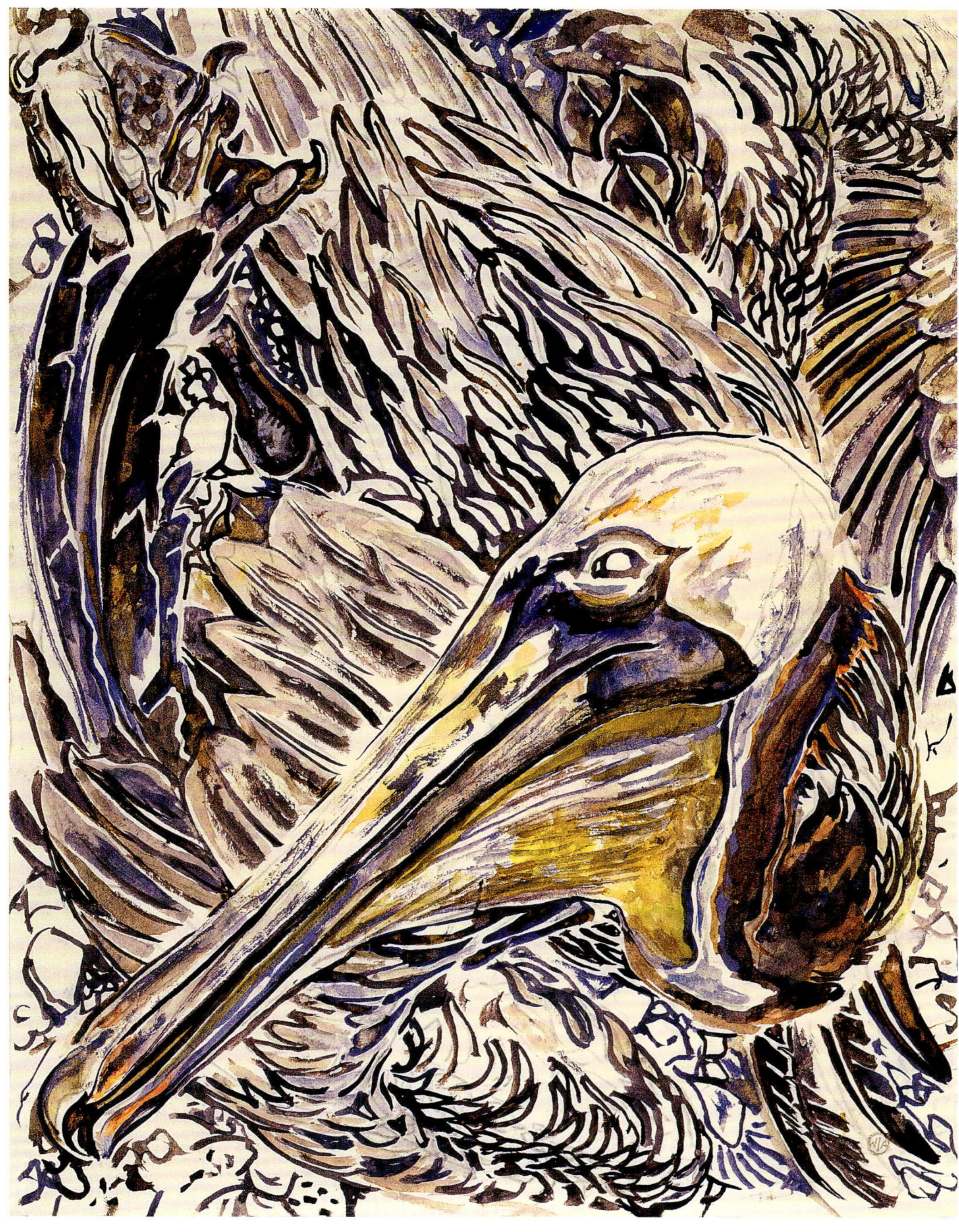

Dead Pelican, ca. 1955

Watercolor on paper, 11 x 8½ in.
Walter Anderson Museum of Art, 75.1.4
On North Key of the Chandeleur Islands, the pelicans nested by the thousands in the 1940s and 1950s. But they were decimated by insecticide effluence from the mouth of the Mississippi River, which contaminated the food chain. By 1965 they had begun to return.

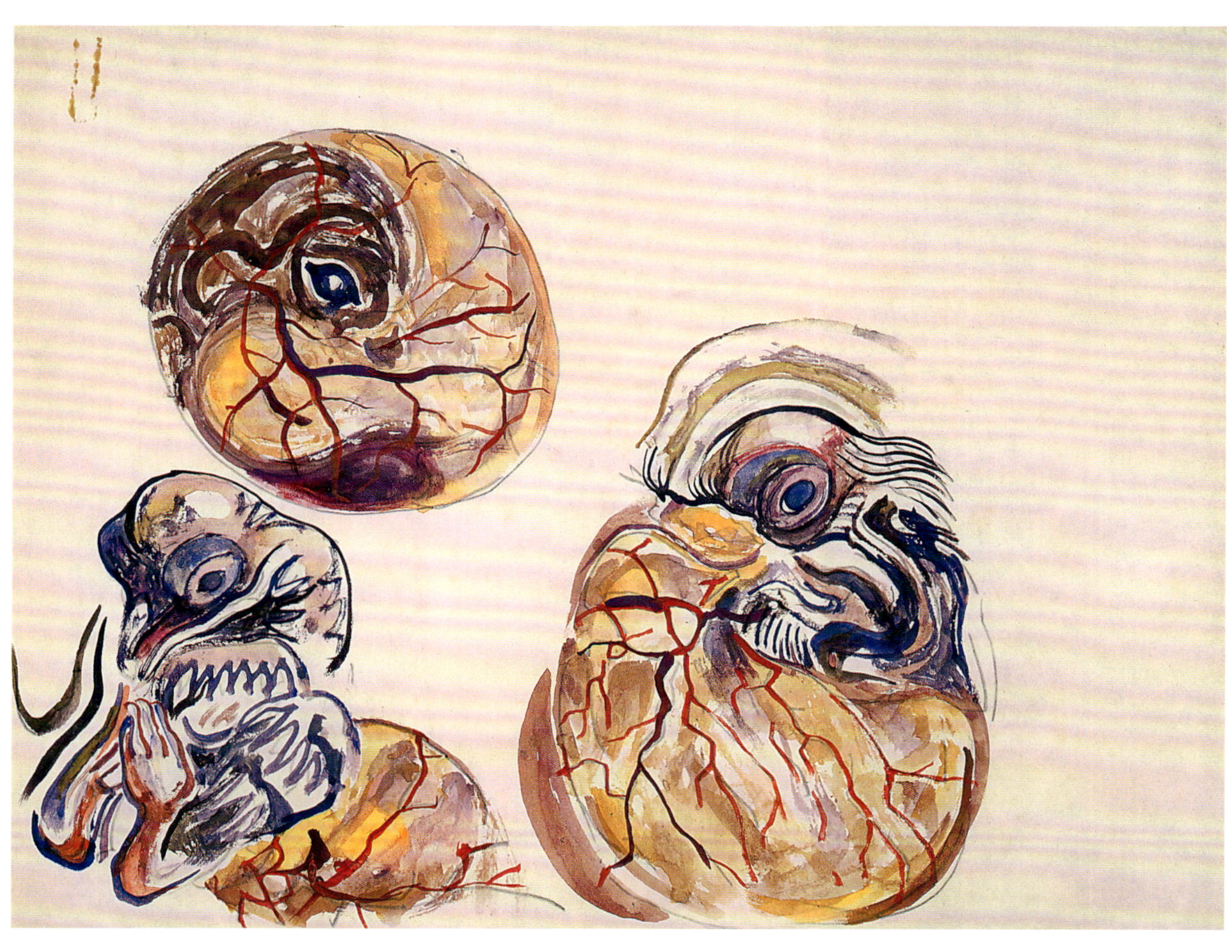

Embryos, Laughing Gulls, ca. 1955

Watercolor on paper, 8½ x 11 in.
The Family of Walter Anderson
"The force of life must find expression in the egg."

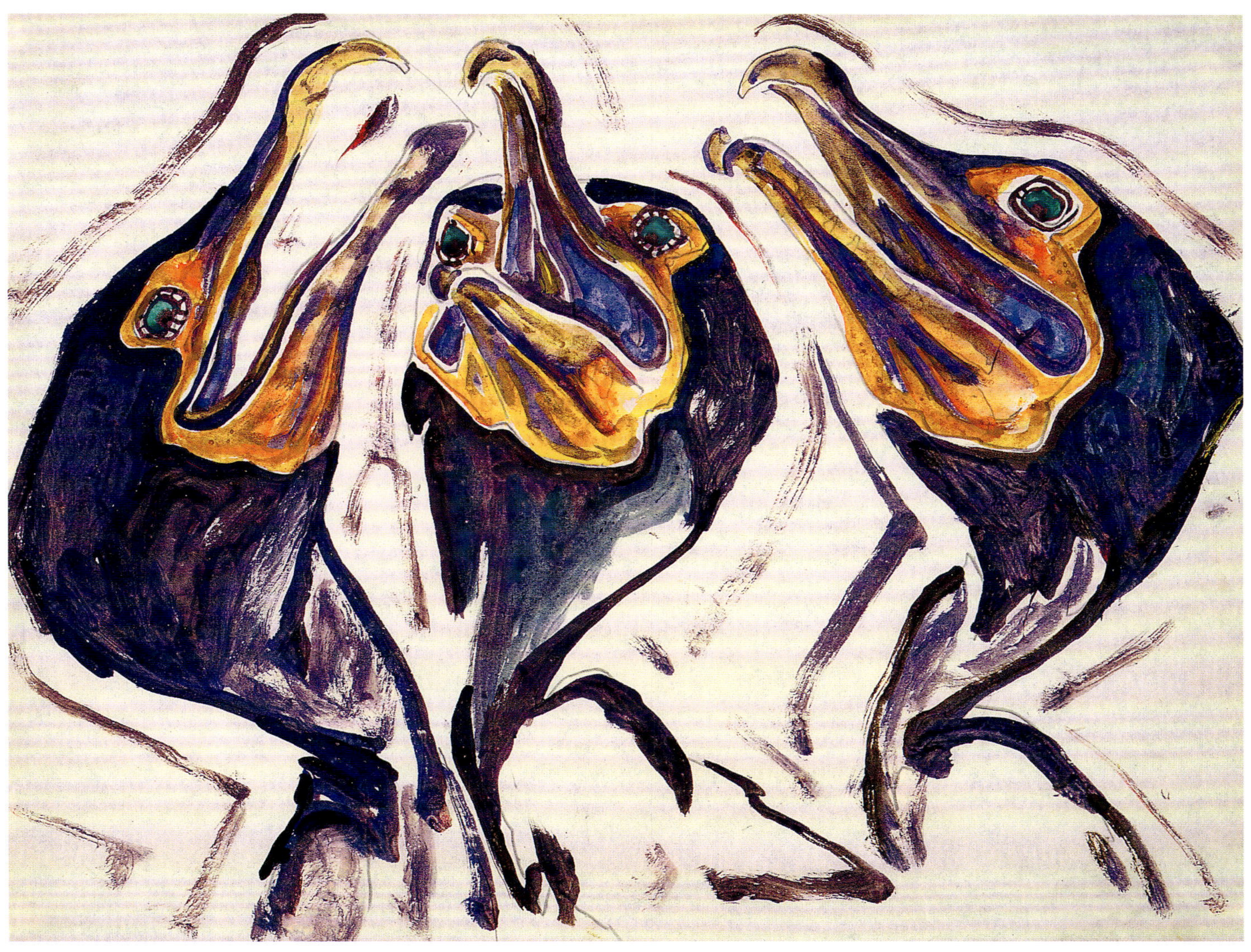

Three Heads of Double Breasted Cormorant, ca. 1962

Watercolor on paper, 8½ x 11 in.
The Family of Walter Anderson
Probably the head of a dead cormorant placed three times in what the artist called "consecutive composition." "He composes very well with himself," he said of multiple images of a single creature.

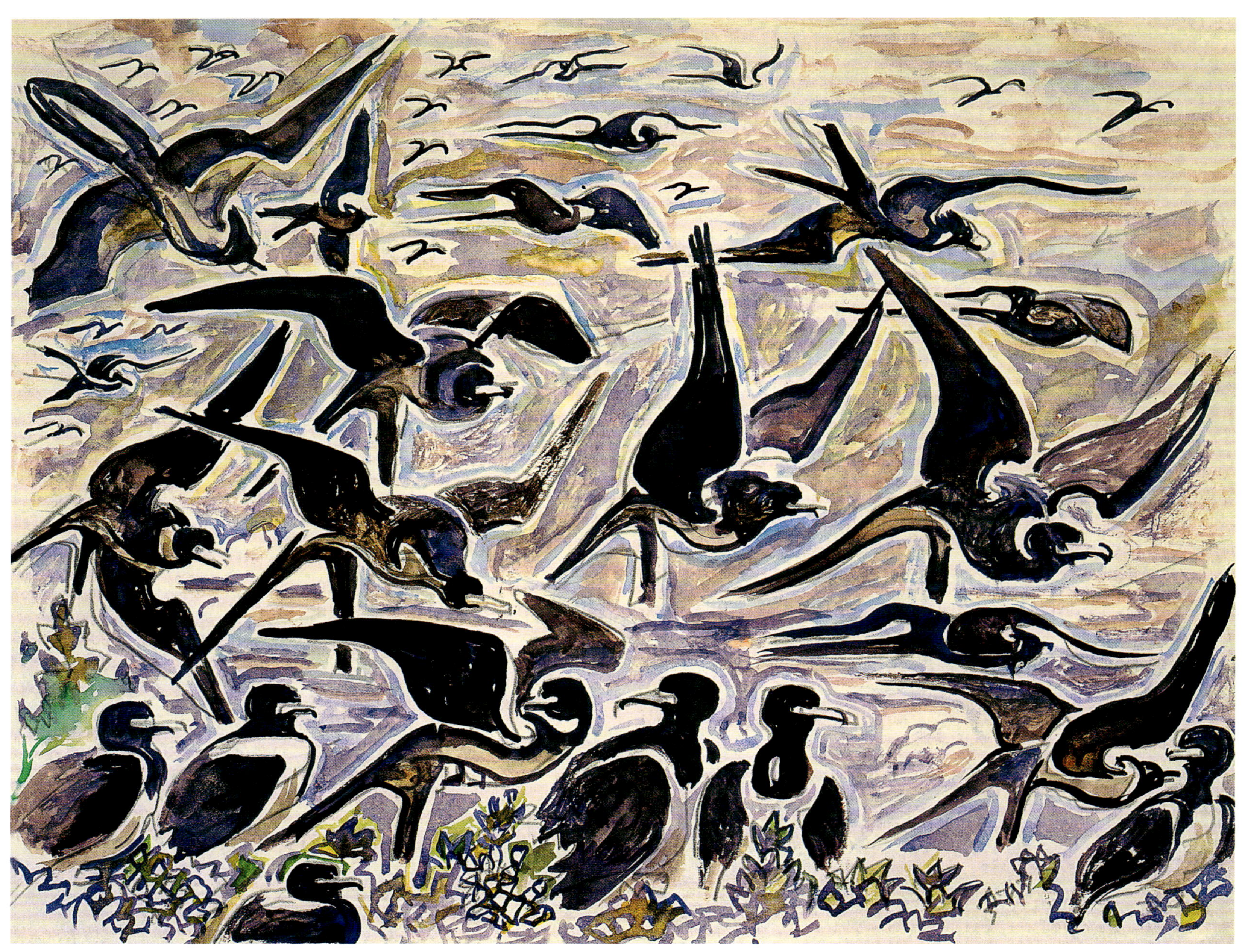

Frigate Birds over North Key, ca. 1954

Watercolor on paper, 8½ x 11 in.
The Family of Walter Anderson
Considered to be weather portents on the coast, these frigates, or man-o'-war birds, were in the mangroves on North Key of the Chandeleur Islands. Anderson writes of them spiraling into the distant air over the island.

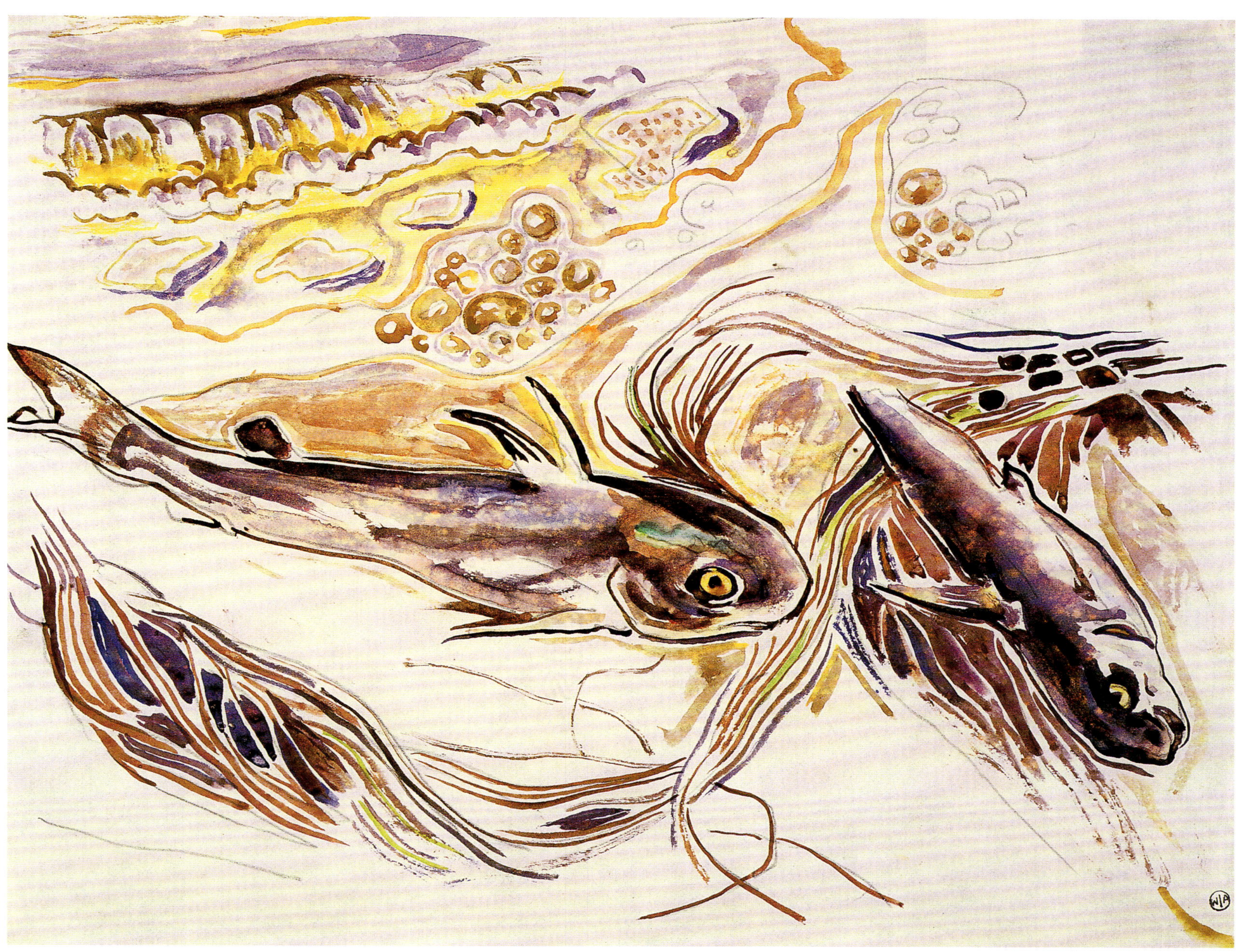

Fish Stranded on Beach, ca. 1960

Watercolor on paper, 8½ x 11 in.
Walter Anderson Museum of Art, 76.3.1

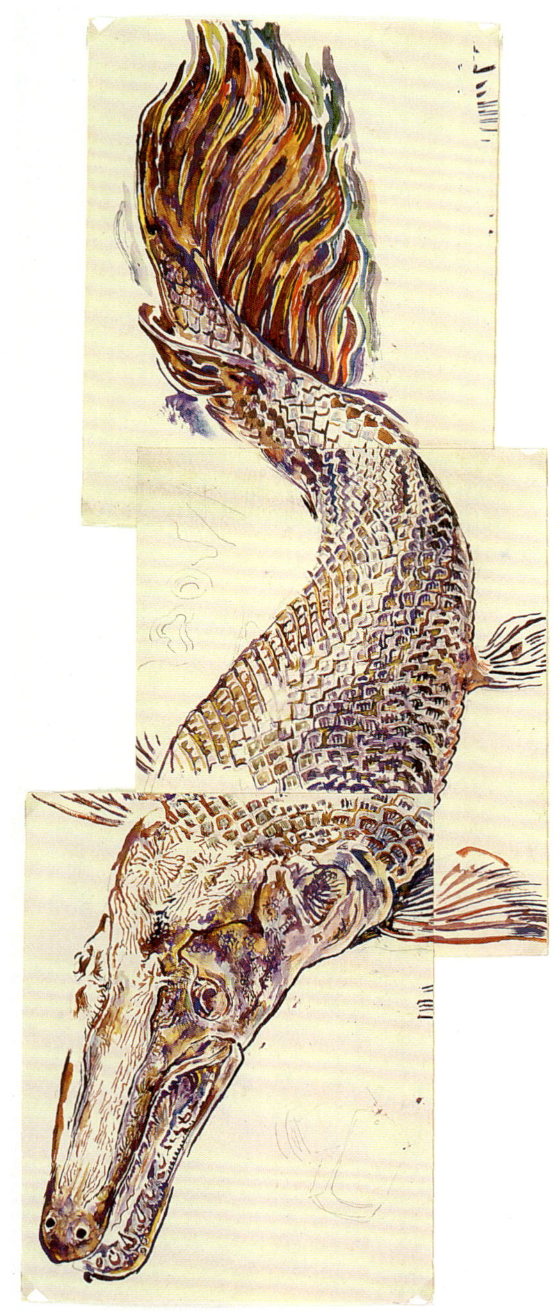

Alligator Gar, ca. 1955

Watercolor on paper, three separate sheets, each 11 x 8½ in.
The Family of Walter Anderson

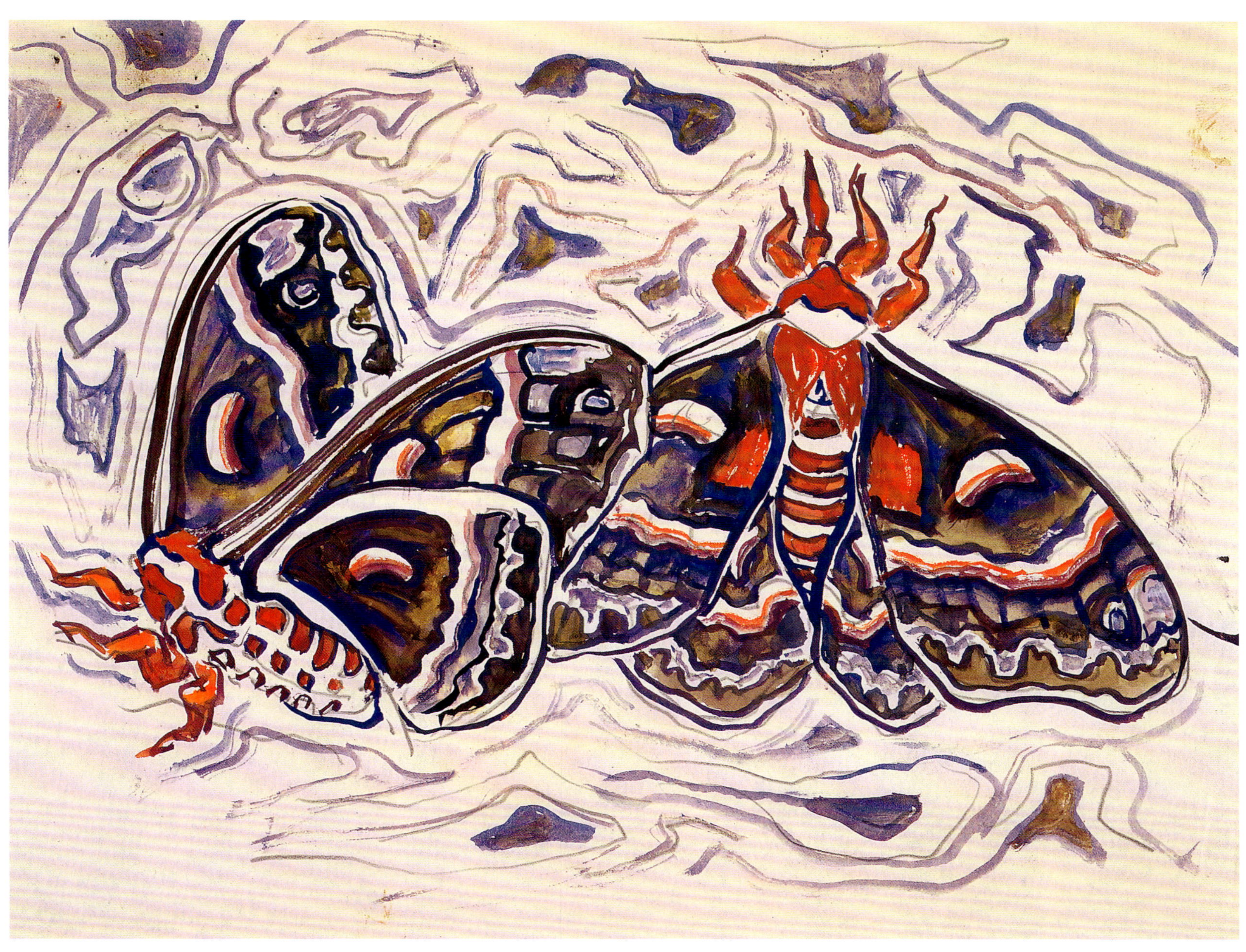

Moths, ca. 1960

Watercolor on paper, 8½ x 11 in.
Walter Anderson Museum of Art, 93.1.9
Gift of the Knight Foundation
Anderson found two cecropia moth cocoons, one on Belle Fontaine Beach and the other on Horn Island, which he placed in a large jar. They hatched the same day and were called "the heavenly twins." He made a series of watercolors of them.

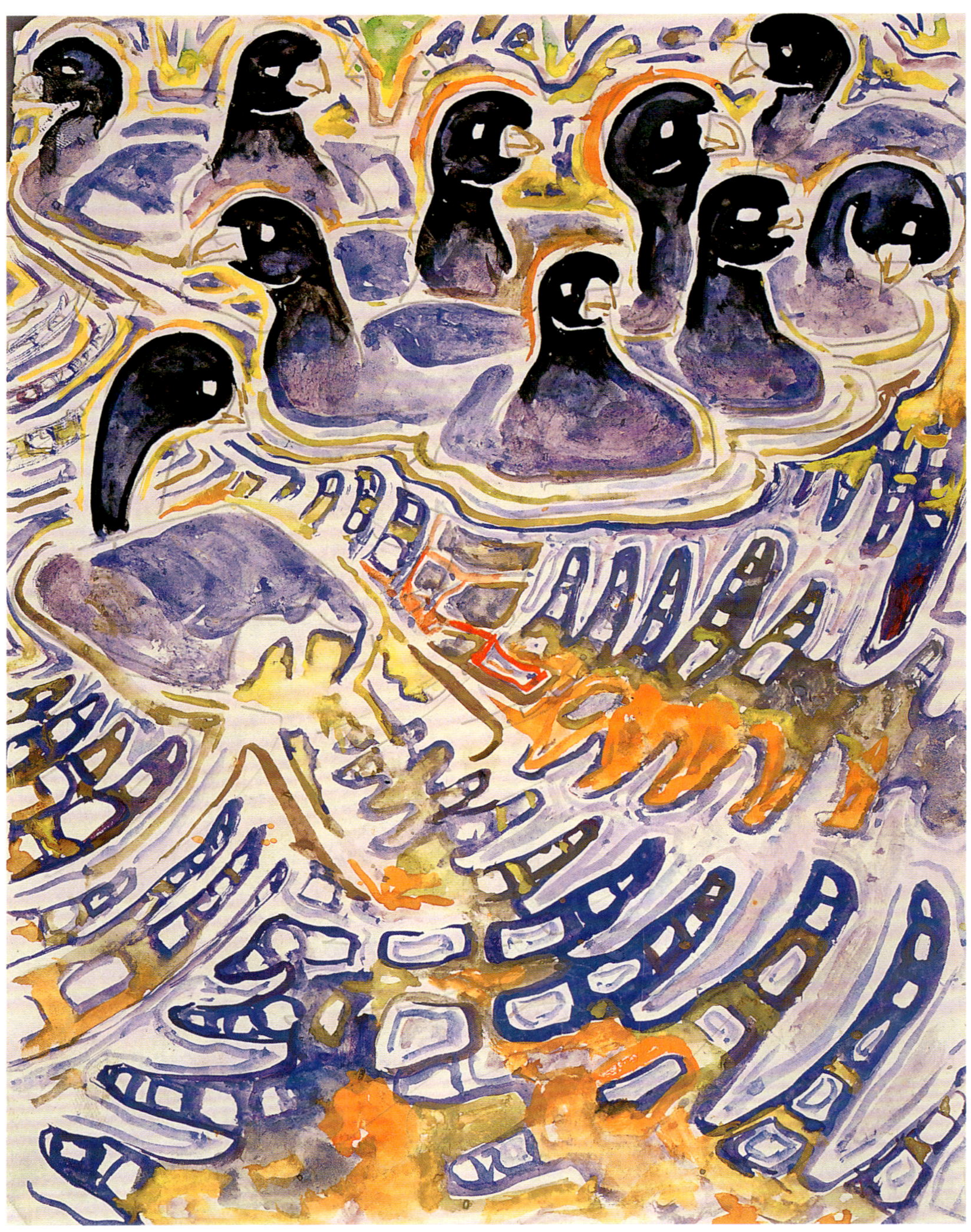

Coots and Waves, ca. 1961

Watercolor on paper, 11 x 8½ in.
The Family of Walter Anderson

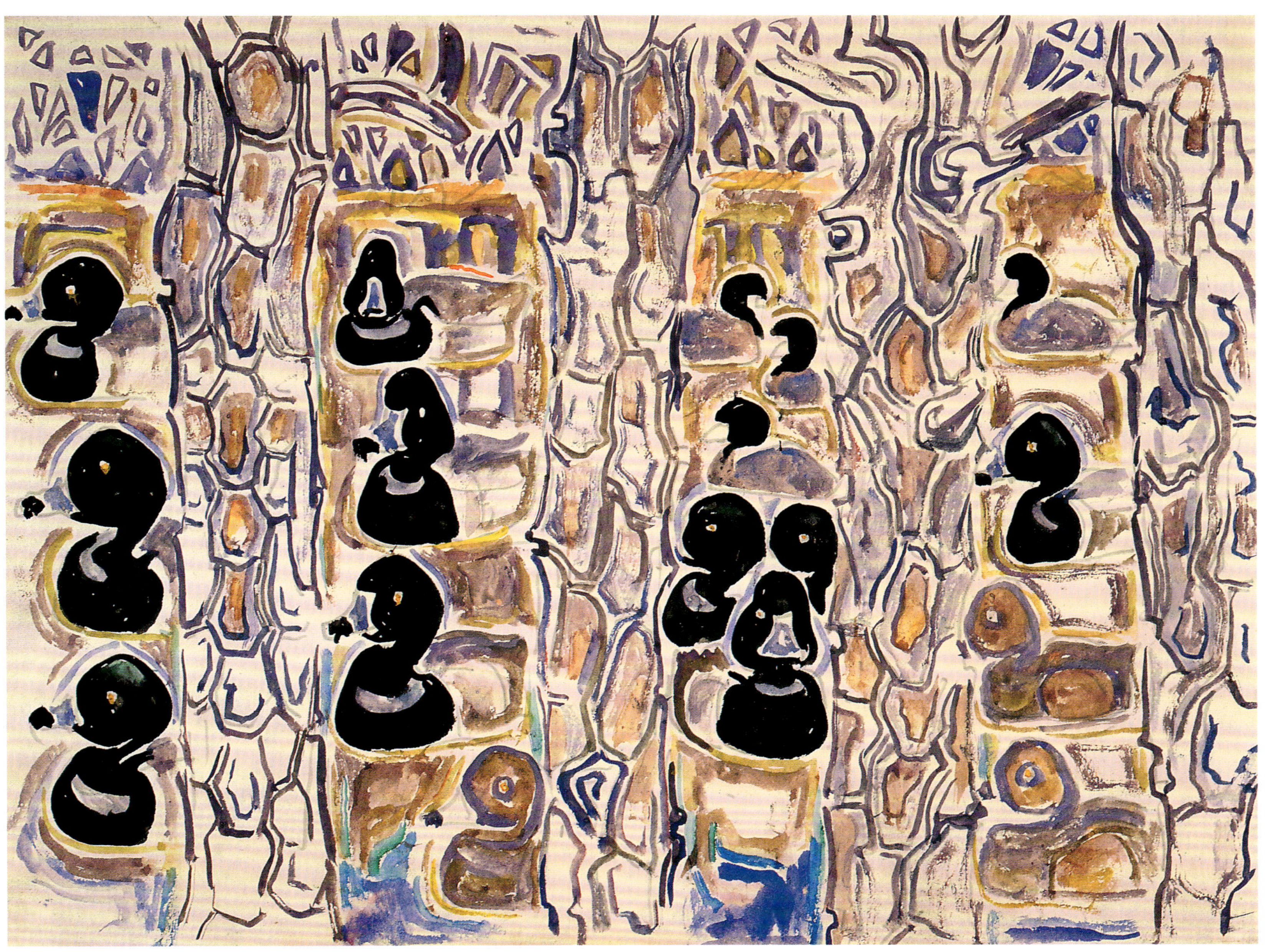

Ducks and Pines, ca. 1952

Watercolor on paper, 8½ x 11 in.
The Family of Walter Anderson
"True art consists in spreading wide the intervals so that imagination may fill the space between the trees."

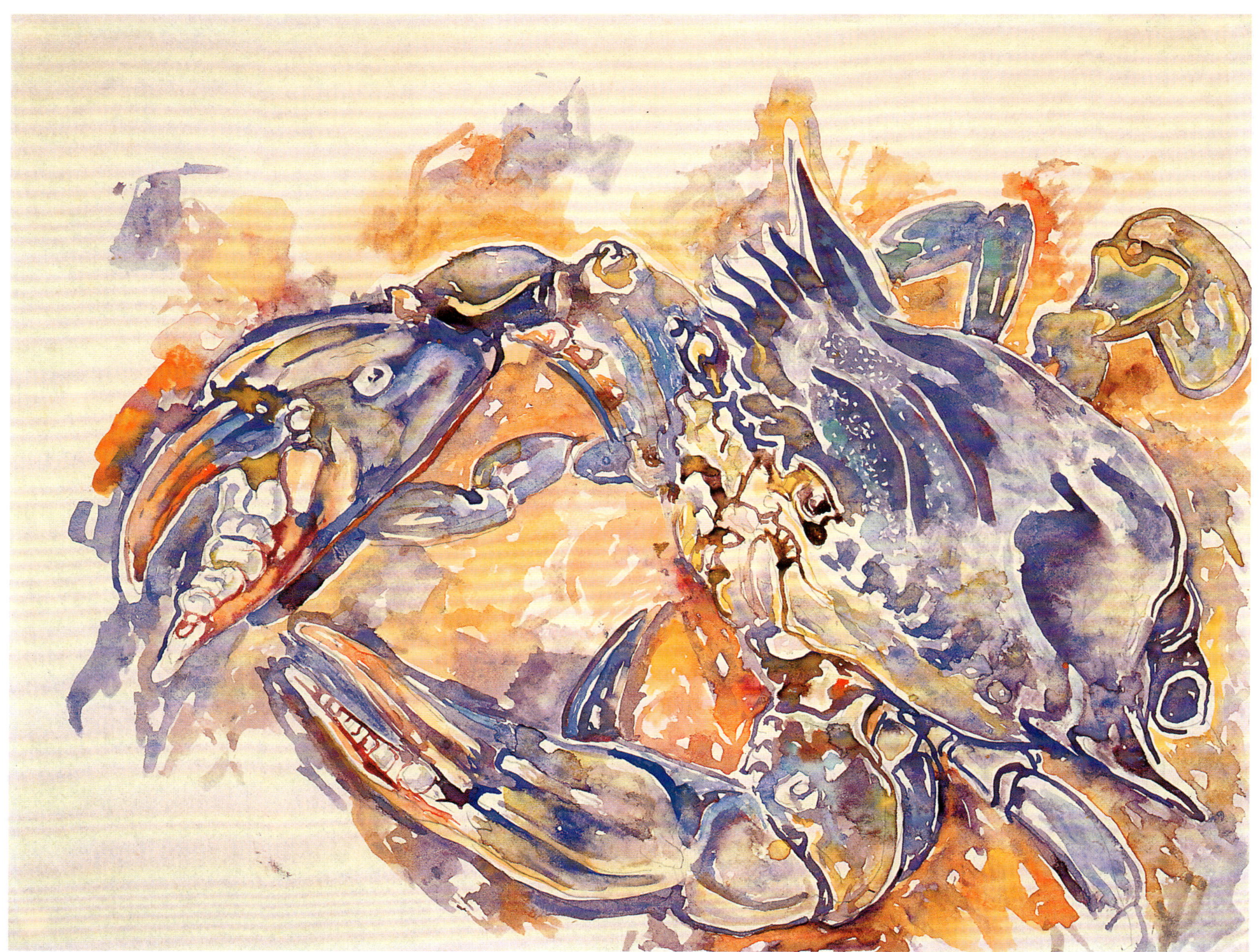

Blue Crab, ca. 1949

Watercolor on paper, 8½ x 11 in.
The Family of Walter Anderson
For Anderson, there was always joy in the mystery of the process. He liked "to paint two things and have them suddenly produce a third." In this watercolor, the claw becomes a vulture's head.

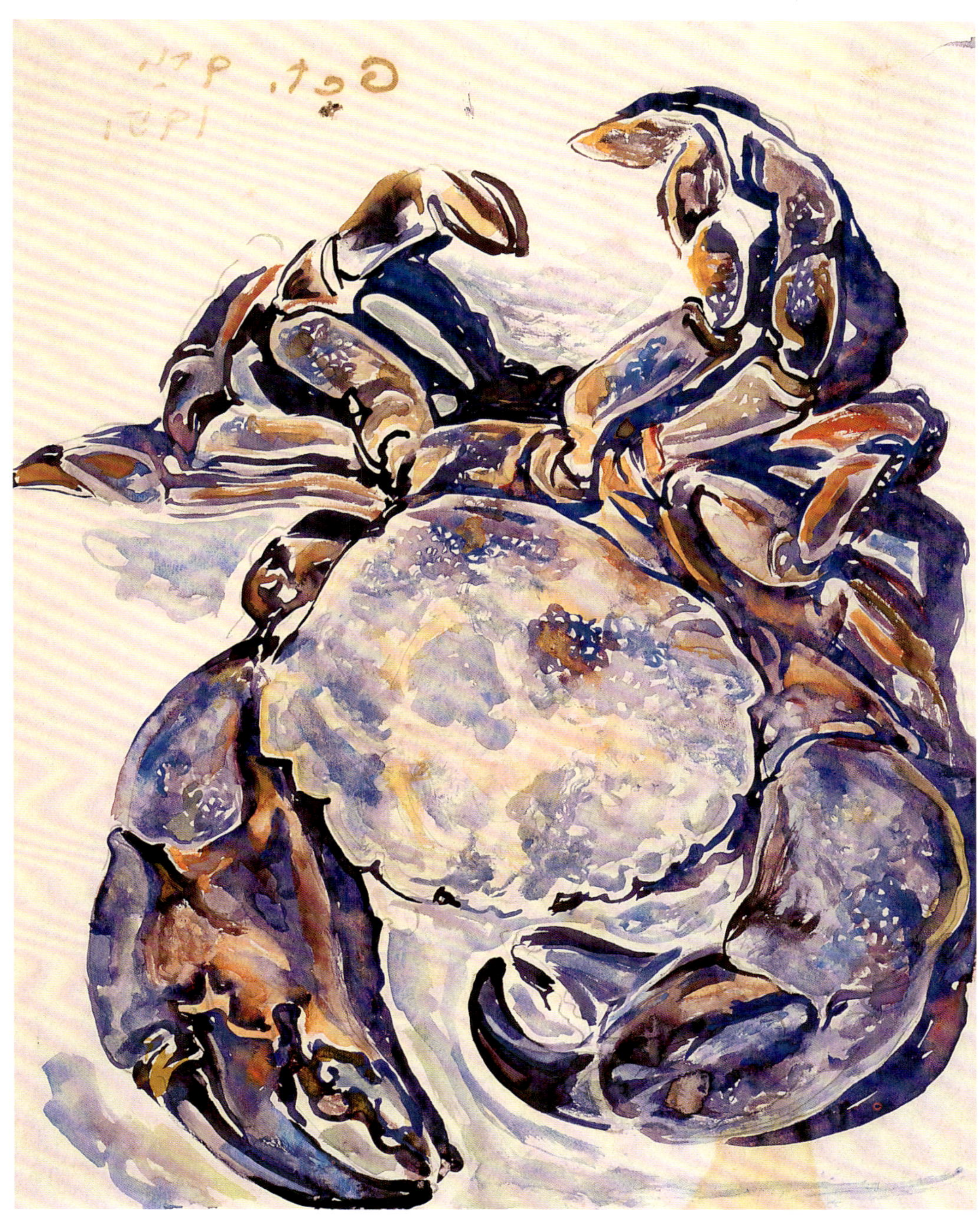

Stone Crab, 1951

Watercolor on paper, 11 x 8½ in.
The Family of Walter Anderson

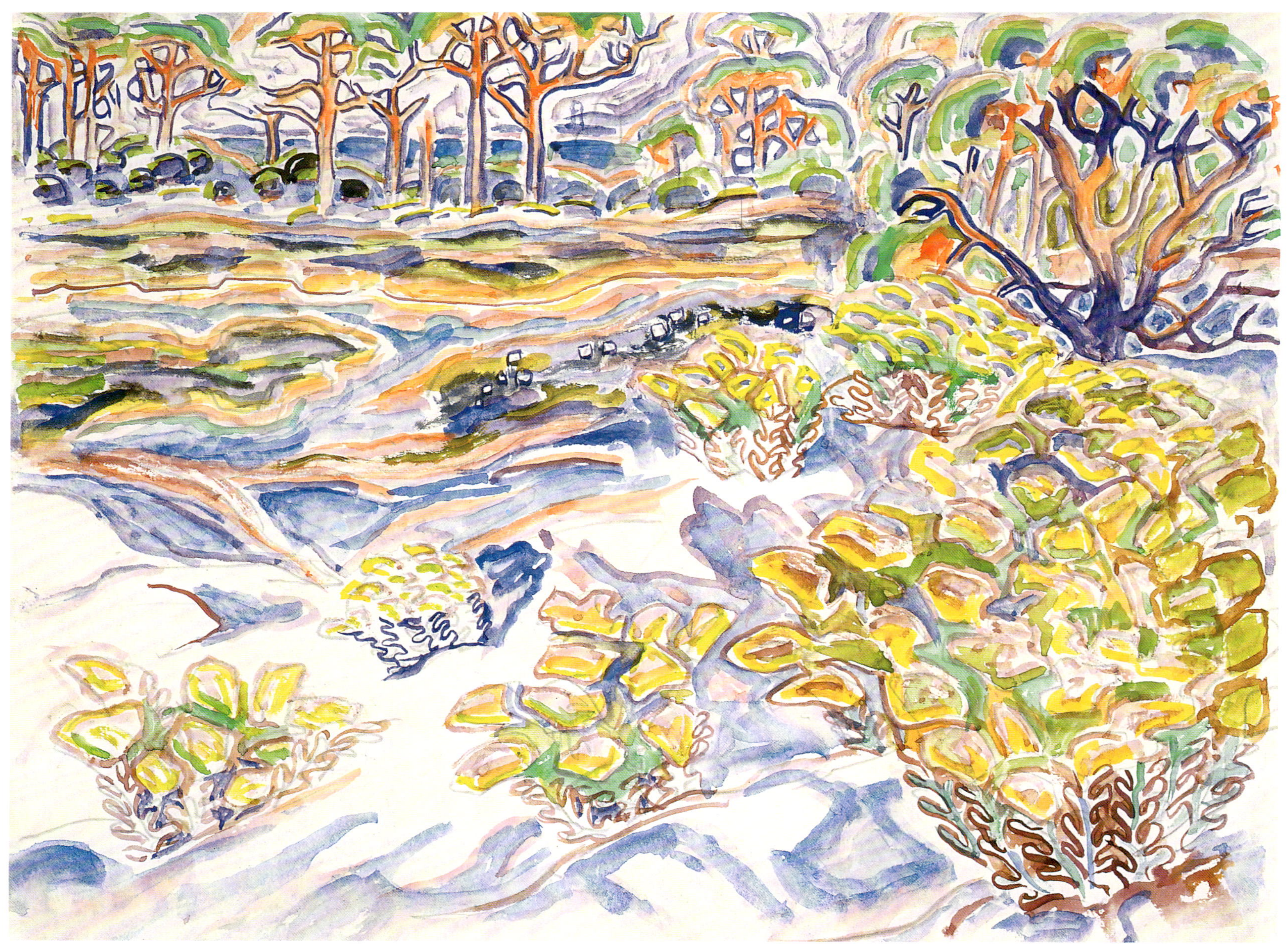

Goldenrod on Horn Island, ca. 1965

Watercolor on paper, 8½ x 11 in.
The Family of Walter Anderson
Horn Island on a fine late September day. "My birthday cake all green and gold with purple candles," he wrote in the logs.

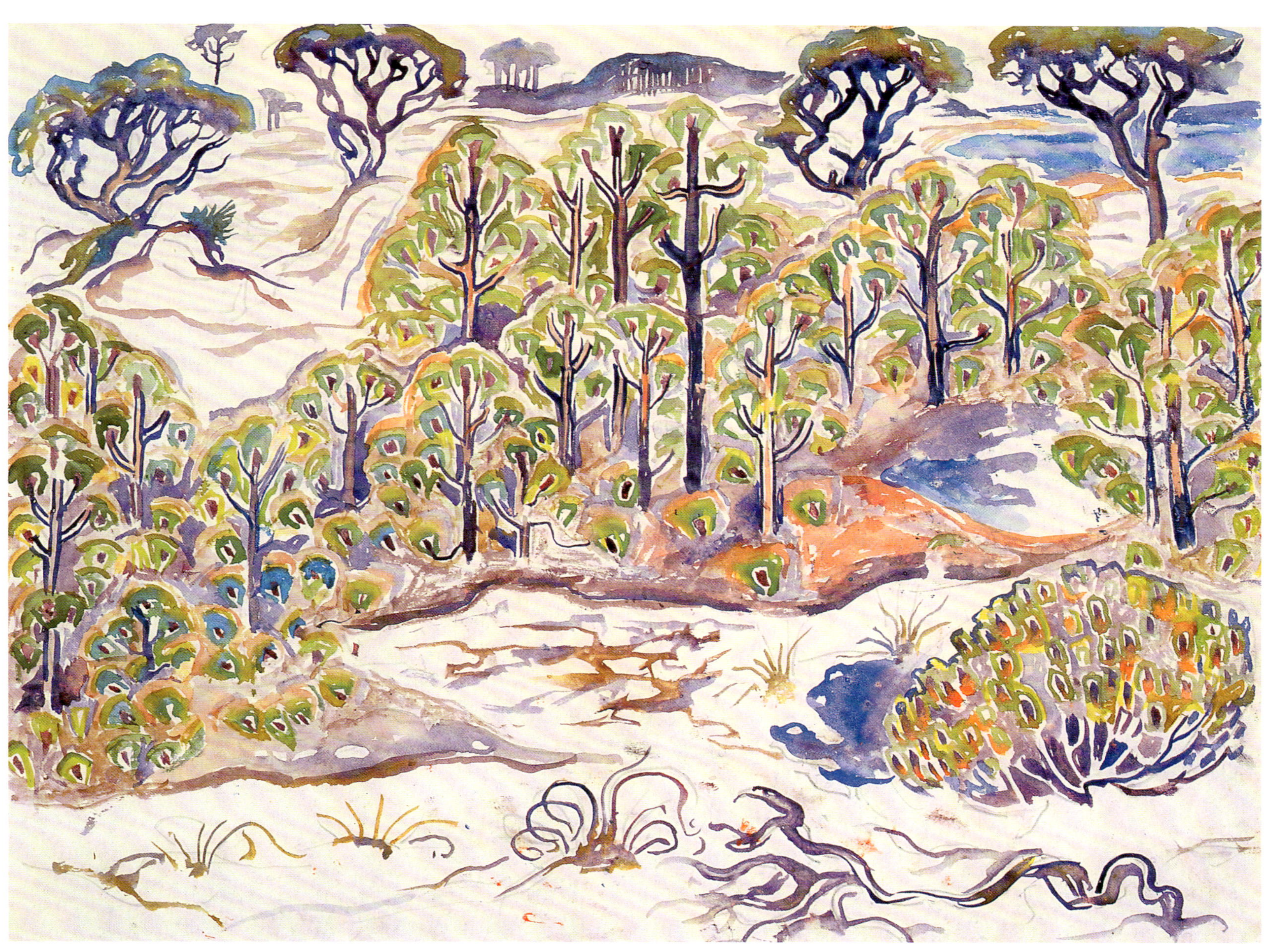

Horn Island, ca. 1955

Watercolor on paper, 8½ x 11 in.
The Family of Walter Anderson

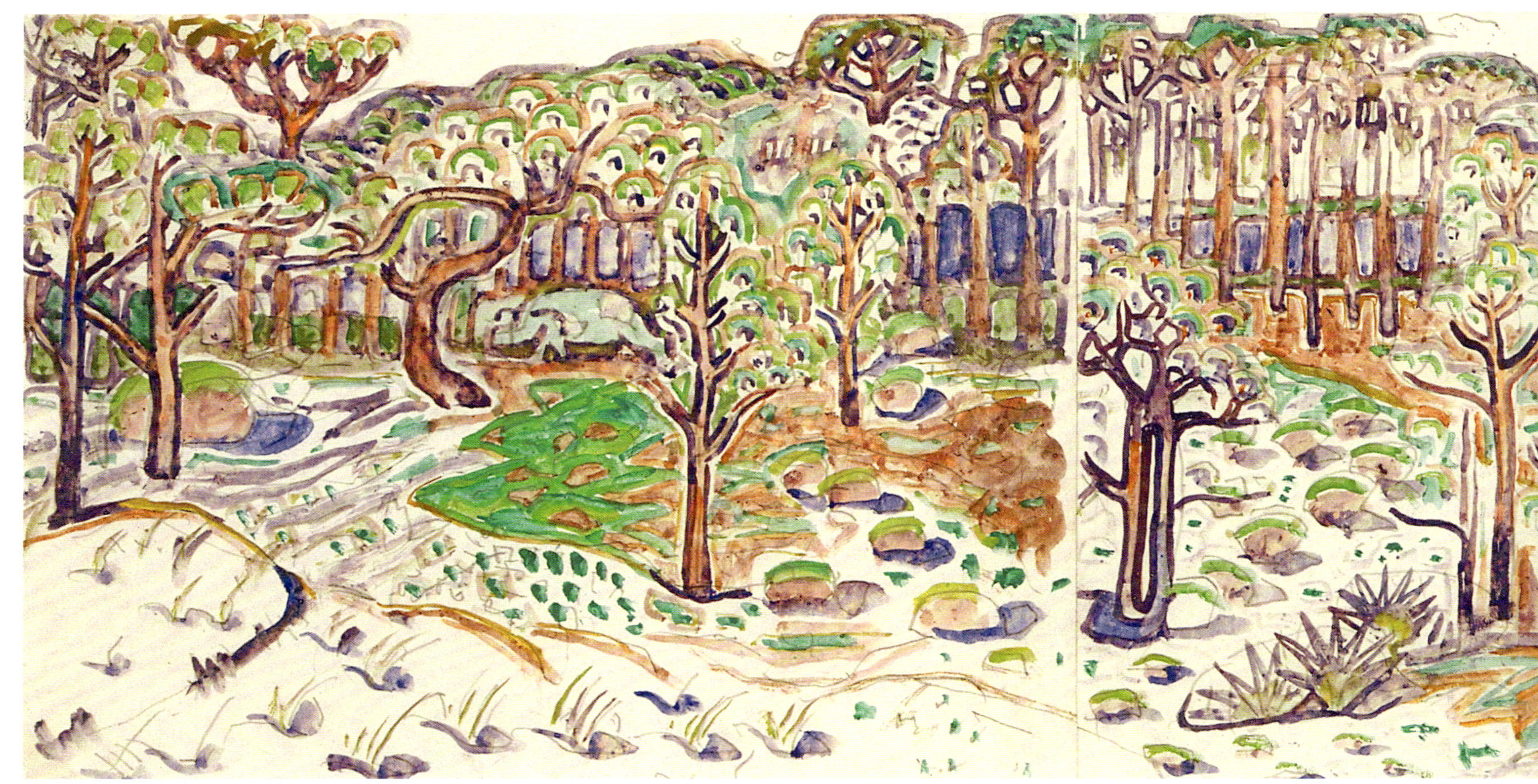

Horn Island, ca. 1960

Watercolor on paper, three separate sheets, each 8½ x 11 in.
Walter Anderson Museum of Art, 99.1.1
Anderson did several triptychs showing the relationships between the trees and undergrowth, among the dunes and water and sky. Paintings of Horn Island frequently required more than one page.

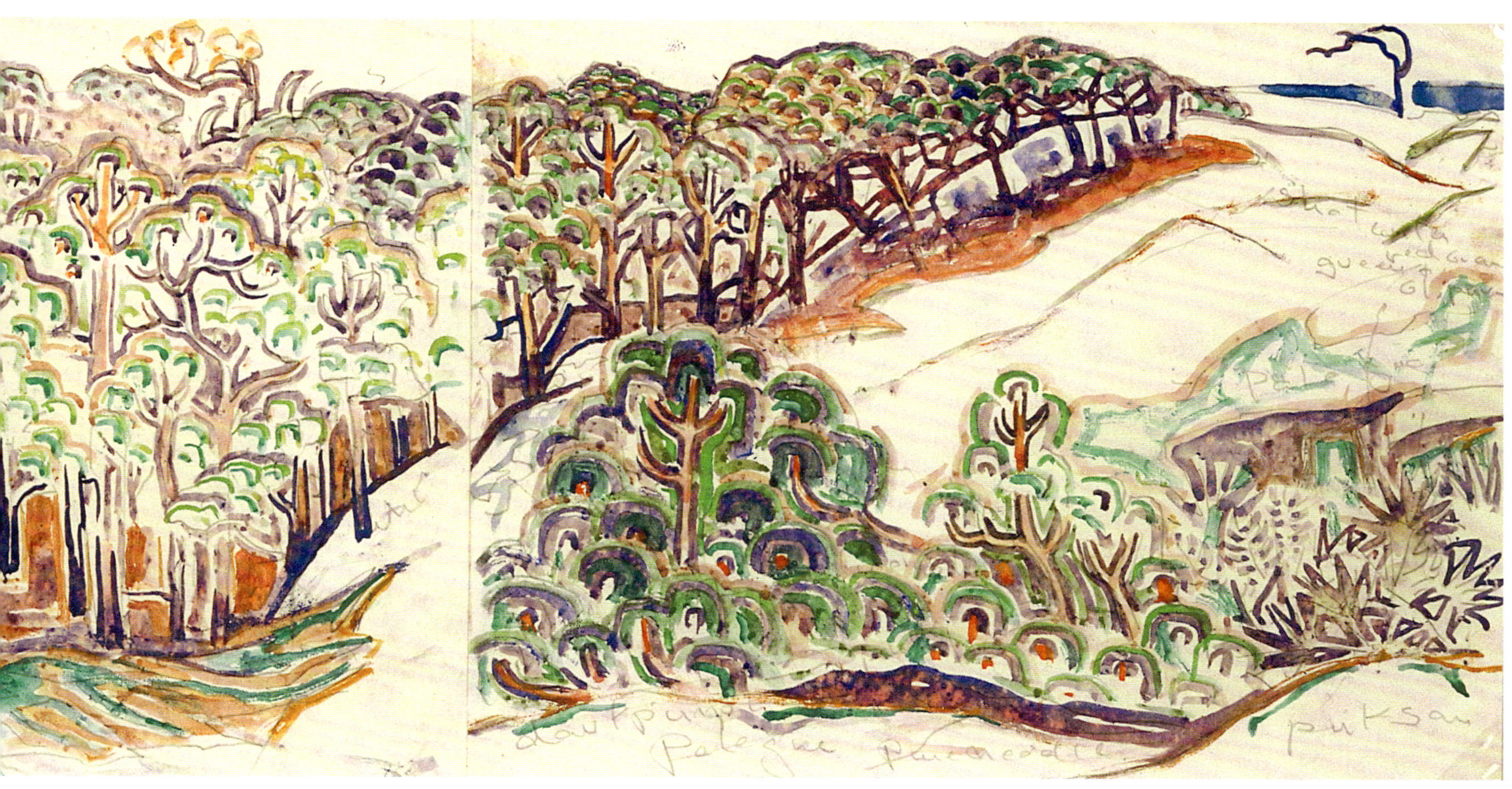

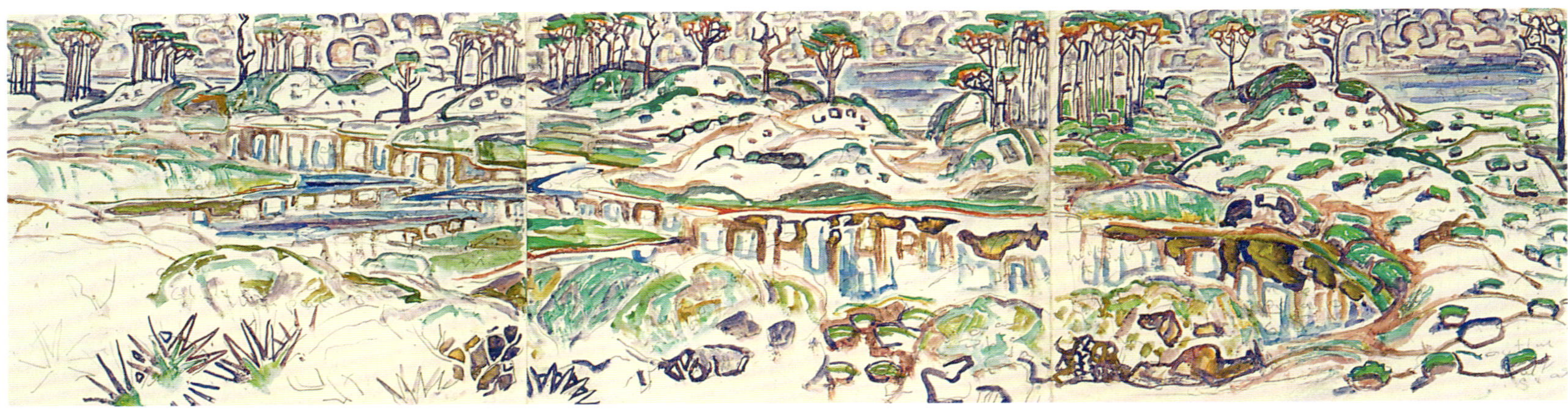

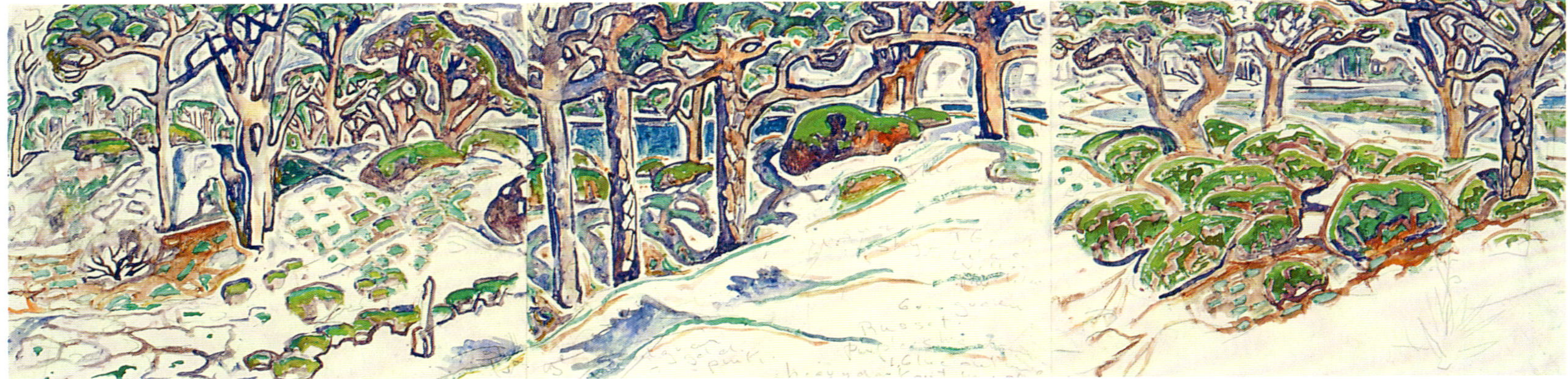

The Long Lagoon, ca. 1960

Watercolor on paper, three separate sheets, each 8½ x 11 in. The Family of Walter Anderson

Horn Island, ca. 1960

Watercolor on paper, three separate sheets, each 8½ x 11 in.
The Family of Walter Anderson

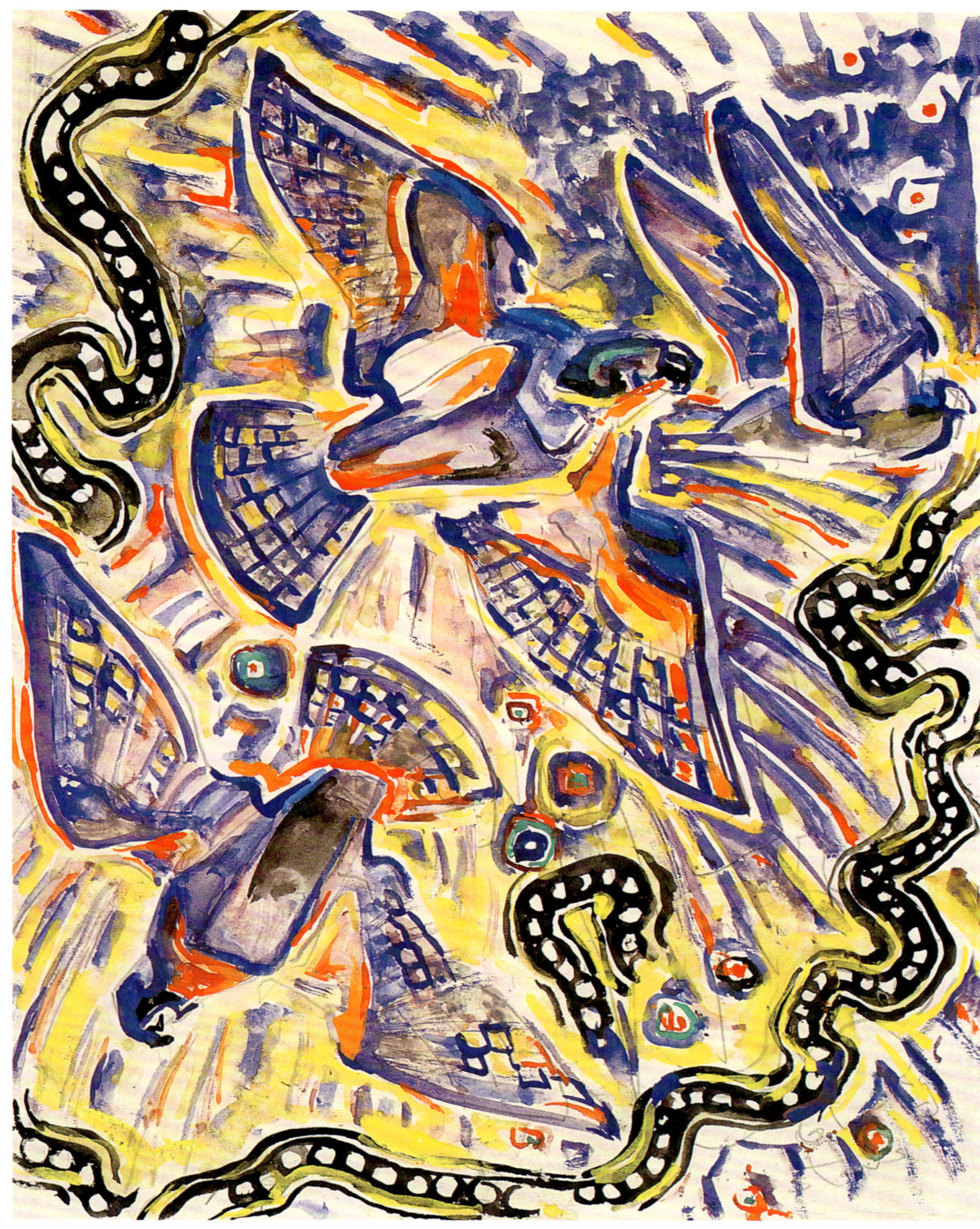

Hawks at Sunrise, ca. 1960

Watercolor on paper, 11 x 8½ in.
The Family of Walter Anderson
In his logs, the artist notes hearing an osprey's call at daybreak and ponders when the bird had to rise "to be the first to greet the sun."

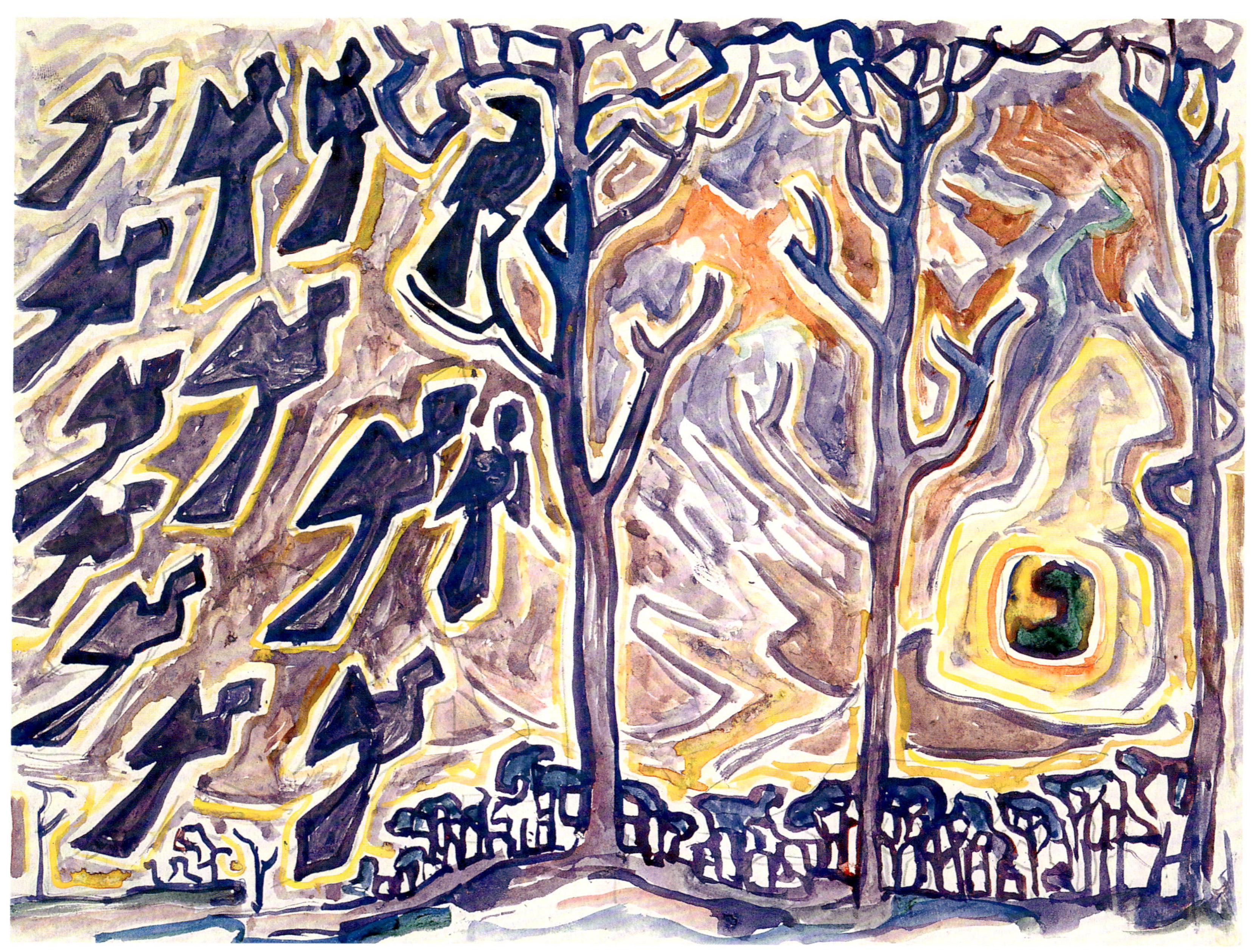

Boat Tailed Grackles at Sunrise, 1965

Watercolor on paper, 8½ x 11 in.
The Family of Walter Anderson

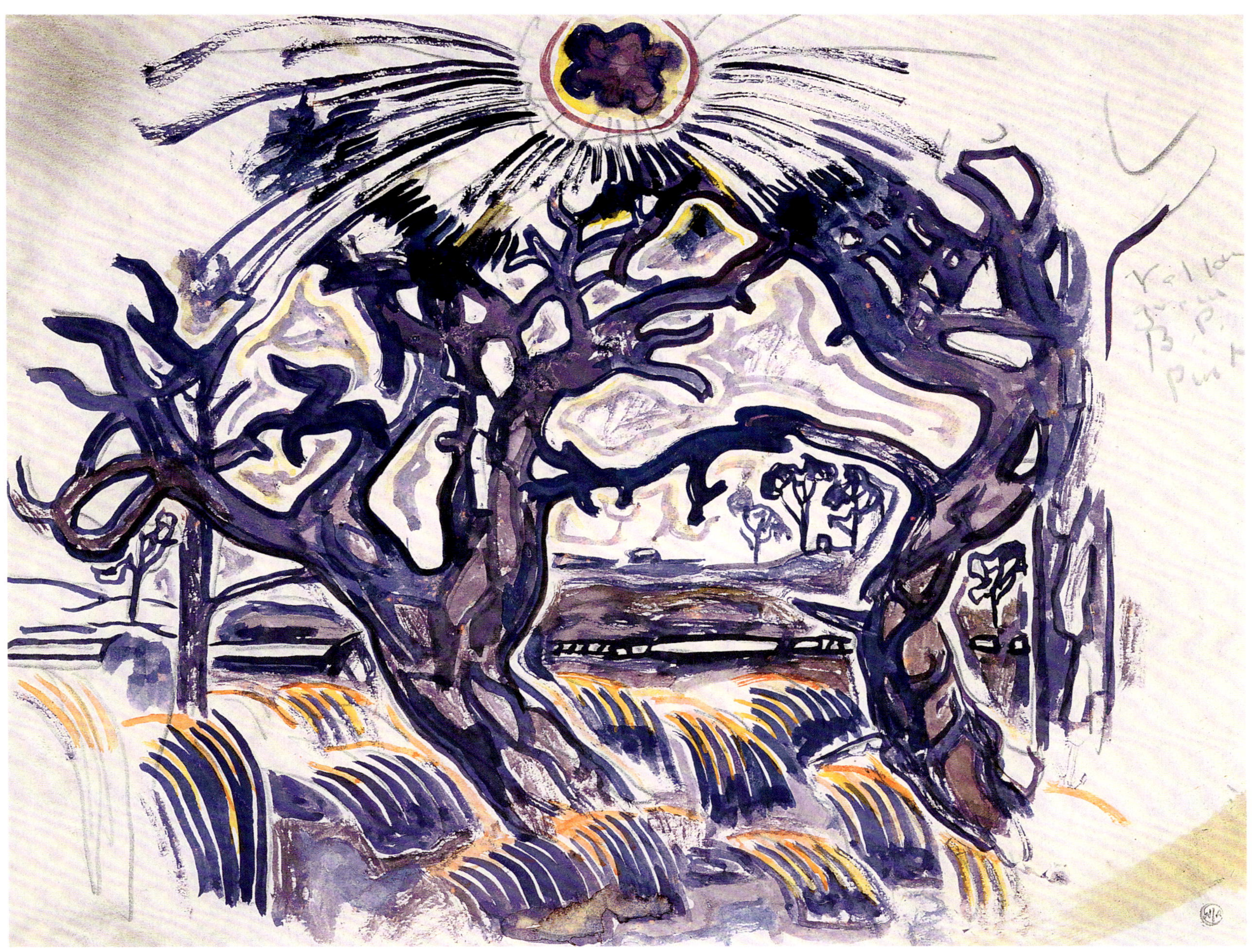

Sun Behind the Clouds, 1965

Watercolor on paper, 8½ x 11 in.
The Family of Walter Anderson

After you have lived on the island for a while there comes a time when ~~th~~ you realize that the pelican holds everything for you It has the song of the thrush the form and understanding of man, the tenderness and gentleness of the dove the mystery and dynamic quality of the night jar. and the potential qualities of all life

In a word you lose your heart to it. It becomes your child and the hope and future of the world depend upon it.

You share in all of its reactions and conditions of life, you awake with it you feel the change from the cave of sleep to the beginning of consciousness and desire You hear its cries of hunger with the need to cry to the

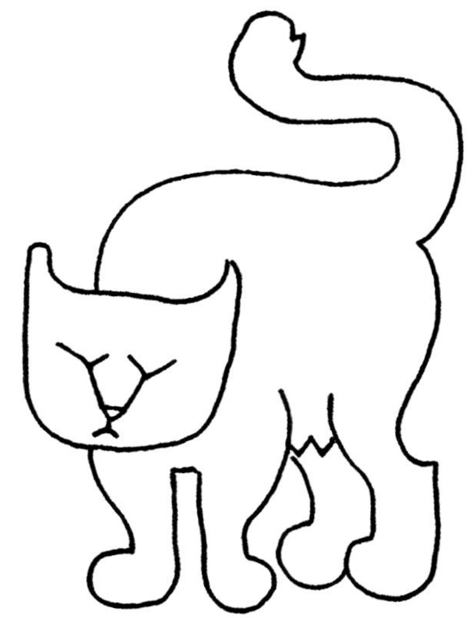

THE WRITINGS OF WALTER ANDERSON

ERNEST PINSON

The first poetry is written against the wind by sailors and farmers who sing with the wind in their teeth.
The second poetry is written by scholars and wine drinkers who learned to know a good thing.
The third poetry is sometimes never written but when it is, it is by those who have brought nature and art together into one thing! [1]
—Walter Anderson

"Why do I write this?"[2] inquired Mississippi artist Walter Anderson in his logs on Saturday, October 30, 1959, as he roamed, a solitary, on a small deserted island. It may to the unalerted ear sound frivolous, but to Anderson, age fifty-six, only six years away from his untimely death, it was more than a mere question of boredom. It was a question of self-assessment and of philosophical purpose. "I think writing has a cleansing effect and although it is easy enough to keep the body clean the mind seems to grow clogged." And then, as if to call attention to his playful wit, he claimed special powers for writing: "Writing may have an hypnotic effect on nature; a mosquito hawk has just lit on my big toe."[3] Later he was to observe more astutely: "Unless the artist can identify his art with poetry he had better keep away from the people, for he will always be identified with patronage of heaven."[4]

Anderson, who earlier had labeled himself a "decorator," now developed a psychic closeness to nature, a yearning to literally merge with the bird's flight, to create a

Manuscript page from an essay on pelicans, 1948
Ink on paper, 11 x 8½in.
The Family of Walter Anderson

dictionary of pelican language, to swim in alligator bubbles, to ride the back of sea waves. The artist/writer must experience Nature first before he can wed it, before he can turn it into art. And so in a small rural town midway between Mobile and New Orleans a young, budding painter carved out for himself a concept of art rooted in a blend of nature and primal self. He made a claim for a unity in all things, of all animals, of all art forms even though they come from different angles of vision, from different inner worlds. He proceeded to act out this dramatic dialogue with godly Nature ten miles offshore on his fourteen-mile-long, one-half-mile-wide island-stage that brooked no audience or rehearsals. "If I destroy nature," he wrote, "and if nature is my source, I destroy myself."[5] Nature was perceived as perfect and archetypal, alive and knowable, universal and organic, unified and individualized in its parts.

It seemed to Anderson that he must try all mediums available to him to capture what the mind fails to grasp but the feelings sense. And try them he did: pen-and-ink drawings, watercolor, ceramics, wood carving, tile making, block prints, book illustrations, children's tales, aphorisms, poetry, short stories, logs, drama, acting, dancing.

This essay intends two things: (1) to focus on the source of Anderson's artistic creed and illustrate this creed with his verbal art, and (2) to illuminate the writings of his logs, aphorisms, stories, poems, and plays by interpreting certain ones in each genre.

I. ARTISTIC CREED

"E=mc^2 . . . means that everything is one."[6]

Throughout history, Horace's famous "Ut Pictura Poesis" ("as in painting, so in poetry") has had its advocates and its adversaries. But unity of the arts, indeed, of all things is at the heart of Anderson's intense feelings of compatibility with nature. In his April 1950 log he penned one of his most profound statements: "The love of bird or shell which might have restored [man's] life flies away . . . and in that fraction of a second man and the bird are real. . . . And he, man, exists and he is almost as wonderful as the thing he sees."[7]

But there is another part to his creed that is often forgotten. He felt a deep responsibility to produce art for society, a call from nature for mankind to share his talents with his fellow creatures. Agnes, his betrothed in 1931, speaks of Anderson's "fairly well-developed theory of an artist's obligation to society. He felt this work [pottery designing] would fulfill for him the duty of an artist to produce inexpensive but good works that would provide satisfying decoration for the home of the average man."[8] Anderson's rendering of a full-scale mural on the walls of the Ocean Springs Community Center in 1951 for the ridiculous charge of one dollar is a prime indication of this sense of obligatory art.

Where, then, is the source of this creed? While it seems clear that it is tied in with his cosmic godly view of Nature, his view of art must have developed early in his studies in Philadelphia and France. We go back in time to 1875, the place Moscow, and the person Madam Helena Petrovna Blavatsky, founder of a movement called the Theosophical Society. By 1910, again in Moscow, George Ivanovitch Gurdjieff had started the Institute for the Harmonious Development of Man (almost surely one of several splinter groups from Madam Blavatsky's Theosophical Society), and its influence spread to Georgia (Russia), Constantinople, Berlin, Dresden, and Paris, France, at the Chauteau du Prieuré near Fountainebleau. From there it spread to England and was carried across the Atlantic to the United States. Gurdjieff himself came to New York in 1923 where for seven years he preached the "harmony of the universe" gospel in lecture halls and private homes. Anderson visited a "camp" several times in Trenton, New Jersey, which was run by A. R. Orage, a disciple of Gurdjieff. We know that Anderson received a Cresson award for study abroad and went to France in 1927 where it is probable that he attended some lectures by Gurdjieff and engaged in discussions at the time. Anderson was especially drawn to the ancient culture, art, and religious murals in China and Tibet, and since Gurdjieff taught that Asia was the root of all ancient knowledge, it is likely that Anderson wished to pursue these ideas in his travels to the Orient.

It was his wife's belief that the name Gurdjieff came up only when Anderson became mentally ill in 1937 (cited by Redding S. Sugg, Jr., to whom all of us are indebted for uncovering this whole line of thinking about Anderson's philosophy at this time).[9] But whether or not Anderson became embarrassed about his connections with Gurdjieff, as his wife seemed to conclude, his art, nevertheless, reveals strong characteristics of the movement. This is not pantheism, nor transcendental mysticism, although both have certain affinities with theosophy, which comes from the Greek words *theos* (god) and *sophos* (wise), and, therefore, literally means one "wise in divine matters." It has two major movements—one Western and fairly recent (fifteenth century) is tied in with the writings of Paracelsus, Rudolf Steiner, and Emanuel Swedenborg, while the other Oriental and very ancient one is tied to Buddhism, Brahmanism, Vedic Hinduism, Islamic Sufism, and Neoplatonism. It has many branches, all of which believe in the universal unity of all things, especially in the blurring of spirit and matter, body and soul, mind and senses. *The Cambridge Dictionary of Philosophy* ties in Madam Blatavsky to Swedenborg and Steiner and notes that her views were strongly influenced by mystical elements of Indian philosophy and by the book *The Theosophy of the Orient of Light* by Islamic philosopher-writer Suhrawardi.[10]

However, none of this circumstantial evidence of Anderson's readings and travel would be important if we could not trace the evidence of theosophy in his art and writings. One of the basic tenets of all branches of theosophy is the unity of all things. Throughout Anderson's writing are such key words as "oneness," "unity," "harmony," "rhythms of the universe," "I and the night are one." He once told his wife Agnes, "I become one with all things when I blend water and my sense of touch."[11] At least five poems deal with heavenly harmony and the divine symphony of the universe. One poem begins:

> Every little movement, each discovery
> is a part of the heavenly music
> and if my ears
> were functioning properly
> I would hear . . . an orderly and recognizable harmony.[12]

(Often Anderson did not put his poems in stanza form, and for this and subsequent poems I rely upon past research and formulation done by Patricia Pinson except as otherwise noted.)

Another poem sings out:

> All movement is to invisible music
> although few people hear it.
> It comes from the sun and the wind
> and the movement of water and
> a running rabbit and a crowing cock,
> and together it is a part
> of a great symphony.[13]

Second, most branches of theosophy also urge a belief in a self-perpetuating, primordial essence from which everything emerges, a kind of demiurge. Rudolf Steiner, one of the early theoreticians, argued that all reality is organic, evolving from itself. Our knowing is, therefore, intuitive rather than discursive, and all forms, matter and spirit, emerge from the One.

> As the turtle emerged from the fish,
> so the hills rose above the waters.

As the bird rose above the turtle
and lit in a tree, so the stream rose
from the hills when they were left bare.
As the bird lost its wings and became a beast,
so the vapor left the hills in rain, and
as the rain rose to the sun,
so the beast became man . . .
all part of the divine symphony.[14]

To some minds, this leads to a belief in the mystical wonder of the god/spirit that, in Wordsworth's words, "moves in and through all things"—a desire to interconnect all apparent opposites: body and soul, matter and spirit, logic and feeling, animals and plants—in short, a human sensitivity to Nature's "presences." "Air and spirit are one," Anderson told Agnes. "There is a soaring quality to both spirit and intellect."[15] Gurdjieff taught that man "has everything within him. I have inside me the sun, the moon, God. I am—all life in its totality."[16]

But Anderson's attempt to marry this theosophic unity to his Christian heritage produced a strange kind of mysticism. In the winter of 1934, after having reread some of G. K. Chesterton (a writer he had known since his "old school days"), he evidently tried to resolve the Christian dualism of soul/body, Heaven/Hell, good/evil, God/Satan via "the Prince of Peace, the Baby, symbol of love all-conquering." This had been a fundamental conflict—his Christian upbringing with Gurdjieff's theosophical teachings. Agnes tells us that "time and again throughout his life [Walter] was in a hairsbreadth of following" Chesterton's conversion to Roman Catholicism.[17] Suddenly, inexplicably, he shouted to Agnes in a moment of excited exhilaration: "The elements were man's gods, you see, until the event of love. I got it now. It's such a beautiful paradox. Chesterton would have loved it. All this terrific strength and suddenly the Babe, the son of Mary."[18] Here, by this act, the unity of all things is mysteriously cemented with love; and here was the solace, serenity, peace, and relief he sought from conflict, the solution that would erase the internal struggle he found on shore. And here, Anderson escaped not from others, but from his own struggle to resolve the contradictions. So he writes:

I can leap
   and I can play
With all things the day
   has left behind
And the deadness
of the day has

gone
Gone down with
the sun
And I and night are one
The music and
the mystery
are mine.[19]

Tied in with mysticism is the emphasis on relying on the intuitive senses for insights, as taught by Gurdjieff, because they stem from primordial nature. He believed, as did Steiner, "that patient observation of the physical reality leads to an awareness of the spiritual reality behind physical appearances. . . . Every flower when properly observed will reveal secrets."[20] So, says Anderson assuredly, "The realization of form and space is through feeling."[21] Agnes tells us that through a process called "realizations," Anderson claimed "he could become one with tree or insect or any living thing. It was connected with the use he made of his five senses while he was creating paintings, drawings, any kind of art."[22] "Stop thinking," he shouted to Agnes when she tried to explain her fear of drowning. "Can't you feel at all? . . . Don't you see what it was? It was like finding yourself, your primal self, knowing exactly where you come from."[23] Much later he was to write, "The heart is the thing that counts. The mingling of my heart with the heart of the wild bird: to become one with the thing I see."[24]

Finally, in the philosophy of theosophy one must accept the natural world as not only primordial but organic and cathartic (pantheism), for "man's salvation depended upon his discovery of the natural world and his recognition of his own role within it."[25] But while acceptance seemed easy enough on the one hand, man's misuse of nature, on the other hand, made that relationship rather obscure to Anderson:

What is man's relationship to nature?

If he makes friends with it, does he lose the careless relationship that is so important as every farmer knows—the careless sowing of seeds?

If nature becomes a god, will it not also become a demon and destroy him with the same careless brutality with which man destroys fish?

If the brute is to be necessary, who is to be the brute?

So Music and Art are the answer.[26]

So the artist's chore of peeling off the outer layers of matter to get at the inner spiritual core of truth becomes quite a burden. Trying to blend the "oneness" of things in nature with its seeming contradictions proved illusive. Death, sorrow, pain, rejection, fear kept raising their nasty heads. The death of his father in February 1937 was one of the most traumatic experiences in his life, and Anderson's desire to escape the pain can all be tied to this search for purpose. Such hurt is well encapsulated in this poem.

> The mind is a serpent moving slowly
> while the quick birds fly overhead
> scolding its slowness. Once it was a
> turtle protected from the birds by its
> shell. Now its strength is its only
> protection. It longs for the night and
> the end of the world, the rising sea,
> or some catastrophe which will
> destroy its pain.[27]

For weeks after his father's funeral, Anderson's "sleepless nights were full of long descriptions of his father and tales of childhood." One night he cried out, "Who is my God? Is it my father who is dead? Is it the cat of your dreams? They say the spiral goes the other way on the other side of the equator. Still a spiral. My God is a spiral without beginning or end." A spiral, of course, is a symbol of infinity, and often represents a god in ancient religions. Noticing how the spirals of the waves curled, he picked up a conch shell and showed Agnes how the twisted end repeated the spiral in a wave, a grapevine, a pinecone, a maple seed, and the coil of ferns.[28] At other times his god is symbolic: "I thought of god, and a white Heron flew up . . . ,"[29] or god can be playfully Greek: "Ah Psyche, I have felt thy aid,"[30] or at times the "elements were man's gods."[31] But most often by Anderson's words or by actions, God is that unifying Spirit of Nature.

Hence, Anderson's view of art goes much deeper than a mere "Ut Pictura Poesis," for his talents came out of a deep, personal, philosophical immersion of the self in creative acts that have not yet been fully understood by reviewers. Professor Redding Sugg came close to identifying it when he observed that Anderson performed "dramatic" painting, "for he thought of painting as the part he played in the drama of Nature. He regarded it as his ecological function, no more and no less important than the function of the other creatures, plants, and wheeling seasons. He thought of himself as painting catalytically, in order to help nature to 'realize' itself."[32] After all, the function of the ancient poet is seer, visionary, explorer, "mystics, or ecstatic devotees of the Muse," which he had learned from reading Robert Graves's book *The White*

Goddess.[33] And it was on Horn Island that this dramatic mingling with nature took place; that was where, observed his wife, Agnes, "the images came more frequently and with greater intensity. . . . He first went to Horn Island as an observer, then he tried to join in . . . to become one with nature."[34]

II. MODELS OF ANDERSON'S WRITING STYLES

Art is incredible stuff—not for itself, but in changing the artist's relation to other things—perspective.[35]

—Walter Anderson

Here we will follow Anderson's creative process in motion by using examples of his own writing. Professor Sugg has noted Anderson's "Blakean turn for aphorism," writing that Anderson "habitually scrawled his inspirations on sheets and scraps which he pinned to his walls. . . ."[36] It is another kind of contemplation found scattered throughout his logs, stories, poems, letters, and diaries.

A. Aphorisms

Man's eyes are windows and may be closed.

Ducks are trained to rise against the wind.
So don't be surprised if they oppose everything they are taught.

Homer related hysteria to order and made it poetry—
how much depended on his blindness it is hard to say.

From what I have found out in my life I realize that clouds still come between me and the sun.

B. Small, constricted aphorisms turned into three- or four-line meditations

The green fire of the night possessed me
until suddenly the cock crew,
and I knew that the sun still lived.[37]

Some walk on the earth,
Others on water.
Still others need clouds to walk on.[38]

Lost to virtue and to art
I must make another start again, again, again.
I must fall down with the rain
I must leave my cloud again
And descend like gentle rain again, again, again.[39]

C. Poems of deeper development

These aphoristic poems graduate into the more mature poems. Despite the simplistic rhyme of the little poem below, it has its subtle theme and its Emily Dickinson metaphor, and may remind one of Blake's "A Poison Tree."

But if thou canst not love thy friends,
Thou still mayst love thy foe.
For he hath brought thee low.
And taught thy ear to know
The voice of growing grass.[40]

The incident in the next poem, called "Cypress Knees," literally happened to Anderson. This is one of his better poems, for it not only plays upon frogs as "benevolent old men," whereupon "a real old man appears," but it also has the nice double entendre image of frogs that "climb up on his knees"—but wait! Which knees? The old man's or the cypress's? This clever paradox is achieved by his beginning with the "Cypress knees" and ending with the "old man's knees," neatly deepening the mystery. Does Nature use the knees of the cypress as a device to get frogs and the old man to be friends? Or do cypress knees need the "anthropomorphic quality . . . of benevolent old men" to attract the frogs? Or is this a metapoem showing how "frogs are drawn"?

Cypress knees need
the anthropomorphic quality—
until frogs are drawn—

then as if they were benevolent old men—
then the chorus accomplished—
a real old man appears
and the frogs climb up
on his knees.[41]

D. Anderson's versatile nature

Below are five different types of work on the subject of cats: a short story, a poem, a kind of riddle, a painting, a ceramic piece. Anderson's stories are always short, light, clever, fairytalesque vignettes often designed to instruct and entertain children.

The Cat Who Was the Sun

The cat who left the sun and walked among the flowers was at one time the sun itself. But because of its love of flowers, it left its place in the sky and came to earth where it admired and loved the flowers and birds while one of the flowers took its place in the sky.

It cared for the flowers and watered and manured them until they were able to care for themselves and then looking very much like a flower itself, it wished to return to its place in the sky.

It thought of all the ways it might do this. It finally decided that the only way was to drink up the milky way. As soon as it began, the stars let down a rope ladder. The cat climbed up it and tomorrow morning you will see it in its usual place. But ever since then, cats have been very partial to milk, but as far as I know it has had very little effect on them.[42]

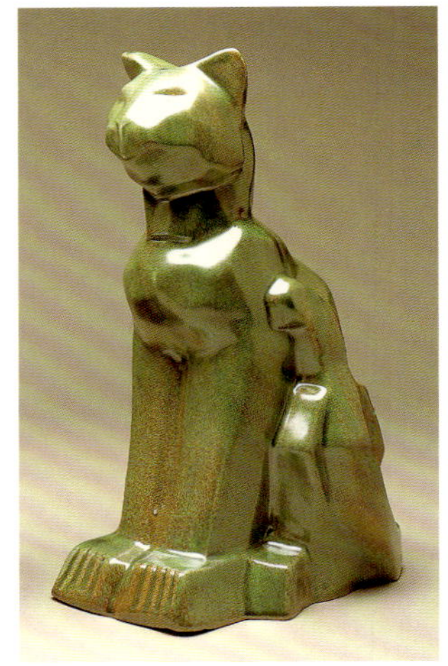

To the Cat
Thou who carries the sun for a head
A serpent for a tail
And for feet, four flowers
which follow thee wherever thou doest go.[43]

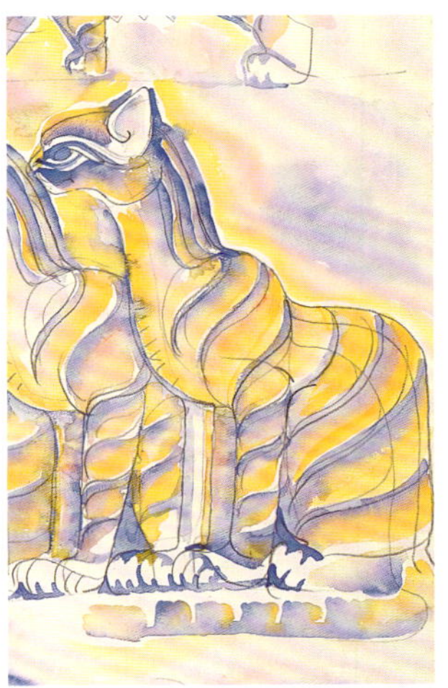

Form
The little boy understood cats,
and realized how much man had sacrificed
in order to grow into a man.
Wings to the birds

and light
and fur
and grace to the cats.[44]

E. Other medium matchups (painting-poem-story-ceramic-woodcut)

A variety of topics—"man running," "symphony of movements," frogs, turtles, birds, pelicans, cows, blades of grass—are used repeatedly in different mediums. But while those "matchups" are usually playful in childlike tones, Anderson can be serious and complex, as seen in the following examples. This poem is subtle, catchy, profound, and quite modern in technique, personifying the world, sun, stars, and colors into a theme of "rebellious" envy. The imagery of the poem has parallels to the art on pages 167, 170, 178, 229, and 230.

The world was
    Quite embarrassed
Turning from pink
    to red and then
                to brown
But when the sun
        has set
It will black
    with rebellious
        stars to say
the night should
    be as bright
        as day.[45]

F. Drama

In a letter to his mother on February 12, 1923, Anderson writes: "[George Bernard] Shaw says that an artist is either a poet or a scalawag. Which one do you prefer? If I have to choose, I think I'll take the scalawag."

Walter Anderson's mother was herself well trained in music and art and appreciated architecture and drama. Mary Anderson Pickard, his older daughter, says that her grandmother often had friends over who "spoke the same language," and they danced, played games, and sang while she played the piano, which she did quite well. She was an ardent Episcopalian who believed in doing things that would heal the mind, and so she taught her grandchildren to play the game "concentration" and toyed with the ouija board. Another favorite was a game of cards with geometric designs in which each person had to guess the design before the card was turned over to reveal its secret.[46]

His wife, Agnes (called Sissy), in her book *Approaching the Magic Hour: Memories of Walter Anderson*, mentions that when they moved in 1940 to Oldfields, the antebellum plantation that belonged to her maternal grandfather, a large unfinished attic became Walter's art studio. It was in this attic, too, that he turned playwright, created a puppet play, and so arranged the ropes and pulleys that he was able to become a one-man show—playing the music and telling the story, while pulling all the ropes and maneuvering the puppets with fishing lines. Agnes remembered "the sun rising, with dramatic pauses, and the worshipping dances of the flora and the fauna . . . the ludicrous leaping of the frogs and the slow lumbering of the turtles, [and] the dreadful tension engendered by the many pursuits, which centered upon the patterned moths."[47] But Mary remembered how the "large frogs, turtles, and insects leaped, crawled and clicked to music provided by the artist on pipes he had made from bamboo."[48] So taken were the children and viewers that Walter performed it several times with chants, grunts, chirps, fluting, and drumming.

Later he cut out a large three-foot Greek ship with oars and Ulysses for the children to use in acting out a drama scene. His interest in drama, while not consistent, was extensive. According to his daughter Mary, one of his favorites was the Scottish playwright Sir James Barrie, best remembered for his play *Peter Pan*,[49] and we know from his letters while he was at school in 1923 that he had read playwrights like Sophocles, Racine, Molière, Ibsen, Maeterlinck, Chekhov, and Shaw. We also learn from his logs that he played charades, read Shakespeare in the 1940s, and drew ninety-nine illustrations for *Hamlet.*

Below is a short excerpt from this puppet play which uses a frog, lizard, moth, turtle, flower, and mostly sounds of animals rather than human dialogue. Mary reminds us that her father thought animals talked a language among themselves, perhaps even better than ours, and that he later attempted to create a pelican language dictionary.[50]

A frog appears and suddenly in the center of the stage (silence)
Frog (up!—Silence)—
Frog (up!—Silence)—
Off stage more frogs
Frogs (up! —urr-uup)

child's song up—urr-up upp
Slowly the sun rises
Frog chorus becomes a regular chant

*Chorus
Sun Sun. Hail to the sun
We come, we come
to greet the sun
The day is begun
We greet the sun
We dance to the sun
one by one
day is begun
(The dance subsides while the sun climbs higher)
(a hawk flies over)
(screams)
Then the sun rose and he found the morning star
in a drop of dew holding the light from the sun.[51]

Aside from this play, he did create and perform in a family Christmas play, and although he and his wife often read to each other in a dramatic style, he was never again to accept the challenge of being a dramatist.

III. CONCLUSION

Poets walk with webbed feet when it rains and talk with the frogs.[52]
—Walter Anderson

After e. e. cummings learned to be a painter, he became a poet and carried with him in this transition a painter's eye for space. His poems expanded out—more vertical than horizontal, his lines were broken up, he abandoned punctuation, and he tried to paint verbal images—attracting the ear as well as the eye, much as we witnessed in Anderson's puppet drama. Everything is related, unified, even the arts, Anderson wrote in a poem, "[b]ut the artist knows that for him to be successful, art and nature must become one."[53] The role of an artist is to relate "the parts to the strange and transient unity,"[54] he wrote, but "the duty of the poet is to give words to the bells."[55]

An image can come in a splash of color or a cascade of words. So a poem or story can seek to resemble a painting, interpret it, or use the same image/subject as its own. W. B. Yeats, in his famous poem "Ego Dominus Tuus," writes, "I seek an image, not a book." Earlier in the poem, he says, "By the help of an image / I call to my own opposite, summon all / That I have handled least, least looked upon." Yeats just happened to be Anderson's favorite poet, and the concept of the image was picked up. It is July 1959. Anderson, in retreat to his island, sees a young heron climb a tree using feet, wings, and bill: "It seemed that with very little it would climb the cloud and take the kingdom of heaven by force. . . . I drew it in ecstasy. It was a concentrated image that nothing could take from me. If it was not poetry it was the image asked for by Yeats from which poetry is made."[56]

Sugg's theory that Anderson's "fulfillment came in the ecstatic experiences involving dance, song, and mystical identification with the *genius loci* of which the logs, the drawings, and the paintings are the surviving evidences" is difficult to refute.[57] And indeed, there are certain scenes like this scattered through his logs: "a pouldeau became a song, and I danced to it—feet still firmly planted—it was a restoring experience—my shadow danced with me,—blue shadow against the copper bullrushes."[58] It is evident that life for Anderson on his beloved island was always an adventure, and seldom a lonely one, for he had his "companions" of Nature. Writes Agnes, "As long as he was on Horn Island he was in tune with the rhythms of the universe. He was a part of the changing seasons. He was filled with the ecstasy of creation. He recorded it all, working endlessly. It became his world."[59] In 1965 Anderson and his world became one. He now lies buried in Evergreen Cemetery in Ocean Springs.

NOTES

1. "Yellow Butterflies: A Reading of Excerpts from the Writings of Walter Inglis Anderson" (Ocean Springs, MS: The Walter Anderson Estate), n.p. (Hereafter referred to as "Yellow Butterflies.")

2. Redding S. Sugg, Jr., ed., *The Horn Island Logs of Walter Inglis Anderson*, rev. ed. (Jackson: University Press of Mississippi, 1985), p. 156.

3. Sugg, *Horn Island Logs*, p. 156.

4. From Walter Anderson's handwritten manuscripts at the Mississippi Department of Archives and History, Jackson, Mississippi, collected by Patricia Pinson, 23 May 1996. (Hereafter referred to as Archives.)

5. Walter Anderson, *A Symphony of Animals* (Jackson: University Press of Mississippi, 1996), p. 91.

6. Agnes Grinstead Anderson, *Approaching the Magic Hour: Memories of Walter Anderson*, ed. Patti Carr Black (Jackson: University Press of Mississippi, 1989), p. 140.

7. Sugg, *Horn Island Logs*, p. 82.

8. Agnes Anderson, *Approaching the Magic Hour*, p. 6.

9. Sugg, *Horn Island Logs,* p. 14.

10. *The Cambridge Dictionary of Philosophy* (Cambridge: Cambridge University Press, 1999), p. 915.

11. Agnes Anderson, *Approaching the Magic Hour*, p. 36.

12. "Yellow Butterflies," n.p.

13. Walter Anderson, *A Symphony of Animals*, p. 1.

14. Walter Anderson, *A Symphony of Animals*, p. 101.

15. Agnes Anderson, *Approaching the Magic Hour*, p. 46.

16. G. I. Gurdjieff, *Views from the Real World* (New York: E. P. Dutton & Co., 1973), p. 102.

17. Agnes Anderson, *Approaching the Magic Hour*, p. 44.

18. Agnes Anderson, *Approaching the Magic Hour*, p. 44.

19. Archives, n.p.

20. Quoted by Anthony Storr, *Feet of Clay: Saints, Sinners, and Madmen: A Study of Gurus* (New York: The Free Press, 1996), p. 75.

21. Walter Anderson, *A Symphony of Animals*, p. 37.

22. Agnes Anderson, *Approaching the Magic Hour*, p. 45.

23. Agnes Anderson, *Approaching the Magic Hour*, p. 35.

24. Agnes Anderson, *Approaching the Magic Hour*, p. 138.

25. Mary Anderson Pickard, introduction to *Birds*, by Walter Anderson (Jackson: University Press of Mississippi, 1990), p. xxvi.

26. "Yellow Butterflies," n.p.

27. Walter Anderson, *A Symphony of Animals*, p. 88.

28. Agnes Anderson, *Approaching the Magic Hour*, pp. 55–56.

29. Sugg, *Horn Island Logs*, p. 52.

30. Sugg, *Horn Island Logs*, p. 83.

31. Agnes Anderson, *Approaching the Magic Hour*, p. 46.

32. Redding S. Sugg, Jr., ed., *Walter Anderson's Illustrations of Epic and Voyage* (Carbondale, IL: Southern Illinois University Press, 1980), p. xiv.

33. Robert Graves, *The White Goddess: A Historical Grammar of Poetic Myth* (New York: Farrar, Straus & Cudaly, 1948), p. 447.

34. Agnes Anderson, interview by John Driscoll, August 1984.

35. Archives, n.p.

36. Sugg, *Horn Island Logs*, p. 10.

37. "Yellow Butterflies," n.p.

38. "Yellow Butterflies," n.p.

39. "Yellow Butterflies," n.p.

40. "Yellow Butterflies," n.p.

41. Archives, n.p.

42. Archives, n.p.

43. "Yellow Butterflies," n.p.

44. Archives, n.p.

45. Archives, n.p.

46. Mary Anderson Pickard, interview by author, 23 December 2002.

47. Agnes Anderson, *Approaching the Magic Hour*, pp. 85–86.

48. Mary Anderson Pickard, afterword to *Robinson: The Pleasant History of an Unusual Cat*, by Walter Anderson (Jackson: University Press of Mississippi, 1982), n.p.

49. Mary Anderson Pickard, interview.

50. Mary Anderson Pickard, interview.

51. Archives; this text was copied from Anderson's handwritten note by Patricia Pinson.

52. Walter Anderson, *A Symphony of Animals*, p. 41.

53. Walter Anderson, *A Symphony of Animals*, p. 45.
54. Quoted by Patti Carr Black in her introduction to *Approaching the Magic Hour*, p. viii.
55. "Yellow Butterflies," n.p.
56. Sugg, *Horn Island Logs*, p. 139.
57. Sugg, introduction to *Horn Island Logs*, p. 18.
58. Sugg, *Horn Island Logs*, February 1963, n.p.
59. Agnes Anderson, *Approaching the Magic Hour*, p. 148.

CHRONOLOGY

Christopher Maurer

This chronology is based upon Christopher Maurer and María Estrella Iglesias, *Dreaming in Clay on the Coast of Mississippi: Love and Art at Shearwater* (New York: Doubleday, 2000), and on my biography, *Fortune's Favorite Child: The Uneasy Life of Walter Anderson* (Jackson: University Press of Mississippi, 2003). Both of these books draw on Agnes Grinstead Anderson's poignant memoir, *Approaching the Magic Hour: Memories of Walter Anderson*, and on the expert knowledge of Mary Anderson Pickard, Redding S. Sugg, Jr., and others. I am indebted to Mary Anderson Pickard for her writing and teaching about the life and work of her father. Because Walter Anderson seldom dated his works or his letters, it is not always possible to assign definitive dates. Only a few of them—enough to orient the reader—are included here. The letters and numbers in parentheses refer to illustrations of the works in this catalogue and in the following books:

AMH Agnes Grinstead Anderson. *Approaching the Magic Hour: Memories of Walter Anderson*. Jackson: University Press of Mississippi, 1989.

B Walter Anderson. *Birds*. Introductory essay by Mary Anderson Pickard. Jackson: University Press of Mississippi, 1990.

HIL *The Horn Island Logs of Walter Inglis Anderson*. Edited by Redding S. Sugg, Jr. Rev. ed., Jackson: University Press of Mississippi, 1985.

IEV *Walter Anderson's Illustrations of Epic and Voyage*. Edited and with an introduction by Redding S. Sugg, Jr. Carbondale: Southern Illinois University Press; London: Feffer & Simmons, 1980.

MC *The Magic Carpet and Other Tales*. Retold by Ellen Douglas, with the illustrations of Walter Anderson. Jackson: University Press of Mississippi, 1987.

PP Redding S. Sugg, Jr. *A Painter's Psalm: The Mural from Walter Anderson's Cottage*. Rev. ed., Jackson: University Press of Mississippi, 1992.

RI *Walter Anderson: Realizations of the Islander*. Selections of paintings and essay by John Paul Driscoll. The Walter Anderson Estate, 1985.

SA Walter Anderson. *A Symphony of Animals*. Introduction by Mary Anderson Pickard. Jackson: University Press of Mississippi, 1996.

VR *The Voluptuous Return: Still Life by Walter Inglis Anderson*. Foreword by Patti Carr Black. Ocean Springs, MS: Family of Walter Anderson, 1999.

WL Anne R. King. *Walls of Light: The Murals of Walter Anderson*. Jackson: University Press of Mississippi and the Walter Anderson Museum of Art, 1999.

1903

Born in New Orleans, September 29, the second son of George Walter Anderson (1865–1937), a New Orleans grain dealer, and Annette McConnell Anderson (1867–1964), who had studied art at Newcomb College (class of 1900) and possibly with William Merritt Chase and J. Alden Weir. WIA's brothers are Peter Anderson (1901–1984) and James McConnell ("Mac") Anderson (1907–1998).

1905

The Andersons move to 553 Broadway, near Audubon Park. As a child, WIA attends a small private school run by family friends, the Finney sisters. Childhood drawings (*WL* 15; *SA* viii; *B* 10).

1914–1915

WIA attends R. M. Lusher Public School, New Orleans.

1915–1919

In summer 1915, WIA and Peter enroll at St. John's School, Manlius, New York. WIA takes a course on landscape painting at E. Ambrose Webster's Summer School of Art, Provincetown, Massachusetts. In June 1918, Annette McConnell Anderson purchases Fairhaven, a property on the Bay of Biloxi, in Ocean Springs, Mississippi.

1919–1922

Studies at Isidore Newman Manual Training School, New Orleans. In August 1920, WIA nearly drowns while sailing his catboat from Ocean Springs to Chef Menteur. *Elephant Chest* (*SA* ix); carved figures of people and animals (*SA* xi).

1922–1923

Studies commercial art at New York School of Fine and Applied Art, later known as Parsons School of Design, and lives in a boardinghouse on the Upper West Side. Course on Jay Hambidge's "dynamic symmetry," taught by Howard Giles. Attends 1923 Independents Exhibition; frequents the American Museum of Natural History, the Hispanic Society of America, the Metropolitan Museum of Art, and other museums and exhibitions. Reads voraciously and works on woodcarving, watercolors, and tempera painting.

1923

Summer: the Andersons move to Fairhaven, Ocean Springs.

1924–1928

Studies at the Pennsylvania Academy of the Fine Arts, Philadelphia, on a scholarship from the New Orleans Art Association, and studies with Henry McCarter, Daniel Garber, Hugh Breckenridge, and Arthur B. Carles. Friendship with Frank Baisden, Francis Speight, Walter and Cyril Gardner, Archie Bonge, and Conrad Roland. Works on school drawings of animals, drawings from cast and life, carved saints, paintings (*Portrait of a Girl*, Walter Anderson Museum of Art), and others reproduced in 1928 and 1929 academy catalogues.

1924

President's Prize, Packard Competition for Animal Drawing.

1925

Second Prize, Packard Competition. In summer, returns home in a canoe down the Mississippi River. Peter Anderson builds a "groundhog kiln" at Fairhaven and fires his first pieces.

1926

Annette McConnell Anderson organizes a summer art colony at Fairhaven, under the direction of Daniel G. Whitney, an artist from New Orleans. Peter studies pottery with Edmund DeForest Curtis in Wayne, Pennsylvania, and, upon his return, begins to build the future Shearwater Pottery.

1927

With Schuyler Jackson and Frank Baisden, attends lectures by A. R. Orage (spokesman and fund-raiser for the Armenian visionary George Ivanovitch Gurdjieff) in Trenton and New York. In the summer, travels through France and Spain on Cresson Traveling Fellowship from the Pennsylvania Academy of the Fine Arts. Visits caves of Les Eyzies, Mont-Saint-Michel, Chartres, and the Louvre and Prado. Brief visit to the Institute for the Harmonious Development of Man, directed by Gurdjieff. Peter studies under Charles F. Binns at the School of Clay-Working and Ceramics at Alfred, New York.

1928

Shearwater Pottery opens to the public. In 1928–1929, WIA designs his earliest ceramic pieces: pelican and crab bookends, lamp bases (*SA* xvi), *Resting* and *Sitting Geometric Cats* (*SA* 23), "rounded" cats, a fish, *Horse and Rider* (*SA* 55), a horse, and numerous plates and vases. His work as a designer and decorator at Shearwater Pottery, from now until his death, will include incised pieces, sgraffito work, and underglaze decoration (examples of pottery in *SA* xi, 10, 19, 20 and passim; *B* 65, 80, 85, 92; *WL* 25). Woodcarvings of saints, carved *Nativity,* copies of African/Polynesian art, early furniture designs.

1929

Peter and WIA meet Patricia and Agnes ("Sissy") Grinstead at Shearwater; they are daughters of William Wade Grinstead, a Pittsburgh lawyer and trust officer, and Agnes Marjorie Deuel Hellmuth. WIA paints in oil. Early works include *Dark Flowers*, *Dark-Haired Woman in Red Dress*. At the pottery, WIA, remembering the cave paintings of Les Eyzies, makes *Vase with Horses* (*SA* 18), and gives it to Sissy or her mother. He also does the cast piece *Bacchante*, pelican doorstop, and pirate figurines.

1930

Peter Anderson marries Patricia Grinstead (April 16). WIA corresponds with Sissy, a fine arts major at Radcliffe College (class of 1931), telling her about his painting, his woodcarving (figures in cedar), and his admiration for primitive art, including African sculpture.

1931

Opening of Shearwater Annex, where WIA and James McConnell Anderson produce a series of "Negro figurines" (widgets). In November, the figurines are included in an exhibition of contemporary American ceramics at W. & J. Sloane, a department store on Fifth Avenue in New York, bringing publicity in the *New York Times*, the *Christian Science Monitor*, and other national publications, but WIA dismisses them as "perfectly worthless." At Shearwater, WIA discusses primitive art with Tulane archaeologist Franz Blom. In the summer, he and Sissy are engaged. His carved vases *Jazz* and *Bacchante* are exhibited in March at the Municipal Art Gallery, Jackson.

1933

Marries Sissy at St. Pierre's Episcopal Church, Gautier (April 29). Honeymoon at Oldfields, the Grinstead family home in Gautier, Mississippi.

1934

In spring, paints mural in the auditorium of the Ocean Springs Public School (*Ocean Springs: Past and Present*) on a commission from the Public Works of Art Project

(*WL* 17–40) (see Francis V. O'Connor, pp. 48–51). Peter Anderson and James McConnell Anderson create a ceramic mural for the entrance of the school (*WL* 21). WIA paints *Indians Hunting* (*WL* 26) and *Jockeys Riding Horses* (*WL* 25, 27). Other early paintings include at least four oil portraits of Sissy, 1933–37, *Black Skimmer* (*B* 68–69), *Androcles and Lion* (*SA* 54), *Man on Horse* (*SA* 57), and *Achilles* (Memphis Brooks Museum of Art). Watercolors of flowers, animals, and birds. Bird studies for a projected book on birds of the southeastern United States (*B* xi, 7, 12, 21, 51–55, 57–58). Block prints, including *Tourist Cards, Alphabet* (*SA* xvii, 72), nursery rhymes, *On the River, Valkyries, Butterfly Book,* scenes from Shearwater Pottery.

In summer 1934, WIA and Sissy attend Bach Festival in Bethelehem, Pennsylvania, with Dr. and Mrs. Edwards A. Park. They visit Sissy's Grinstead relatives in Louisville, Kentucky, and make an excursion to Baltimore, where he orders supplies for the construction of paper lamp shades (example in the Walter Anderson Museum of Art). They attempt to return to Ocean Springs in a canoe on the Ohio and Mississippi rivers. WIA is stricken with malaria, and the trip is broken off in Lake Village, Arkansas.

1935

Submits preliminary sketches for a mural in the Jackson, Mississippi, post office and courthouse (*WL* 28) (see Francis V. O'Connor, pp. 51–53). Weaves numerous hooked rugs, from 1929 through the early 1940s (*WL* 20). Two copper-red carved vases are exhibited in the Robineau Memorial Exhibition, sponsored by the Syracuse Museum of Fine Arts (other pieces are displayed regularly in this exhibition throughout the 1930s). Work from Shearwater Pottery, including decorated work by WIA, is shown in the California Pacific Exposition, San Diego.

1936

Undulant fever. Renovation of the cottage, with furniture designed by WIA. Mural designs are rejected in Jackson, Mississippi, post office and courthouse competition. Submits designs for PWA mural (never completed) at the Indianola, Mississippi, post office (*WL* 28) (see Francis V. O'Connor, pp. 53–54).

1937

Death of his father, George Walter Anderson (February 23.) After a psychotic episode in March, enters Henry Phipps Psychiatric Clinic, Johns Hopkins University (April 1), where he is treated by Adolf Meyer, Norman Cameron, Henry Mead, and a team of distinguished psychiatrists. The diagnosis is hypothymergasia (depression in which the patient displays feelings of guilt and inadequacy and the desire to harm himself). Hooks rugs, models in clay, "plays at the piano." December 8: birth of his first child, Mary. That month, a showing of Shearwater

Pottery at the Virginia Museum of Fine Arts. Among WIA's pieces are "a powerful, blunt lion in a beautiful dull-glazed green shade," "two pelican heads," "panels of rhythmic rounded nymphs dancing in ivory glaze around a pale blue vase and the same nymphs in green on a dull green vase" (*Bacchante?*), "a bold, crude and arresting presentation of the adoration of the Shepherds and Wise Men," Negro figurines, pirates, and "a sleepy cat in the subtle dull gun-metal shade" (*Richmond Times-Dispatch*, December 15, 1937).

1938

Discharged from Phipps after eighteen months of treatment (October). Returns to Shearwater, where he paints and draws. The pottery figure *Rima* (suggested by W. H. Hudson's *Green Mansions*) is submitted to the Robineau Memorial Exhibition. In December, Peter Anderson enters Henry Phipps Psychiatric Clinic, where he will remain for nine months.

1939

Admitted to Mississippi State Hospital at Whitfield (February) and diagnosed with "dementia praecox, catatonic type." Escapes from Whitfield in April. In May, he is admitted to the Sheppard and Enoch Pratt Hospital, Baltimore, where he is diagnosed with schizophrenia. Works on wallpaper designs, drawing, modeling in clay, and reads extensively. Escapes on July 1. In October, returns to Shearwater and is readmitted to Whitfield. Birth of son, William Walter.

Escapes from Whitfield. Lives with Annette McConnell Anderson and an attendant in a house on Moss Avenue in Jackson, Mississippi. Writes a series of illustrated letters to Sissy (*AMH* 14), designs dresses, oil painting *Don Quixote*, important series of pencil drawings (*AMH* 33, 43, 50, etc.). Paints with Marie Hull.

1940

In February, escapes from mother's care in Jackson and walks to Shearwater. Resumes pottery decoration there, working in black and white. Many works by WIA are shown at an exhibition entitled *Anderson Brothers' Shearwater Pottery*, May 19–31 at the Number 10 Gallery, New York. Among the figurines are *Chesty Horse*, *Tibetan Cats*, pirates and Negro figurines, *Trojan Horses*, *Sea Gulls*, and *Pelicans*. Carved pieces include *Sea, Earth and Sky*, *Thrasher Vase*, *Bacchante*, and *Flying Duck* and *Flying Gull* plates.

Begins a translation of *Summa Artis,* a multivolumed history of art by the Spaniard José Pijoan. First trips to the Chandeleurs (barrier islands) to observe pelicans (*B* 86). Block-prints a children's book, *Robinson: The Pleasant History of an Unusual Cat* (*SA* x). Sissy briefly separates from him while she visits Hellmuth relatives in Chicago and lives with the two children at the house of painter Dusti Bonge in Biloxi.

1941

In April, Sissy moves to the Grinstead family home, Oldfields, with her father, Mary, and Billy. That summer WIA joins Sissy at Oldfields, and begins to participate fully in life with his family on a coastal farm. Studies Adolfo Best-Maugard, *A Method for Creative Design*, and Jay Hambidge's works on "dynamic symmetry" (*SA* 34) and incorporates Best-Maugard's "seven motifs" into his work (*SA* xiv; *HIL* 15), for example, into the series (both in ink and in color) *Calendar Drawings,* a journal in images of his life at Oldfields, 1941–43 (*SA* xvii, 6, 34, 46–47, 58, 65; *B* 87, 91, 93–100). He also works on ink, pencil, and crayon drawings illustrating scenes from his readings in Pope's translation of Homer's *Iliad*, Coleridge's "Rime of the Ancient Mariner," *Alice in Wonderland*, *Hamlet*, *Paradise Lost* and *Paradise Regained*, *Faust*, the works of Ossian, *Don Quixote*, Bulfinch's *Legends of Charlemagne*, Dante's *Divine Comedy*, and Darwin's *Voyage of the Beagle* (*IEV*). Ink drawings of plants and animals, sea creatures, people (*WL* 43). Collaborates with Sissy on illustrated poems.

1942

Fall: bicycle trip to New York, to sketch and visit museums. Admires Egyptian antiquities at the Metropolitan, "things from Cyprus and Crete," Etruscan art, early Greek figures, and Mesopotamian pottery. Revisits the American Museum of Natural History. Upon his return to Oldfields he builds a kiln in the carriage house, and designs, models, fires, and decorates a new series of figurines (*SA* 29.)

1943

Bicycle trip to New Orleans, where he does preliminary sketches for city scenes he will paint in watercolors at Oldfields (*WL* 59). He combines many of these into composite mural-like scenes. Also does series of plants and animals at Oldfields in the primary colors, in which the figures are surrounded by an aura of lemon-yellow light (*SA* 2, 4, 5, 25, 28, 53, 106–107; *B* vi, 101, 115, 118; *RI* plates 1–7). Several distinct series emerge, including *Nativity at the Barn* (*SA* 120–21), *Pines and Oaks*, *Pecan Trees with Doves*, and *Garden*. Probable date of *The Road to Oldfields*. In June he stages a puppet show in the attic at Oldfields about animal and plant life in the cutover lands (clear-cut by loggers). Interest in Hambidge develops into ink drawings—dominated by spirals—of animals and plants.

1944

In January, walks from Oldfields to see the Mississippi sandhill cranes, and writes an essay about the experience. Exhibition of Shearwater Pottery by Peter Anderson, decorated by Walter Anderson, Brooks Memorial Art Gallery, Memphis, Tennessee. Sketches pelicans in the Chandeleurs (*HIL* 43–53). May 23: birth of daughter Leif, whom he names for Leif Eriksson.

1945

Large, bold tempera paintings, often on wallpaper, of birds, people, fall foliage, animals, pelicans, sea creatures, fairy tale figures (*WL* 42, 46). Large linoleum block prints of fish and animals, birds, clouds, trees, cutover land, wildflowers, fairy tales, nursery rhymes, myth, *Arabian Nights*, etc. (*MC*; *SA* 16–17, 32–33, 48–49; *B* viii, 72, 74, 78, 79; *WL* 47). Large watercolors like *Monkey in Jungle* (*SA* 76) and *Cow* (*SA* 95). In August, bicycle trip to western Texas, where he sketches the landscape. Chair designs.

1947

Birth of son, John Grinstead, March 12. In 1946 or 1947 WIA leaves Oldfields and moves into the cottage at Ocean Springs. Summer: gives volunteer art classes at a hospital in Gulfport.

1948

Trip to Chandeleurs to observe nesting pelicans. Essay on pelicans, drawings of pelicans in sepia ink on typewriter paper (*B* 56, 83, 85; *HIL* 76). Carves *The Swimmer* (Walter Anderson Museum of Art) from a tree blown down in the 1947 hurricane, as well as a series of carved and painted animals (*SA* 19, 38–39, 116, 121, and *Squirrel*, Memphis Brooks Museum of Art). Paints numerous still lifes (*VR*). Begins regular trips to Horn Island.

1949

Folktales and Fantasy: Modern Scroll Prints by Walter Anderson, exhibition of block prints, two sculpted, wooden cats, and ceramics, at Brooklyn Museum, May 26–October 1. In 1949–50, some of the carved pieces go on sale in the Bertha Schaefer Gallery in New York. August–September: travels to China, with the intention of looking at Tibetan murals. His belongings and passport are stolen, and the trip ends early, with a return to Hong Kong and a visit to Macao. In Hong Kong, before departing for the United States, he does a series of ink drawings illustrating his travels and a series of remarkable watercolors of sea creatures (*RI* plates 8–9; *VR* plate 2).

1950

In July, WIA puts up *The River* (group of wood sculptures, including *Father Mississippi*) at Shearwater (*SA* xviii, 119). Designs and builds furniture (pelican chair, blue jay table; *B* 21, 30; chests), carves assorted animals, and creates fairy-tale figurines. Probable date of decorative mural in the bathroom of the cottage (*SA* 104.) In November, exhibition of block prints and watercolors at Mississippi Delta Art Association, Greenwood, Mississippi.

In September, a comprehensive exhibition sponsored by the American Association of University Women, organized by Lura Beam, opens at Brooks

Memorial Art Gallery, Memphis, Tennessee, with an enthusiastic review ("A genius is amongst us") by Guy Northrop, art critic of the Memphis *Commercial Appeal*. Over the next two years sixty pieces—fairy-tale block prints, woodcarvings, watercolors, and line drawings—tour twenty cities in Mississippi, Minnesota, New Hampshire, Tennessee, Alabama, and Oklahoma. When the tour comes to an end, an ink drawing of a pelican is included in another AAUW exhibition, *Contemporary American Drawing*, at the Whitney Museum of American Art.

1951

AAUW show exhibited in newly built Ocean Springs Community Center, January 31–February 2. First showing of his works in Ocean Springs. On March 10, begins work on Community Center murals, commissioned in mid-February and executed for the sum of one dollar. By April, finishes preliminary drawings on walls of the Community Center. In June, Guy Northrop interviews him about Community Center murals (*WL* 51–90). That summer, WIA travels to Costa Rica, where he sketches and paints and gathers orchids and other plants. In September, exhibition of prints, large and small watercolors, and Shearwater Pottery in Lauren Rogers Museum, Laurel, Mississippi.

1951?–1953

Before October 1954, probably paints mural in "Little Room" of cottage at Shearwater (cf. *PP*; *WL* 91–103). From now until the end of his life, frequent trips to Horn Island, where he draws, paints watercolors, and meditates on art and nature.

1952

Exhibits a scroll print—*Jack the Giant Killer*—at Mississippi State College for Women, Columbus, Mississippi, and it is acquired for their permanent collection.

1953

Train and bicycle trip to Philadelphia and New York (April) to see artwork by his old teacher Henry McCarter and visit with Francis Speight, a friend from the Pennsylvania Academy of the Fine Arts. Bicycle trip to Memphis, Tennessee (August).

1955

In January, "paintings, drawings and craftwork" by WIA go on display in the little gallery at the Newcomb, in New Orleans. Exhibits watercolors (*Sea Turtles*, *Man of War Birds*, *Baby Pelicans on Chandeleur Islands*, *Pitcher Plants*, *Shoes and Onions*, *Oranges*, *Shrimp*, *Possum*, *Pansies*, *Fruit*, and *Turkey*, as well as block prints on paper and cloth at the Mississippi Art Colony, Allison's Wells, in Way,

Mississippi (August). Series of watercolor studies for plate designs (*SA* 42–43; *B* 62), many of which are painted in underglaze decoration at Shearwater (*B* 67, 71). In September, he is hospitalized at De Paul Sanitarium, New Orleans. During his month there, he does numerous watercolor portraits of fellow patients and possibly a self-portrait.

1960

Bicycle trip to Florida, to visit Kay and Frank Baisden and to paint with Baisden (December). Contact with Schuyler Jackson and Laura Riding in Florida and with the psychiatrist Norman Cameron at Shearwater. Large painting entitled *Map of Horn Island* (*WL* 110) done for his brother Peter and sister-in-law Patricia.

1962

Trip to New Orleans. Upon his return he paints scenes from Mardi Gras, zoo animals (*SA* 30–31), and *Under the Umbrella* (Memphis Brooks Museum of Art). Bitten by a water moccasin on Horn Island.

1964

Death of Annette McConnell Anderson. Frank Baisden organizes an exhibition entitled *Fledgling Birds* at Hunter Museum in Chattanooga, Brooks Memorial Art Gallery in Memphis, and Jackson, Mississippi.

1965

Weathers Hurricane Betsy on Horn Island. Trip to New Orleans, where he paints tropical birds and other animals at zoo. November 30, dies in New Orleans from complications arising from an operation for lung cancer. Buried in Evergreen Cemetery, Ocean Springs.

1967

The World of Walter Anderson, a 587-piece retrospective curated by Robert J. McKnight, opens at the Brooks Memorial Art Gallery. Travels 1968–69.

1989

Agnes Grinstead Anderson publishes her memoir, *Approaching the Magic Hour: Memories of Walter Anderson*, begun in 1967 and edited by Patti Carr Black.

1991

Walter Anderson Museum of Art in Ocean Springs, Mississippi, opens to the public.

EXHIBITIONS

1944

Shearwater Pottery, Brooks Memorial Art Gallery, Memphis, Tennessee

1949

Folktale and Fantasy: Modern Scroll Prints by Walter Anderson, Brooklyn Museum, Brooklyn, New York

1950–1952

Block Prints, Watercolors, Drawings and Wood Carvings by Walter I. Anderson, Brooks Memorial Art Gallery, Memphis, Tennessee. Traveled under the auspices of the American Association of University Women over the next two years to twenty cities in Minnesota, New Hampshire, Tennessee, Alabama, Oklahoma, and Mississippi, including Ocean Springs, where at the Ocean Springs Community Center it was the first showing of Anderson's work.

1955

Watercolors and block prints at the Mississippi Art Colony, Allison's Wells, Way, Mississippi

1964

Fledgling Birds, Brooks Memorial Art Gallery, Memphis, Tennessee; Hunter Museum, Chattanooga, Tennessee; and Jackson, Mississippi

1967

The World of Walter Anderson, Brooks Memorial Art Gallery, Memphis, Tennessee

1968–1969
The World of Walter Anderson traveling exhibit
1970–1978
Frequent small exhibitions uncatalogued
1979
The Shearwater Legacy, Mississippi State Historical Museum, Jackson, Mississippi
1980
Sea, Earth, Sky: The Art of Walter Anderson, Mississippi State Historical Museum, Jackson, Mississippi
1982
The Birds of Walter Anderson, Percy H. White Art Center, Fairhope, Alabama
1983
The Birds of Walter Anderson, Louisiana Nature Center, New Orleans, Louisiana
1984
Walter Anderson for Children, Mississippi State Historical Museum, Jackson, Mississippi
1984
Walter Anderson's New Orleans, Louisiana World Exposition, New Orleans, Louisiana
1985
Walter Anderson: Realizations of the Islander, Pennsylvania Academy of the Fine Arts and traveling, Philadelphia, Pennsylvania
1986
Walter Anderson's Calendar, Mississippi State Historical Museum, Jackson, Mississippi; traveled under the auspices of the Southern Arts Federation
1987
The Birds of Walter Anderson; traveled to universities and to art and nature centers
1988
Walter Anderson's New Orleans, New Orleans Museum of Art, New Orleans, Louisiana
1989
An American Master: Walter Anderson of Mississippi, Memphis Brooks Museum of Art and Jackson, Mississippi
1989
The Birds of Walter Anderson, Fairhope, Alabama
1989
Walter Anderson: The Birds, Luise Ross Gallery, New York, New York
1989
Walter Anderson: Witness to Wilderness, University Art Museum, Lafayette, Louisiana

1989

Walter Anderson, Tilden-Foley Gallery, New Orleans, Louisiana

1989

Walter Anderson for Children, Greenville County Museum of Art, Greenville, South Carolina

1989

The Walter Anderson Collection, Mississippi Museum of Art Gulf Coast, Biloxi, Mississippi

Exhibitions of Walter Anderson's Work at the Walter Anderson Museum of Art, Ocean Springs, Mississippi

1991

Walter Inglis Anderson: A Conscious Adventurer

Opening exhibition for the Walter Anderson Museum of Art, Ocean Springs, Mississippi

1992

Anderson's Saints: Carvings and Religious Imagery

Celebrating the Child with Gifts of Generous Spirit

Birds: Walter Inglis Anderson

1993

Carousel Animals and Walter Anderson's Exotic Creatures

The Rhythm of Insects

Our Vanishing Heritage: The Harmonious Bog

1994

Spirit Lines: Graphite Images of Gendron Jensen and Walter Anderson

Across the Lake: The Woodward Brothers and Annette McConnell Anderson

Potpourri of Walter Anderson

Pine Trees in the Wind

1995

Walter Anderson's "A Host of Angels"

At the Edge of the Sea

1996

Interior Images: The Influence of the Cave Paintings in France on the Work of Walter Anderson

Strong on Design: The Decorative Work of Walter Anderson

Art Blooms at the Walter Anderson Museum

The Good Earth: Folk Art and Artifacts from the Chinese Countryside
Walter Anderson: Creatures of the Air
1997
Between the Blades of Grass
A Succession of Flowers
A Symphony of Animals
Seeking the Sublime: The People of Walter Anderson
1998
Motion Detection: The Visual Rhythms of Walter Anderson and the Kinetic Sculpture of James Seawright
A Shared Dream: The Friends of Walter Anderson (1975–1980)
Shearwater at Seventy: A Living Legacy Exhibition
1999
Voluptuous Return: Still Life by Walter Anderson
Walls of Light: The Murals of Walter Anderson
Repaying the Debt: The Work of Walter Anderson
2000
Vanishing Point: The View from Horn Island
The Private Eye: Walter Anderson from Individual Collections
Child's Play: Crayon Drawings of Walter Anderson
More about Motifs: The Influence of Best-Maugard's Seven Archetypical Symbols on the Work of Walter Anderson
The Third Poetry: Watercolor and Drawings of Walter Anderson
2001
A Modernist Spirit: Walter Anderson and His American Contemporaries
Hamlet and Beyond: Literature of Walter Anderson
On the Walls for Fifty Years: Community Center Studies (1951–2001)
Views from the Mainland
2002
Visions of Nature: The World of Walter Anderson
Motifs of Time: Mississippi Artists Invitational
Soaring Spirits: The Birds of Walter Anderson
2003
Journeys of a Lifetime: The Travels of Walter Anderson

Walter Anderson Museum of Art Traveling Exhibitions

1999

Thunder & Enlightenment: Highlights of the Walter Anderson Museum of Art Collection

The University of Southern Mississippi Museum of Art, Hattiesburg, Mississippi

2001

Visions of Nature: The World of Walter Anderson

The Mississippi Museum of Natural Science, Jackson, Mississippi

Walter Anderson Museum of Art Long-Term Exhibitions

An objective in the original concept for the Walter Anderson Museum of Art was to bring the artist's three major murals together in one place for permanent display, preservation, and study.

Ocean Springs: Past and Present, 1934

The Public Works of Art Project murals were commissioned for the Ocean Springs High School auditorium. Grant funding was received to conserve and relocate the six murals on canvas to the museum in 1991.

The Ocean Springs Community Center Murals, 1951–1952

The largest single work by Walter Anderson. The Community Center is owned by the city of Ocean Springs, but daily supervision of the facility is achieved through a partnership between the museum and the city.

The Little Room Murals, 1951–1953

This room from the artist's cottage was relocated to the Walter Anderson Museum of Art in 1991 to go on permanent display.

Group Exhibitions Including Works by Walter Anderson

1951–1952

Contemporary American Drawings, American Association of University Women art program, circulating exhibitions; Whitney Museum of American Art, New York, New York

1981

Southern Works on Paper, Louisiana State University, Baton Rouge, Louisiana; traveled

Paintings in the South: 1564–1980, Virginia Museum of Fine Arts, Richmond, Virginia

The South on Paper, traveled under the auspices of Robert M. Hicklin, Jr., Inc.

1988

The Watercolorists: Walter Anderson and His Peers, Luise Ross Gallery and Vanderwoude Tanabaum Gallery, New York, New York

1988

Show & Tell: Artists' Illustrated Letters—1450–1968, The Grey Art Gallery, New York University, New York, New York

PERMANENT COLLECTIONS

Art Institute of Chicago, Chicago, Illinois
Brooklyn Museum of Art, Brooklyn, New York
Columbus Museum of Art, Columbus, Georgia
Fitchburg Art Museum, Fitchburg, Massachusetts
Greenville County Museum of Art, Greenville, South Carolina
Lauren Rogers Museum of Art, Laurel, Mississippi
Memphis Brooks Museum of Art, Memphis, Tennessee
Mississippi Museum of Art, Jackson, Mississippi
Mobile Museum of Art, Mobile, Alabama
Montgomery Museum of Fine Arts, Montgomery, Alabama
New Orleans Museum of Art, New Orleans, Louisiana
Ogden Museum of Southern Art, New Orleans, Louisiana
Pennsylvania Academy of the Fine Arts, Philadelphia, Pennsylvania
Smithsonian Institution, Washington, D.C.
Wake Forest University Collection, Wake Forest, North Carolina
Whitney Museum of American Art, New York, New York

SELECTED BIBLIOGRAPHY

Anderson, Agnes Grinstead. *Approaching the Magic Hour: Memories of Walter Anderson.* Edited by Patti Carr Black. Jackson: University Press of Mississippi, 1989.

Anderson, Walter. *Robinson: The Pleasant History of an Unusual Cat.* With an afterword by Mary Anderson Pickard. Jackson: University Press of Mississippi, 1982.

———. *An Alphabet.* Jackson: University Press of Mississippi, 1984.

———. *The Walter Anderson Birthday Book.* Jackson: Mississippi State Historical Society, 1986.

———. *Birds.* With an introduction by Mary Anderson Pickard. Jackson: University Press of Mississippi, 1990.

———. *A Symphony of Animals.* With an introduction by Mary Anderson Pickard. Jackson: University Press of Mississippi, 1996.

———. *The Walter Anderson Cat's Address Book.* Jackson: Edge Press, 1999.

Backes, Clarus. "Artist in the Eye of a Hurricane." *Chicago Tribune Magazine,* 17 August 1969, section F, 3, 24–31.

Black, Patti Carr. "Depression and War, 1929–1945." In *Art in Mississippi, 1720–1980* (Jackson: University Press of Mississippi in association with the Mississippi Historical Society and the Mississippi Department of Archives and History, 1998).

Burton, Marda Kaiser. "Portraitist of Nature." *Horizon,* March 1982, 44–49.

Campbell, Lawrence. "Walter Inglis Anderson at Luise Ross." *Art in America* 75 (April 1987): 227.

"Capturing the Magic of the Gulf Coast." *Chronicle of Higher Education,* 3 September 1999, B132.

Carroll, Lewis. *Anderson's Alice: Walter Anderson Illustrates Alice's Adventures in Wonderland.* With a foreword by Mary Anderson Pickard. Jackson: University Press of Mississippi, 1983.

Charbonnet, Grace R. "The Anderson Story . . . Splendor in Mississippi." *Delta Review*, November–December 1966, 40, 43, 52, 58.

Cohrs, Timothy. "Walter Anderson at Luise Ross Gallery." *Arts Magazine*, June 1988, 109.

Douglas, Ellen, with the illustrations of Walter Anderson. *The Magic Carpet and Other Tales*. Jackson: University Press of Mississippi, 1987.

Driscoll, John Paul. Introduction to *Walter Anderson: Realizations of the Islander*. Foreword by Dan Miller. Ocean Springs, MS: Estate of Walter Anderson, 1985.

Gilbert, Bil. "Stalking the Blue Bear: The Fine Art of Walter Anderson." *Smithsonian*, October 1994, 108–119.

Glade, Luba. "The Anderson Museum of Art: A Safe Bet on the Coast." *Arts Quarterly* 15, no. 4 (October–December 1993): 20–21.

"Islander: Walter Anderson and His Watercolors." *Perspective* 1, no. 2 (fall 1989): 2–7.

King, Anne R. *Walls of Light: The Murals of Walter Anderson*. With a foreword by Stephen Ambrose. Jackson: University Press of Mississippi and the Walter Anderson Museum of Art, 1999.

Larson, Kay. "Natural Man." *New York Magazine*, 20 April 1992, 96.

Maurer, Christopher, with María Estrella Iglesius. *Dreaming in Clay on the Coast of Mississippi: Love and Art at Shearwater.* New York: Doubleday, 2000.

McKnight, Robert J. Introduction to *The World of Walter Anderson.* Traveling exhibition catalogue. Memphis: Brooks Memorial Art Gallery, 1967.

Pickard, Edward. "Realizations." In "Walter Anderson: A Tribute." *Mississippi Coast*, June/July 1991, 91–106.

Pickard, Mary Anderson. "Yellow Butterflies: A Reading of Excerpts from the Writings of Walter Inglis Anderson." Ocean Springs, MS: The Walter Anderson Estate, n.d.

———. Introduction to *Sea, Earth, Sky: The Art of Walter Anderson*. With a preface by Patti Carr Black. Exhibition catalogue. Jackson: Mississippi Department of Archives and History, 1980.

———."Possessed of a Vision." In "Walter Anderson: A Tribute." *Mississippi Coast*, June/July 1991, 91–106.

———. Introduction to *The Voluptuous Return: Still Life by Walter Inglis Anderson*. With a foreword by Patti Carr Black. Exhibition catalogue. Ocean Springs, MS: The Family of Walter Inglis Anderson, 1999.

Rudloe, Jack. "The Nature of a Painter." *Natural History*, February 1990, 62–69.

Russell, John. "The Art of Walter Anderson." *New York Times*, 5 April 1985.

Sozanski, Edward J. "A Watercolorist Possessed by his Work." *Philadelphia Inquirer*, 14 February 1985, 10c.

Sugg, Redding S., Jr. "His Exquisite Wilderness Drawings Were His Way of Being a Part of the Chain of Nature." *Southern Voices*, March–April 1974, 3–10.

———. *A Painter's Psalm: The Mural from Walter Anderson's Cottage*. 1978. Rev. ed., Jackson: University Press of Mississippi, 1992.

———, ed. *The Horn Island Logs of Walter Anderson*. 1973. Rev. ed., Jackson: University Press of Mississippi, 1985.

———, ed. *Walter Anderson's Illustrations of Epic and Voyage*. Carbondale: Southern Illinois University Press; London: Feffer & Simmons, 1980.

Thompson, Carole E., ed. *An American Master: Walter Anderson of Mississippi*. Exhibition catalogue. Memphis: Memphis Brooks Museum of Art, 1988.

Toops, Connie. "In Ecstasy: The Watercolors and Diaries of Walter Inglis Anderson." *Southern Exposure*, May/June, 1982, 3–6.

Watson, Marie. "Brushes Aside No More." *Americana*, February 1992, 52–57.

———. "The Sunshine of Walter Anderson." *Biloxi-Gulfport Daily Herald*; *Riviera Review Magazine*, 24 July 1971, 2–8, 14–15.

CONTRIBUTORS

KEVIN BERNE (B.S., University of California, Davis) has a degree in environmental design and got his start in photography by claiming first prize in the American Photography Metropolitan Life competition. After a year of travel abroad and then study at the Academy of Art in San Francisco, he launched his career in architectural and editorial photography. He currently has his own company and is retained by such clients as American Conservatory Theater, National Semiconductor, Pacific Marketing Associates, California State Automobile Association, San Francisco Museum of Modern Art, and the National Multiple Sclerosis Society. He has been part of six group exhibits and has had three one-man shows, including a joint exhibition with his artist mother in Tokyo, Japan.

COLIN EISLER (Ph.D., Harvard University) is currently Robert Lehman Professor of Fine Arts at New York University. He was Distinguished Visiting Professor at George Washington University and Senior Fellow at the Center for Advanced Studies in the Visual Arts in 1988–1989. His major interest is in early Netherlands painting and Renaissance drawing and prints. He has published over fifteen books, including *Masterworks from Berlin: A City's Paintings Reunited*; *Paintings in the Hermitage*; *Treasures of the Jewish Museum*; *Dürer's Animals*; *The Seeing Hand*; *Flemish and Dutch Drawings from the 15th to the 18th Century*; *The Genius of Jacopo Bellini: The Complete Paintings and Drawings*; and *The Master of the Unicorn: The Life and Work of Jean Duvet*. He is a member of the College Art Association and the Renaissance Society of America and is on the editorial board of the *Renaissance Quarterly*.

SUSAN C. LARSEN (Ph.D., Northwestern University) is currently Collector, Archives of American Art, the Smithsonian Institution. She has been Chief Curator for the Farnsworth Art Museum, Rockland, Maine; Curator of the Permanent Collection, Whitney Museum of American Art, New York; professor and chair of the Department of Art History, University of Southern California; and assistant professor of art history at Carleton College. Her publications include *Abstract Painting and Sculpture in America 1927–1944*, of which she is coauthor, and articles or editorial responsibility in forty-six exhibition catalogues for museums including the Tokyo Museum and the Whitney Museum of American Art. In addition, she has published numerous brochures as well as articles and reviews in journals and magazines including *Architectural Digest*, *Art News*, *Art in America*, and *Art International*, and has been a regular reviewer for *Artforum*.

CHRISTOPER MAURER (Ph.D., University of Pennsylvania) is chair of the Department of Spanish, French, Italian and Linguistics at the University of Illinois, Chicago. He has also been chair of the Department of Spanish and Portuguese at Vanderbilt University, and has taught at Harvard University. He is a noted scholar on Spanish poetry and on the work of Federico García Lorca, and has published over sixteen book-length volumes, including Lorca's collected poems and complete letters. His work on Lorca covers the drawings, plays, poems, letters, and prose works. He has written, with María Estrella Iglesias, a book on the history of the Anderson family and Shearwater Pottery, *Dreaming in Clay on the Coast of Mississippi: Love and Art at Shearwater*, and is the author of the only full-length biography of Walter Anderson, *Fortune's Favorite Child: The Uneasy Life of Walter Anderson*; he has also lectured on Walter Anderson in Spain and in the United States. He has been published in *Hispanic Review*, the *New Republic*, *Romance Notes*, and the *New York Times*, and in foreign journals including *El País* (Madrid) and *Magazin Littéraire* (Paris).

FRANCIS V. O'CONNOR (Ph.D., Johns Hopkins University) is an independent historian of American art who has published widely on Jackson Pollock and abstract expressionism, the New Deal art programs of the 1930s, government art patronage, the history of the American mural, and the psychodynamics of the creative process. He has taught at the University of Maryland, George Washington University, and Williams College and has held fellowships from the National Endowment for the Arts, the National Endowment for the Humanities, the Smithsonian Institution, the Institute for Medical Humanities of the University of Texas, the U.S. Capitol Historical Society, and the National Humanities Center. He is the editor of O'Connor's Page on the Internet, where a complete career narrative and bibliography can be found at <http://members.aol.com/FVOC > under Services.

MARY ANDERSON PICKARD (B.A., Delta State University) is the oldest of four children born to Walter Anderson and Agnes Grinstead Anderson. With a degree in English literature, she taught school for seventeen years; she acted in many plays and directed the children's theater for the Anderson Players in Ocean Springs. She served as curator for her father's estate for many years and has written major essays for books on Anderson's life and art and for exhibition catalogues and periodicals. She has also given tours and lectures at the New Orleans Museum of Art, the Walter Anderson Museum of Art, the Memphis Brooks Museum of Art, and the Pennsylvania Academy of the Fine Arts, as well as presenting papers at symposia and conferences on art and other fields. Her watercolors, along with those of her son, Christopher Stebly, are often shown in exhibitions throughout the state.

ERNEST PINSON (Ph.D., Ohio University) has recently returned from teaching English at the University of Nanjing, China. He has also taught at William Carey College on the Coast, Union University, and Bluefield College, and served in the U.S. Army Intelligence at the Pentagon. He has written forty critical reviews on music, drama, and books for the *Harbinger*, a newspaper in Mobile, Alabama, and sixty reviews for the *Jackson Sun*, a newspaper in Jackson, Tennessee, as well as articles on fiction writer Jacques Futrelle, Italian artist Simone Martini, Italian writer Mario Praz, Austrian writer Hugo von Hofmansthal, and Shakespeare. He also authored a multimedia play celebrating the 150th anniversary of Union University. He has received six Mellon Foundation summer grants at Vanderbilt University, four awards from the National Science Foundation, two grants for Folger Institute Symposia, and a National Endowment for the Humanities grant for study at the University of Virginia.

PATRICIA PINSON (Ph.D., Ohio University) is currently Curator at the Walter Anderson Museum of Art in Ocean Springs, Mississippi. She has taught art (including courses on Walter Anderson at the museum and at William Carey College on the Coast), music, and fine arts courses at Bluefield College, Ohio University, Union University, where she was also dean of the School of Fine Arts, and William Carey College on the Coast, where she was vice president and dean. She was the director of the Honors Interdisciplinary Programs at Union University and the Charles Goodson Honors Consultant and Lecturer at Ouachita Baptist University. She has received grants from the National Science Foundation, Mellon Foundation, Tennessee Endowment for the Humanities, and Danforth Foundation. She has published articles in the *Southern Baptist Educator* and art reviews in the *Harbinger*, and has written gallery guides for the Walter Anderson Museum of Art since 2000.

LINDA CROCKER SIMMONS (M.A., University of Delaware; completing dissertation for Ph.D., University of Virginia) has worked in the art museum field for more than thirty years, during which she was Curator for the Corcoran Gallery of Art, where she is now Curator Emeritus. She is an expert in American painting of the eighteenth and nineteenth centuries, focusing in her research and publications on artists of the Washington, D.C., area, eighteenth- and nineteenth-century American women artists, painters of the Shenandoah Valley, American nonacademic painters, African American painters, and the painters of the Peale family. She is Senior Scholar in the Peale Paintings Project at the Maryland Historical Society and was guest curator for an exhibition devoted to the early African American painter Joshua Johnston at the Winterthur Museum. She serves on four boards, including the Black Heritage Museum of Arlington, the Arlington Heritage Center Task Force, and the Arlington Historical Affairs and Landmark Review Board. She has received numerous grants and awards, including three grants from the National Endowment of the Arts, and has published over thirty-five articles in journals and magazines, including essays for the catalogue of the Sewell Biggs Museum and articles in *American Painting: The Philadelphia Collection LXVIII*, the Schwartz Gallery, Philadelphia.

INDEX

Numbers in **boldface** indicate an illustration on that page.